lonely planet

USA National Parks

PLAN YOUR TRIP

SQUIRREL, CRATER LAKE P224

THOMAS WINZ /GETTY IMAGES ©

BRANDYWINE FALLS P347

FDASTUDILLO /GETTY IMAGES ©

USA'S NATIONAL PARKS

Contents

SPECIAL FEATURES

USA'S NATIONAL PARKS

TOTEM POLE, SITKA P250

Contents

Welcome to USA's National Parks

*'In wildness is the
preservation of the world.'*

– Henry David Thoreau

Uniquely American

The Grand Canyon. Yellowstone. Yosemite. These names represent more than just scenic beauty. They represent American ideals at their best: the preservation of life and liberty, the pursuit of happiness for all. That we are able to enjoy these special places today may seem like a matter of course, but the establishment of the national park system was no sure thing. These were the first expanses of public wilderness preserved anywhere in the world, and there were no blueprints for their creation, no guides suggesting how to best manage such huge tracts of land. Challenges have been present every step of the way, and many threatened to derail the entire experiment. But, until now, our best instincts have prevailed. Given the awe-inspiring majesty of these 59 parks, we couldn't accept anything less.

Superlatives...

The moment you roll up to a national-park entry kiosk, you feel it. You're entering a special place. Maybe it's the mountain air or the smell of the trees. Most likely, it's because you're about to see something *big*. Something indescribable: a canyon so deep you can see two billion years of geological history in its walls; trees so massive you could fit buildings inside them; rock formations so strange they can only be called 'hoodoos.' America's national parks hold some of the most spectacular scenery on earth. A collection of superlatives, they encompass the highest and lowest points in North America. One park is home to the greatest concentration of geothermic features on the planet. Another encompasses the world's densest collection of natural stone arches. These national parks – and the plants and animals they protect – are our greatest treasure.

...and Sanctuaries

Each visitor brings back something different from these wild sanctuaries. For some, it is an opportunity to experience primordial beauty; to grasp, if only for a minute, a sense of the sublime. For others, it is a place to enjoy life to its fullest, to feel the rush of adventure, to overcome a personal challenge. And for still others, it may be a place to seek refuge or to heal, to connect with the deeper pulse that runs through our planet, beyond the reach of the modern world. Whatever it is that you feel or think during your stay, take the time to thank the parks by keeping them just as they were when you arrived – because the person following you is entitled to exactly the same experience.

Right: Havasu Falls, Grand Canyon National Park

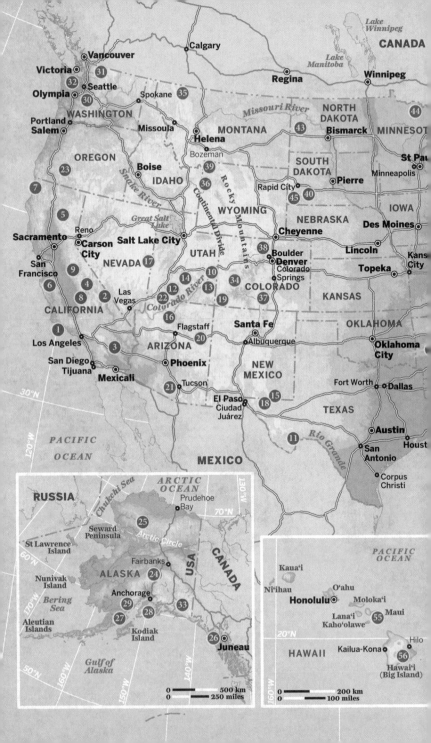

ELEVATION

	13,000ft
	12,000ft
	11,000ft
	8000ft
	5000ft
	2000ft
	1000ft
	0

0 — 500 km
0 — 250 miles

1. Channel Islands
2. Death Valley
3. Joshua Tree
4. Kings Canyon
5. Lassen Volcanic
6. Pinnacles
7. Redwood
8. Sequoia
9. Yosemite
10. Arches
11. Big Bend
12. Bryce Canyon
13. Canyonlands
14. Capitol Reef
15. Carlsbad Caverns
16. Grand Canyon
17. Great Basin
18. Guadalupe Mountains
19. Mesa Verde
20. Petrified Forest
21. Saguaro
22. Zion
23. Crater Lake
24. Denali
25. Gates of the Arctic & Kobuk Valley
26. Glacier Bay
27. Katmai
28. Kenai Fjords
29. Lake Clark
30. Mount Rainier
31. North Cascades
32. Olympic
33. Wrangell-St Elias
34. Black Canyon of the Gunnison
35. Glacier
36. Grand Teton
37. Great Sand Dunes
38. Rocky Mountain
39. Yellowstone
40. Badlands
41. Cuyahoga Valley
42. Isle Royale
43. Theodore Roosevelt
44. Voyageurs
45. Wind Cave
46. Acadia
47. Biscayne
48. Congaree
49. Dry Tortugas
50. Everglades
51. Great Smoky Mountains
52. Hot Springs
53. Mammoth Cave
54. Shenandoah
55. Haleakalā
56. Hawai'i Volcanoes
57. American Samoa
58. Virgin Islands

USA's National Parks'
Top 15

Yosemite Valley, Yosemite

1 In Yosemite Valley (p116), the national-park system's crown jewel, massive granite rock formations tower thousands of feet over the Merced River. Wild creeks plummet from the cliff tops, creating a spectacle of waterfalls unlike anywhere on earth. And presiding over it all stand the iconic and mighty sentinels of rock, including El Capitan, Half Dome, the Royal Arches, the Three Brothers and Cathedral Rocks. No matter what people tell you about the summer crowds, the sights of Yosemite Valley are so astonishing that almost nothing can detract from the experience.

Going-to-the-Sun Road, Glacier

2 Going-to-the-Sun Rd (p288) offers steely-nerved motorists the drive of their life. Chiseled out of the mountainside and punctuated by some of the sheerest and most vertiginous drop-offs in the US, this 50-mile, vista-laden strip of asphalt offers drivers access to some of the most astounding sights in the Rockies.

Sunset, Grand Canyon

3 When Bob Dylan wrote of God and Woody Guthrie, he said 'I may be right or wrong / You'll find them both / In the Grand Canyon / At sundown.' Of all the places to watch the sunset in the world, few can measure up to the Grand Canyon (p172). Lipan Point is one of the finest spots to do it. Or, if you're feeling leisurely, simply grab a drink and a porch swing on the patio of El Tovar lodge, where you can watch the sunset in style.

Wildlife Watching, Yellowstone

4 No matter how many nature shows you've seen, nothing can prepare you for the first time you spot a moose in the wild. And in Yellowstone (p318), if you don' see a moose – or a bison or a herd of elk or a bear – you probably have your eyes closed. On par with the Galápagos, the Serengeti and Brazil's Pantanal, Yellowstone is one of the world's premier wildlife-watching destinations. Big mammals are everywhere. The knowledge that grizzlies, wolves and mountain lions are among them simply adds to the rush. Right: Bison bull

Bryce Amphitheater, Bryce Canyon

5 Proof that nature has a wild imagination, hoodoos are among the strangest formations on the planet. From the rim of southern Utah's Bryce Amphitheater (p157) you can look down upon thousands of these bizarre, ancient rock spires as they tower out of the so-called Silent City, a conglomeration of hoodoos so vast that you'd be forgiven for thinking you'd landed on another planet. Sunrise over the amphitheater is one of life's treats.

Rock Climbing, Joshua Tree

6 Whether you're a rock-climbing novice or a bouldering goddess, you'll find heaven above earth when you take to Joshua Tree's granite (p77). With more than 8000 established climbing routes, this is truly one of the world's rock meccas. There are classes for beginners, and the 400-plus climbing formations offer endless fun for seasoned enthusiasts. Amid the giant boulders and sweaty climbers, the bizarre Joshua trees themselves lend the scenery an otherworldly character.

Wildlife Watching on Snake River, Grand Teton

7 Spilling down from Jackson Lake beneath the mighty Teton Range, the wild and scenic Snake River offers some of the most dramatic mountain scenery in the country. Not only are its waters the perfect place to gawk at the Tetons themselves (including the 13,770ft Grand Teton), but they're prime for wildlife watching (p297). Numerous outfitters offer float trips ranging from gentle to giant water. No matter which you choose, prepare to be awed.

8

The Narrows, Zion

8 Check your claustro-phobia at the door and prepare to get wet on this hike up the Virgin River into a 2000ft-deep slot canyon (p206). As you make your way upriver, the cliffs press inward, towering higher and higher until, finally, you reach Wall Street, where the width of the canyon narrows to less than 30ft.

Kayaking, Glacier Bay

9 Blue-water paddling – kayaking in Alaskan coastal areas, which are characterized by extreme tidal fluctuations, cold water and the possibility of high winds and waves – is the means of escape into areas such as Glacier Bay's Muir Inlet (p240). Everywhere you turn, a tide-water glacier seems to be calving in this grand park, where you may also see humpback whales, black bears, seals and bald eagles.

Wildflower Season, Mt Rainier

10 Mt Rainier (p254) gets over 650in of snow annually. It's covered in glaciers, and the high meadows are blanketed in white for nearly nine months of the year. Once the snow finally melts and the meadows are exposed, wildflowers, somehow knowing they have only a short time to do their thing, explode into bloom. Avalanche lilies, beargrass, bog orchids, wood nymphs and dozens of other flow-ers turn the slopes of the Cascade's highest moun-tain into a rainbow of color. July and August are peak season. Right: Hoary marmot in wildflowers, Mt Rainier

Longs Peak, Rocky Mountain

11 Whether you hike to the top of its 14,259ft summit or just ogle its glaciated slopes from below, Longs Peak (p313) is truly a feast for the eyes. Given it's the highest peak in the park, it should be. Those who attempt the ascent via the Keyhole Route must first brave the hair-raising Ledges, before conquering the Trough and inching across the Narrows, which finally give way to the (whew!) Homestretch. The views from the top are mind-boggling.

Hoh Rainforest, Olympic

12 Embrace the rain! It's what makes this temperate rainforest (p258), in all its Tolkienesque beauty, one of the greenest places in North America. With an average rainfall of up to 170in (that's 14ft), it is also one of the wettest. This tremendous amount of water creates a forest covered in mosses, lichens and ferns, with a canopy so dense the forest floor seems trapped in the perpetual lowlight of dusk. Pack your rain jacket and watch for the Roosevelt elk.

11

Sunrise, Cadillac Mountain, Acadia

13 Catching the country's 'first sunrise' from the top of Cadillac Mountain (p375) is, hands down, one of the finest ways to kick off a day. At 1530ft, Cadillac Mountain is the highest point on Maine's Mount Desert Island, and the views over the Atlantic are sublime. The island is one of the easternmost points in the USA, and, while it's technically not the *first* place that catches the morning sun, we prefer to do what everyone else up top does at sunrise: ignore the technicalities and bliss out.

Paddling, Everglades

14 The country's third-largest national park (p396) is a paddler's paradise, with kayak and canoe 'trails' meandering through mangrove swamps and freshwater marshes that teem with wildlife. Crocodiles, alligators, turtles, cormorants, herons, egrets and fish are just some of the wildlife boaters come across while paddling around this subtropical park. Thanks to the National Park Service's handy (and free) kayak and canoe trail maps, navigating the waters is fairly straightforward.

13

Cliff Palace, Mesa Verde

15 This grand engineering achievement, the largest cliff dwelling (p192) in North America, has 217 rooms and 23 kivas, and once provided shelter for 250 to 300 Ancestral Pueblo people. To access it, visitors must climb down a stone stairway and four 10ft ladders, as part of an hour-long ranger-led tour. It's a great place to puzzle out the clues left by its former inhabitants – who vacated the site in AD 1300 for reasons still not fully understood.

Best Hiking

Nothing encapsulates the spirit of the national parks like hiking. Thousands of miles of trails crisscross the parks, offering access to their most scenic mountain passes, highest waterfalls, deepest canyons and quietest corners. Trails run the gamut of accessibility, from the flat, paved paths of Yosemite's Loop Trails to the infamous, thigh-busting grunt up to Zion's Angels Landing.

Vernal & Nevada Falls, Yosemite

Take in unmatched views of Yosemite's most stunning waterfalls.

Iceberg Lake, Glacier

An azure lake sits beneath a massive glacial cirque

Grandview Trail, Grand Canyon

A rugged and steep trail with switchbacks of cobblestone and epic canyon views.

Cascades Pass Trail, North Cascades

High-altitude scenery at its best in the lightly trodden Pacific Northwest wilderness.

Angels Landing, Zion

Exposed scrambling and unrivaled panoramas on a chain-assisted climb to heaven.

1. Iceberg Lake, Glacier **2.** Angels Landing, Zion
3. Vernal Falls, Yosemite

KEVIN SCHAFER / GETTY IMAGES ©

1. Brown bear trapping salmon **2.** Bull moose, Grand Teton
3. Blue heron, Everglades **4.** Hoary marmot, Denali

CHRISTER FREDRIKSSON / GETTY IMAGES ©

Best Wildlife Watching

North America is home to creatures both great and small, from the ferocious grizzly bear to the industrious beaver, with colossal bison, snowy owls, soaring eagles, howling coyotes and doe-eyed manatees all part of the great American menagerie. The USA's national parks are by far the best places to see them.

Lamar Valley, Yellowstone

Bison, moose, wolves and elk roam the 'American Serengeti.' Yellowstone is one of the world's premier wildlife-watching destinations.

Park Road, Denali

One of the best places to spot wildlife in Alaska, this road takes you into the heart of Denali.

Brooks Camp, Katmai

Watch brown bears pluck salmon straight from the falls in this ursine paradise.

Oxbow Bend, Grand Teton

Moose, elk, bald eagles, trumpeter swans, blue herons and more can be seen at this special place in Grand Teton.

Anhinga Trail, Everglades

Spot alligators soaking up the sun and watch for the trail's namesake birds as they spear their prey with their razor-sharp bills.

DON LANDWEHRLE / GETTY IMAGES ©

1. Sunrise, Haleakalā 2. Inspiration Point, Bryce Canyon
3. Cape Royal Point, Grand Canyon
4. Mt Le Conte, Great Smoky Mountains

ROBERTO SONCIN GEROMETTA / GETTY IMAGES ©

Best Views

With sweeping panoramas, deep canyons and sky-high peaks, it's easy to get distracted by viewpoints at almost every turn. Early-morning and late-afternoon light add depth, color, dimension and drama.

Cape Royal Point, Grand Canyon

The earth seems to disappear beneath your feet.

Island in the Sky, Canyonlands

A wide sandstone mesa hemmed by precipitous cliffs that drop over 1000ft to the floor below.

Inspiration Point, Bryce Canyon

Mysterious hoodoos tower up from the Silent City below.

Sunrise, Haleakalā

Watch the sun wake up from the mighty volcano's rim and see the lunarlike surface and multicolored cinder cones.

Mt Le Conte, Great Smoky Mountains

The Great Smoky's third highest peak, visible from practically every viewpoint, and accessible only by foot.

BILL BIRTWHISTLE / GETTY IMAGES ©

1. Sunset, Yosemite Valley 2. Deer in Yellowstone
3. Snow in Rocky Mountain

Best Winter Wonderlands

After you've double-checked parks' accessibility during the colder months, think cross-country skiing, snowshoeing, and picturesque winter wilderness. Not to mention fewer visitors.

Yosemite Valley

Frozen waterfalls, snowy cliffs and a silent, magical white valley await winter visitors.

Yellowstone

Without the crowds, wildlife watching in the nation's very first national park is even better.

Rocky Mountain

You'll practically have this pristine wilderness to yourself if you wait until winter arrives.

Grand Teton

Miles of cross-country ski trails snake beneath massive peaks.

Everglades

A subtropical paradise for those who want to be warm in winter.

1. Canyoneering, Zion 2. Mountaineering, Mt Rainier
3. Rafting, Grand Canyon 4. Swamp in the Everglades

DANNY WARREN / GETTY IMAGES ©

Best Adventures

With environments ranging from the subtropics of the Everglades to the glacial snowfields of the Pacific Northwest, the USA's national parks have no shortage of spectacular settings for a bit of adventure.

Rafting the Colorado River, Grand Canyon

Rafting this stretch of the Colorado River is a virtual all-access pass to the Grand Canyon, in all its wildness, peace and ancient glory.

Paddling, Everglades

Paddle the 99-mile Wilderness Waterway, a labyrinth of mangroves, swamps and the waterways of the Ten Thousand Islands.

Canyoneering, Zion

Rappelling 100ft over the lip of a sandstone bowl, tracing a slot canyon's sculpted curves, staring up at a ragged gash of blue sky – canyoneering is beautiful, dangerous and sublime all at once.

Snorkeling, Dry Tortugas

The Florida Keys reef system is the third largest in the world and it's swarming with barracuda, sea turtles and sunken ships.

Mountaineering, Mt Rainier

The snowcapped summit and forest-covered foothills boast numerous hiking trails, huge swaths of flower-carpeted meadows, and an alluring conical peak that presents a formidable challenge for aspiring climbers.

GREG VAUGHN / GETTY IMAGES ©

1. Hawai'i Volcanoes National Park 2. Pronghorn antelope, Lamar Valley 3. Mammoth Cave

Best Family Experiences

There's something inherently gratifying about bringing kids to a national park. Seeing your child spot a moose or a roaring waterfall can be as thrilling as the experience itself. Along with the natural wonders that will dazzle even the most Xbox-addicted child, national parks have educational programs and activities designed to engage children in the environments around them.

Wildlife Watching, Lamar Valley, Yellowstone

If you don't see a moose – or a bison or a herd of elk or a bear – you probably have your eyes closed. One of the world's premier wildlife-watching destinations.

Rock Climbing, Yosemite Mountaineering School, Yosemite

The world's holy grail of rock climbing, made accessible to all. The school is a gold mine of opportunity, and a constructive way to turn the kids loose for a day.

Cave Tour, Mammoth Cave

Longer than any other known cave, with vast interior cathedrals, bottomless pits and strange, undulating rock formations.

Sand Sledding, Great Sand Dunes

Landscapes collide here in a shifting sea of sand – you might wonder whether a spaceship has whisked you to another planet.

Lava Spotting, Hawai'i Volcanoes National Park

The world's most active volcano has been erupting since 1983. With any luck, you'll witness the primal event of molten lava tumbling into the sea.

USA'S NATIONAL PARKS

NAME	STATE	DESCRIPTION
Acadia National Park	Maine	The only national park in New England encompasses an unspoiled wilderness of undulating coastal mountains, towering sea cliffs, surf-pounded beaches and quiet ponds.
Arches National Park	Utah	Giant sweeping arcs of sandstone frame snowy peaks and desert landscapes; explore the park's namesake formations in a red-rock wonderland.
Badlands National Park	South Dakota	This otherworldly landscape, softened by its rainbow hues, is a spectacle of sheer walls and spikes stabbing the dry air.
Big Bend National Park	Texas	Traversing Big Bend's 1252 sq miles, you come to appreciate what 'big' really means. This is a land of incredible diversity, and vast enough to allow a lifetime of discovery.
Biscayne National Park	Florida	A portion of the world's third-largest reef sits here off the coast of Florida, along with mangrove forests and the Florida Keys.
Black Canyon of the Gunnison National Park	Colorado	No other canyon in America combines the narrow openings, sheer walls and dizzying depths of the Black Canyon.
Bryce Canyon National Park	Utah	Bryce Canyon's sights are nothing short of otherworldly: repeated freezes and thaws have eroded soft sandstone and limestone into a landscape that's utterly unique.
Canyonlands National Park	Utah	A forbidding and beautiful maze of red-rock fins, bridges, needles, spires, craters, mesas and buttes, Canyonlands is a crumbling, decaying beauty – a vision of ancient earth.
Capitol Reef National Park	Utah	Giant slabs of chocolate-red rock and sweeping yellow sandstone domes dominate the landscape of Capitol Reef, which Fremont Indians called the 'Land of the Sleeping Rainbow.'
Carlsbad Caverns National Park	New Mexico	Scores of wondrous caves hide under the hills at this unique national park. The cavern formations are an ethereal wonderland of stalactites and fantastical geological features.
Channel Islands National Park	California	Tossed like lost pearls off the coast, the Channel Islands are California's last outpost of civilization; the islands have earned themselves the nickname 'California's Galápagos.'
Congaree National Park	South Carolina	The lush trees growing here are some of the tallest in the eastern USA, forming one of the highest temperate deciduous forest canopies left in the world.
Crater Lake National Park	Oregon	The gloriously blue waters of Crater Lake reflect surrounding mountain peaks like a giant dark-blue mirror, making for spectacular photographs and breathtaking panoramas.
Cuyahoga Valley National Park	Ohio	Along the winding Cuyahoga River, between Cleveland and Akron, this park is one of Ohio's nicest surprises.
Death Valley National Park	California	The name itself evokes all that is harsh and hellish, yet closer inspection reveals water-sculpted canyons, windswept sand dunes, palm-shaded oases, jagged mountains and wildlife aplenty.
Denali National Park	Alaska	Here is probably your best chance in the Interior (if not in the entire state) of seeing a grizzly bear, moose or caribou.
Dry Tortugas National Park	Florida	Your efforts to get here (by boat or plane only) will be rewarded with amazing snorkeling, diving, bird-watching and stargazing.
Everglades National Park	Florida	This is not just a wetland, or a swamp, or a lake, or a river, or a prairie, or a grassland – it is all of the above.

SIZE	ENTRANCE FEE	FEATURES	PAGE
62 sq miles	7-day pass per vehicle $25		p374
116 sq miles	7-day pass per vehicle $25		p132
379 sq miles	7-day pass per vehicle $15		p344
1252 sq miles	7-day pass per vehicle $25		p144
270 sq miles	Free		p380
48 sq miles	7-day pass per vehicle $15		p280
56 sq miles	7-day pass per vehicle $30		p150
527 sq miles	7-day pass per vehicle $25		p162
378 sq miles	7-day pass per vehicle $10		p168
73 sq miles	Adult/child $10/free		p170
390 sq miles	Free		p64
35 sq miles	Free		p386
287 sq miles	7-day pass per vehicle $15		p224
51 sq miles	Free		p346
5270 sq miles	7-day pass per vehicle $20		p70
9500 sq miles	7-day pass per adult/child $10/free		p226
100 sq miles	7-day pass per adult/child $10/free		p388
2344 sq miles	7-day pass per vehicle $20		p396

NAME	STATE	DESCRIPTION
Gates of the Arctic & Kobuk Valley National Parks	Alaska	These parks are part of a contiguous wilderness harboring no roads and a population of precisely zero.
Glacier Bay National Park	Alaska	Eleven tidewater glaciers spill out of the mountains and fill the sea with icebergs of all shapes, sizes and shades of blue.
Glacier National Park	Montana	Glacier is the only place in the lower 48 states where grizzly bears still roam in abundance, and smart park management has kept the place accessible yet at the same time authentically wild.
Grand Canyon National Park	Arizona	The Grand Canyon embodies the scale and splendor of the American West, captured in its dramatic vistas and inner canyons.
Grand Teton National Park	Wyoming	Simply put, this is sublime and crazy terrain, crowned by the dagger-edged Grand (13,770ft).
Great Basin National Park	Nevada	Rising abruptly from the desert, and dominating Great Basin National Park, 13,063ft Wheeler Peak creates an awesome range of life zones and landscapes within a very compact area.
Great Sand Dunes National Park	Colorado	Landscapes collide in a shifting sea of sand at Great Sand Dunes National Park, making you wonder whether a spaceship has whisked you to another planet.
Great Smoky Mountains National Park	North Carolina & Tennessee	The iconic Great Smoky Mountains National Park offers visitors a chance to experience deep, mysterious old-growth forests.
Guadalupe Mountains National Park	Texas	Guadalupe Mountains National Park is a Texas high spot, both literally and figuratively. At 8749ft, Guadalupe Peak is the highest point in the Lone Star State.
Haleakalā National Park	Hawaii	It's impossible not to be awed by the raw beauty of this ancient place, a haven for wildlife and surefooted hikers.
Hawai'i Volcanoes National Park	Hawaii	This fantastic park dramatically reminds you that nature is very much alive and in perpetual motion.
Hot Springs National Park	Arkansas	Hot Springs borders a city that has made an industry out of the park's major resource: mineral-rich waters of hot springs.
Isle Royale National Park	Michigan	This is certainly the place to go for peace and quiet; the 1200 moose creeping through the forest are all yours.
Joshua Tree National Park	California	Like figments from a Dr Seuss book, Joshua trees welcome visitors to this park where the Sonora and Mojave Deserts converge.
Katmai National Park	Alaska	Stand spine-tinglingly close to 1000lb brown bears, who use their formidable power to paw giant salmon out of the river.
Kenai Fjords National Park	Alaska	Crowning this park is the massive Harding Ice Field; from it, tidewater glaciers pour down, carving the coast into fjords.
Kings Canyon National Park	California	Kings Canyon is one of North America's deepest canyons, plunging over 8000ft.
Lake Clark National Park & Preserve	Alaska	An awesome array of tundra-covered hills, mountains, glaciers, coastline, the largest lakes in the state, and two active volcanoes.
Lassen Volcanic National Park	California	Anchoring the southernmost link in the Cascades' chain of volcanoes, this alien landscape bubbles over with roiling mud pots, noxious sulfur vents, steamy fumaroles, colorful cinder cones and crater lakes.
Mammoth Cave National Park	Kentucky	With hidden underground rivers and more than 400 miles of explored terrain, the world's longest cave system shows off sci-fi-looking stalactites and stalagmites up close.

SIZE	ENTRANCE FEE	FEATURES	PAGE
15,974 sq miles	Free		p232
5036 sq miles	Free		p238
1584 sq miles	7-day pass per vehicle $25 ($15 in winter)		p282
1902 sq miles	7-day pass per vehicle $30		p172
484 sq miles	7-day pass per vehicle $30		p294
120 sq miles	Free		p184
55 sq miles	7-day pass per vehicle $15		p306
815 sq miles	Free		p398
135 sq miles	7-day pass per adult/child $5/free		p186
60 sq miles	3-day pass per vehicle $15		p430
328 sq miles	7-day pass per vehicle $15		p438
8.67 sq miles	Free		p404
210 sq miles	1-day pass per person $4		p350
1240 sq miles	7-day pass per vehicle $20		p76
6400 sq miles	Free		p244
1685 sq miles	Free		p246
721 sq miles	7-day pass per vehicle $20		p78
5625 sq miles	Free		p252
166 sq miles	7-day pass per vehicle $20 ($10 in winter)		p90
83 sq miles	Free		p410

NAME	STATE	DESCRIPTION
Mesa Verde National Park	Colorado	Shrouded in mystery, Mesa Verde is a fascinating, if slightly eerie, place, with a complex of cliff dwellings, some accessed by sheer climbs.
Mount Rainer National Park	Washington	Mt Rainier (elevation 14,411ft) is the USA's fourth-highest peak (outside Alaska) and arguably its most awe-inspiring.
National Park of American Samoa	American Samoa	The National Park of American Samoa is unlike any other, spreading itself across three rainforest-clad South Pacific islands.
North Cascades National Park	Washington	The lightly trodden North Cascades National Park has no settlements, no overnight accommodations and one unpaved road.
Olympic National Park	Washington	Home to one of the world's only temperate rainforests, this notoriously wet national park is as 'wild' and 'west' as it gets.
Petrified Forest National Park	Arizona	Home to an extraordinary array of fossilized ancient logs and the multicolored sandscape of the Painted Desert.
Pinnacles National Park	California	Pinnacles National Park is a study in geologic drama, with craggy monoliths, sheer-walled canyons and ancient volcanic remnants.
Redwood National Park	California	The world's tallest living trees have been standing here from time immemorial; prepare to be impressed.
Rocky Mountain National Park	Colorado	Rocky Mountain National Park showcases classic alpine scenery, with wildflower meadows and serene mountain lakes set under snowcapped peaks.
Saguaro National Park	Arizona	An entire army of the majestic saguaro plant is protected in this two-part desert playground.
Sequoia National Park	California	With trees as high as 20-story buildings, this is an extraordinary park with soul-sustaining forests and vibrant wildflower meadows.
Shenandoah National Park	Virginia	In spring and summer the wildflowers explode; in fall the leaves burn bright; and in winter a beautiful hibernation period sets in.
Theodore Roosevelt National Park	North Dakota	A tortured region known as the 'badlands' whose colors seem to change with the moods of nature.
Virgin Islands National Park	US Virgin Islands	Virgin Islands National Park covers two-thirds of the islands of St John, plus 5650 acres underwater. It's a tremendous resource, offering miles of shoreline, pristine reefs and hiking trails.
Voyageurs National Park	Minnesota	Voyageurs National Park is an outstanding mix of land and waterways formed from earthquakes, volcanoes and glaciers.
Wind Cave National Park	South Dakota	Beneath the mixed-grass prairie and pine forest lies one of the world's longest, most complex cave systems.
Wrangell-St. Elias National Park	Alaska	Comprising more than 20,000 sq miles of brawny ice-encrusted mountains, this is the second-largest national park in the world.
Yellowstone National Park	Wyoming	The real showstoppers here are the geysers and hot springs, but at every turn this land of fire and brimstone breathes, belches and bubbles like a giant kettle on the boil.
Yosemite National Park	California	It's hard to believe so much natural beauty can exist in the one place. The jaw-dropping head-turner of USA national parks, Yosemite garners the devotion of all who enter.
Zion National Park	Utah	From secret oases of trickling water to the hot-pink blooms of a prickly pear cactus, Zion's treasures turn up in the most unexpected places.

SIZE	ENTRANCE FEE	FEATURES	PAGE
80 sq miles	7-day pass per vehicle $10-15		p187
368 sq miles	7-day pass per vehicle $25		p254
20 sq miles	Free		p450
788 sq miles	Free		p256
1406 sq miles	7-day pass per vehicle $20		p258
42,085 sq miles	7-day pass per vehicle $20		p196
40 sq miles	7-day pass per vehicle $10		p94
172 sq miles	Free		p96
415 sq miles	1-/7-day pass per vehicle $20/30		p312
143 sq miles	7-day pass per vehicle/ bicycle $10/5		p198
631 sq miles	7-day pass per vehicle $20		p102
310 sq miles	7-day pass per vehicle $20		p412
110 sq miles	7-day pass per vehicle $20		p352
20 sq miles	Free		p452
340 sq miles	Free		p356
44 sq miles	Free		p358
20,625 sq miles	Free		p260
3472 sq miles	7-day pass per vehicle $30		p318
1169 sq miles	7-day pass per vehicle $30 ($25 November to March)		p114
231 sq miles	7-day pass per vehicle $30		p200

Month by Month

TOP EVENTS

Cody Stampede, July

Spring Wildflowers, April

Strawberry Music Festival, May

Grand Teton Music Festival, July

Frozen Dead Guy Days, March

January

Strap on your snowshoes or cross-country skis and enjoy the white winter magic in Yellowstone, Glacier and Grand Teton. Joshua Tree is lovely, and the subtropical Everglades are sublime.

🏃 Snowshoeing

Leave the crowds behind and take to the trails of the national parks with snowshoes on your feet. Seeing the high-elevation and northern parks when they're blanketed in snow is a magical experience. Rangers at some of the parks even host guided snowshoe hikes.

March

The biting cold of winter fades from the desert parks, and wildflowers begin to bloom at lower elevations. Snow activities are still good at high elevations.

★ Frozen Dead Guy Days

Join the living in Nederland (near Rocky Mountain National Park) and celebrate a dead guy – a Norwegian named Grandpa Bredo Morstoel – who is cryo-genically frozen in a local lab, patiently awaiting reanimation. The festival (go to 'events' at www.frozendeadguydays.org) spans three days in early March and includes music and coffin races.

April

Wildflowers are in full swing at lower elevations, and waterfalls begin pumping at full force with the beginning of the snowmelt. Weather in the desert parks is beautiful.

◉ Spring Wildflowers

Wildflowers put on dazzling springtime displays at the lower-elevation parks, especially at Death Valley, Shenandoah, Great Smoky Mountains, Zion and sometimes Joshua Tree. Check the National Park Service websites for wildflower walks, talks and celebrations.

◉ Yosemite Waterfalls

Most people who visit Yosemite in July and August have no idea – until they get there – that the Valley's famous falls are but a trickle of their springtime selves. April, May and June are the best months to see the falls in full force.

★ National Park Week

For an entire week every April, admission to the national parks is free. Early in the year, the US president announces when National Park Week will fall that year. Many of the parks also host free activities.

May

Temperatures in Zion, Bryce, Grand Canyon, Yosemite Valley, Death Valley and Joshua Tree are delightful. The summer crowds have yet to materialize, waterfalls are at their peak, and river and stream levels are high.

🎵 Strawberry Music Festival

Twice a year (Memorial Day and Labor Day weekend), lovers of country and folk music make a beeline to this wildly popular music festival (www.strawberrymusic.com) held in a meadow at Camp Mather, 10 miles west of Yosemite's Big Oak Flat Entrance.

🎵 Joshua Tree Music Festival

Over a long weekend in May, numerous bands rock Joshua Tree Lake Campground during a family-friendly indie music fest (www.joshuatreemusicfestival.com). It's followed by a soulful roots celebration in mid-October.

June

It's still possible to beat the crowds of summer in early June. By late June, the parks are jammed but the weather is stellar in many of them. Upper-elevation roads are still closed in the Sierras and Rocky Mountains.

🎭 Utah Shakespeare Festival

Near Zion National Park, Cedar City kicks off its three-month-long Shakespeare Festival (www.bard.org) in late June, bringing famed actors to the stage for dozens of top-notch performances. Activities include classes, literary seminars, magic shows and more.

July

High-elevation sectors of the Rockies, Sierras and Cascades begin opening. It's prime hiking time in the high country, where wildflowers are at their peak. Desert parks, including Grand Canyon, are sweltering.

🏃 Cody Stampede

In Yellowstone's gateway communities, rodeo is the major cultural event of the year. Cowboys take to the saddle throughout June, July and August in various communities. The largest rodeos are the Cody Stampede (www.codystampederodeo.com) and the Wild West Yellowstone Rodeo (www.yellowstone-rodeo.com).

🎵 North American Indian Days

In the second week of July, head to the Blackfeet Indian Reservation, immediately east of Glacier National Park, for traditional drumming, dancing and the annual crowning of the year's Miss Blackfeet. The four-day festival (www.browningmontana.com/naid.html) is a wonderful display of Blackfeet traditions.

☉ Summer Wildflowers

There's nothing like hiking through high-country meadows that are blanketed in wildflowers. In high-elevation parks such as Glacier, Rocky Mountain, Yellowstone, Grant Teton and parts of Yosemite, wildflowers bloom intensely during the short growing season between snows.

🎵 Grand Teton Music Festival

Over 40 classical music concerts are held throughout the Jackson Hole region near Grand Teton National Park. Everything from children's concerts to full orchestras are on the menu. Concerts take place almost nightly throughout July and into August. See www.gtmf.org for calendars and to purchase tickets.

August

Hello crowds! It's the height of summer, it's blazing hot, and every hotel and campsite is reserved. First-come, first-served campgrounds are your best bet. Head to the high country, where the weather is superb.

🎵 Christmas in August

Join the Christmas caroling in one of the parks' oddest celebrations, Yellowstone's Christmas in August (celebrated on the 25th). The event dates back to the turn of the last century, when a freak August snowstorm stranded a group of visitors in the Upper Geyser Basin.

September

The crowds begin to thin out, and by the end of the month things are pretty quiet. If you don't mind brisk evenings, this can be a beautiful time to visit the parks. High-country sectors close by the end of the month.

✸ Mountain Life Festival

Participate in hearth cooking demonstrations and help make historic farm staples like hominy, apple butter, apple cider and soap. The event is celebrated every year in mid-September at the Mountain Farm Museum in Great Smoky Mountains National Park.

October

From Yosemite to the Great Smoky Mountains, fall color is nothing short of fabulous in many of the parks. Grand Canyon, Zion, Joshua Tree and Death Valley are especially beautiful. Crowds are nonexistent and the temperatures are dropping quickly. High-elevation sectors are closed.

✸ Pioneer Days

On the third weekend in October, the town of Twentynine Palms, near Joshua Tree National Park, celebrates Pioneer Days (www.visit29.org) with an Old West–themed carnival featuring a parade, arm-wrestling and a giant chili dinner.

Top: Thistle flower, Rocky Mountain National Park
Bottom: Winter hiking, Bryce Canyon National Park

Top: Mountain Farm Museum, Great Smoky Mountains National Park
Bottom: Vernal Falls, Yosemite National Park

November

Winter is creeping in quickly. The best parks to visit are those in southern Utah, Arizona and the California deserts, where the weather is cool but still beautiful.

✿ Death Valley '49ers

In early or mid-November, Furnace Creek hosts this historical encampment (www.deathvalley49ers. org), featuring cowboy poetry, campfire sing-alongs, a gold-panning contest and a Western art show. Show up to this Death Valley festival early to watch the pioneer wagons come thunderin' in.

December

Winter is well under way in most of the parks. High-elevation roads and park sectors are closed, and visitor-center and business hours are reduced. Think snowshoeing and cross-country skiing.

✿ National Audubon Society Christmas Bird Count

Every year around Christmastime, thousands of people take to the wilds to look for and record birds for the Audubon Society's annual survey. Many of the parks organize a count and rely on volunteers to help. Check the National Park Service websites for information.

Get Inspired

Books

Our National Parks (1901) The words of John Muir inspired a nation to embrace national parks.

Ranger Confidential: Living, Working, & Dying in the National Parks (2010) Former park ranger Andrea Lankford tells you what it takes to fill the shoes of our favorite park employee.

Lost in My Own Backyard (2004) Chuckle your way around Yellowstone with Tim Cahill.

A Sand County Almanac (1949) Aldo Leopold's nature-oriented classic embodies the conservation ethic that lies at the heart of the USA's national parks.

Films

American Experience: Ansel Adams (2002) Inspire your snapshots with this PBS documentary.

Vacation (1983) Perfect comedy kick-starter for any family vacation.

Thelma & Louise (1991) The classic American road-trip flick is a joy to watch, despite the terrible circumstances.

Into the Wild (2007) Follow Chris McCandless as he kisses his possessions goodbye and hitchhikes to Alaska.

Music

Classic Old-Time Fiddle (2007) Perfect fiddle compilation for trips to Great Smoky Mountains and Shenandoah.

Joshua Tree (1987) Crank up this U2 classic, whether you're heading to Joshua Tree or not.

Beautiful Maladies (1998) Nothing spells 'road trip' like a good Tom Waits tune.

This Land is Your Land: The Asch Recordings, Vol. 1 (1997) Woodie Guthrie sings everything from 'This Land is Your Land' to 'The Car Song'.

Websites

Lonely Planet (www.lonely-planet.com) Hotel bookings, traveler forum and more.

RoadsideAmerica.com (www.roadsideamerica.com) Don't miss all those weird roadside attractions.

The National Parks (www.pbs.org/nationalparks) Online portal of Ken Burns' national park PBS classic.

Short on Time?

This list will give you an instant insight into the national parks.

➜ **Read** *Adam Ansel in the National Parks* (2010) is the next best thing to being there.

➜ **Watch** Ken Burns' 12-hour PBS miniseries, *The National Parks, America's Best Idea* (2009) is a must.

➜ **Listen** Dig into the blues, folk and country roots of America with Harry Smith's *Anthology of American Folk Music* (1952).

➜ **Log on** National Park Service websites (www.nps.gov) are jammed with information on everything from hiking to stargazing.

Lower Yesllowstone Falls, Yellowstone National Park

Need to Know

Entry Fees
Free (Great Smoky) to $30 per vehicle (Yosemite); valid for seven consecutive days.

America the Beautiful Annual Pass
$80 per vehicle valid for all national parks for 12 months from purchase. Buy through National Park Service (☏888-275-8747, ext 3; www.nps.gov).

ATMs
Most parks have at least one ATM; widely available in gateway towns.

Credit Cards
Major credit cards widely accepted; Forest Service, BLM and other campgrounds accept cash and/or checks only.

Cell Phones
Coverage inside parks is spotty at best.

Wi-Fi
Some park lodges have wireless. Outside the parks, most cafes and hotels offer free wireless. Chain hotels charge.

Tipping
Tip restaurant servers 15–20%; porters $2 per bag; hotel maids $2 to $5 per night.

When to Go

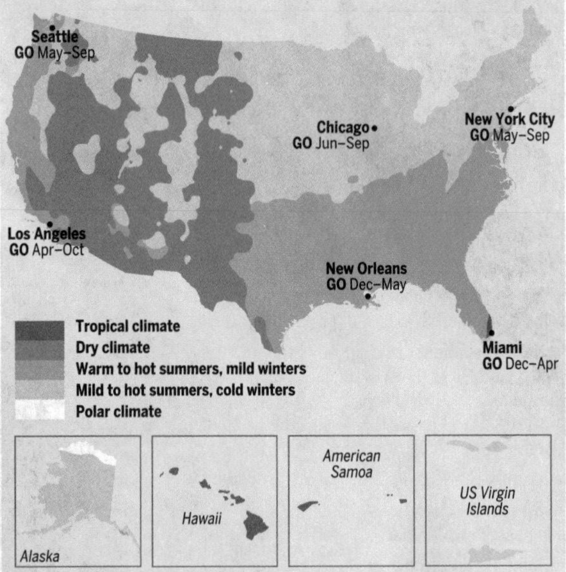

Seattle GO May–Sep
Chicago GO Jun–Sep
New York City GO May–Sep
Los Angeles GO Apr–Oct
New Orleans GO Dec–May
Miami GO Dec–Apr

Tropical climate
Dry climate
Warm to hot summers, mild winters
Mild to hot summers, cold winters
Polar climate

Alaska
Hawaii
American Samoa
US Virgin Islands

High Season
(Jun–early Sep)
→ High-country sectors in the Rockies, Sierras and Cascades are guaranteed to be open.
→ July and August are crowded; reservations are a must.

Shoulder
(May–mid-Jun & mid-Sep–Oct)
→ Waterfalls in Yosemite and Great Smoky Mountains are at their peak in spring.
→ High-elevation roads are still closed in spring.

Low Season
(mid-Sep–May)
→ Cross-country skiing and snowshoeing are excellent in the Rockies and Sierras.
→ High season for the subtropical Everglades.

Advance Planning

➡ **Twelve months before** Reserve campsites and historic lodge accommodations.

➡ **Six months before** Reserve hotel rooms in satellite towns if visiting in summer. Book flights.

➡ **Three months before** Start training if planning to backpack. If you haven't reserved sleeping arrangements, do so.

➡ **One month before** Secure rental car. Take your own car in for a safety inspection and tune-up if planning a long drive.

What to Bring

➡ **Rain jacket** Thin shell that's easy to pack; afternoon thundershowers are common in summer.

➡ **Layers** Layered clothing keeps you warmest and is best for adjustability.

➡ **Binoculars** A must for wildlife watching.

➡ **Insect repellent** Critical for high country in summer, when mosquitoes and blackflies are out. Also use for ticks in woodsy, low-elevation areas.

➡ **Camp chair** Relax in style.

➡ **Sun protection** Hat, sunglasses and sunblock.

➡ **First aid kit** Buy one or make your own.

➡ **Flashlight** Critical for campers.

Exchange Rates

Australia	A$1	US$0.75
Canada	C$1	US$0.79
Euro zone	€1	US$1.10
Japan	¥100	US$0.82
New Zealand	NZ$1	US$0.67
UK	£1	US$1.53

For current exchange rates see www.xe.com.

Daily Costs

Budget:
Less than $100

➡ Campsites: $10–25

➡ Park entrance fees: Free–$30

➡ Plenty of self-catering options in gateway towns; pricier at stores inside parks

➡ Park shuttles and visitor sites free with admission

➡ Gas costs depend on distances and vehicle

Midrange:
$100–250

➡ Double room in budget or chain hotel, or B&B: $50–200

➡ Cafe meals $15-25; diners and local restaurants $25–50

➡ Activities: $15–50

➡ Standar car rental: from $30 excluding insurance and gas

Top End:
More than $250

➡ Better B&Bs and four-star hotels: over $200

➡ Meal in a high-end restaurant in a gateway town: $50

Arriving at a National Park

➡ **Information** Pick up a park newspaper at the entry kiosk and hang onto it; they're packed with useful information.

➡ **Camping** If you're going for a first-come, first-served site, head straight to the campground. Try to arrive no later than mid-morning Friday.

➡ **Parking** People not spending the night inside a park will find parking difficult. Arrive early, park and take free shuttles whenever possible.

➡ **Visitor Centers** Best places to start exploring the parks. Purchase books and maps, ask rangers questions, check weather reports and trail and road conditions.

Getting Around

➡ **Car** Most convenient way to travel between the parks. A few park roads are gravel. Traffic inside some parks can be horrendous.

➡ **Park Shuttles** Many parks have excellent shuttle systems with stops at major visitor sites and trailheads.

➡ **Bicycles** Some parks have rentals. Good for getting around developed areas. Elsewhere, roads can be steep and shoulders narrow.

Accommodations

➡ **Campsites** Reservation and first-come, first-served sites both available in all parks. Flush toilets are common, hot showers are not. Full hookups for RVs usually found outside parks.

➡ **Park Lodges** Wonderful experience. Usually lack TV; some have wi-fi.

➡ **B&Bs** Available in gateway towns outside parks; often excellent and usually include wi-fi.

➡ **Hotels** Occasionally inside parks; most in gateway towns. Nearly all have wi-fi.

Useful Websites

National Park Service (www.nps.gov) Comprehensive guide to parks around the country.

Lonely Planet (www.lonelyplanet.com) Hotel bookings, traveler forum and more.

USA
BY REGION

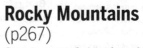

Rocky Mountains
(p267)

Gasp at postcard views from the high country, and explore frontier history, pristine lakes, natural geysers and celebrity ski resorts.

Pacific Northwest
(p213)

Lose yourself amid snow-topped volcanoes, bubbling hot springs, wind-whipped beaches and deep coastal rainforest.

California (p51)

Cruise by the surf-tossed Pacific and reach for the sky in the Sierra Nevada on your way through nine of the USA's national parks.

Great Lakes & Great Plains (p331)

Wind past lakefront beaches and lighthouses, bison and bighorn. Take in tales of the Wild West, Native American traditions and endless miles of golden prairie.

The East (p361)

Search out craggy coastlines strung with fishing villages, brilliant fall foliage and Civil War battlefields. The natural beauty rolls inland through rural Appalachia and Cajun country.

Southwest (p127)

Gaze at boundless horizons from the Grand Canyon, between Monument Valley's buttes or by the banks of the Rio Grande.

Hawaii & US Territories (p427)

Volcanoes, subtropical forests, coral reefs, idyllic beaches and unique island wildlife: the US Virgin Islands, Hawaii and American Samoa are well worth the trip.

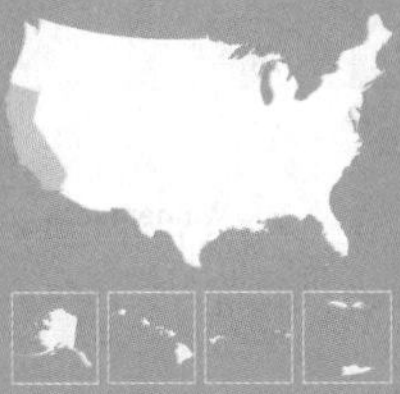

California

Thunderous waterfalls, glacier-carved valleys and the world's tallest, biggest and oldest trees are just some of the natural wonders that California offers. This is a state that has it all: the highest peak in the Lower 48, Mt Whitney, tumbles all the way down to Badwater Basin, the nation's lowest point below sea level. The arid expanses of the Mojave Desert reach almost to the underwater kelp forests of the Pacific, while mighty redwoods line the northern coast.

Throw in all the ecosystems in between, and it's no surprise that California has more national parks than anywhere else in the United States. Yosemite and Sequoia became the state's first in 1890, and today there are seven more: Kings Canyon, Death Valley, Joshua Tree, Channel Islands, Redwood, Lassen Volcanic and Pinnacles.

Santa Barbara island, Channel Islands National Park
BILL PERRY/SHUTTERSTOCK ©

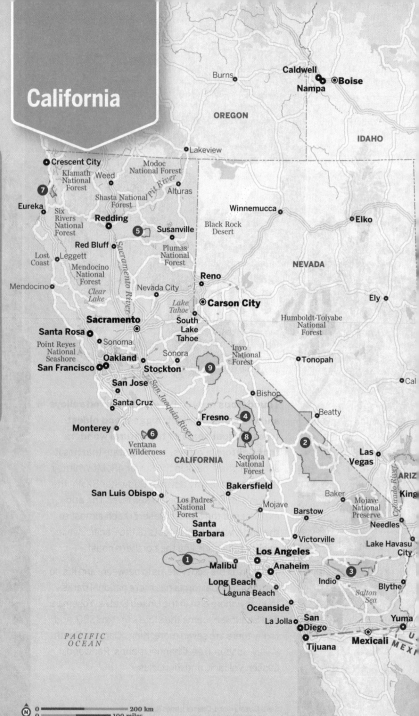

California

① Channel Islands National Park
Remote and rugged islands off the coast of California. (p64)

② Death Valley National Park
Singing sand dunes, shady oases and endemic wildlife. (p70)

③ Joshua Tree National Park
Whimsical Joshua trees in a climber's paradise. (p76)

④ Kings Canyon National Park
Giant sequoias, sheer granite cliffs and one of America's deepest canyons. (p78)

⑤ Lassen Volcanic National Park
Otherwordly, off-the-beaten-path and quietly impressive. (p90)

⑥ Pinnacles National Park
Talus caves, endangered condors and towering spires. (p94)

⑦ Redwood National Park
The tallest trees on earth along the foggy Northern California coast. (p96)

⑧ Sequoia National Park
Gigantic mountains and sequoia-filled forests. (p102)

⑨ Yosemite National Park
Waterfalls, granite peaks and dreamlike landscapes. (p114)

✔ DON'T MISS

Yosemite Valley
Home of the big sights: Half Dome, Yosemite Falls, El Capitan and the Royal Arches. See them all in **Yosemite National Park**.

Rock Climbing
From boulders to cracks to multipitch faces, there are more than 8000 established routes in **Joshua Tree National Park**.

Walking Among Redwoods
Crane your neck at the world's tallest trees in **Redwood National Park**.

Moro Rock
Climb the quarter-mile staircase to this viewpoint and marvel at the Great Western Divide in **Sequoia National Park**.

Zumwalt Meadow
Take in the sweeping Sierra Nevada views from beside the Kings River in **Kings Canyon National Park**.

Yosemite Falls Triple-tiered, thi
waterfall is North America's talles

Yosemite, Sequoia & Kings Canyon National Parks

Drive up into the lofty Sierra Nevada, where glacial valleys and ancient forests overfill the windshield scenery. Go climb a rock, pitch a tent or photograph wildflowers and wildlife.

TRIP HIGHLIGHTS

70 miles

Tuolumne Meadows
Drive over the rooftop of the Sierra Nevada

15 miles

Yosemite Valley
Where waterfalls tumble over giant granite cliffs

Tunnel View — START

Glacier Point

Wawona

325 miles

Cedar Grove
Drop into California's deepest river canyon

Grant Grove

Fresno

Mineral King Valley — FINISH

Giant Forest
Circumambulate the world's biggest trees

345 miles

**5–7 DAYS
450 MILES/725KM**

GREAT FOR...

BEST TIME TO GO

April and May for waterfalls; June to August for mountain highlands.

ESSENTIAL PHOTO

Yosemite Valley from panoramic Tunnel View.

BEST SCENIC DRIVE

Kings Canyon Scenic Byway to Cedar Grove.

Classic Trip

Yosemite, Sequoia & Kings Canyon National Parks

Glacier-carved valleys resting below dramatic peaks make Yosemite an all-ages playground. Here you can witness earth-shaking waterfalls, clamber up granite domes and camp out in high-country meadows where wildflowers bloom in summer. Home to one of the USA's deepest canyons and the biggest tree on the planet, Sequoia & Kings Canyon National Parks justify detouring further south into the Sierra Nevada, which conservationist John Muir called 'The Range of Light.'

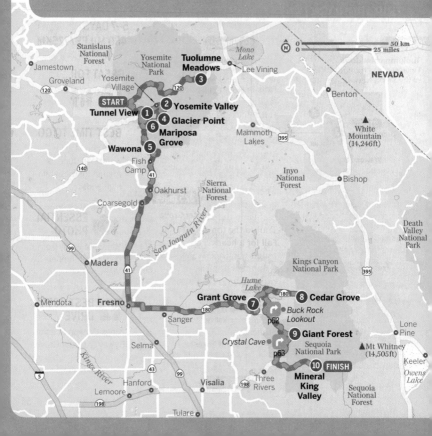

❶ Tunnel View

Arriving in **Yosemite National Park** (☎209-372-0200; www.nps.gov/yose; 7-day pass per vehicle $30; 🚻) at the Arch Rock entrance station, follow Hwy 140 east. Pull over at **Tunnel View** for your first look into Yosemite Valley, which has inspired painters, poets, naturalists and adventurers for centuries. On the right, Bridalveil Fall swells with snowmelt in late spring, but by late summer it's a mere whisper, often lifted and blown aloft by the wind. Spread below you are the pine forests and meadows of the Valley floor, with the sheer face of El Capitan rising on the left, and in the distance straight ahead, iconic granite Half Dome.

The Drive ≫ Merge carefully onto Wawona Rd, which continues downhill into Yosemite Valley, full of confusingly intersecting one-way roads. Drive east along the Merced River on Southside Dr past the Bridalveil Fall turnoff. Almost 6 miles from Tunnel View, turn left and drive across Sentinel Bridge to Yosemite Village's day-use parking lots. Ride free shuttle buses that circle the Valley.

TRIP HIGHLIGHT

❷ Yosemite Valley

From the bottom looking up, this dramatic valley cut by the meandering Merced River is song-inspiring, and not just for birds: rippling meadow grasses; tall pines; cool, impassive pools reflecting granite monoliths; and cascading, glacier-cold whitewater ribbons. At busy **Yosemite Village**, start inside the **Yosemite Valley Visitor Center** (⏰10am-6pm late May–early Sep, 9am-5pm early Sep–late May; 🚻), with its thought-provoking history and nature displays and free *Spirit of Yosemite* film screenings. At the nearby **Yosemite Museum** (⏰9am-5pm), Western landscape paintings are hung beside Native American baskets and beaded clothing.

The Valley's famous waterfalls are thunderous cataracts in May, but mere trickles by late July. Triple-tiered **Yosemite Falls** is North America's tallest, while **Bridalveil Fall** is hardly less impressive. A strenuous, often slippery staircase beside **Vernal Fall** leads you, gasping, right to the top edge of the waterfall, where rainbows pop in clouds of mist. Keep hiking up the same Mist Trail to the top of **Nevada Fall** for a heady 6-mile round-trip trek.

In midsummer, you can rent a raft at Curry Village and float down the **Merced River**. The serene stretch between Stoneman Bridge and Sentinel Beach is gentle enough for kids. Or take the whole family to see the stuffed wildlife mounts at the hands-on **Nature Center at Happy Isles** (⏰usually 9:30am-5pm late May–Sep; 🚻), east of Curry Village.

The Drive ≫ From Yosemite Village, drive west on Northside Dr, passing Yosemite Falls and El Capitan. After 6 miles, turn right onto Big Oak Flat Rd/Hwy 120. For almost 10 miles, the road curves above the valley into the forest. Near Crane Flat gas station, turn right to follow Tioga Rd/Hwy 120 east (open summer and fall only). Continuing straight ahead, Big Oak Flat Rd/Hwy 120 west exits the park, leading past the turnoff to Hetch Hetchy.

TRIP HIGHLIGHT

❸ Tuolumne Meadows

Leave the crushing crowds of Yosemite Valley behind and escape to the Sierra Nevada high country along Tioga Rd, which follows a 19th-century wagon road and Native American trading route. **Warning!** Completely closed by snow in winter, Tioga Rd is usually open *only* from May or June through October.

About 45 miles from Yosemite Valley, stop at **Olmsted Point**. Overlooking a lunar-type landscape of glaciated granite, gaze deeply down Tenaya Canyon to the backside of Half Dome. A few miles further east, a sandy half-moon beach wraps around **Tenaya Lake**,

Classic Trip

tempting you to brave some of the coldest swimming in the park. Sunbathers lie upon the rocks that rim the lake's northern shore.

About a 90-minute drive from Yosemite Valley, **Tuolumne Meadows** is the Sierra Nevada's largest subalpine meadow, with fields of wildflowers, bubbling streams, ragged granite peaks and cooler temperatures at an elevation of 8600ft.

Hikers and climbers find a paradise of trails and granite domes to tackle, or unpack a picnic basket by the stream-fed meadows.

The Drive ≫ From Tuolumne Meadows, backtrack 50 miles to Yosemite Valley, turning left on El Portal Rd, then right on Northside Dr and right again on Wawona Rd. Follow narrow Wawona Rd/Hwy 41 up out of the valley. After 9 miles, turn left onto Glacier Point Rd at the Chinquapin intersection, driving 15 more miles to Glacier Point.

- - - - - - - - - - - - - - - -

❹ Glacier Point

In only an hour, you can zip from Yosemite Valley up to head-spinning

Glacier Point. **Warning!** Glacier Point Rd is closed by snow in winter, usually not opening again until May. Between November and April, the road remains open as far as Badger Pass ski area, but snow tires and tire chains may be required.

Rising over 3000ft above the valley floor, dramatic **Glacier Point** (7214ft) practically puts you at eye level with Half Dome. Glimpse what John Muir and US President Teddy Roosevelt saw when they camped here in 1903: the waterfall-strewn Yosemite Valley below and the distant

HIKING HALF DOME & AROUND YOSEMITE VALLEY

Over 800 miles of hiking trails in Yosemite National Park fit hikers of all abilities. Take an easy half-mile stroll on the Valley floor or underneath giant sequoia trees, or venture out all day on a quest for viewpoints, waterfalls and lakes in the mountainous high country.

Some of the park's most popular hikes start right in Yosemite Valley, including to the top of **Half Dome** (17-mile round-trip), the most famous of all. It follows a section of the John Muir Trail and is strenuous, difficult and best tackled in two days with an overnight in Little Yosemite Valley. Reaching the top can only be done in summer after park rangers have installed fixed cables; depending on snow conditions, this may occur as early as late May or as late as July and the cables usually come down in October. To limit the cables' notorious human logjams, the park now requires permits for day hikers, but the route is still nerve-wracking as hikers must share the cables. **Advance permits** (✆877-444-6777; www.recreation. gov) go on sale by lottery in early spring, with a limited number available via a daily lottery in hiking season (for use two days later). Permit regulations and prices keep changing; check the park website (http://www.nps.gov/yose) for current details.

The less ambitious or physically fit will still have a ball following the **Mist Trail** as far as Vernal Fall (3-mile round-trip), the top of Nevada Fall (6-mile round-trip) or idyllic Little Yosemite Valley (8-mile round-trip). The **Four Mile Trail** (9-mile round-trip) up to Glacier Point is a strenuous but satisfying climb to a glorious viewpoint. If you've got the kids in tow, nice and easy **Valley walks** include to Mirror Lake (2-mile round-trip) and viewpoints at the base of thundering Yosemite Falls (1-mile round-trip) and lacy Bridalveil Fall (0.5-mile round-trip).

WINTER WONDERLANDS

When the temperature drops and the white stuff falls, there are still tons of fun outdoor activities around the Sierra Nevada's national parks. In Yosemite, strap on some skis or a snowboard and go tubing downhill at Badger Pass; plod around Yosemite Valley or to Dewey Point on a ranger-led snowshoe tour; or just try to stay upright on ice skates at Curry Village. Further south in Sequoia & Kings Canyon National Parks, the whole family can go snowshoeing or cross-country skiing among groves of giant sequoias. Before embarking on a winter trip to the parks, check road conditions on the official park websites or by calling ahead. Don't forget to put snow tires on your car, and always carry tire chains, too.

peaks ringing Tuolumne Meadows. To get away from the crowds, hike a little way down the Panorama Trail, just south of the crowded main viewpoint.

On your way back from Glacier Point, take time out for a 2-mile hike up **Sentinel Dome** or out to **Taft Point** for incredible 360-degree valley views.

The Drive » Drive back downhill past Badger Pass, turning left at the Chinquapin intersection and winding south through thick forest on Wawona Rd/Hwy 41. After almost 13 curvy miles, you'll reach Wawona, with its hotel, visitor center, general store and gas station, all on your left.

----

⑤ Wawona

At Wawona, a 45-minute drive south of the valley, drop by the **Pioneer Yosemite History Center**, with its covered bridge, pioneer-era buildings and historic Wells Fargo office. In summer you can take a short, bumpy stagecoach ride and really feel like

you're living in the past. Peek inside the **Wawona Visitor Center** (⊘8:30am-5pm mid-May–Oct) at 19th-century artist Thomas Hill's recreated studio, hung with romantic Sierra Nevada landscape paintings. On summer evenings, imbibe a civilized cocktail in the lobby lounge of the Wawona Hotel, where pianist Tom Bopp plays tunes from Yosemite's bygone days.

The Drive » In summer, leave your car at Wawona and take a free shuttle bus to Mariposa Grove. By car, follow Wawona Rd/Hwy 41 south for 4.5 miles to the four-way stop by the park's south entrance. Continue straight ahead on Mariposa Rd (closed in winter) for 3.5 miles to the parking lot – when it's full, drivers are turned away.

----

⑥ Mariposa Grove

Wander giddily around the Mariposa Grove, home of the 1800-year-old Grizzly Giant and 500 other giant sequoias that tower above your head. Nature trails wind

through this popular grove, but you can only hear yourself think above the noise of vacationing crowds and motorized tram tours during the early morning or evening.

Notwithstanding a cruel hack job back in 1895, the walk-through California Tunnel Tree continues to survive, so pose your family in front and snap away. If you've got the energy for a 5-mile round-trip hike to the upper grove, the **Mariposa Grove Museum** (⊘10am-4pm May-Sep) has displays about sequoia ecology inside a pioneer cabin.

The Drive » From Yosemite's south entrance station, it's a 120-mile, three-hour trip to Kings Canyon National Park. Follow Hwy 41 south 60 miles to Fresno, then slingshot east on Hwy 180 for another 50 miles, climbing out of the Central Valley back into the mountains. Keep left at the Hwy 198 intersection, staying on Hwy 180 towards Grant Grove.

Classic Trip

JON ARNOLD IMAGES / GETTY IMAGES ©

➐ Grant Grove

Through **Sequoia & Kings Canyon National Parks** (☎559-565-3341; www.nps.gov/seki; 7-day pass per vehicle $20; ♿), roads seem barely to scratch the surface of the twin parks' beauty. To see real treasures, you'll need to get out and stretch your legs. North of Big Stump entrance station in Grant Grove Village, turn left and wind downhill to **General Grant Grove**, where you'll see some of the park's landmark giant sequoia trees along a paved path. You can walk right through the Fallen Monarch, a massive, fire-hollowed trunk that's done duty as a cabin, hotel, saloon and horse stable. For views of Kings Canyon and the peaks of the Great Western Divide, follow a narrow, winding side road (closed in winter, no RVs or trailers) starting behind John Muir Lodge up to **Panoramic Point**.

The Drive ›› Kings Canyon National Park's main visitor areas, Grant Grove and Cedar Grove, are linked by narrow, twisting Hwy 180, which dramatically descends into Kings Canyon. Expect spectacular views all along this outstandingly scenic 30-mile drive. **Warning!** Hwy 180 from the Hume Lake turnoff to Cedar Grove is closed during winter (usually mid-November through mid-April).

Clockwise from top left: Mariposa Grove; Yosemite National Park; Tuolumne Meadows

Classic Trip

TRIP HIGHLIGHT

8 Cedar Grove

Serpenting past chiseled rock walls laced with waterfalls, Hwy 180 plunges down to the Kings River, where roaring whitewater ricochets off the granite cliffs of one of North America's deepest canyons. Pull over partway down at **Junction View overlook** for an eyeful, then keep rolling along the river to **Cedar Grove Village**. East of the village, **Zumwalt Meadow** is the place for spotting birds, mule deer and black bears. If the day is hot and your suit is handy, stroll from Road's End to **Muir Rock**, a large flat-top river boulder where John Muir once gave outdoor talks, now a popular summer swimming hole. Starting from Road's End, a very popular day hike climbs 4.5 miles each way to roaring **Mist Falls**.

The Drive » Backtrack from Road's End nearly 30 miles up Hwy 180. Turn left onto Hume Lake Rd. Curve around the lake past swimming beaches, turning right onto 10 Mile Rd, which runs by US Forest Service (USFS) campgrounds. At Hwy 198, turn left and follow the Generals Hwy (sometimes closed in winter) south for about 23 miles to the Wolverton Rd turnoff on your left.

TRIP HIGHLIGHT

9 Giant Forest

We dare you to try hugging the trees in **Giant Forest**, a 3-sq-mile grove protecting the park's most gargantuan specimens. Park off Wolverton Rd and walk downhill to reach the world's biggest living tree, the **General Sherman Tree**, which towers 275ft into the sky. With sore arms and sticky sap fingers, you can lose the crowds on any of many forested trails nearby. The trail network stretches all the way south to Crescent Meadow, a 5-mile one-way ramble.

By car, drive 2.5 miles south along the Generals Hwy to get schooled on sequoia ecology and fire cycles at the **Giant Forest Museum** (⊙ usually 9am-4.30pm or 6pm mid-May–mid-Oct; 🚻).

Starting outside the museum, Crescent Meadow Rd makes a 6-mile loop out through Giant Forest, passing right through the **Tunnel Log**. For 360-degree views of the Great Western Divide, climb the steep quarter-mile staircase up **Moro Rock**.

Warning! Crescent Meadow Rd is closed to traffic by winter snow; during summer, ride the free shuttle buses around the loop road and between the Giant Forest Museum and Wolverton Rd parking areas, rather than driving yourself.

The Drive » Narrowing, the Generals Hwy drops for almost 20 miles into the Sierra Nevada foothills, passing Amphitheater Point and exiting the park beyond Foothills Visitor Center.

DETOUR: BUCK ROCK LOOKOUT

Start: 8 Cedar Grove

To climb one of California's most evocative fire lookouts, drive east of the Generals Hwy on Big Meadows Rd into the Sequoia National Forest between between Grant Grove and the Giant Forest. Follow the signs to staffed **Buck Rock Lookout** (www. buckrock.org; Forest Rd 13S04; admission free; ⊙usually 9:30am-6pm Jul-Oct). Constructed in 1923, this active fire lookout allows panoramic views from a dollhouse-sized cab lording over the horizon from 8500ft atop a granite rise, reached by 172 spindly stairs. It's not for anyone with vertigo!

Before reaching the town of Three Rivers, turn left on Mineral King Rd, a dizzyingly scenic 25-mile road (partly unpaved, no trailers or RVs allowed) that switchbacks up to Mineral King Valley.

- - - - - - - - - - - - - -

⑩ Mineral King Valley

Navigating almost 700 hairpin turns, it's a winding 1½-hour drive up to glacially sculpted **Mineral King Valley** (7500ft), a 19th-century silver-mining camp and lumber settlement, and later a mountain retreat. Trailheads into the high country begin at the end of Mineral King Rd, where historic private cabins dot the valley floor flanked by massive mountains. Your final destination is just over a mile past the ranger station, where the valley

DETOUR: CRYSTAL CAVE

Start: ⑨ Giant Forest

Off the Generals Hwy, about 2 miles south of the Giant Forest Museum, turn right onto twisting 6.5-mile-long Crystal Cave Rd for a fantastical walk inside 10,000-year-old **Crystal Cave** (www.sequoiahistory.org; tours adult/child from $15/8; ⊗tours May-Nov, weather permitting; 🚻), carved by an underground river. Stalactites hang like daggers from the ceiling, and 10,000-year-old milky-white marble formations take the shape of ethereal curtains, domes, columns and shields. Bring a light jacket – it's 50°F (10°C) inside the cave. You must buy tour tickets in advance from the Lodgepole or Foothills Visitor Centers.

unfolds all of its hidden beauty, and hikes to granite peaks and alpine lakes beckon.

Warning! Mineral King Rd is typically open only from mid-May through late October. In early summer,

marmots like to chew on parked cars, so wrap the undercarriage of your vehicle with a tarp or stake chicken-wire fencing (which can be rented from Silver City Resort) around the outside of your vehicle.

California Tunnel Tree, Mariposa Grove

STATE
California

ENTRANCE FEE
Free

AREA
390 sq miles

GOOD FOR

Elephant seals in Point Bennett, San Miguel island

BOB EVANS / GETTY IMAGES ©

Channel Islands National Park

Tossed like lost pearls off the coast, the Channel Islands are California's last outpost of civilization. Remote and rugged, the islands have earned themselves the nickname 'California's Galápagos'.

Isolated for thousands of years, the Channel Islands are a unique haven for plants, animals and archaeological resources.

The islands support an abundance of marine life, from coral reefs to giant elephant seals, and offer fantastic sea kayaking, scuba diving and snorkeling.

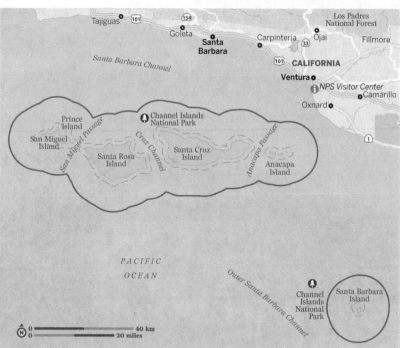

Channel Islands National Park, off the coast of southern California, is made up of five islands and their surrounding ocean: San Miguel, Santa Rosa, Anacapa, Santa Barbara and Santa Cruz.

Anacapa, an hour's boat ride from the mainland, is the best island for day-tripping, with easy hikes and unforgettable views. From **Inspiration Point** you can see the two smaller Anacapa islets and Santa Cruz Island, and from the sea cliffs view sea lions and seals.

Santa Cruz, the biggest island, is ideal for overnight camping excursions, kayaking and hiking.

Other islands require longer channel crossings and multiday trips. **San Miguel** is often shrouded in fog. Tiny **Santa Barbara** supports seabird and seal colonies. So does **Santa Rosa**, which also protects Torrey pine trees.

Snorkeling, Diving & Kayaking

The waters of Santa Barbara, Anacapa and the eastern Santa Cruz Islands are best for underwater exploration. Here you'll find sea caves, coves and kelp forests.

When to Go

Spring, when wildflowers bloom, is a gorgeous time to visit; summer and fall are bone-dry, but the latter brings the calmest water and winds; winter can be stormy.

Wildlife Watching

Point Bennett on San Miguel Island has one of the largest concentrations of wildlife in the world. There are more than 30,000 seals and sea lions here. In the **Santa Barbara Channel**, there are more than 30 different marine mammal species including dolphins, California sea lions, gray whales and elephant seals.

Anacapa Island

Coral reef, Anacapa Island

Humpback whale, Santa Barbara island

Information

Visitors must bring all their own supplies. There are no lodgings or services on the islands. The park's **visitor center** (📞805-658-5730; www.nps.gov/chis; 1901 Spinnaker Dr, Ventura; 🕐8:30am-5pm) is located in the Ventura Harbor, off Hwy 101. Ventura is 70 miles north of Los Angeles and 30 miles south of Santa Barbara.

Boats leave for the islands from Ventura Harbor. The main tour-boat operator is **Island Packers** (📞805-642-1393; www.islandpackers.com; 1691 Spinnaker Dr, Ventura; 3hr cruise adult/child 3-12yr from $36/26); book ahead.

Access

The islands are only accessible by park-managed boats and planes or private boat.

There is no transportation on the islands. All areas must be accessed by foot, kayak or private boat (no bicycles).

Sleeping

Camping is available year-round on all five islands in the national park. There is currently one established campground, managed by the National Park Service, on each island: above the Landing Cove on Santa Barbara, on the east islet of Anacapa, at Scorpion Ranch on Santa Cruz, at Water Canyon on Santa Rosa, and above Cuyler Harbor on San Miguel. Limited backcountry camping is available on Santa Cruz and Santa Rosa Islands. Campground reservations are required; book through recreation.gov.

STATE
California

ENTRANCE FEE
7-day pass per vehicle $20

AREA
5270 sq miles

GOOD FOR

Coyote, Death Valley National Park

Death Valley National Park

The name itself evokes all that is harsh and hellish – a punishing, barren and lifeless place. Yet closer inspection reveals water-sculpted canyons, windswept sand dunes, palm-shaded oases, jagged mountains and wildlife aplenty here.

It's also a land of extremes and superlatives, holding the US records for hottest temperature (134°F, or 57°C), lowest point (Badwater, 282ft below sea level), and largest national park outside Alaska (more than 5000 sq miles). Peak tourist season is when spring wildflowers bloom.

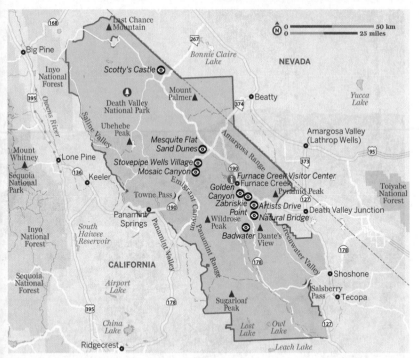

Viewpoints

Southeast of Furnace Creek is **Zabriskie Point**, offering spectacular sunset views across the valley and golden badlands eroded into waves, pleats and gullies. Twenty miles southeast at **Dante's View**, you can simultaneously spot the highest (Mt Whitney, 14,505ft) and lowest (Badwater) points in the contiguous USA. **Badwater** itself, a timeless landscape of crinkly salt flats, is 17 miles south of Furnace Creek.

Scotty's Castle

About 55 miles northwest of Furnace Creek is whimsical **Scotty's Castle** (☎877-444-6777; www.recreation.gov; tours adult/child from $15/7.50;

hgrounds 8:30am-4:15pm, tour schedules vary, closed Tue-Thu mid-May–mid-Aug). Tour guides dressed in historical character bring to life the Old West tales of con man 'Death Valley Scotty' (reservations advised).

Hiking & Scenic Drives

Golden Canyon and **Natural Bridge** are easily explored on short hikes. A 9-mile detour along

Artists Drive through a narrow canyon is best in late afternoon when the eroded hillsides erupt in fireworks of color.

Northwest of Furnace Creek, near Stovepipe Wells Village, trek across Saharan-esque **Mesquite Flat sand dunes** – magical under a full moon – and scramble along the smooth marble walls of **Mosaic Canyon**.

Why Such an Ominous Name?

In the winter of 1849–50, a group of pioneers went missing in what became known as Death Valley. All except one of the pioneers were rescued by two young men, William Lewis Manly and John Rogers. As the rescued party climbed out of the valley, one man turned, looked back and proclaimed, 'Goodbye, Death Valley'.

Sunset at Zabriskie Point

Mesquite Flat sand dunes

Information

The central hub of the park is **Furnace Creek.** Here you'll find a general store, expensive gas station, post office, ATM, coin-op laundromat and pay showers. You can also pick up a free map and newspaper when you show your park ticket receipt at the **visitor center** (☏760-786-3200; www.nps.gov/deva; ☺8am-5pm mid-Oct–mid-Jun, 9am-6pm mid-Jun–mid-Oct).

Stovepipe Wells Village, a 30-minute drive northwest of Furnace Creek, has a general store, expensive gas station, ATM and pay showers. Cell-phone reception is spotty to nonexistent in the park.

For 4WD adventures in the park, talk to **Farabee's Jeep Rentals** (☏760 786 9872; www.farabeejeeps.com; day Jeep rental $195-235; ☺mid-Sep–late May) near the Inn at Furnace Creek.

Five miles west of Grapevine junction, walk around volcanic **Ubehebe Crater** and its younger sibling.

A scenic drive up **Emigrant Canyon**, starting 8 miles west of Stovepipe Wells, passes turnoffs to ghost towns with a 3-mile unpaved stretch up to the historic beehive-shaped **Charcoal Kilns**. Nearby is the trailhead for the 8.4-mile round-trip hike up **Wildrose Peak** (9064ft). At the park's western edge, utterly remote **Panamint Springs** offers panoramic vistas and a 2-mile round-trip hike to tiny Darwin Falls.

Scotty's Castle

Sleeping & Eating

There are nine developed, first-come, first-served campgrounds in Death Valley. All are first come first served except Furnace Creek Campground, which can take reservations (www.recreation.gov) from mid-October through mid-April.

In-park lodging is often booked solid, especially on weekends and during the spring wildflower bloom. The closest town with a few roadside motels is Beatty, NV (40 miles northeast of Furnace Creek); many more accommodations are found in Las Vegas, NV (125 miles southeast) and Ridgecrest, CA (125 miles southwest).

Ranch at Furnace Creek Tailor-made for families, this rambling resort with multiple, motel-style buildings has received a vigorous facelift, resulting in spiffy rooms swathed in desert colors, updated bathrooms and French doors leading to porches with comfortable patio furniture. The grounds encompass a playground, spring-fed swimming pool, tennis courts, restaurants, shops and the Borax Museum. Activities include horseback riding, golf, mountain biking and hot-springs pool swimming.

Stovepipe Wells Village (📞760-786-2387; www.escapetodeathvalley.com; Hwy 190, Stovepipe Wells; RV sites $33, r $117-176) The 83 rooms at this sea-level tourist village are newly spruced-up and have quality linens beneath Death Valley–themed artwork, cheerful Native American–patterned bedspreads, coffeemakers and TVs. The small pool is cool and the cowboy-style **Toll Road Restaurant** (dinner mains $13-26; ⏱7-10am & 6-10pm) serves breakfast and dinner daily.

STATE
California

ENTRANCE FEE
7-day pass per vehicle $20

AREA
1240 sq miles

GOOD FOR

A Joshua tree

FRANK KRAHMER / GETTY IMAGES ©

Joshua Tree National Park

Like figments from a Dr Seuss book, whimsical-looking Joshua trees (actually tree-sized yuccas) welcome visitors to this wilderness park where the Sonora and Mojave Deserts converge.

'J-Tree' is perennially popular with rock climbers and day hikers, especially in spring when the trees bloom with cream-colored flowers. The mystical quality of this stark, boulder-strewn landscape has inspired countless artists, most famously the rock band U2. You'll find most of the main attractions, including all of the Joshua trees, in the park's northern half.

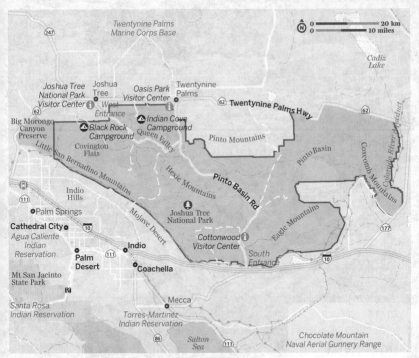

Sights & Activities

Dominating the north side of the park, the epic Wonderland of Rocks calls to climbers, as does Hidden Valley. Sunset-worthy Keys View overlooks the San Andreas Fault; on clear days you can see as far as Mexico.

For pioneer history, tour **Keys Ranch** (☎760-367-5522).

Hikers seek out native desert fan-palm oases like 49 Palms Oasis (3-mile round-trip trail) and Lost Palms Oasis (7.2-mile round-trip trail). Kid-friendly trails include Barker Dam (1.1-mile loop), which passes Native American petroglyphs; Skull Rock (1.7-mile loop); and Cholla Cactus Garden (0.25-mile loop).

For a scenic 4WD route, tackle bumpy 18-mile Geology Tour Road, also open to mountain bikers.

Sleeping

The park itself only has camping. Budget and mid-range motels line Hwy 62.

Joshua Tree National Park Campgrounds (www.nps.gov/jotr; tent & RV sites $10-15; ⊞⊞) has eight campgrounds: Cottonwood and Black Rock have potable water, flush toilets and dump stations; Indian Cove and Black Rock accept reservations, others are first-come, first-served. None have showers.

Backcountry camping (no campfires) is allowed 1 mile from any trailhead or road and 100ft from water sources; free self-registration is required at the park's 12 backcountry boards at trailheads.

Eating

Crossroads Cafe (☎760-366-5414; 61715 Twentynine Palms Hwy, Joshua Tree; mains $5-12; ⊙7am-9pm Mon-Sat, to 8pm Sun; 🐾) The go-to place for carbo-loaded breakfasts, fresh sandwiches and garden salads that make both omnivores (burgers, Reuben sandwich) and vegans (spinach salad) happy.

Pie for the People (☎760-366-0400; www.pieforthepeople.com; 61740 Twentynine Palms Hwy, Joshua Tree; pizzas $11-25; ⊙11am-9pm Mon-Thu, to 10pm Fri & Sat, to 8pm Sun; ⊞) For takeout and delivery thin-crust pizza. Enjoy your pies under the exposed rafters in the wood and corrugated-metal dining room, or under the tree on the back patio.

STATE
California

ENTRANCE FEE
7-day pass per vehicle $20

AREA
721 sq miles

GOOD FOR

Horseback riding, Kings Canyon National Park

Kings Canyon National Park

Carved out of granite by ancient glaciers and a powerful river, Kings Canyon is one of North America's deepest canyons, plunging over 8000ft.

Straddling the southern Sierra Nevada, Kings Canyon National Park has myriad backcountry routes to granite peaks, alpine lakes, high-country meadows and waterfalls. The dramatic landscape caught the eye of pioneering naturalist John Muir in 1873; some years later, in 1940, the park was officially established.

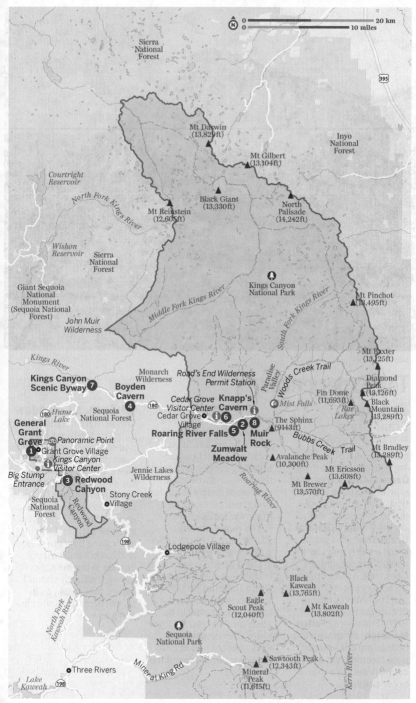

0 — 20 km
0 — 10 miles

Sierra
National
Forest

*Courtright
Reservoir*

North Fork Kings River

Mt Daswin
(13,829ft)

Mt Gilbert
(13,104ft)

Inyo
National
Forest

395

Black Giant
(13,330ft)

Mt Reinstein
(12,605ft)

North
Palisade
(14,242ft)

*Wishon
Reservoir*

Sierra
National
Forest

Giant Sequoia
National
Monument
(Sequoia National
Forest)

Middle Fork Kings River

*John Muir
Wilderness*

Kings Canyon
National Park

South Fork Kings River

Mt Pinchot
(13,495ft)

Kings River

Monarch
Wilderness

Road's End Wilderness
Permit Station

Mt Baxter
(13,125ft)

Woods Creek Trail

Paradise
Valley

Diamond
Peak
(13,126ft)

**Kings Canyon
Scenic Byway** ⑦

**Boyden
Cavern** ④

180

*Cedar Grove
Visitor Center*
Cedar Grove ○
Village

**Knapp's
Cavern**
ⓘ

Mist Falls

Fin Dome
(11,693ft)

*Rae
Lakes*

Black
Mountain
13,289ft)

**General
Grant
Grove**

Panoramic Point

Sequoia
National Forest

*Hume
Lake*

ⓘ ⑥
Roaring River Falls ⑤

② ⑧
**Muir
Rock**

The Sphinx
(9143ft)

Bubbs Creek

Mt Bradley
(13,289ft)

①
Grant Grove Village
*Kings Canyon
Visitor Center* ⓘ

**Zumwalt
Meadow**

Trail

*Big Stump
Entrance*

③ **Redwood
Canyon**

Jennie Lakes
Wilderness

Avalanche Peak
(10,300ft)

Mt Ericsson
(13,608ft)

Mt Brewer
(13,570ft)

Sequoia
National
Forest

*Redwood
Canyon*

Stony Creek
○ Village

Roaring River

198

Lodgepole Village

North Fork Kaweah River

Black
Kaweah
(13,765ft)

Eagle
Scout Peak
(12,040ft)

Mt Kaweah
(13,802ft)

Sequoia
National Park

Mineral King Rd

Kern River

Sawtooth Peak
(12,343ft)

○ Three Rivers

*Lake
Kaweah*

198

Mineral
Peak
(11,615ft)

Zumwalt Meadow

Top Experiences

❶ General Grant Grove

This sequoia grove is nothing short of astounding. The paved half-mile **General Grant Tree Trail** is an interpretive walk that visits a number of mature sequoias, including the 27-story **General Grant Tree**. This giant holds triple honors as the world's second-largest living tree, a memorial to US soldiers killed in war, and the nation's official Christmas tree since 1926. The nearby **Fallen Monarch**, a massive, fire-hollowed trunk you can walk through, has been a cabin, hotel, saloon and horse stables.

To escape the bustling crowds, follow the more secluded 1.5-mile **North Grove Loop**, which passes wildflower patches and bubbling creeks as it gently winds underneath a canopy of stately sequoias, evergreen pines and aromatic incense cedars.

The magnificence of this ancient sequoia grove was nationally recognized in 1890 when Congress first designated it General Grant National Park. It took another half-century for this tiny parcel to be absorbed into much larger Kings Canyon National Park, established in 1940 to prevent damming of the Kings River.

❷ Zumwalt Meadow

This verdant meadow bordered by the Kings River and soaring granite canyon walls offers phenomenal views. In the early morning, the air hums with birdsong, the sun's rays light up the canyon walls, and mule deer and black bears can often be spotted foraging among the long grasses, wildflowers and berry bushes in the meadow. Following the partly shaded nature trail gives you a quick snapshot of the canyon's beauty.

③ Redwood Canyon

Over 15,000 sequoias cluster in Redwood Canyon, making it one of the world's largest groves of these giant trees. In an almost-forgotten corner of the park, this secluded forest lets you revel in the grandeur of the trees away from the crowds while hiking mostly moderate trails. What you won't find here, however, are any of California's coast redwood trees – that's what early pioneers mistook these giant sequoias for, hence the erroneous name.

The trailheads are at the end of a 2-mile bumpy dirt road (closed in winter) that starts across from the Hume Lake/Quail Flat signed intersection on the Generals Hwy, just over 5 miles southeast of Grant Grove Village.

④ Boyden Cavern

While the rooms are smaller and the interiors less eye-popping than Crystal Cave in Sequoia National Park, touring the beautiful and fantastical formations of **Boyden Cavern** (☏888-956-8243; www.caverntours.com/BoydenRt.htm; Hwy 180; tours adult/child from $14.50/8.75; ⊙late Apr–Sep; ♿) requires no advance tickets. Just show up for the basic 45-minute tour, which departs hourly from 10am to 5pm during peak summer season. Reaching the cave entrance requires a short walk up a steep, paved grade.

Panoramic Point

For a breathtaking view of Kings Canyon, head 2.3 miles up narrow, steep and winding Panoramic Point Rd (trailers and RVs aren't recommended). Follow a short paved trail uphill from the parking lot to the viewpoint, where precipitous canyons and the snowcapped peaks of the Great Western Divide unfold below you. Snow closes the road to vehicles during winter, when it becomes a cross-country ski and snowshoe route.

From the visitor center in Grant Grove Village off Hwy 180, follow the paved side road east, turning left after 0.1 miles, then right at the John Muir Lodge.

⑤ Roaring River Falls

A five-minute walk on a paved trail leads to one of the park's most accessible waterfalls, where a 40ft chute gushes into a granite bowl. In late spring and maybe early summer, the strength of this cascade won't disappoint. Look for the parking lot and trailhead on the south side of the road, about 3 miles east of the village, slightly closer to Roads End.

⑥ Knapp's Cavern

During the 1920s, wealthy Santa Barbara businessman George Knapp built this simple wood-shingled cabin to store gear during his extravagant fishing and camping excursions into Kings Canyon. From a signed roadside pullout, about 2 miles east of Cedar Grove Village, a short trail leads to this hidden building, the oldest in Cedar Grove. Come around dusk, when the views of the glacier-carved canyon are glorious.

⑦ Kings Canyon Scenic Byway

Hairpin turns, dizzying drop-offs and sheer granite cliff faces accompany an unforgettable drive to the bottom of one of North America's deepest canyons. The narrow, twisting Hwy 180 links the park's two main visitor areas, Grant Grove and Cedar Grove. Hwy 180 all the way down to Cedar Grove is closed during winter (usually from mid-November until late April), but the stretch from Grant Grove to Hume Lake Rd is open year-round.

⑧ Muir Rock

On excursions to Kings Canyon, John Muir would allegedly give talks on this large flat river boulder, a short walk from the Roads End parking lot and less than a mile past Zumwalt Meadow. A sandy river-beach here is taken over by gleeful swimmers in midsummer. Don't jump in when raging waters, swollen with snowmelt, are dangerous. (Ask at the Roads End ranger station if conditions are calm enough for a dip.)

Ancient sequoia trees

Mist Falls

🏃 Mist Falls Hike

A satisfying long walk along the riverside and up a natural granite staircase highlights the beauty of Kings Canyon. The waterfall is thunderous in late spring and possibly into early summer, depending on the previous winter's snowpack.

Bring plenty of water and sunscreen on this hike, which gains 600ft in elevation before reaching the falls. Get an early morning start, because the return trip can be brutally hot on summer afternoons, and also so you can beat the crowds.

The trail begins just past the **Roads End** wilderness permit station, crossing a small footbridge over **Copper Creek**. Walk along a sandy trail through sparse cedar and pine forest, where boulders rolled by avalanches are scattered on the canyon floor. Keep an eye out for black bears. Eventually the trail enters cooler, shady and low-lying areas of ferns and reeds before reaching a well-marked three-way junction with the Woods Creek Trail, just shy of 2 miles from Roads End.

DURATION 3-5 hours

DISTANCE 9.2 miles round-trip

DIFFICULTY Moderate

START/FINISH Roads End

NEAREST TOWN Cedar Grove Village

TRANSPORTATION Car

SUMMARY A popular day hike, climbing 4.6 miles one way, winding through forest to the Kings River before reaching a gushing Mist Falls.

Turn left (north) toward Paradise Valley and begin a gradual climb that runs parallel to powerful cataracts in the boulder-saturated Kings River. Stone-framed stairs lead to a granite knob overlook, with wide southern views of **Avalanche Peak** and the oddly pointed **Sphinx**, another mountain peak, behind you. Follow cairns up the rock face and continue briefly through shady forest to reach **Mist Falls**, one of the park's largest waterfalls. Warning: don't wade above the waterfall or swim below it, due to the danger of

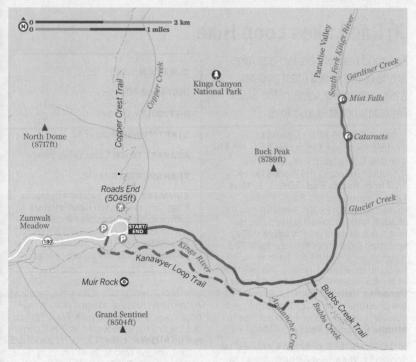

rockfall and swiftwater currents, especially during snowmelt runoff. In late summer, the river downstream from the falls may be tame enough for a dip – use your own best judgment, however.

Retrace your steps just over 2.5 miles downhill to the three-way trail junction. Instead of returning directly to Roads End, bear left and cross the bridge over the Kings River, briefly joining the Bubbs Creek Trail. After less than a quarter-mile, turn right onto the untrammeled Kanawyer Loop Trail, which is mostly flat. After crossing Avalanche Creek on a makeshift log bridge, the tree canopy opens up to show off sprawling talus slopes along the Kings Canyon's southern walls.

Muir Rock and its late-summer swimming hole come into view across the river before you make a short climb to the River Trail junction. Turn right and walk across the red footbridge, below which is another favorite late-summer swimming hole. Follow the path back to the paved highway, turning right to walk back to the Roads End parking lot.

🚶 Rae Lakes Loop Hike

For good reason, this five-day hike is one of the park's most popular trails, traversing some of the Sierra Nevada's finest landscapes.

🚶 DAY 1: ROADS END TO MIDDLE PARADISE VALLEY (4-6 HOURS, 7 MILES)

The Rae Lakes Loop kicks off with a 4.5-mile hike along the Woods Creek Trail from **Roads End** (5045ft) to **Mist Falls**. Beyond the waterfall, a set of rocky switchbacks leads you up into the shadier forest above the river. The trail levels out as it enters **Paradise Valley**, less than 2 miles north of the falls. The Kings River's South Fork flows through forested meadows, inviting you to linger at the backpacker campsites in **Lower Paradise Valley** (6600ft). Continue up the beautiful river valley through mixed-conifer forest just over a mile further to **Middle Paradise Valley** (6700ft).

🚶 DAY 2: MIDDLE PARADISE VALLEY TO WOODS CREEK (4-6 HOURS, 7 MILES)

The trail gradually ascends alongside a grassy meadow before dropping back to the river in **Upper Paradise Valley** (6800ft). Forested campsites appear before the confluence of the Kings River's South Fork and Woods Creek, about 1.5 miles from Middle Paradise Valley.

After crossing a footbridge, the trail steadily ascends switchbacks through a forested valley above Woods Creek. Less than 4 miles from the river crossing, the trail rolls into **Castle Domes Meadow** (8200ft).The trail meanders across the meadow and re-enters pine forest. At the signposted **John Muir Trail (JMT) junction** (8500ft), turn right and cross Woods Creek on the wooden planks of a steel-cable suspension bridge. Backpacker campsites sprawl just south of the bridge.

🚶 DAY 3: WOODS CREEK TO MIDDLE RAE LAKE (4-6 HOURS, 6.5 MILES)

Heading south, the JMT rolls easily on open slopes along the west side of Woods Creek's South Fork, with good views of the granite high country. Crossing a small stream, the trail continues upvalley, rising

> **DURATION** 5 days
>
> **DISTANCE** 40 miles
>
> **DIFFICULTY** Difficult
>
> **START/FINISH** Roads End
>
> **NEAREST TOWN** Cedar Grove Village
>
> **TRANSPORTATION** Car
>
> **SUMMARY** The best backpacking loop in Kings Canyon tours sun-blessed forests and meadows, crosses one mind-bending pass, and skirts a chain of jewel-like lakes beneath the Sierra crest, joining the famous John Muir Trail partway along.

over rocky terrain to reach a small meadow. At the next crossing, a bigger stream cascades over a cleft in the rock. Foxtail pines dot the dry slope above the trail as it continues up to **Dollar Lake** (10,220ft), about 3.5 miles from the Woods Creek crossing. The striking view of **Fin Dome** (11,693ft) above Dollar Lake (camping strictly prohibited) sets the theme of mountain splendor.

Skirting Dollar Lake's west shore, the JMT continues up to arrive at larger **Arrowhead Lake** (10,300ft). It ascends more gradually to enchanting **Lower Rae Lake** (10,535ft). The gently rolling trail crosses several small side streams and passes a spur trail to a seasonal ranger station. Continue to the signed turnoff for campsites above the eastern shore of **Middle Rae Lake** (10,540ft).

🚶 DAY 4: MIDDLE RAE LAKE TO JUNCTION MEADOW (5-7 HOURS, 9 MILES)

Return to the JMT and turn right (south). Walk along the northern shore of **Upper Rae Lake** (10,545ft). Cross the connector stream between the lakes. At a signed trail junction, where a trail to Sixty Lake Basin peels off northwest, keep straight ahead on the JMT, which continues south up well-graded switchbacks above the west side of Upper Rae Lake. Heading higher, even more switchbacks take you up a talus slope to a basin, from where Glen Pass is visible ahead.

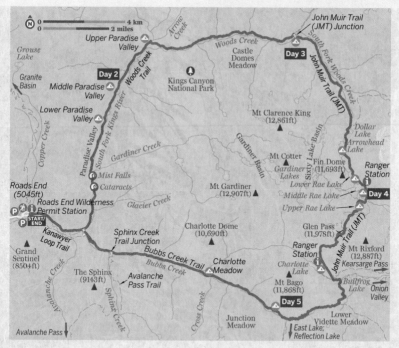

The trail passes several small mountain lakes, then it rises on a series of switchbacks up talus to the very narrow saddle of **Glen Pass** (11,978ft), almost 3 miles from Middle Rae Lake.

Gravelly but well-graded switchbacks take you down from Glen Pass over a steep scree slope toward a pothole tarn at the tree line. Stop to filter water here – the next reliable water is not until the Bullfrog Lake outlet a few miles ahead. Then head down the narrow canyon until the trail swings south, then contours high above Charlotte Lake. A connector trail to Kearsarge Pass appears about 2.5 miles from Glen Pass, after which you'll soon reach a four-way junction with the main Charlotte Lake (northwest) and Kearsarge Pass (northeast) trails. Continue straight (south).

At the head of Bubbs Creek, cross a low rise and then start descending, passing a junction with the trail heading northeast to Bullfrog Lake and Kearsarge Lakes. The scenic descent twice crosses the outlet from Bullfrog Lake to reach **Lower Vidette Meadow** (9480ft). Leaving the JMT, turn right (southwest) and follow the trail down Bubbs Creek. Beneath soaring granite walls on either side of the canyon, the trail drops steadily down to now narrower, rushing Bubbs Creek, continuing to **Junction Meadow** (8500ft). Past the signed junction with the East and Reflection Lakes Trails, you'll find grassy campsites.

🥾 **DAY 5: JUNCTION MEADOW TO ROADS END (5-7 HOURS, 10.5 MILES)**

From the west end of Junction Meadow, the Bubbs Creek Trail meanders downvalley to Charlotte Creek. After crossing the creek, the trail continues downhill for 3 more miles to the **Sphinx Creek Trail junction** (6240ft).

Continuing straight ahead, the Bubbs Creek Trail descends steeply, providing views into **Kings Canyon** and of the pinnacle of the **Sphinx** (9143ft) towering above you. At last reaching the canyon floor, the trail crosses braided Bubbs Creek. Just beyond the steel **Bailey Bridge**, which spans the Kings River's South Fork, is the Paradise Valley Trail junction. Turn left (west) and retrace your steps from Day 1 for less than 2 miles to **Roads End**.

General Grant Grove

Information

Kings Canyon National Park's only entrance is Big Stump. Just over 3 miles north of the Big Stump Entrance in Grant Grove Village is the **Kings Canyon Visitor Center** (☎559-565-4307; Hwy 180, Grant Grove Village; ⊙8am-noon & 1-5pm late May–early Sep, shorter off-season hours). It has a very good selection of books and maps, and staff issue wilderness permits (usually until 30 minutes before closing).

The seven-day entrance fee (per vehicle $20) covers Kings Canyon National Park as well as neighboring Sequoia National Park and nearby Hume Lake District of the Sequoia National Forest.

The park is only accessible by car from the west, and no roads cross the Sierra Nevada mountain range, only trails. There is no public transportation into the park.

Sleeping & Eating

There are stores in Grant Grove and Cedar Grove selling firewood, camping supplies and packaged food, with a small selection of fruits and veggies. Cedar Grove has a snack bar that serves hot meals and there's a restaurant and coffee cart in Grant Grove.

Camping

All park campgrounds are first-come, first-served. The Sequoia National Forest, Hume Lake, Princess and Landslide campgrounds accept reservations (highly recommended in summer).

Campfires are allowed only in existing fire rings. When the risk of wildfires is high, all campfires may be prohibited.

Hume Lake Campground

(reservations ☎877-444-6777, 518-885-3639; www.recreation.gov; Hume Lake Rd; tent & RV sites $24-26; ⊙mid-May–mid-Sep; ⊛) Almost always full yet still managing a laid-back atmosphere, this campground

offers almost 75 relatively uncrowded, shady campsites, a handful with lake views. It's on the lake's northern shore. Reservations highly recommended.

Sunset Campground

(Generals Hwy; tent & RV sites $18; ⊙mid-May–early Sep; ⊛) Grant Grove's biggest campground has more than 150 shady sites set among evergreen trees. There are ranger campfire programs in summer, and it's a five-minute walk from the village.

Sheep Creek Campground

(Hwy 180; tent & RV sites $18; ⊙mid-May–mid-Oct) Just a short walk west of the visitor center and village, Cedar Grove's second-biggest campground has shady waterfront loops that are especially popular with RVers. Don't expect much quiet at night, though.

Lodgings

John Muir Lodge

(☎559-335-5500, 866-807-3598; www.visitsequoia.com; off Hwy 180, Grant Grove Village; r from $170; ⊙year-round; ⊛) An atmospheric wooden building hung with historical black-and-white photographs, this year-round hotel is a place to lay your head and still feel like you're in the forest. Wide porches have wooden rocking chairs, and homespun rooms contain rough-hewn wood furniture and patchwork bedspreads. Cozy up to the big stone fireplace on chilly nights with a board game.

Cedar Grove Lodge

(☎559-565-3096, 866-807-3598; www.visitsequoia.com; Hwy 180, Cedar Grove Village; r from $130; ⊙early May–mid-Oct; ⊛⊛) The only indoor sleeping option in the canyon, this riverside lodge offers 21 unexciting motel-style rooms. A recent remodel has dispelled some of the frumpy decor. Three ground-floor rooms with shady furnished patios have spiffy river views and kitchenettes. All rooms have phones and TVs.

STATE
California

ENTRANCE FEE
7-day pass per vehicle $20
($10 in winter)

AREA
166 sq miles

GOOD FOR

Bumpass Hell

Lassen Volcanic National Park

Anchoring the southernmost link in the Cascades' chain of volcanoes, this alien landscape bubbles over with roiling mudpots, noxious sulfur vents, steamy fumaroles, colorful cinder cones and crater lakes.

You won't find the crowds of more famous national parks at this off-the-beaten-path destination, but Lassen still offers peaks to be conquered, azure waters to be paddled, forested campsites for pitching your tent, and boardwalks through Bumpass Hell that will leave you awestruck.

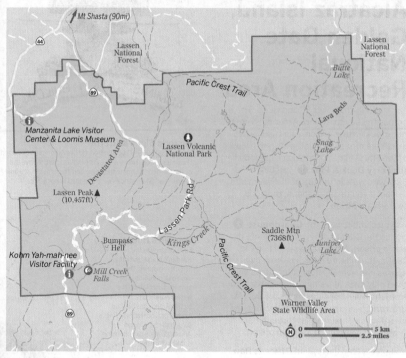

Sights & Activities

The dry, smoldering, treeless terrain stands in stunning contrast to the cool conifer forest that surrounds it. (That's the summer; in winter snow ensures you won't get far inside park borders.)

Entering the park from the southwest entrance is to suddenly step into another world.

Hwy 89, the road through the park, wraps around **Lassen Peak** on three sides and provides access to dramatic geothermal formations, pure lakes, gorgeous picnic areas and remote hiking.

In total, the park has 150 miles of **hiking trails**, including a 17-mile section of the Pacific Crest Trail. Experienced hikers can attack the Lassen Peak Trail (at least 4½ hours; 5 miles round-trip); the first 1.3 miles up to the Grandview viewpoint is suitable for families. The 360-degree view from the top is stunning. Early in the season you'll need snow and ice-climbing equipment to reach the summit.

Near the Kohm Yah-mah-nee visitor facility, a gentler 2.3-mile trail leads through meadows and forest to Mill Creek Falls. Further north on Hwy 89 you'll recognize the roadside sulfur works by its bubbling mudpots, hissing steam vent, fountains and fumaroles.

Sleeping & Eating

If you're coming to the park from the north on Hwy 89, you won't see many gas/food/lodgings signs after Mt Shasta City. Your best option is to stock up en route and camp.

Lassen Peak

The world's largest plug-dome volcano rises 2000ft over the surrounding landscape to 10,457ft above sea level. Classified as an active volcano, its most recent eruption was in 1917, when it spewed a giant cloud of smoke, steam and ash 7 miles into the atmosphere. The national park was created the following year to protect the newly formed landscape. Some areas destroyed by the blast, including the aptly named Devastated Area on the northeast side of the peak, are recovering impressively.

Alcatraz Island, Golden Gate National Recreation Area

Book a ferry from Pier 33 and ride 1.5 miles across the bay to explore America's most notorious former prison. The trip itself is worth the money, providing stunning views of the city skyline. Once you've landed at the **Ferry Dock & Pier** ❶, you begin the 580-yard walk to the top of the island and prison; if you're out of shape, there's a twice-hourly tram.

As you climb toward the **Guardhouse** ❷, notice the island's steep slope; before it was a prison, Alcatraz was a fort. In the 1850s, the military quarried the rocky shores into near-vertical cliffs. Ships could then only dock at a single port, separated from the main buildings by a sally port (a drawbridge and moat in what became the guardhouse). Inside, peer through floor grates to see Alcatraz' original prison.

Volunteers tend the brilliant **Officer's Row Gardens** ❸ an orderly counterpoint to the overgrown rose bushes surrounding the burned-out shell of the **Warden's House** ❹. At the top of the hill, by the front door of the **Main Cellhouse** ❺, beautiful shots unfurl all around, including a view of the **Golden Gate Bridge** ❻. Above the main door of the administration building, notice the **historic signs & graffiti** ❼, before you step inside the dank, cold prison to find the **Frank Morris cell** ❽, former home to Alcatraz' most notorious jail-breaker.

TOP TIPS

➡ Book at least one month prior for self-guided daytime visits, longer for ranger-led night tours. For info on garden tours, see www.alcatraz-gardens.org.

➡ Be prepared to hike; a steep path ascends from the ferry landing to the cell block. Most people spend two to three hours on the island. You need only reserve for the outbound ferry; take any ferry back.

Historic Signs & Graffiti
During their 1969–71 occupation, Native Americans graffitied the water tower: 'Home of the Free Indian Land.' Above the cellhouse door, examine the eagle-and-flag crest to see how the red-and-white stripes were changed to spell 'Free.'

Warden's House
Fires destroyed the warden's house and other structures during the Indian Occupation. The government blamed the Native Americans; the Native Americans blamed agents provocateurs acting on behalf of the Nixon Administration to undermine public sympathy.

Parade Grounds

Officer's Row Gardens
In the 19th century soldiers imported topsoil to beautify the island with gardens. Well-trusted prisoners later gardened – Elliott Michener said it kept him sane. Historians, ornithologists and archaeologists choose today's plants.

FRANK VAN DEN BERGH / GETTY IMAGES ©

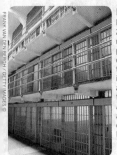

Main Cellhouse
During the mid-20th century, the maximum-security prison housed the day's most notorious troublemakers, including Al Capone and Robert Stroud, the 'Birdman of Alcatraz' (who actually conducted his ornithology studies at Leavenworth).

FRANCKREPORTER / GETTY IMAGES ©

6
Recreation Yard
Water Tower
Power House
5
Officers' Club
8
7
ghthouse
3
4
2
Guard Tower
1

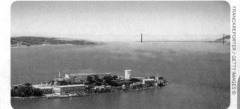

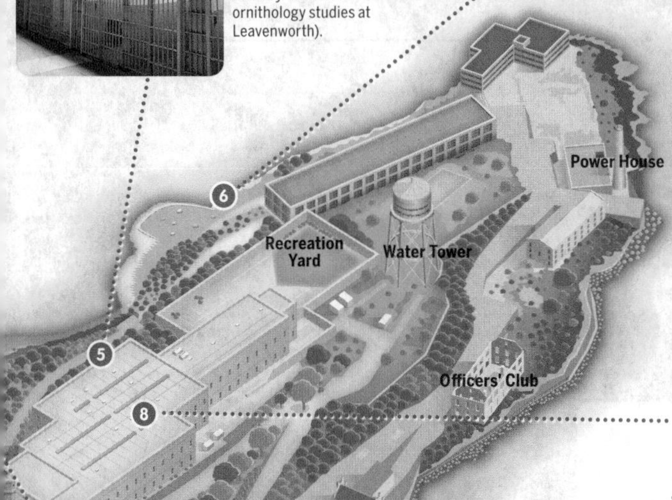

View of Golden Gate Bridge
The Golden Gate Bridge stretches wide on the horizon. Best views are from atop the island at Eagle Plaza, near the cellhouse entrance, and at water level along the Agave Trail (September to January only).

Frank Morris Cell
Peer into cell 138 on B-Block to see a re-creation of the dummy's head that Frank Morris left in his bed as a decoy to aid his notorious – and successful – 1962 escape from Alcatraz.

Guardhouse
Alcatraz' oldest building dates to 1857 and retains remnants of the original drawbridge and moat. During the Civil War the basement was transformed into a military dungeon – the genesis of Alcatraz as prison.

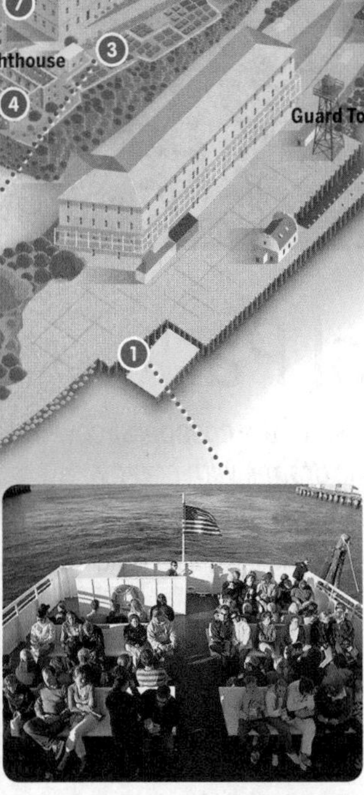

DAVID CLAPP / GETTY IMAGES ©

Ferry Dock & Pier
A giant wall map helps you get your bearings. Inside nearby Bldg 64, short films and exhibits provide historical perspective on the prison and details about the Indian Occupation.

MORTEN FALCH SORTLAND / GETTY IMAGES ©

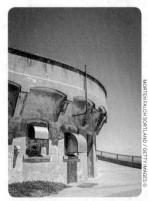

STATE
California

ENTRANCE FEE
7-day pass per vehicle $10

AREA
40 sq miles

GOOD FOR

High Peaks

DAVID MADISON / GETTY IMAGES ©

Pinnacles National Park

Named for the towering spires that rise abruptly out of the chapparal-covered hills, Pinnacles National Park is a study in geologic drama, with craggy monoliths, sheer-walled canyons and ancient volcanic remnants.

On the way to nowhere, petite Pinnacles is worth a big detour for a chance to see endangered California condors soaring above spiring rock formations. The park's other biggest attractions are hiking, rock climbing and two talus caves, formed by piles of boulders. The best time to visit the park is during spring or fall – summer heat and humidity are extreme.

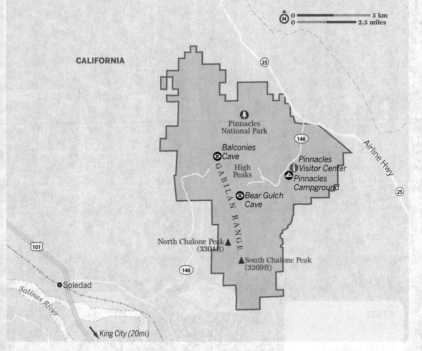

Talus Caves

Balconies Cave is almost always open for exploration. Scrambling through it is not an exercise recommended for claustrophobes, as it's pitch-black inside, making a flashlight essential. Be prepared to get lost a bit too.

The cave is found along a 2.5-mile hiking loop from the west entrance. Nearer the east entrance, **Bear Gulch Cave** is closed seasonally, so as not to disturb a resident colony of Townsend's big-eared bats.

Hiking

To really appreciate Pinnacles' stark beauty, you need to hike. Moderate loops of varying lengths and difficulty ascend into the High Peaks and include thrillingly narrow clifftop sections. In the early morning or late afternoon, you may spot endangered California condors soaring overhead. Get an early start to tackle the 9-mile round-trip trail to the top of Chalone Peak, granting panoramic views.

Rangers lead guided full-moon hikes and stargazing programs on some weekend nights, usually in spring or fall. Reservations are required: call ☎831-389-4485 in advance or check for last-minute vacancies at the visitor center.

Camping

A **campground** (www.recreation.gov) with a seasonal swimming pool lies near the park's east entrance, off Hwy 25 about 30 miles northwest of King City on Hwy 101.

Getting There & Around

There is no road connecting the two sides of the park. To reach the less-developed west entrance (⊙7:30am-8pm), exit Hwy 101 at Soledad and follow Hwy 146 northeast for 14 miles. The east entrance (⊙24hr), where you'll find the visitor center and campground, is accessed via lonely Hwy 25 in San Benito County, southeast of Hollister and northeast of King City.

STATE
California

ENTRANCE FEE
Free

AREA
172 sq miles

GOOD FOR

Giant redwood trees

Redwood National Park

The world's tallest living trees have been standing here from time immemorial, predating the Roman Empire by over 500 years. Prepare to be impressed.

Redwood National Park is part of a patchwork of forested public lands. Be awed by the towering ancient stands of coast redwoods along the often foggy Northern California coast. And spot shaggy Roosevelt elk foraging in woodland prairies, then go tide pooling along rugged beaches.

hours for the round-trip, which includes a 6-mile drive down a rough dirt road (speed limit 15mph) and a steep 1.3-mile one-way hike, which descends 800ft to the grove.

Several longer trails include the awe-inspiring **Redwood Creek Trail**, which also reaches Tall Trees Grove. You'll need a free backcountry permit to hike and camp (highly recommended, as the best backcountry camping on the North Coast), but the area is most accessible from Memorial Day to Labor Day, when summer footbridges are up. Otherwise, getting across the creek can be perilous or impossible.

Sleeping

Elk Meadow Cabins
(☎866-733-9637; www. redwoodadventures.com; 7 Valley Green Camp Rd, Orick; cabins $179-279; 🛜🐾) Offers bright cabins with equipped kitchens and all the mod-cons in a perfect mid-park location. Expect to see elk on the lawn in the mornings. Cabins sleep six to eight people.

Information

Unlike most national parks, there are no fees and no highway entrance stations at Redwood National Park, so it's imperative to pick up the free map at the park headquarters in Crescent City or at the visitor center in Orick. Rangers here issue permits to visit Tall Trees Grove and loan bear-proof containers for backpackers.

Just north of the southern visitor center, turn east onto Bald Hills Rd and travel 2 miles to **Lady Bird Johnson Grove**, one of the park's most spectacular groves, and also one of the busiest, accessible via a gentle 1-mile loop trail. Continue for another 5 miles up Bald Hills Rd to **Redwood Creek Overlook**. On the top of the ridgeline, at 2100ft, get views over the forest and the watershed – provided it's not foggy. Just past the overlook lies the gated turnoff for **Tall Trees Grove**, the location of several of the world's tallest trees. Rangers issue 50 vehicle permits per day. Pick one up, along with the gate-lock combination, from the visitor centers. Allow four

Diverse Landscapes

From snowy peaks to scorching deserts, and golden-sand beaches to misty redwood forests, California is home to a bewildering variety of ecosytems, flora and fauna.

Muir Woods National Monument

Wander among an ancient stand of the world's tallest trees at 550-acre Muir Woods National Monument (☏415-388-2595; www.nps.gov/muwo; 1 Muir Woods Rd, Mill Valley; adult/child $10/free; ☉8am-sunset), 10 miles northwest of the Golden Gate Bridge. Easy hiking trails loop past thousand-year-old coast redwoods at Cathedral Grove. By the entrance, a cafe (☏415-388-7059; www.muirwoodstradingcompany.com; 1 Muir Woods Rd, Mill Valley; items $3-11; ☉from 9am daily, closing varies 4pm to 7pm; ♿) ✿ serves light lunches, snacks and drinks. Come midweek to avoid crowds, or arrive early morning or before sunset. Take Hwy 101 to the Hwy 1 exit, then follow the signs.

The Muir Woods Shuttle (Route 66F; www.marintransit.org; round-trip adult/child $5/free; ☉weekends & holidays Apr–Oct) operates weekends and holidays from April through October (daily in peak summer season), connecting with Hwy 101 and Sausalito's ferry terminal.

Point Reyes National Seashore

The windswept peninsula of Point Reyes National Seashore (www.nps.gov/pore) FREE juts 10 miles out to sea on an entirely different tectonic plate, protecting over 100 sq miles of beaches, lagoons and forested hills. A mile west of Olema, Bear Valley Visitor Center (☏415-464-5100; www.nps.gov/pore; ☉10am-5pm Mon-Fri, from 9am Sat & Sun) has maps, information and natural-history displays. The 0.6-mile Earthquake Trail, which crosses the San Andreas Fault zone, starts nearby.

Crowning the peninsula's westernmost tip, Point Reyes Lighthouse (☏415-669-1534; ☉lighthouse 10am-4:30pm Fri-Mon, lens room 2:30-4pm Fri-Mon) FREE is ideal for winter whale-watching. Off Pierce Point Rd, the 10-mile round-trip Tomales Point Trail rolls atop blustery bluffs past herds of tule elk to the peninsula's northern tip. To paddle out into Tomales Bay, Blue Waters Kayaking (☏415-669-2600; www.bluewaterskayaking.com; rentals/tours from $50/68; ♿) launches from Inverness and Marshall.

....

1. Muir Woods National Monument
2. Point Reyes Lighthouse

Nature lovers bunk at the only in-park lodging, HI Point Reyes Hostel (☎415-663-8811; www.norcalhostels.org/reyes; 1390 Limantour Spit Rd; dm $26-29, r $87-130, all with shared bath; @) ✈, 8 miles inland from the visitor center. In the coastal town of Inverness, the Cottages at Point Reyes Seashore (☎415-669-7250, 800-416-0405; www.cottagespointreyes.com; 13275 Sir Francis Drake Blvd; r $129-239; 🛜🐾👶) is a family-friendly place tucked away in the woods. The West Marin Chamber of Commerce (☎415-663-9232; www.pointreyes.org) checks availability at more cozy inns, cottages and B&Bs.

Two miles north of Olema, the tiny town of Point Reyes Station has heart-warming bakeries, cafes and restaurants. Gather a picnic lunch at Tomales Bay Foods & Cowgirl Creamery (www.cowgirlcreamery.com; 80 4th St; sandwiches $6-12; ⏱10am-6pm Wed-Sun; 🚗) 🌿 or 2 miles west of town at Perry's Deli (http://perrysinvernessparkgrocery.com; 12301 Sir Francis Drake Blvd, Inverness Park; sandwiches $5-11; ⏱7am-8pm Mon-Thu, to 9pm Fri & Sat, 8am-8pm Sun).

Lava Beds National Monument

Site of California's last major Native American conflict and a half-million years of volcanic destruction, Lava Beds National Monument (☎530-667-8113; www.nps.gov/labe; 7-day pass per vehicle $15) is a peaceful monument to centuries of turmoil. This park's got it all: lava flows, cinder and spatter cones, volcanic craters and amazing lava tubes. It was the site of the Modoc War, and ancient Native American petroglyphs are etched into rocks and pictographs painted on cave walls. Pick up info and maps at the visitor center (☎530-667-8113; www.nps.gov/labe; Tulelake; ⏱8am-6pm late May–early Sep, to 5pm mid-Sep–mid-May), which sells basic spelunking gear (borrow flashlights for free). Nearby is the park's basic campground (tent & RV sites $10; 🐾), where drinking water is available. Over 20 miles northeast of the park, the dusty town of Tulelake off Hwy 139 has basic motels, roadside diners and gas.

1. Native American petroglyphs, Lava Beds National Monument 2. Flowering yucca, Santa Monica Mountains National Recreation Area

Santa Monica Mountains National Recreation Area

A haven for hikers, trekkers and mountain bikers, the northwestern-most stretch of the Santa Monica Mountains National Recreation Area (www.nps.gov/samo) FREE is where the nature gets bigger and wilder, with jaw-dropping red-rock canyons, and granite outcrops with sublime sea views. Of course, the best trails are in Pacific Palisades, Topanga and Malibu. The Backbone Trail (www.nps.gov/samo/planyourvisit/backbonetrail.htm) is the longest trail in the range, linking – and accessible from – every state park. It's 68 miles all told, running from Will Rogers to Pt Mugu State Park. The hike takes place two Saturdays a month, January through April and is led by the National Park Service. Hikers need to register their interest in the trail and then go into the hiker lottery to see if they've scored a place.

There are two visitor centers. Santa Monica Mountains Anthony C. Beilenson Interagency Visitor Centre (805-370-2301; 26876 Mulholland Hwy, Calabasas; 9am-5pm) also has a bookstore. At the Satwiwa Native American Indian Culture Center (Rancho Sierra Vista/Satwiwa, Newbury Park), a Native American guest host or park ranger is available to answer questions on weekends from 9am to 5pm. Workshops, programs and art shows are held here throughout the year.

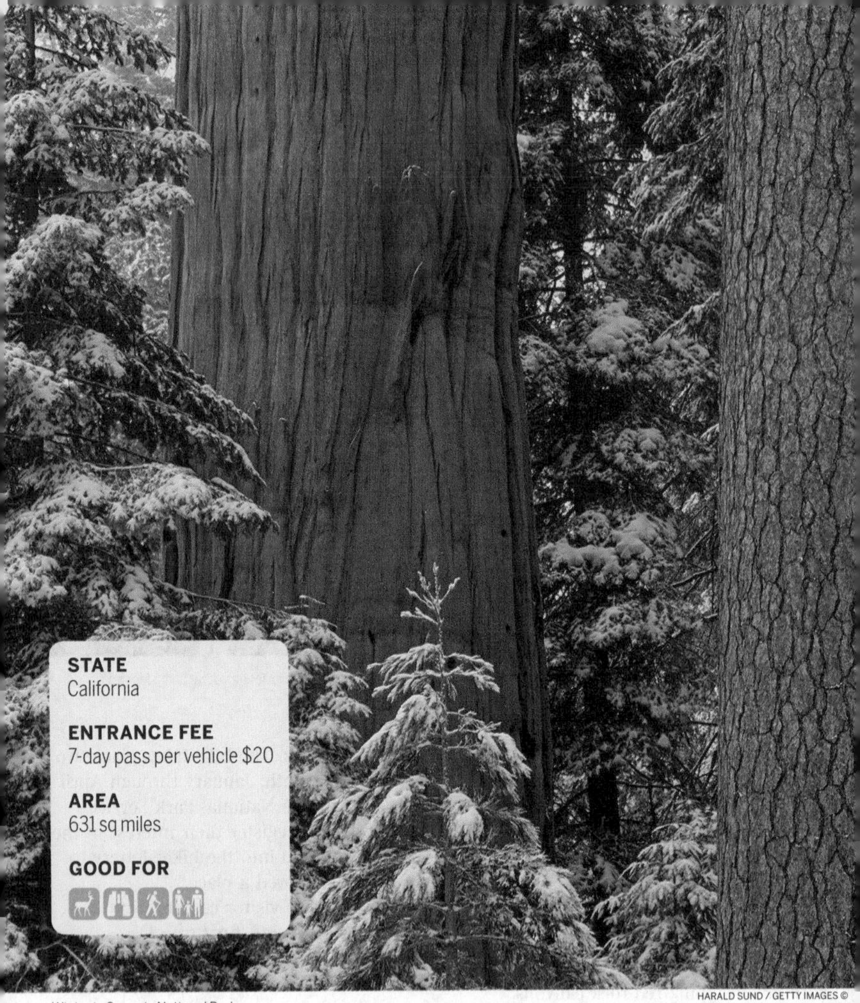

STATE
California

ENTRANCE FEE
7-day pass per vehicle $20

AREA
631 sq miles

GOOD FOR

HARALD SUND / GETTY IMAGES ©

Winter in Sequoia National Park

Sequoia National Park

With trees as high as 20-story buildings and as old as the Bible, this is an extraordinary park with five-star geological highlights, soul-sustaining forests and vibrant wildflower meadows.

Neighbouring the Kings Canyon National Park, here, giant sequoia trees are bigger and more numerous than anywhere else in the Sierra Nevada. Tough and fire-charred, they'd easily swallow two freeway lanes each. Giant, too, are the mountains – including the western slope of Mt Whitney (14,505ft), the tallest peak in the lower 48 states. The park receives less than half as many annual visitors as Yosemite, its more iconic northern neighbor, making it easier to find solitude among the geological wonders.

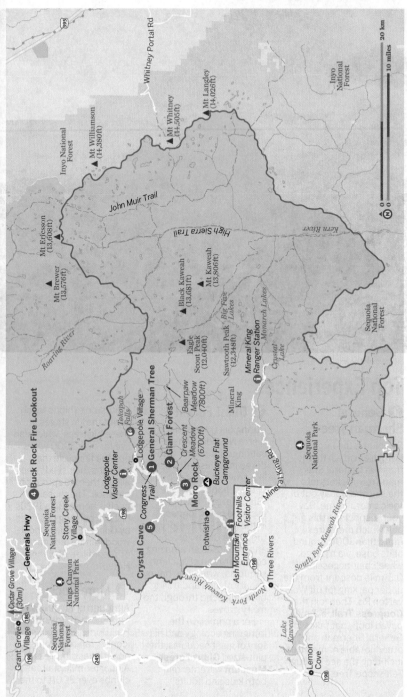

Sunset from Moro Rock

Top Experiences

❶ General Sherman Tree

By volume the largest living tree on earth, the massive General Sherman Tree rockets into the sky and *waaay* out of the camera frame. Pay your respects to this giant, which measures more than 100ft around at its base, via a paved, wheelchair-accessible 0.5-mile descent from the upper parking lot off Wolverton Rd. Then join the **Congress Trail**, a 2-mile paved loop that takes in General Sherman and other notable named trees, including the see-through Telescope Tree.

❷ Giant Forest

During his travels in the Sierra Nevada, conservationist John Muir wandered into this cathedral-like grove of giant sequoias in 1875, baptizing it the 'Giant Forest.' Having escaped being logged in the late 19th century, today the Giant Forest encompasses an amazing concentration of ancient sequoias, where the happy shouts of kids and trilling birdsong echo through the misty groves.

For a primer on the intriguing ecology and history of giant sequoias, the pint-sized **Giant Forest Museum** will entertain both kids and adults.

Hands-on exhibits teach about the life stages of these big trees, which can live for over 3000 years, and the fire cycle that releases their seeds and allows them to sprout on bare soil. The museum itself is housed in a 1920s historic building designed by Gilbert Stanley Underwood, famed architect of Yosemite's Ahwahnee Hotel.

❸ Moro Rock

Although not nearly as mammoth as Yosemite's Half Dome, Sequoia's iconic granite dome is nonetheless impressive. A quarter-mile staircase climbs over 300ft to the

Giant sequoias

top for mind-boggling views of the Great Western Divide, running north–south through the middle of the park, splitting the watersheds of the Kaweah River to the west from the Kern River to the east. Due to pollution drifting up from the Central Valley, this spectacular vantage point is sometimes obscured by thick haze, especially during summer.

Historical photos at the trailhead show the rock's original rickety wooden staircase, erected in 1917. You'll be grateful that the current staircase, built in 1931 by the Civilian Conservation Corps, has nearly 400 steps solidly carved into the granite with sturdy handrails for gripping.

From the Giant Forest Museum, the trailhead is 2 miles up narrow, twisty Moro Rock–Crescent Meadow Rd.

④ Buck Rock Fire Lookout

Built in 1923, this active fire lookout is one of the finest restored watchtowers you could ever hope to visit. Here, 172 stairs lead to a dollhouse-sized wooden cab on a dramatic 8500ft granite rise; it's staffed during the wildfire season. From the Generals Hwy, turn east onto Big Meadows Rd (FR-14S11). At around 2.5 miles, turn north on the dirt road (FR-13S04) then drive another 3 miles to the parking area.

⑤ Crystal Cave

Accidentally discovered in 1918 by two park employees who were going fishing, this unique marble cave was carved by an underground river, and has formations estimated to be 10,000 years old. Stalactites hang like daggers from the ceiling, and milky white marble formations take the shape of ethereal curtains, domes, columns and shields. The cave is also a unique biodiverse habitat for spiders, bats and tiny aquatic insects that are found nowhere else on earth.

Giant Sequoias

In California you can see the world's oldest trees (bristlecone pines) and its tallest (coast redwoods), but the record for biggest in terms of volume belongs to giant sequoias (Sequoiadendron giganteum). They grow only on the western slope of the Sierra Nevada range and are most abundant in Sequoia, Kings Canyon and Yosemite National Parks. John Muir called them 'Nature's forest masterpiece,' and anyone who's ever craned their neck to take in their vastness has probably done so with the same awe. These trees can grow to almost 275ft tall and 100ft in circumference, protected by bark up to 2ft thick.

Boardwalk, Sequoia National Park

Monarch Lake

🥾 Monarch Lakes Hike

This exceptionally scenic out-and-back high-country route reaches two alpine lakes below jagged Sawtooth Peak. Although it's not very long, the trail can be breathtakingly steep.

A steep climb kicks off this higher-altitude trek. At the Timber Gap Trail junction just over a half-mile in, you can see Mineral King Rd back below and snow-brushed peaks looking south. Turn right, following the signs for Sawtooth Pass. Corn lilies and paintbrush speckle **Groundhog Meadow**, named for the whistling marmots that scramble around the granite rocks seemingly everywhere you look during this hike.

Leaving the meadow, rock-hop across burbling Monarch Creek. On its far bank, a shady wooded spot is the perfect place for a picnic lunch. From there, begin ascending a stretch of loose and lazy switchbacks with goose-bump views. It's a slow, steady climb through red fir and pine forest that won't leave you too winded, though you'll feel the altitude the higher you climb. Blue grouse may be spotted on the hillsides.

DURATION 4-6 hours

DISTANCE 8.4 miles round-trip

DIFFICULTY Difficult

START/FINISH Sawtooth/Monarch trailhead parking area

NEAREST TOWN Silver City

TRANSPORTATION Car

SUMMARY A challenging high-country hike to an alpine lake beneath Sawtooth Peak. A marmot-lover's paradise.

At about 2.5 miles there's a signed junction for the Crystal Lake Trail, which takes a hard and steep right. Bear left and continue straight up toward Sawtooth Pass instead. After flipping to the opposite side of the ridgeline, the trail rounds **Chihuahua Bowl**, an avalanche-prone granite basin named after a Mexican mining region. The tree line wavers and fades away, opening up gorgeous views of Monarch Creek canyon, Timber Gap and the peaks of the Great Western Divide.

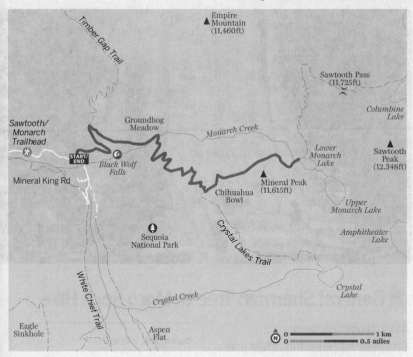

The distinctive pitch of Sawtooth Peak (12,348ft) is visible ahead. A walk through a large talus field and some stream crossings brings you to **Lower Monarch Lake** (10,400ft), where round-topped Mineral Peak (11,615ft) points up directly south. The maintained trail stops here, but **Upper Monarch Lake** (10,640ft) can be reached by a steep trail heading up the hillside. Established backpacker campsites are by the lower lake; for overnight camping, a wilderness permit is required.

When you're ready, retrace your steps to return. If you're looking for extremely challenging cross-country treks with some steep drop-offs and rock scrambling required, detour up scree-covered **Sawtooth Pass** (11,725ft) or make an alternate return route via **Crystal Lake** (10,900ft). But ask for route advice and safety tips at the Mineral King ranger station first.

General Sherman Tree

🥾 General Sherman Tree to Moro Rock Hike

A deviation from the popular Congress Trail loop, this rolling one-way hike takes in huge sequoias, green meadows and the pinnacle of Moro Rock. Expect stretches of blissful solitude and potential black bear sightings.

Keep in mind that hiking this route in one direction is possible only when the free seasonal park shuttle buses are running, usually from late May until late September.

From the General Sherman parking lot and shuttle stop off Wolverton Rd, just east of the Generals Hwy, a paved trail quickly descends through towering sequoias. At an overlook on the way down you'll get the best view of the **General Sherman Tree**. After walking up to the giant's trunk, turn around and walk downhill on the western branch of the Congress Trail loop. (If you end up on the eastern branch by mistake, jog right then left at two minor trail junctions that appear about 0.5 miles south of the General Sherman Tree.)

DURATION 3-4 hours

DISTANCE 6 miles one way

DIFFICULTY Moderate

START Wolverton Rd parking lot/shuttle stop

FINISH Moro Rock parking lot/shuttle stop

NEAREST TOWN Lodgepole Village

TRANSPORTATION Shuttle, car

SUMMARY One-way hike with great rock climbing, peaceful meadows, huge sequoias and the top of Moro Rock.

At a five-way junction by the **McKinley Tree**, continue straight ahead south on the dirt trail towards **Cattle Cabin**. Pass the hollow-bottom **Room Tree** and the pretty cluster of the **Founders Group** as you walk through tufts of ferns and corn lilies. Approaching the bright green strip of 'C'-shaped **Circle Meadow**, there are no more crowds, and all you can hear is the breeze and birdsong. Trace the east-

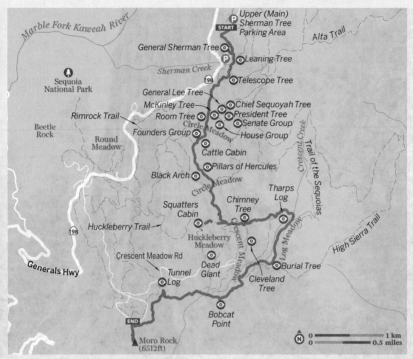

ern edge of the meadow toward another well-named tree group, the **Pillars of Hercules**. Stand between them and look up for a heroic view.

The trail then passes the huge charred maw of the **Black Arch** tree. Continue south, veering slightly right and then left at the next two trail junctions. At a three-way intersection, lush Crescent Meadow finally comes into view. Go straight at this junction and the next one to continue, or make a 0.6-mile round-trip detour to the **Squatters Cabin** by going right on the trail marked 'Huckleberry Meadow.' On the north side of Crescent Meadow stands the hollow-bodied **Chimney Tree**. Continue east past **Tharp's Log**, which

once was a pioneer cabin, then turn right (south) on a paved trail along the east side of **Log Meadow**.

Before reaching the Crescent Meadow parking lot, head left then right onto the signed High Sierra Trail, heading west for more marvelous ridge views. Stop at **Bobcat Point** overlook to take in the Great Western Divide and Kaweah Canyon. In 0.2 miles, cross Crescent Creek on a log to join the Sugar Pine Trail. Go left (west) and follow it for 0.9 miles to **Moro Rock**. Climb the granite dome for some of the park's best views, then return to your starting point via shuttle buses.

Admiring Sequoia National Park's giant trees

Entrances & Access

The park is only accessible by car from the west, and no roads cross the Sierra Nevada mountain range, only trails. The main entrance is at Ash Mountain in the foothills. All park entrances are open 24 hours a day year-round. Some roads – including Mineral King Rd beyond Three Rivers and Big Meadows Rd in the Sequoia National Forest off the Generals Hwy – are closed during winter. Exact opening and closing dates vary by area of the park and on the weather from year to year. The most remote and hazardous roads may be inaccessible from autumn's first snowfall until the snow melts in late spring or early summer.

The seven-day entrance fee (per vehicle $20) covers Sequoia National Park, Kings Canyon National Park and the nearby Hume Lake District of the Sequoia National Forest.

Sleeping & Eating

The markets at Lodgepole, Grant Grove and Cedar Grove have limited groceries. Lodgepole and Cedar Grove snack bars serve basic, budget-friendly meals. Grant Grove has a simple restaurant and espresso cart.

Outside Sequoia's southern entrance, mostly well-worn cabins and chain motels, as well as down-home eateries, line Hwy 198 through Three Rivers town.

Camping

Lodgepole, Potwisha and Buckeye Flat Campgrounds and both Stony Creek campgrounds in the national forest offer reservations. All other campgrounds are first-come, first-served.

Where reservations are accepted, they can be made via recreation.gov or by calling ☑877-444-6777, ☑518-885-3639. Reservations are strongly recommended in summer (late May to September).

Lodgepole Campgrounds

(Generals Hwy; tent & RV sites $22; ◷late Mar–mid-Oct) Closest to the Giant Forest area with over 200 closely packed sites, this place fills quickly because of proximity to Kaweah River swimming holes and Lodgepole Village amenities. A dozen or so walk-in sites are more private.

Potwisha Campground

(Generals Hwy; tent & RV sites $22; ◷year-round; ▦) Popular campground with decent shade near swimming spots on the Kaweah River. It's 3 miles northeast of the Ash Mountain entrance, with 42 sites.

Buckeye Flat Campground

(off Generals Hwy; tent sites $22; ◷late Mar–late Sep; ▦) This tent-only campground is in an open stand of oaks, about 6 miles northeast of the Ash Mountain entrance, down a winding road that's off-limits to RVs and trailers.

Cold Springs Campground

(Mineral King Rd; tent sites $12; ◷late May–late Oct; ▦) A short walk from the Mineral King ranger station, this campground has a peaceful creekside location with ridge views and a gorgeous forest setting of conifers and aspen. If you spend the night here at 7500ft, you'll be well on your way to acclimatizing for high-altitude hikes. It often fills up on summer weekends, including its secluded walk-in sites.

Lodgings

Wuksachi Lodge

(☑559-565-4070, 866-807-3598; www.visitsequoia.com; 64740 Wuksachi Way, off Generals Hwy; r $185-290; ◷year-round ☎) Built in 1999, Wuksachi Lodge is the park's most upscale lodging and dining option. But don't get too excited – the wood-paneled atrium lobby has an inviting stone fireplace and forest views, but charmless motel-style rooms with coffeemakers, mini-fridges, oak furniture and thin walls have an institutional feel. The lodge's location nearby Lodgepole Village, however, can't be beat.

Silver City Mountain Resort

(☑559-561-3223; www.silvercityresort.com; Mineral King Rd; cabins with/without bath from $195/120, chalets from $250; ◷late May–late Oct; ☎) The only food and lodging option anywhere near these parts, this rustic, old-fashioned place rents everything from cute and cozy 1950s-era cabins to modern chalets that sleep up to eight. Bring your own sheets and towels (otherwise, rentals cost $45 per cabin). There's a ping-pong table, outdoor playground and a small pond. It's 3.5 miles west of the ranger station. Most cabins don't have electricity, and the property's generator usually shuts off around 10pm.

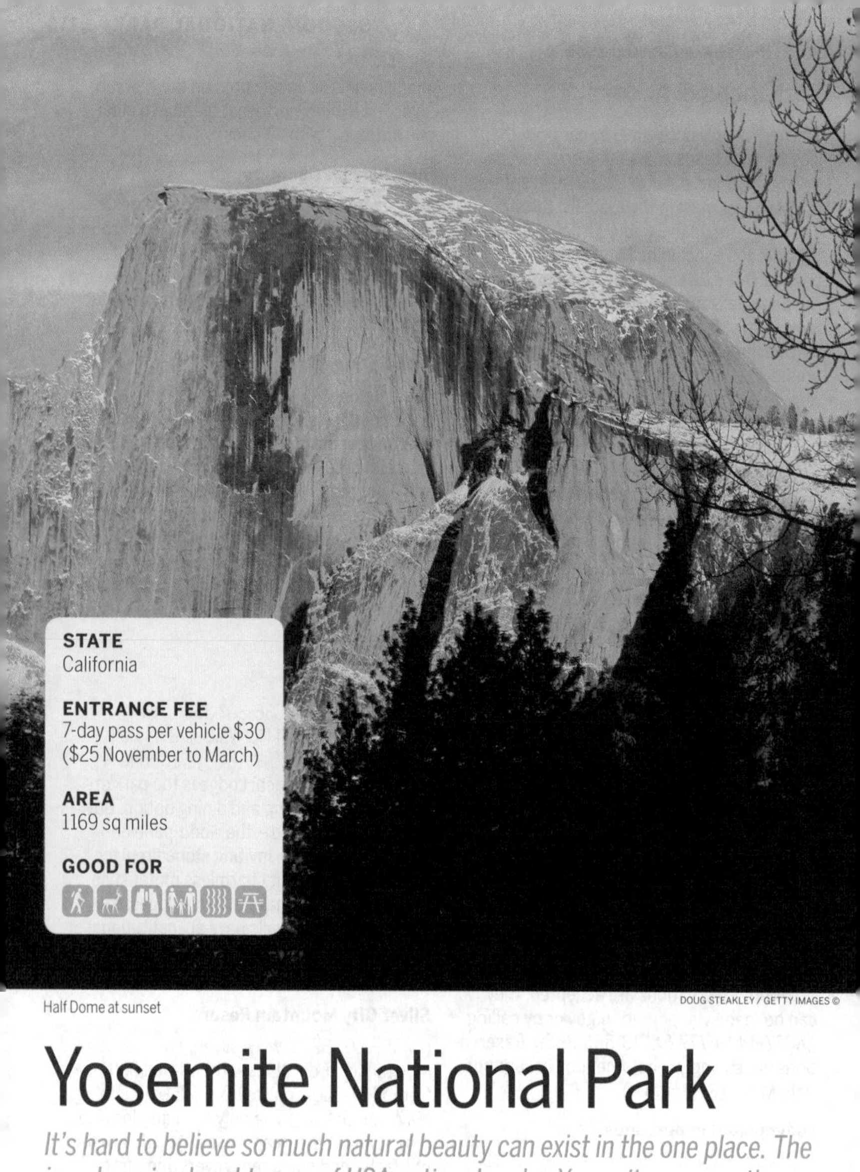

STATE
California

ENTRANCE FEE
7-day pass per vehicle $30
($25 November to March)

AREA
1169 sq miles

GOOD FOR

Half Dome at sunset

DOUG STEAKLEY / GETTY IMAGES ©

Yosemite National Park

It's hard to believe so much natural beauty can exist in the one place. The jaw-dropping head-turner of USA national parks, Yosemite garners the devotion of all who enter.

Yosemite's beauty gave birth to the idea of setting aside land as a protected park. It inspired writers and artists like John Muir and Ansel Adams to produce their finest work. And to the indigenous Miwok, it was a land of forest and river spirits and of thousands of years of ancestral beauty.

Don't be deterred by the park's four million visitors each year. Lift your eyes ever so slightly above the crowds, seek out the park's serene corners or explore its miles of roadless wilderness and you'll feel your heart instantly moved by unrivaled splendors.

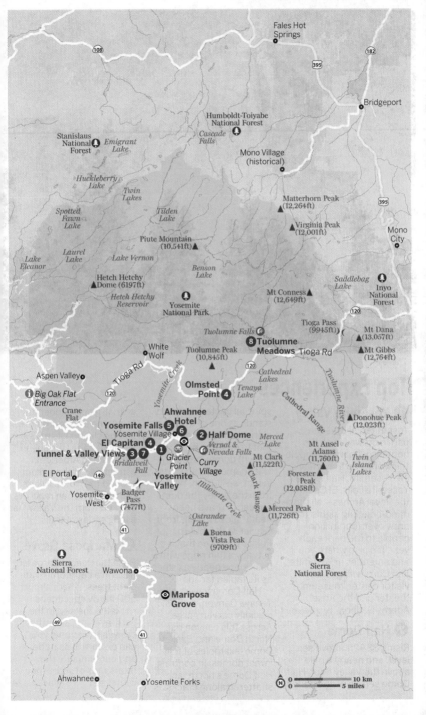

Fales Hot Springs

108

182

395

Bridgeport

Humboldt-Toiyabe National Forest

Cascade Falls

Stanislaus National Forest

Emigrant Lake

Mono Village (historical)

Huckleberry Lake

Twin Lakes

Tilden Lake

Matterhorn Peak (12,264ft)

395

Spotted Fawn Lake

Piute Mountain (10,541ft)

Virginia Peak (12,001ft)

Mono City

Laurel Lake

Lake Vernon

Benson Lake

Mt Conness (12,649ft)

Saddlebag Lake

Inyo National Forest

Lake Eleanor

Hetch Hetchy Dome (6197ft)

Hetch Hetchy Reservoir

Yosemite National Park

Tioga Pass (9945ft)

Mt Dana (13,057ft)

120

Tuolumne Falls

8 Tuolumne Meadows

Mt Gibbs (12,764ft)

White Wolf

Tuolumne Peak (10,845ft)

Tioga Rd

Tuolumne River

Aspen Valley

Tioga Rd

120

Cathedral Lakes

Olmsted Point 4

Tenaya Lake

Cathedral Range

Donohue Peak (12,023ft)

Big Oak Flat Entrance

120

Yosemite Creek

Ahwahnee Hotel

Crane Flat

Yosemite Falls 5 6

Yosemite Village

2 Half Dome

Merced Lake

Mt Ansel Adams (11,760ft)

Twin Island Lakes

El Capitan 4

Vernal & Nevada Falls

El Portal

140

Tunnel & Valley Views 3 7 1

Bridalveil Fall

Glacier Point

Curry Village

Yosemite Valley

Mt Clark (11,522ft)

Forester Peak (12,058ft)

Clark Range

Yosemite West

Badger Pass (7477ft)

Illilouette Creek

Merced Peak (11,726ft)

41

Ostrander Lake

Buena Vista Peak (9709ft)

Sierra National Forest

Wawona

Sierra National Forest

49

Mariposa Grove

41

Ahwahnee

Yosemite Forks

N

0   10 km
0   5 miles

El Capitan

Top Experiences

① Yosemite Valley

Yosemite Valley is the park's crown jewel. It's home to what most people think of when they imagine Yosemite: Half Dome, Yosemite Falls, El Capitan, the Royal Arches – all those mind-boggling sights that draw over four million people to the park each year. It's also where you'll find amenties in Yosemite and Curry villages, the visitor center, museum, theater and the Ansel Adams Gallery.

② Half Dome

Rising 8842ft above sea level, and nearly a mile above the Valley floor, Half Dome serves as the park's spiritual centerpiece and stands as one of the most glorious and monumental (not to mention best-known) domes on earth.

Its namesake shape is, in fact, an illusion. While from the Valley the dome appears to have been neatly sliced in half, from Glacier or Washburn Points you'll see that it's actually a thin ridge with a back slope nearly as steep as its fabled facade.

Half Dome towers above Tenaya Canyon, a classic, glacially carved gorge. Across this canyon rise North Dome and Basket Dome, examples of fully intact domes. In contrast, Half Dome's north face shattered along cracks as a small glacier undercut the dome's base. The resulting cliff boasts a 93% vertical grade (the sheerest in North America), attracting climbers from around the world. Hikers with a permit can reach its summit from the Valley via a long series of trails.

③ Mariposa Grove

Pace the needle-carpeted trails in a cathedral of ancient trees, where almost 500 hardy specimens rocket to the sky. In the early evening, after the crowds have gone, you can explore in solitude and contemplate the thousands of years they've witnessed. Fire scars blaze the trunks, and you can walk through the heart of the still-living California Tunnel Tree and wonder at the girth of the Grizzly Giant. Snowshoe or ski here after the road closes for winter to see its yearly hibernation, and snow camp beneath a giant. The grove has been closed for restoration works and is due to reopen in spring 2017.

④ Classic Roadside Views

For some of the very best views over Yosemite Valley, you don't even have to stroll far from your car. The best all-around photo op of the Valley can be had from **Tunnel View**, a large, busy parking lot and viewpoint at the east end of Wawona Tunnel, on Hwy 41. It's just a short drive from the Valley floor. The vista encompasses most of the Valley's greatest hits: El Capitan on the left, Bridalveil Fall on the right, the green Valley floor below, and glorious Half Dome front and center.

Valley View offers a bottom-up (rather than top-down) view of the Valley and is a lovely spot to dip your toes in the Merced River and bid farewell to sights like Bridalveil Fall, Cathedral Rocks and El Capitan. Look carefully to spot the tip-top of Half Dome in the distance.

Olmsted Point is a knock-out viewpoint of a lunar landscape of glaciated granite with a stunning view down Tenaya Canyon to the backside of Half Dome. It's midway between the May Lake turnoff and Tenaya Lake.

⑤ El Capitan

At nearly 3600ft from base to summit, El Capitan ranks as one of the world's largest granite monoliths. Its sheer face makes it a world-class destination for experienced climbers, and one that wasn't 'conquered' until 1958. Since then, it's been inundated. Look closely and you'll probably spot climbers reckoning with El Cap's series of cracks and ledges, including the famous 'Nose.' At night, park along the road and dim your headlights; once your eyes adjust, you'll easily make out the pinpricks of headlamps dotting the rock face. Listen, too, for voices.

⑥ Yosemite Falls

One of the world's most dramatic natural spectacles, Yosemite Falls is a marvel to behold. Naturalist John Muir devoted entire pages to its changing personality, its myriad sounds, its movement with the wind and its transformations between the seasons. No matter where you are when you see it (and it regularly pops into view from all over the Valley), the 2425ft falls will stop you in your tracks.

⑦ Ahwahnee Hotel

Almost as iconic as Half Dome itself, the elegant Ahwahnee Hotel has drawn well-heeled tourists through its towering doors since 1927. Of course, you needn't be wealthy to partake of its many charms. In fact, a visit to Yosemite Valley is hardly complete without a stroll through the **Great Lounge** (aka the lobby), which is handsomely decorated with leaded glass, sculpted tile, Native American rugs and Turkish kilims.

The site of the hotel was chosen for its exposure to the sun and its views of Half Dome, Yosemite Falls and Glacier Point.

⑧ Tuolumne Meadows

Arriving at Tuolumne Meadows after the drive up from Yosemite Valley is like stepping into another world, even though the two areas are only about 55 miles apart. Instead of being surrounded by waterfalls and sheer granite walls, you emerge in a subalpine wonderland marked by jagged peaks, smooth granite domes, brilliant blue lakes and the meadows' lush grasses and wildflowers. The flowers, which peak in July, are truly a highlight of any visit to Yosemite. (Tuolumne Meadows is only open in summer and dates depend on snowmelt.)

Lake of Shining Rocks

Tenaya Lake (8150ft) is one of Yosemite's biggest (and prettiest) natural lakes. It takes its name from Chief Tenaya, the Ahwahneechee chief who aided white soldiers, only to be driven from the land by white militias in the early 1850s. Tenaya allegedly protested use of his name, pointing out that the lake already had a name – Pywiack ('Lake of Shining Rocks') for the polished granite that surrounds it. A 2-mile loop trail skirts the south shore and makes for a very pleasant one-hour stroll.

Yosemite Valley

Hikers passing Vernal Fall on the Mist Trail

🚶 Vernal & Nevada Falls Hike

Don't miss this day hike (especially if it's springtime). Not only are Vernal and Nevada Falls two of Yosemite's most spectacular waterfalls, but Yosemite Falls and Illilouette Fall both make appearances in the distance from select spots on the trail. If you prefer a shorter excursion, stop at the top of Vernal Fall.

DURATION 4-6 hours

DISTANCE 6.5 miles round-trip

DIFFICULTY Moderate–difficult

START/FINISH Vernal & Nevada Falls/ John Muir Trailhead

NEAREST JUNCTION Happy Isles

TRANSPORTATION Shuttle stop 16

SUMMARY Affording views that are unmatched anywhere else in the park, this well-trodden partial loop ascends the so-called Giant Staircase: the route of the Merced River as it plunges over Nevada and Vernal Falls.

There are two ways to hike this loop: up the **Mist Trail** and down the **John Muir Trail** (in a clockwise direction) or vice versa. It's easier on the knees to climb rather than descend the plethora of steep granite steps along the Mist Trail, so it's best to go for the clockwise route. Then you can lollygag along the John Muir Trail – which has astounding views of both falls – on the way down. The granite slabs atop Nevada Fall make for a superb lunch spot (as close to the edge as you want), with the granite dome of **Liberty Cap** (7076ft) towering above.

From the Happy Isles shuttle stop, cross the road bridge over the Merced River, turn right at the trailhead and follow the riverbank upstream. As the trail

steepens, watch over your right shoulder for Illilouette Fall (often dry in summer), which peels over a 370ft cliff in the distance. From a lookout, you can gaze west and see Yosemite Falls. After 0.8 miles you arrive at the **Vernal Fall footbridge**, which offers the first view of 317ft Vernal Fall upstream.

Shortly beyond the Vernal Fall footbridge (just past the water fountain and restrooms), you'll reach the junction of

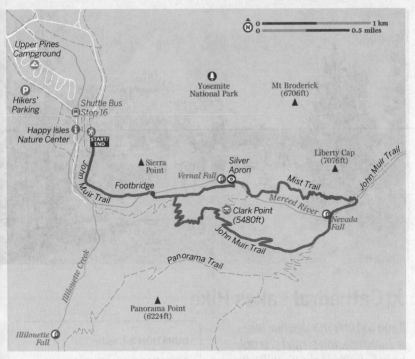

the John Muir and Mist Trails. To do the trail clockwise, hang a left and shortly begin the steep 0.3-mile ascent to the top of **Vernal Fall** by way of the Mist Trail's granite steps. If it's springtime, prepare to get drenched in spray – wear some waterproof clothing – and peer behind you as you near the top to see rainbows in the mist.

Above the falls, the Merced whizzes down a long ramp of granite known as the **Silver Apron** and into the deceptively serene Emerald Pool before plunging over the cliff. No matter how fun the apron looks on a hot day, *don't enter the water:* underwater currents in Emerald Pool have whipped many swimmers over the falls.

From above the apron, it's another 1.3 miles via granite steps and steep switchbacks to the top of the Mist Trail, which meets the John Muir Trail, about 0.2 miles northeast of the falls. From this junction, it's 2.5 miles back to Happy Isles via the Mist Trail or 4 miles via the John Muir Trail.

Shortly after joining the John Muir Trail, you'll cross a footbridge (elevation 5907ft) over the Merced. Beneath it, the river whizzes through a chute before plummeting 594ft over the edge of **Nevada Fall**. Nevada Fall is the first of the series of steps in the Giant Staircase, a metaphor that becomes clear when viewed from afar at Glacier Point. Plant yourself on a slab of granite for lunch and views, and be prepared to fend off the ballsy Steller's jays and squirrels that will have your jerky in their jaws in no time, should you let down your guard.

Returning back from Nevada Fall along the John Muir Trail offers a fabulous glimpse of Yosemite Falls. The trail passes the Panorama Trail junction and traverses a cliff, offering awesome views of Nevada Fall as it winds down the canyon. Soon you'll reach **Clark Point** and a junction that leads down to the Mist Trail. From here it's just over 2 miles downhill, through Douglas firs and canyon live oaks to Happy Isles.

If you choose to do this hike in summertime, be sure to hit the trail early to avoid the crowds and afternoon heat.

Cathedral Peak from the shores of Cathedral Lake

🥾 Cathedral Lakes Hike

If you can only manage one hike in Tuolumne, this should probably be it. Cathedral Lake (9588ft), the lower of the two lakes, sits within a mind-blowing glacial cirque, a perfect amphitheater of granite capped by the iconic spire of nearby Cathedral Peak (10,911ft).

From the lake's southwest side, the granite drops steeply away, affording views as far as Tenaya Lake, whose blue waters shimmer in the distance. Although it's only about two hours to this lower lake, you could easily spend an entire day exploring the granite slopes, meadows and peaks surrounding it. Continuing to the upper lake (9585ft) adds less than an hour to the hike and puts the round-trip walk at 8 miles, including the stop at Cathedral Lake. Admittedly, the upper lake is less spectacular when measured against the lower lake, but by all other standards it's utterly sublime.

Parking for the Cathedral Lakes Trailhead is along the shoulder of Tioga Rd, 0.5 miles west of Tuolumne Meadows

DURATION 5-7 hours

DISTANCE 8 miles round-trip (upper lake)

DIFFICULTY Moderate

START/FINISH Cathedral Lakes Trailhead

NEAREST TOWN Tuolumne Meadows

TRANSPORTATION Tuolumne Meadows hikers' bus; Tuolumne Meadows shuttle stop 7

SUMMARY Easily one of Yosemite's most spectacular hikes, this steady climb through mixed conifer forest ends with glorious views of Cathedral Peak from the shores of two shimmering alpine lakes.

Visitor Center. Due to the popularity of this hike, parking spaces fill up fast, so arrive early or take the free shuttle. Camping is allowed at the lower lake (despite what some maps show), but be absolutely certain you're 100ft from the water *and* the trail, and that you choose an already

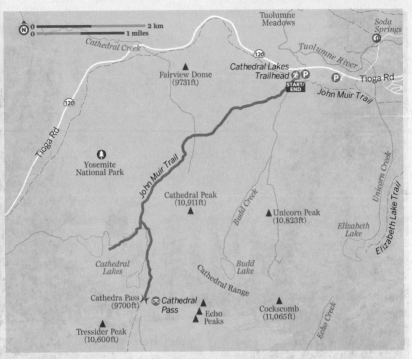

impacted site to prevent further damage. Better yet, camp somewhere near the upper lake or off the pass.

From the Cathedral Lakes Trailhead on Tioga Rd, the hike heads southwest along the John Muir Trail. Almost immediately, it begins to climb through forest of lodgepole pine, mountain hemlock and the occasional whitebark pine. After ascending over 400ft, the trail levels out and a massive slab of granite – the northern flank of Cathedral Peak – slopes up from the left side of the trail. Soon you'll see Fairview Dome (9731ft) through the trees to your right.

Before long, the trail begins its second ascent, climbing nearly 600ft before leveling off and affording outstanding views of Cathedral Peak. Three miles from the trailhead, you'll hit the junction that leads 0.5 miles southwest to Cathedral Lake. This trail crosses a stunning meadow (turn around as you cross it for the head-on view of Cathedral Peak) before arriving at the granite shores of the lake. Be sure to follow the trail around the lake and take in the views from the southwest side.

To visit the upper lake, backtrack to the main trail, turn right (southeast) and, after about 0.5 miles, you'll hit the lake. If you wish to stretch the hike out even further, you can continue past the upper lake to Cathedral Pass (9700ft), where you'll be rewarded with a stellar side-view of Cathedral Peak and Eichorn Pinnacle (Cathedral's fin-like west peak). This side trip adds about 0.6 miles to the trip.

Merced River

Entrances

The park has four main gates. From the west: Big Oak Flat Entrance (Hwy 120 West) and Arch Rock Entrance (Hwy 140). From the east: South Entrance (Hwy 41) near Wawona, and Tioga Pass Entrance (Hwy 120 East).

Tioga Pass (9945ft) is the highest roadway across the Sierra, and Tioga Rd/Hwy 120 East is usually open only between early June and mid-November, though the dates vary every year. In high snow years, the road may not open until July, so check the status of the road before driving across the park in springtime.

Visitor Centers

Rangers staff the park visitor centers and can answer questions and suggest suitable hiking trails, activities and sights. The visitor centers offer excellent displays on park history and the local environment, as well as a range of maps, hiking and climbing guides, geology and ecology books, and gift items. While less extensive, the centers at Big Oak Flat and Wawona are still good places to ask questions, get your bearings and purchase useful books and maps.

Big Oak Flat Information Station
(☏209-379-1899; ⊗8am-5pm late May–Sep) Also has a wilderness permit desk.

Tuolumne Meadows Visitor Center
(☏209-372-0263; ⊗9am-6pm Jun-Sep) Near the campground entrance.

Wawona Visitor Center (☏209-375-9531; ⊗8:30am-5pm May-Sep) On Chilnualna Falls Rd. Issues wilderness permits.

Yosemite Valley Visitor Center
(☏209-372-0200; Yosemite Village; ⊗9am-5pm) The main office, with exhibits and free film screenings in the theater. In the day-use parking lot near Camp Curry.

Information

Yosemite Village, Curry Village and Wawona stores all have ATMs. Drivers should fill up before entering the park. High-priced gas is sold at Wawona and Crane Flat year-round and at Tuolumne Meadows in summer. Cell-phone service is spotty throughout the park. Check the free park newspaper for wi-fi hot spots and pay-as-you-go internet terminals.

Sleeping

There are 13 campgrounds in Yosemite; reservations are accepted at some, while others operate a first-come, first-served system.

Reservations for all campgrounds within the park are handled by **Recreation.gov** (☏877-444-6777, 518-885-3639; www.recreation.gov; ⊗7am-7pm Nov-Feb, to 9pm Mar-Oct).

From mid-March through mid-October or November, many park campgrounds accept or require reservations which are available starting five months in advance. Campsites routinely sell out online within minutes. In summer most campgrounds are noisy and booked to bulging.

All campgrounds have bear-proof lockers and campfire rings; most have potable water.

Nearly all the other lodging in Yosemite National Park is managed by the park concessionaire. The concessionaire was in the process of changing at the time of research, so check the park website (www.nps.gov/yose/planyourvisit/eatingsleeping.htm) for reservations contact information. If you arrive at the park without a room reservation, the Yosemite Valley Visitor Center and all the lodging front desks have courtesy phones so you can inquire about room availability throughout the park. That said, it's important to remember that rooms rarely become available midsummer.

Eating

There are a number of restaurants and other dining options in Yosemite Valley and seasonally at Wawona, Badger Pass, Glacier Point, White Wolf and Tuolumne Meadows. Groceries are available year-round in Yosemite Valley, Wawona, Crane Flat and El Portal, and seasonally at Tuolumne Meadows.

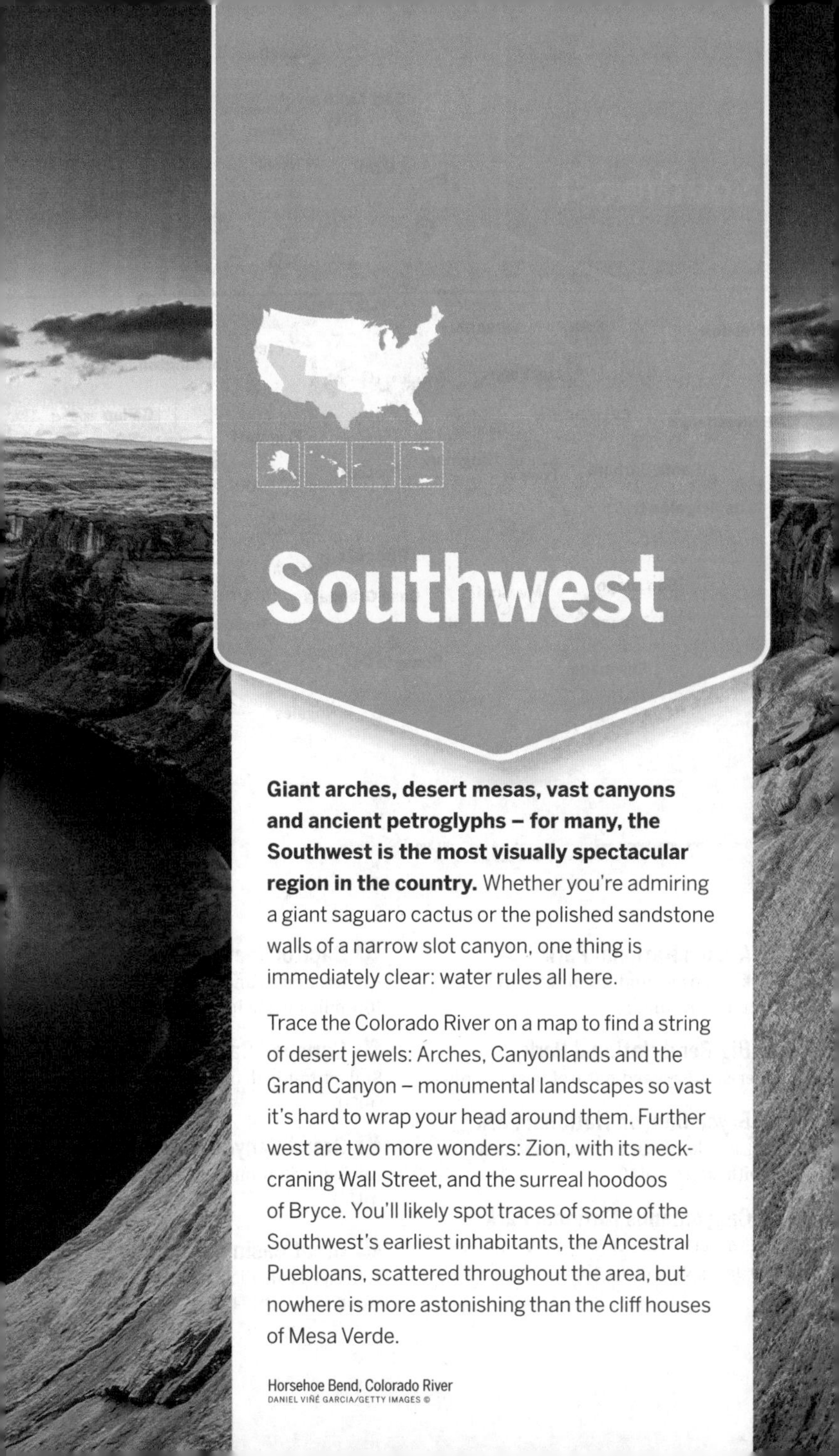

Southwest

Giant arches, desert mesas, vast canyons and ancient petroglyphs – for many, the Southwest is the most visually spectacular region in the country. Whether you're admiring a giant saguaro cactus or the polished sandstone walls of a narrow slot canyon, one thing is immediately clear: water rules all here.

Trace the Colorado River on a map to find a string of desert jewels: Arches, Canyonlands and the Grand Canyon – monumental landscapes so vast it's hard to wrap your head around them. Further west are two more wonders: Zion, with its neck-craning Wall Street, and the surreal hoodoos of Bryce. You'll likely spot traces of some of the Southwest's earliest inhabitants, the Ancestral Puebloans, scattered throughout the area, but nowhere is more astonishing than the cliff houses of Mesa Verde.

Horsehoe Bend, Colorado River
DANIEL VIÑÉ GARCIA/GETTY IMAGES ©

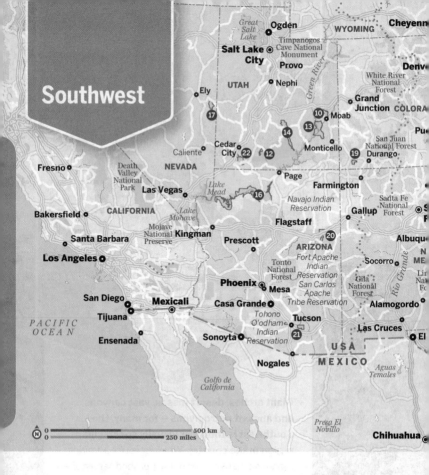

Southwest

10 Arches National Park
Stark, exposed, and unforgettably spectacular. (p138)

11 Big Bend National Park
Super-sized rugged natural beauty. (p144)

12 Bryce Canyon National Park
A bizarre landscape of nature's own ampitheaters. (p150)

13 Canyonlands National Park
High-desert wilderness carved into vast serpentine canyons. (p162)

14 Capitol Reef National Park
Arches, domes and monoliths decorate a 100-mile buckle in the earth's crust. (p168)

15 Carlsbad Caverns National Park
Stalactite-filled, underground wonderland. (p170)

16 Grand Canyon National Park
Ancient and immense with epic views. (p172)

17 Great Basin National Park
Wheeler Peak, glacial lakes and bristle-stone pines. (p184)

✔ DON'T MISS

Hiking Rim to Rim
Hike the classic corridor route through **Grand Canyon National Park**.

Inspiration Point
A hypnotising view of the Silent City's hoodoos in **Bryce Canyon National Park**.

Cliff Palace & Balcony House
Ancient and mysterious cliff dwellings of the Ancestral Puebloan civilization in **Mesa Verde National Park**.

The Narrows
Follow the Virgin River into a narrow slot canyon on this quintessential hike in **Zion National Park**.

Cavernous Caves
Explore the ethereal cave world at **Carlsbad Caverns National Park**.

Bryce Canyon National Park
Sandcastle-like spires

Zion & Bryce Canyon National Parks

From canyon floor to cliff-top perches, the red-rock country in southwestern Utah will delight your eyes and challenge your muscles.

TRIP HIGHLIGHTS

0 miles

Kolob Canyon
A scenic drive at the top of Zion National Park

160 miles

Bryce Canyon National Park
Overlooking sorbet-colored spindles and spires

START ①

8 **Tropic** **FINISH**

Virgin **5**

Glendale

St George

Zion Canyon
Day-hikers heaven: stunning scenery, challenging trails

82 miles

6 DAYS
178 MILES / 286KM

GREAT FOR...

BEST TIME TO GO

In April and September you'll likely have warm weather both at low and high elevations.

ESSENTIAL PHOTO

The amphitheater's color at sunrise on Fairyland Point.

BEST FOR HIKING

Zion Canyon has easy river walks to strenuous, canyon-climbing hikes.

Classic Trip

Zion & Bryce Canyon National Parks

Standing in the umber earth atop Observation Point (6507ft), Zion Canyon spreads before you. The sinuous green river belt snakes through towering crimson cliffs, and hikers below on Angels Landing resemble ants. If you climbed the 4-mile trail up 2148ft from the canyon floor – *bravo!* But insiders know that the views look just as sweet if you hiked the backcountry East Mesa trail and descended to the point.

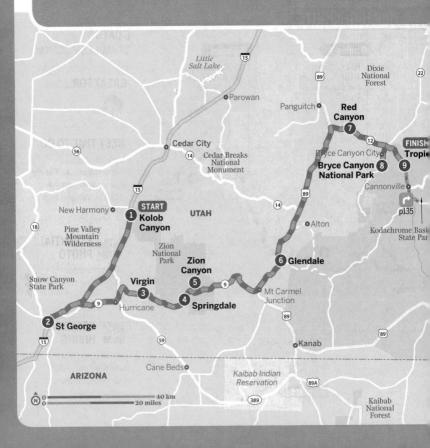

❶ Kolob Canyon

Start your visit at the **Kolob Canyons Visitor Center** (☎435-586-0895; www.nps.gov/zion; Kolob Canyons Rd, Zion National Park; 7-day vehicle pass $30; ⊙park 24hr, center 8am-6pm Jun-Sep, to 4:30pm Oct-May), gateway to the less-visited, higher-elevation section of Zion National Park off I-15. Even in peak season you'll see relatively few cars on the scenic 5-mile **Kolob Canyon Road**, a high-plateau route where striking canyon and rangeland views alternate. The road terminates at **Kolob Canyon Overlook** (6200ft), from there the **Timber Creek Trail** (1-mile round-trip) follows a 100ft ascent to a small peak with great views of the Pine Valley Mountains beyond. In early summer the trail area is covered with wildflowers. Note that the upper section of the road may be closed due to snow from November through May.

The best longer hike in this section of the park is the **Taylor Creek Trail** (5-mile round-trip), which passes pioneer ruins and crisscrosses a creek, with little elevation change.

The Drive » Distant rock formations zoom by as you cruise along at 70-plus mph on I-15. St George is 41 miles south.

❷ St George

A spacious Mormon town with an eye-catching temple and a few pioneer buildings, St George sits about equidistant between the two halves of Zion. The **Chamber of Commerce** (☎435-628-1658; www.stgeorgechamber.com; 97 E St George Blvd; ⊙9am-5pm Mon-Fri) can provide information on the historic downtown. Otherwise, use this time to stock up on food and fuel in this trip's only real city (population 75,561). Eleven miles north of town, **Snow Canyon State Park** (☎435-628-2255; http://stateparks.utah.gov; 1002 Snow Canyon Dr, Ivins; per vehicle $6; ⊙day-use 6am-10pm; ⊕) is a 7400-acre sampler of southwest Utah's famous land features. Easy trails that are perfect for kids lead to tiny slot canyons, cinder cones, lava tubes and fields of undulating slickrock.

The Drive » Off the interstate, Hwy 9 leads you into canyon country. You'll pass the town of Hurricane before sweeping curves give way to tighter turns (and slower traffic). Virgin is 27 miles east of St George.

❸ Virgin

The tiny-tot town of Virgin, named after the river (what else?), has an odd claim to fame – in 2000 the city council passed a largely symbolic law requiring every resident (about 600 of them) to own a gun. You can't miss the **Virgin Trading Post** (☎435-635-3455; 1000 W Hwy 9; village entry $2; ⊙9am-7pm), which sells homemade fudge, ice cream and every Western knickknack known to man. Stop and have your picture taken in the 'Virgin Jail' or 'Wild Ass Saloon' in the replica Old West village here. It's pure, kitschy fun.

The Drive » Springdale is 14 miles further along Hwy 9 (55 minutes from St George).

❹ Springdale

Stunning orangish-red mountains, including the **Watchman** (6555ft), form the backdrop for a perfect little park town. Here eclectic cafes and eateries are big on locally sourced ingredients. Galleries and artisan shops line the long main drag, interspersed with indie motels, lodges and a few B&Bs. Make this your base for three nights exploring Zion Canyon and surrounds. Outfitters **Zion Rock**

Classic Trip

& Mountain Guides
(📞435-772-3303; www.
zionrockguides.com; 1458
Zion Park Blvd; 🕐8am-8pm
Mar-Oct, hours vary Nov-Feb)
and **Zion Adventure
Company** (📞435-772-1001;
www.zionadventures.com; 36
Lion Blvd; 🕐8am-8pm Mar-
Oct, 9am-noon & 4-7pm Nov-
Feb) lead canyoneering,
climbing and 4WD trips
outside the park; the
latter has inner-tube
rentals for summer float
trips. They both outfit
for backcountry hikes
through the Narrows.

Three times daily,
**Zion Canyon Giant
Screen Theatre** (www.
zioncanyontheatre.com;
145 Zion Park Blvd; adlut/
child $8/6) shows the
40-minute *Zion Canyon:
Treasure of the Gods*. The
film's light on substance
but long on beauty.

The Drive » The entrance to
the Zion Canyon section of Zion
National Park is only 2 miles
east of Springdale. Note that
here you're at about 3900ft,
the lowest (and hottest) part of
your trip.

TRIP HIGHLIGHT

❺ Zion Canyon

More than 100 miles
of trails cut through
the surprisingly well-
watered, deciduous
tree-covered Virgin
River canyon section

of Zion National Park.
Map out your routes
at the **Zion Canyon
Visitor Center** (📞435-
772-3256; www.nps.gov/
zion; Hwy 9, Zion National
Park; 7-day vehicle pass
$30; 🕐8am-7:30pm late
May–early Sep, to 5pm
late Sep–early May). Your
first activity should
be the 6-mile **Scenic
Drive**, which pierces the
heart of the park. From
April through October,
using the free shuttle
is mandatory, but you
can hop off and on at
any of the scenic stops
and trailheads along
the way.

The paved, mile-long
one-way **Riverside Walk**
at the end of the road
is an easy stroll. When
the trail ends, you can
continue hiking along
in the Virgin River for
5 miles. Alternatively, a
half-mile one-way trail
leads up to the lower of
the **Emerald Pools** where
water tumbles from
above a steep overhang
stained by desert
varnish.

The strenuous, 5.4-
mile round-trip **Angels
Landing Trail** (four
hours, 1400ft elevation
gain) is a vertigo-
inducer with narrow
ridges and 2000ft sheer
drop-offs. Succeed
and the exhilaration is
unsurpassed. Canyon
views are even more
phenomenal from the
top of the even higher
Observation Point

(8 miles round-trip;
2148ft elevation change).

For the 16-mile
one-way trip down
through the **Narrows**,
spectacular slot
canyons of the Virgin
River, you need to plan
ahead. An outfitter,
shuttle and gear – see
Springdale (p272) – plus
a backcountry permit
from the park are
required; make advance
reservations via the
park website.

The Drive » Driving east,
Hwy 9 undulates over bridges
and up 3.5 miles of tight
switchbacks before reaching
the impressive gallery-dotted
Zion–Mt Carmel Tunnel. From
there until the east park
entrance, the canyon walls
are made of etched, light-
colored slickrock, including
Checkerboard Mesa. Glendale
lies 32 miles (50 minutes)
northwest of Zion Canyon.

❻ Glendale

Several little towns
line Hwy 89 north of
the Hwy 9 junction. As
you drive, look for little
rock shops, art galleries
and home-style cafes.
Glendale is a small
Mormon settlement
founded in 1871. **Buffalo
Bistro** (📞435-648-2778;
www.buffalobistro.net; 305 N
Main St; burgers & mains $8-
24; 🕐4-9:30pm Thu-Sun mid-
Mar–mid-Oct) conjures a
laid-back Western spirit
with a breezy porch,
sizzling grill and eclectic
menu that includes

wild boar ribs and elk burgers. Reservations recommended.

The Drive » Hwy 89 is a fairly straight shot through pastoral lands; turn off from there onto Scenic Byway 12 where the red rock meets the road. Red Canyon is 41 miles northeast of Glendale.

---

⑦ Red Canyon

Impossibly red monoliths rise up roadside as you reach **Red Canyon** (☏435-676-2676; www.fs.usda.gov/recarea/dixie; Scenic Byway 12, Dixie National Forest; admission free; ☺park 24hr, visitor center 9am-6pm Jun-Aug, 10am-4pm May & Sep). These parklands provide super-easy access to eerie, intensely colored formations. Check out the excellent geologic displays and pick up maps at the visitor center, where several moderate hiking trails begin. The 0.7-mile one-way **Arches Trail** passes 15 arches as it winds through a canyon. Legend has it that outlaw Butch Cassidy once rode in the area; a tough 8.9-mile hiking route, **Cassidy Trail**, bears his name.

The Drive » Stop to take the requisite photo before you drive through two blasted-rock arches to continue on. Bryce Canyon National Park is only 9 miles down the road.

DETOUR:
KODACHROME BASIN STATE PARK

Start: ⑨ Tropic

Dozens of red, pink and white sandstone chimneys punctuate **Kodachrome Basin State Park** (☏435-679-8562; www.stateparks.utah.gov; off Cottonwood Canyon Rd; day-use per vehicle $6; ☺day-use 6am-10pm), named for its photogenic landscape by the National Geographic Society in 1948. The moderately easy, 3-mile round-trip **Panorama Trail** provides an overview of the otherworldly formations. Be sure to take the side trails to **Indian Cave**, where you can check out the handprints on the wall (cowboys' or Indians'?), and **Secret Passage**, a short spur through a narrow slot canyon. **Red Canyon Trail Rides** (☏800-892-7923; www.redcanyontrailrides.com; Kodachrome Basin State Park; 1hr ride $40; ☺Mar-Nov) offers horseback riding in Kodachrome.

The park lies 26 miles southeast of Bryce Canyon National Park, off Cottonwood Canyon Rd, south of Cannonville.

TRIP HIGHLIGHT

⑧ Bryce Canyon National Park

The pastel-colored, sandcastle-like spires and hoodoos of **Bryce Canyon National Park** (☏435-834-5322; www.nps.gov/brca; Hwy 63; 7-day vehicle pass $30; ☺24hr, visitor center 8am-8pm May-Sep, to 4:30pm Oct-Apr) look like something straight out of Dr Seuss' imagination. The 'canyon' is actually an amphitheater of formations eroded from the cliffs. **Rim Road Scenic Drive** (18 miles one way) roughly follows the canyon rim past the visitor center (8000ft), the lodge, incredible overlooks and trailheads, ending at **Rainbow Point** (9115ft). From early May through early October, an optional free shuttle bus (8am until at least 5:30pm) departs from a staging area just north of the park.

The easiest walk would be to follow the **Rim Trail** that outlines Bryce Amphitheater from Fairyland Point to Bryce Point (up to 5.5 miles one way). Several sections are paved and wheelchair accessible, the most level being the half-mile between Sunrise and Sunset Points.

A number of moderate trails descend below the rim to the maze of fragrant juniper and undulating high-mountain desert. The **Navajo Loop** drops 521ft from Sunset Point. To avoid a super-steep ascent, follow the **Queen's Garden Trail** on the desert floor and hike up 320ft to Sunrise Point. From there take the shuttle, or follow the Rim Trail back to your car (2.9-mile round-trip).

Note that the high altitude means cooler temperatures – 80°F (27°C) average in July – here than at scorching Zion National Park.

The Drive » Only 11 miles east of Bryce Canyon, the town of Tropic is 2000ft lower in elevation – so expect it to be 10°F/5°C warmer there.

9 Tropic

A farming community at heart, Tropic does offer a few services for park-goers. There's a grocery store, a couple of restaurants and several motels. Basing yourself here for two nights is definitely less expensive than staying in the park.

Clockwise from top: Bridge across the Virgin River, Zion National Park; The Narrows, Zion National Park; Rock tower, Kodachrome Basin State Park

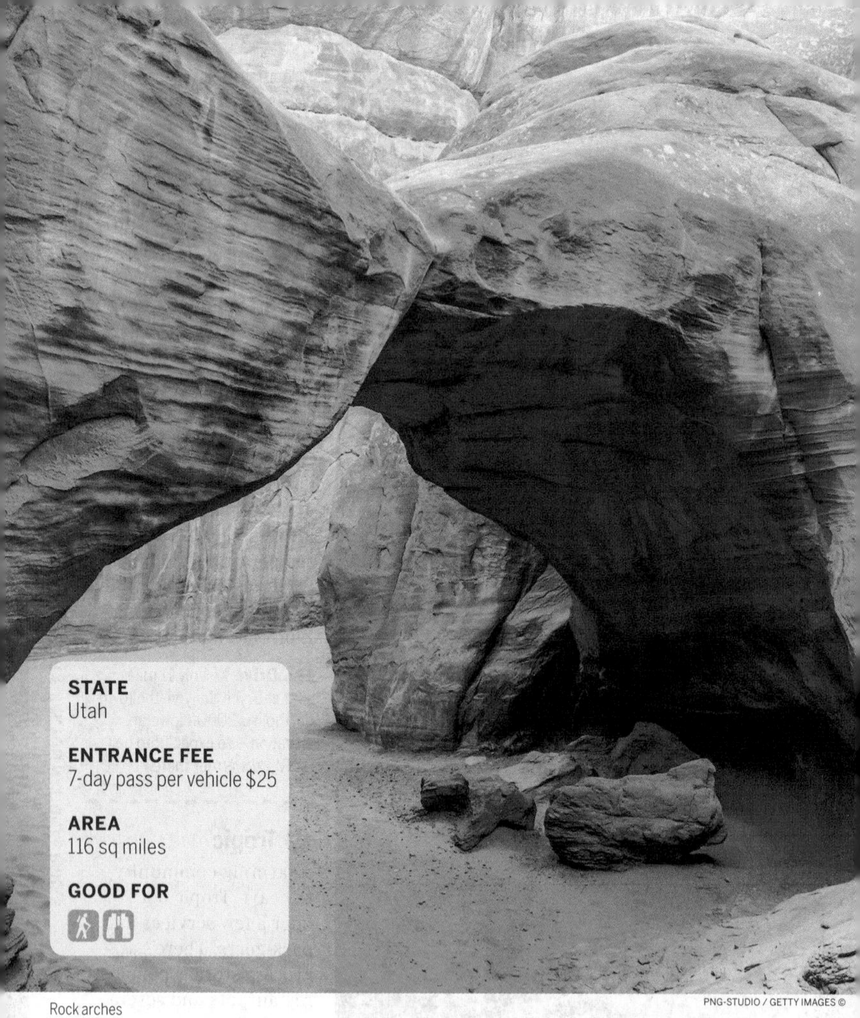

STATE
Utah

ENTRANCE FEE
7-day pass per vehicle $25

AREA
116 sq miles

GOOD FOR

Rock arches

Arches National Park

Giant sweeping arcs of sandstone frame snowy peaks and desert landscapes at Arches National Park, where you can explore the park's namesake formations in a red-rock wonderland.

Arches National Park boasts the highest density of rock arches anywhere on earth: more than 2000 in a 116-sq-mile area. You'll lose perspective on size at some, such as the thin and graceful Landscape Arch, which stretches almost 300ft across (it's one of the largest in the world). Others are tiny – the smallest only 3ft across. An easy drive makes the spectacular arches accessible to all. Fiery Furnace is a not-to-be-missed guided-tour-only area of the park, where you can weave your way through narrow canyons and soaring fin-like rocks.

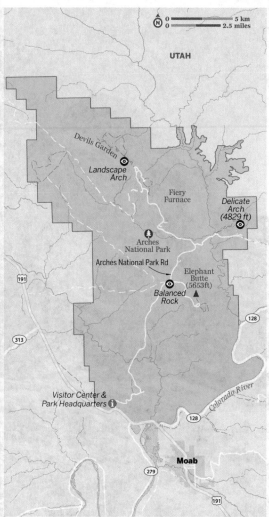

UTAH

Devils Garden

Landscape Arch

Fiery Furnace

Delicate Arch (4829 ft)

Arches National Park

Arches National Park Rd

Elephant Butte (5653ft)

Balanced Rock

191

313

128

Visitor Center & Park Headquarters

Colorado River

128

Moab

279

191

strenuous, 3-mile round-trip trail that ascends the slickrock to reach the unofficial state symbol, **Delicate Arch**. You've seen it before; it's featured on just about every piece of Utah tourist literature.

❷ Fiery Furnace

Further along the road, the spectacularly narrow canyons and maze-like fins of the Fiery Furnace are most safely explored on the three-hour, ranger-led hikes, for which advance reservation is usually necessary. This is no walk in the park. (Well, it is, but...) Be prepared to scramble up and over boulders, shimmy down between rocks and navigate narrow ledges.

Top Experiences

❶ Arches Scenic Drive

The park's main scenic drive is paved and visits all sorts of strange forms and flaming desert land-

scapes. It's packed with photo ops and short walks to arches and iconic landmarks. The full 43-mile drive (including spurs) takes two to three hours if you're not taking any hikes.

Highlights along the way include **Balanced Rock**, precariously perched beside the road, and, for hikers, the moderate-to-

North Window, Windows Trail

Devils Garden

❸ Devils Garden

The scenic drive ends 19 miles from the visitor center at Devils Garden. The trailhead here marks the start of several hikes (ranging from 2 to 7.7 miles, round-trip), pass-ing at least eight arches, though most hikers only go the relatively easy 1.3 miles to **Landscape Arch**, a gravity-defying, 290ft-long behemoth.

❹ Windows Trail

If you're tight on time, the Windows section of the park is a good option, with stunning arches that take very little effort to reach. The 0.6-mile round-trip trail brings you up to the most famous formations. Stand be-neath North Window and look out to the canyon views beyond, or frame North Window within South for a stunning pic-ture. Don't forget Double Arch, right across the parking lot.

Dead Horse Point State Park

Tiny but stunning **Dead Horse Point State Park** (www. stateparks.utah.gov; Hwy 313; park day use per vehicle $10; tent & RV sites $25; ⊙park 6am-10pm, visitor center 8am-6pm Mar-Oct, 9am-4pm Nov-Feb) has been the setting for numerous movies, including the climactic scenes of *Thelma & Louise*. It's not a hiking destination, but mesmerizing views merit the half-hour drive (especially if taken as a short detour off Hwy 313 en route to the Island in the Sky in Canyonlands National Park, see p162): look out at red-rock canyons rimmed with white cliffs, the Colorado River, Canyonlands and the distant La Sal Mountains. The 21-site campground has limited water (bring your own if possible); no showers, no hookups. Reserve ahead.

WHIT RICHARDSON / GETTY IMAGES ©

Petroglyphs

Sleeping & Eating

For stays between March and October, advance reservations are a must for the **Devils Garden Campground** (📱877-444-6777; www.recreation.gov; tent & RV sites $20). Don't expect much shade, nor showers or hookups.

Otherwise, base yourself in Moab (aka activity central – a town built for mountain biking, river running and four-wheel driving), for access to both Arches and Canyonlands National Parks.

Most lodgings in Moab have bike storage facilities and hot tubs. Despite having an incredible number of motels, Moab does fill up; reservations are highly recommended March through October.

Foodwise, Moab holds everything from backpacker coffeehouses to gourmet dining rooms; pick up the *Moab Menu Guide* (www.moabmenuguide.com) at area lodgings.

BLM campsites (📱435-259-2100; www.blm.gov/utah/moab; Hwy 128; tent sites $15; ⊙year-round) First-come, first-served. In peak season, check with the Moab Information Center to see which sites are full.

Cali Cochitta (📱435-259-4961, 888-429-8112; www.moabdreaminn.com; 110 S 200 East Moab; cottages $140-180; ❄🛜) Charming and central, these adjoining brick cottages offer snug rooms fitted with smart decor. A long wooden table on the patio makes a welcome setting for community breakfasts. You can also take advantage of the porch chairs, hammock or backyard hot tub. The vibe is warm but the innkeepers live off-site, leaving you alone to enjoy the house.

Getting There & Away

The park entrance station lies off Hwy 191, 5 miles northwest of Moab. Arches has no shuttle system, and no public buses run to the park.

STATE
Texas

ENTRANCE FEE
7-day pass per vehicle $25

AREA
1252 sq miles

GOOD FOR

Canoeing on the Rio Grande

DAVID NEVALA / GETTY IMAGES ©

Big Bend National Park

Traversing Big Bend's 1252 sq miles, you come to appreciate what 'big' really means. This is a land of incredible diversity, laced with well-placed roads and trails, and vast enough to allow a lifetime of discovery.

Like many popular US parks, Big Bend has one area – the Chisos Basin – that absorbs the overwhelming crunch of traffic. The Chisos Mountains are beautiful, and no trip here would be complete without an excursion into the high country.

But any visit to Big Bend should also include time in the Chihuahuan Desert, home to curious creatures and adaptable plants, and the Rio Grande, providing a watery border between the US and Mexico. These three distinct ecosystems provide something for everyone.

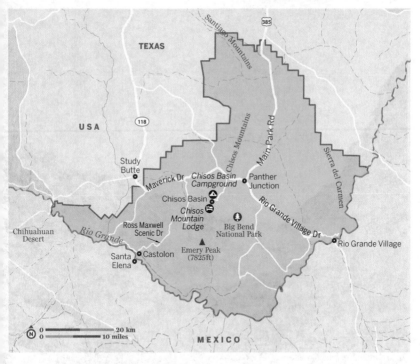

Top Experiences

1 Scenic Drives

With 110 miles of paved and 150 miles of dirt roads, scenic driving is the park's most popular activity.

Maverick Drive The 22-mile stretch between the west entrance and park headquarters is notable for its desert scenery and wildlife. Just west of Basin Junction, a side trip on the gravel Grapevine Hills Rd leads to fields of oddly shaped boulders.

Ross Maxwell Scenic Drive This 30-mile route leaves Maverick Dr midway between the west entrance and park HQ. The Chisos Mountains provide a grand panorama, and the big payoff is the view of Santa Elena Canyon and its 1500ft sheer rock walls.

Rio Grande Village Drive This 20-mile drive leads from park headquarters toward the Sierra del Carmen range, running through the park toward Mexico. The best time to take this drive is at sunrise or sunset, when the mountains glow brilliantly with different hues.

Boquillas: Crossing into Mexico

For years, one of the added draws of Big Bend was crossing the Rio Grande into the quaint Mexican village of Boquillas. After more than a decade of closure, the border has again opened to visitors. A boatman will row you across ($5 round-trip), once on the other side you can hire a burro ($8 round-trip), walk or take a truck for the 1 mile to Boquillas village. There you need to get stamped in at the Mexican immigration office. You can have lunch, peruse local handicrafts and wander around the town before heading back to the river (leave by 5pm to avoid getting stranded). The border opens from 9am to 6pm Wednesday to Sunday. You'll need your passport. For more info, check www.discoverboquillas.wordpress.com.

Chihuahuan Desert

Hikers in the Chihuahuan Desert

❷ Hiking

With over 200 miles of trails to explore, it's no wonder hiking is big in Big Bend. From short, easy trails with views of the Chisos Basin or the Rio Grande, to fascinating desert hikes to rock formations and Native American pictographs and petroglyphs, there are options to suit everyone from non-hikers to serious backpackers.

❸ Birdwatching

More than 450 bird species have been spotted in the park, with prime sites including the Rio Grande Valley, the Sam Nail Ranch, the Chisos Basin and Castolon near Santa Elena Canyon.

The Big Bend region may be best known for its peregrine falcons, which – while still endangered – have been making a comeback. A dozen known nests are found within or near the park.

Among other Big Bend bird celebrities, the Colima warbler has its only US nesting spot in the Chisos Mountains, where it lives from April through mid-September.

Some more common Big Bend species include golden eagles, cactus wrens, ravens, Mexican jays, roadrunners, acorn woodpeckers, canyon towhees and a whole bunch of warblers and hummingbirds.

Bear in Mind...

There's a slim chance you'll encounter a black bear in the park. If you do, don't run away; instead make lots of noise and look as big as possible by waving your hands above your head. If you see cubs, back away slowly so the mother won't fear an attack. To keep bears from joining you for dinner, store all food, coolers, cooking utensils and toiletries in the trunk of your car or in the special bear-proof lockers, and discard trash in the bear-proof containers provided at campsites and near trailheads.

Mexican jay

Sleeping & Eating

In the heart of the park, **Chisos Mountain Lodge** (📞432-477-2291; www.chisosmountainslodge.com; lodge & motel r $156, cottages $174; 📶📺) offers lodging in the sought-after Roosevelt Stone Cottages or in one of two motel-style lodges. There's also a **dining room** (Lodge Dining Room; mains $10-24; ⏱7-10am, 11am-4pm & 5-8pm) within the complex, as well as a **camp store** (📞432-477-2291; ⏱8am-9pm) with basic supplies.

For tent campers or smaller RVs that don't require hookups, there are three main campgrounds, some of which can be reserved, some of which are first-come, first-served. When everything's full, rangers direct tent campers to primitive sites throughout the Big Bend backcountry. Thanks to its mountain climate, the **Chisos Basin Campground** (📞877-444-6777; www.recreation.gov; sites $14) is the most popular.

Getting There & Away

Park headquarters and the **main visitor center** (📞432-477-2251; ⏱8am-6pm) are at Panther Junction, 29 miles south of the Persimmon Gap entrance and 22 miles east of the Maverick entrance near Study Butte. A Chevron station offers fuel, repairs and a small stock of snacks and beverages.

From Panther Junction, it's a (relatively) short 10-mile drive to the Chisos Basin. Sharp curves and steep grades make Basin Rd unsuitable for recreational vehicles longer than 24ft and trailers longer than 20ft.

There is no public transportation to, from or within the park. The closest buses and trains run through Alpine, 108 miles northwest of Panther Junction. The nearest major airports are in Midland (230 miles northeast) and El Paso (325 miles northwest).

The border patrol has checkpoints for vehicles coming from Big Bend. If you're not a US citizen, presenting your passport will help avoid delays (ie prove you're not coming from Mexico).

STATE
Utah

ENTRANCE FEE
7-day pass per vehicle $30

AREA
56 sq miles

GOOD FOR

Early morning at Bryce Canyon

Bryce Canyon National Park

Though it's the smallest of southern Utah's national parks, Bryce Canyon stands among the most prized. Its sights are nothing short of otherworldly. Repeated freezes and thaws have eroded soft sandstone and limestone into a landscape that's utterly unique.

Not actually a canyon, Bryce comprises the eastern edge of an 18-mile plateau. Its Pink Cliffs mark the top step of the Grand Staircase, a giant geologic terrace reaching to the Grand Canyon. Trails descend through 1000ft amphitheaters of pastel daggers into a maze of fragrant juniper and sculpted high-mountain desert.

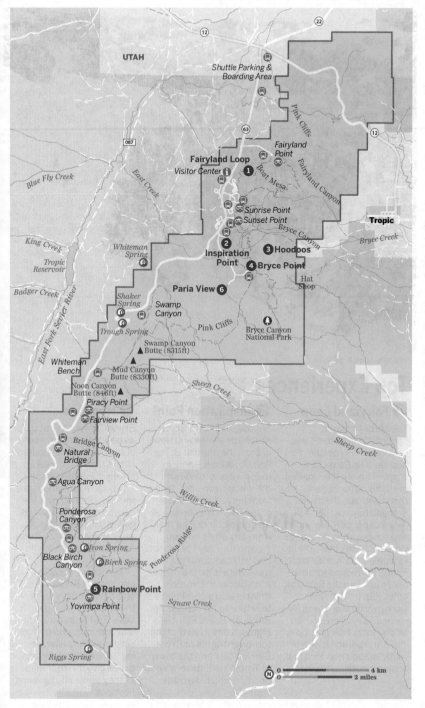

Snowfall at Natural Bridge

Top Experiences

❶ Fairyland Loop

The sorbet-colored, sandcastle-like spires and hoodoos of Bryce Canyon pop like a Dr Seuss landscape. Though the smallest of Utah's national parks, this is perhaps the most immediately visually stunning, particularly at sunrise and sunset when an orange wash sets the otherworldly formations ablaze. Search for the perfect panoramic photo op from the Rim Trail, or let your imagination work overtime on the aptly named Fairyland Loop, an all-day foray that gets up close and personal with wildly shaped hoodoos and ancient bristlecone pines.

❷ Inspiration Point

This overlook into Bryce Amphitheater may sit lower than the popular Bryce Point overlook – and, in many ways, provides much the same view – but seen from here, the hoodoos of the Silent City below are more compelling than from any other rim-top viewpoint. They feel closer, and you can make out more details on the canyon floor below. Inspiration Point is also a great place to return to for stargazing. Although Bryce Point is higher, it sits in view of the too-bright lights of Bryce Canyon City and the town of Tropic, an unfavorable position which dims the starlight.

❸ Hoodoos

Bryce Canyon is famous for its hoodoos: narrow spires of rock that stand hundreds of feet high and create an utterly surreal landscape. The bizarre formations are formed as runoff over the canyon rim carves parallel gullies with narrow rock walls, known as fins. These fins ultimately erode into columns.

The layers of earth in and around Bryce are so soft that in heavy rains they would quickly dissolve the fins into muddy little mounds, except that siltstone layers alternating with resilient limestone bands give them strength as they erode into towering hoodoos.

Hat Shop rock formation

➍ Bryce Point

If you stop nowhere else along Bryce Canyon Scenic Drive, be sure to catch the stunning views from Bryce Point. You can walk the rim above Bryce Amphitheater for awesome views of the Silent City, an assemblage of hoodoos so dense, gigantic and hypnotic that you'll surely begin to see shapes of figures frozen in the rock. Be sure to follow the path to the actual point, a fenced-in promontory that juts out over the forested canyon floor, 1000ft below. The extension allows a broad view of the hoodoos. This rivals any overlook in the park for splendor and eye-popping color. An interpretive panel tells the story of Ebenezer Bryce, the Mormon pioneer for whom the canyon was named, and his wife Mary.

➎ Rainbow Point

On a clear day you can see more than 100 miles from this overlook at the southernmost end of Bryce Canyon Scenic Drive. The viewpoint provides jaw-dropping views of canyon country. Giant sloping plateaus, tilted mesas and towering buttes jut above the vast landscape, and interpretive panels explain the sights. On the northeastern horizon look for the Aquarius Plateau – the very top step of the Grand Staircase – rising 2000ft higher than Bryce. The viewpoint is reachd on a short, paved, wheelchair-accessible path at the far end of the parking lot.

➏ Paria View

This is *the* place for sunset photos, where hoodoos are set aflame by the last light. Three miles north of Swamp Canyon, signs point to the Paria View viewpoint, which lies 2 miles off the main road. If you're tired of RVs and buses, you'll be pleased to learn that this small overlook is for cars only – though it's reserved for cross-country skiers in winter, when the access road isn't plowed. Sunsets are the best here. Most of the hoodoo amphitheaters at Bryce face east, making them particularly beautiful at sunrise, but not sunset. The amphitheater here, small by comparison but still beautiful, faces west toward the Paria River watershed.

Silent City

Bryce's most impressive conglomeration of hoodoos is called the Silent City, and it is best viewed from Bryce Point or Inspiration Point.

Navajo Loop Trail

🚗 Bryce Canyon Scenic Drive

The scenic drive winds south for 17 miles and roughly parallels the canyon rim, climbing from 7894ft at the visitor center to 9115ft at Rainbow Point, the plateau's southern tip at road's end.

> **DURATION** 2 hours
>
> **DISTANCE** 34 miles round-trip
>
> **START/FINISH** Visitor Center
>
> **NEAREST TOWN** Tropic
>
> **TRANSPORTATION** Car
>
> **SUMMARY** Spanning the length of the park, this out-and back route hits all the park highlights.

Head directly to Rainbow Point (a 35-minute drive from the visitor center), then stop at the scenic overlooks and turnouts as you return. Visit ❶ **Rainbow Point** via a short, paved, wheelchair-accessible path at the far end of the parking lot. The overlook offers a jaw-dropping glimpse of canyon country, with giant sloping plateaus, tilted mesas and towering buttes jutting above the vast landscape. At the other end of the parking lot another short, paved, wheelchair-accessible trail leads to ❷ **Yovimpa Point**, one of the park's windiest spots. The southwest-facing view reveals more forested slopes and less eroding rock. Look for Molly's Nipple, an eroded sandstone dome often mistaken for a volcano. Dipping below the horizon is the Kaibab Plateau, marking the Arizona border and the Grand Canyon.

Take the easy 1-mile ❸ **Bristlecone Loop Trail** from Rainbow Point. Yovimpa Point also offers a great picnic area.

Just north of mile marker 16, at 8750ft, the small ❹ **Black Birch Canyon** overlook shows precipitous cliffs roadside. It also offers your first up-close look at hoodoos – though modest ones. There are no trailheads here, only a small lookout.

Higher than the previous stop, ❺ **Ponderosa Canyon** offers long vistas like those at Rainbow Point. Below, note the namesake giant ponderosa pines, some as tall as 150ft. This small amphitheater of hoodoos and burnt-orange cliffs is breathtaking, especially in morning light. If you're feeling ambitious, descend a stretch of the moderately strenuous ❻ **Agua Canyon Connecting Trail**, a lightly traveled, steep trail that drops past woods into a brilliant amphitheater of hoodoos before joining the ❼ **Under-the-Rim Trail**.

One of the best stops at this end of the park, the ❽ **Agua Canyon** viewpoint overlooks two large formations of precariously balanced, top-heavy hoodoos that could tip at any time. Note the precipitous drop-off at your feet. On the ridge above, distinct sedimentary lines stripe iron-rich red rock and white limestone.

The parking lot at ❾ **Natural Bridge** is the biggest since Rainbow Point, and with good reason: a stunning span of eroded, red-hued limestone juts from the edge of the overlook.

The stop at ❿ **Fairview Point** offers a grand view of the tree-studded rises, giant plateaus, blue-hued mesas and buttes that extend from the skirts of Bryce into the Grand Staircase, as far as the eye can see. On clear days you can see 160 miles to Arizona's Black Mesas. A short walk among vanilla-scented pines leads to another overlook at ⓫ **Piracy Point**. There are toilets but no running water.

The overlook at ⓬ **Swamp Canyon** sits in a forested dip between two ridgelines that extend into the canyon. From the turnout you can take a short walk through the trees and descend slightly to towering pink-orange cliffs of crumbling limestone. Nature lovers like the variety of plant and animal life here; kids like the steep trail into the canyon. This is also the jumping-off point for the scenic ⓭ **Swamp Canyon Connecting Trail**.

Three miles north of Swamp Canyon, turn right and follow signs to the ⓮ **Paria View** viewpoint. This small overlook is for cars only – though it's reserved for cross-country skiers in winter, when the access road isn't plowed. This is the place to come for sunsets. Most of the hoodoo amphitheaters at Bryce face east and are best viewed at sunrise. The amphitheater here faces west toward the Paria River watershed.

If you make just one stop, make it ⑮ **Bryce Point**. You can walk the rim above ⑯ **Bryce Amphitheater** for awesome views of the Silent City, an assemblage of hoodoos resembling figures frozen in the rock. Be sure to follow the path to the actual point, a fenced-in promontory that juts over the forested canyon floor, 1000ft below. This rivals any overlook in the park for splendor and eye-popping color.

Bryce Point marks the beginning of the 5.5-mile ⑰ **Rim Trail** and the ⑱ **Peekaboo Loop Trail**. There's also a pit toilet.

At ⑲ **Inspiration Point** a short ascent up a paved path takes you to another overlook into Bryce Amphitheater. Inspiration Point sits lower than Bryce Point and provides much the same view, though the Silent City is most compelling from here. The hoodoos feel closer, and you can make out more details on the canyon floor. Inspiration Point is a great place to return for stargazing.

Views into Bryce Amphitheater at ⑳ **Sunset Point** are as good as they get, but don't expect solitude. It's at the core of the park, near campgrounds, the lodge and all visitor services. Aside from great views of the Silent City, this point is known for ㉑ **Thor's Hammer**, a big square-capped rock balanced atop a spindly hoodoo. This is the starting point for the ㉒ **Navajo Loop Trail**, the park's most popular hike, and you'll find restrooms, drinking water and picnic tables. Don't be fooled by the name of this point. Because it faces east, sunrises are better here than sunsets.

Marking the north end of Bryce Amphitheater, the southeast-facing ㉓ **Sunrise Point** offers great views of hoodoos, the Aquarius Plateau and the Sinking Ship, a sloping mesa that looks like a ship's stern rising out of the water. Keep your eyes peeled for the ㉔ **Limber Pine**, a spindly tree whose roots have been exposed through erosion, but which nonetheless remains anchored to the receding sand.

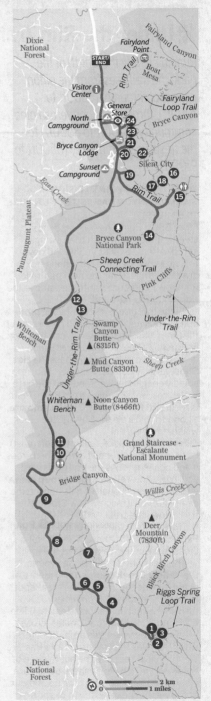

🚶 Under-the-Rim Trail

Running nearly the length of the park, the trail rises from the piñon juniper community (6600ft to 7000ft), through the ponderosa pine community (7000ft to 8500ft) to the fir-spruce community (8500ft to 9100ft).

DURATION 3 days

DISTANCE 22.9 miles one way

DIFFICULTY Moderate–difficult

START Bryce Point

FINISH Rainbow Point

NEAREST TOWNS Tropic, Panguitch

TRANSPORTATION Park shuttle

SUMMARY Ideal for getting away from it all, this multiday hike skirts beneath cliffs, through amphitheaters and amid pines and aspens.

🚶 **DAY 1: BRYCE POINT TO RIGHT FORK SWAMP CANYON CAMPSITE (4-6 HOURS, 10.5 MILES)**

From Bryce Point the trail descends steeply almost due east, then swings south. After 0.5 miles you'll wind down to a ridge, where the earth changes from gray to orange. Over the next half-mile Rainbow Point comes into view above the ridge in the foreground.

As the trail traces a south-facing promontory, look north for a grand panorama of the Pink Cliffs. On the right (west) the Right Fork Yellow Creek forms a steep-sided drainage. Two miles in you'll pass the **Hat Shop**, its gray boulder caps perched atop spindly conglomerate stands. At the base of this descent, 2.8 miles from Bryce Point, is the **Right Fork Yellow Creek campsite**, a good spot in a clearing beside the creek, which runs all year.

From the campsite, follow the left (east) bank of the creek for half a mile, then cross it and bear south. As the trail turns west, you'll pass the **Yellow Creek group campsite** on the left. A quarter-mile beyond the campsite, you'll reach Yellow Creek. The trail follows the creek and climbs toward the Pink Cliffs at the head of the creek and Paria View, 1000ft above. The trail soon crosses the creek; cairns point the way.

Another quarter-mile brings you to the **Yellow Creek campsite**, in plenty of shade beside the creek. It's a great spot to watch the sunset. From here you'll turn southwest up a short, steep hill. The trail undulates for about 2 miles, crossing a slope between two amphitheaters. After 1.5 miles the trail drops into Pasture Wash. Follow cairns to the south edge of the wash and look for a sharp uphill turn, where the trail visibly zigzags up and out of the wash. The view (north to south) of Swamp Canyon, Mud Canyon and Noon Canyon Buttes will reward your effort.

Descend into the valley to the junction with the **Sheep Creek Connecting Trail**, which climbs 2 miles to the scenic drive. A well-marked spur leads 0.5 miles south to the **Sheep Creek campsite**, its beauty second only to the Yellow Creek site; you can usually find water here.

From the junction, the trail climbs 150ft then descends into Swamp Canyon amid a stand of large quaking aspens. On the left (southeast), in a clearing among large ponderosa pines, is the **Right Fork Swamp Canyon campsite**.

🚶 **DAY 2: RIGHT FORK SWAMP CANYON CAMPSITE TO NATURAL BRIDGE CAMPSITE (1½-2½ HOURS, 4.6 MILES)**

One hundred yards past the campsite is the junction with the mile-long Swamp Canyon Connecting Trail. From the connecting trail junction, you'll climb steadily south, then turn west up switchbacks. Just beyond, at 8200ft, is the **Swamp Canyon campsite**.

Beyond camp, the trail passes aspens and pines, then descends to the base of Farview Cliffs. From here you'll skirt **Willis Creek** for a mile until it turns southeast. You may find it difficult to distinguish the trail from other small creeks; bear south and west.

The trail ducks into Dixie National Forest, then curves sharply east to climb an eroded sandstone slope southwest of Willis Creek. At the top, the sandy trail snakes around

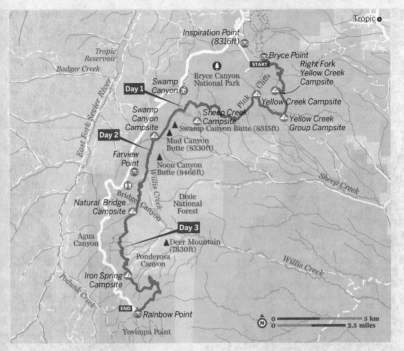

the east edge of a promontory for gorgeous views of the **Pink Cliffs**.

Descend to a southern tributary of Willis Creek and continue 0.5 miles to the **Natural Bridge campsite**, which lacks water.

🏕 **DAY 3: NATURAL BRIDGE CAMPSITE TO RAINBOW POINT (3-5 HOURS, 7.8 MILES)**
Half a mile out of camp, the trail traverses a sage meadow toward Agua Canyon. Crossing this canyon may prove tricky: on older topo maps, the trail turns slightly west and cuts straight across the canyon, but due to floods you now need to hike up the canyon 0.75 miles, then switchback up the canyon's south ridge. When in doubt, follow the cairns. The switchbacks are snowed under until late spring. Atop this ridge, the Agua Canyon Connecting Trail climbs 1.6 miles to the scenic drive.

From the connecting trail junction, you'll skirt a pink promontory, descend into Ponderosa Canyon, then zigzag up and down to South Fork Canyon. Just past the head of the canyon, you'll reach the **Iron Spring campsite** on your right; the east-facing ridge leaves little room to spread out. Amid a grove of aspens 600ft up-canyon (southwest) from the campsite, **Iron Spring** supplies year-round water.

The trail continues its undulating rhythm, dipping to cross both arms of Black Birch Canyon. After clambering over the lower slopes of a northwest-jutting promontory, you'll enter the southernmost amphitheater of the Pink Cliffs.

The trail traces the hammer-shaped ridge below Rainbow Point, climbing steadily and offering unsurpassed views. Ascend the final 1.5 miles up the back (south) side of the amphitheater to the rim.

Navajo Loop Trail

Entrance

The park's sole vehicle entrance is 3 miles south of Utah Hwy 12, via Hwy 63. Bryce Canyon is open 24 hours a day, 365 days a year. The park gate is always open, though entrance booths are not staffed at night.

Because of severe traffic issues, the park has implemented parking restrictions on RVs and trailer vehicles in high season. Those affected should check the park website for details on any restrictions between May and September.

Information

Radio station AM 1590 broadcasts current general park information.

Bryce Canyon National Park Visitor Center

(📞435-834-5322; www.nps.gov/brca; Hwy 63; ⊙8am-8pm May-Sep, 8am-6pm Oct & Apr, 8am-4:30pm Nov-Mar) Check here for weather, hiking and road conditions and campground availability. Exhibits show plant, animal life and geologic displays and there's an excellent 20-minute orientation video. The park headquarters are here, as are first aid, phones and wi-fi in the lobby.

Bryce Canyon Natural History Association

(📞435-834-4600; www.brycecanyon.org) A nonprofit that aids the park service with educational, scientific and interpretive activities. The association operates the bookstore, and staff answer questions in the visitor center.

Sleeping

The park is home to two campgrounds and a lodge. However, most visitors stay at lodgings just north or west of the park, or 11 miles east in the town of Tropic. If nearby lodgings are full, consider staying in or around Panguitch, 24 miles west of the park, or Kodachrome Basin State Park, 19 miles east.

Sunset Campground

(📞877-444-6777; www.recreation.gov; Bryce Canyon Rd; tent/RV site $15/30; ⊙Apr-Sep) Just south of Sunset Point, this 102-site campground offers more shade than North Campground but has few amenities beyond flush toilets. Inquire about availability at the visitor center, and secure your site early.

Twenty tent sites can be reserved up to six months ahead.

North Campground

(📞877-444-6777; www.recreation.gov; Bryce Canyon Rd; tent & RV sites $30) Near the visitor center, this year-round trailside campground is enormous, with 101 sites that have campfire rings. A short walk from the campground takes you to showers, a coin laundry and a general store. A fee-for-use sanitary dump station ($5) is available in summer months at the south end. RV reservations are available six months out.

Bryce Canyon Lodge

(📞435-834-8700, 877-386-4383; www. brycecanyonforever.com; Hwy 63, Bryce Canyon National Park; r & cabins $208-256; ⊙Apr-Oct; @🛜) Built in the 1920s, the main park lodge exudes rustic mountain charm, with a large stone fireplace and exposed roof timbers. Most rooms are in two-story wooden satellite buildings with private balconies. The walls prove thin if the neighbors are noisy. In the perfect woodsy setting, the retro-cool Western cabins have gas fireplaces and creaky porches. No TVs. Wi-fi operates in parts of the main lodge.

Eating

The food around Bryce isn't nearly as good as the scenery. Service may be poky, coffee watered-down and vegetables possibly limited to the speck of garnish alongside your chicken-fried steak. Particularly for vegetarians, it's worth traveling with a cooler of fresh fruit and vegetables.

Bryce Canyon General Store & Snack Bar

(Bryce Canyon Rd, nr Sunrise Point; dishes $3-9; ⊙noon-10pm) In addition to foodstuff and sundries, the general store near Sunrise Point sells hot dogs, cold drinks, packaged sandwiches, chili, soup and pizza.

Bryce Canyon Lodge

(📞435-834-5361; Bryce Canyon Rd; breakfast & lunch $10-20, dinner $18-35; ⊙7am-10pm Apr-Oct) While service may lag, meals deliver, with excellent regional cuisine ranging from fresh green salads to bison burgers, braised portobellos and steak. All food is made on-site and the certified green menu offers only sustainable seafood. The wine list is decent and, best of all, the low-lit room is forgiving if you come covered in trail dust.

STATE
Utah

ENTRANCE FEE
7-day pass per vehicle $25

AREA
527 sq miles

GOOD FOR

La Sal Mountains

Canyonlands National Park

A forbidding and beautiful maze of red-rock fins, bridges, needles, spires, craters, mesas and buttes, Canyonlands is a crumbling, decaying beauty – a vision of ancient earth.

Vast serpentine canyons tipped with white cliffs loom high over the Colorado and Green Rivers, their waters a stunning 1000ft below the rim rock. Skyward-jutting needles and spires, deep craters, blue-hued mesas and majestic buttes dot the landscape.

Overlooks are easy enough to reach, but to explore further you'll need to contend with difficult dirt roads, great distances and limited water resources. You can hike, raft and 4WD here, but be sure that you have plenty of gas, food and water.

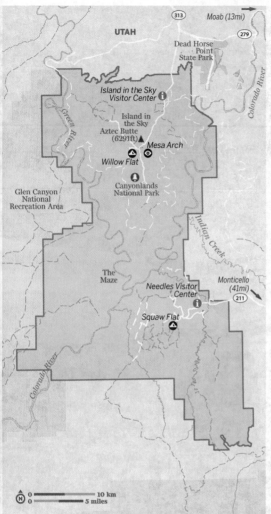

Orientation

The Colorado and Green Rivers form a Y that divides the park into three separate districts, inaccessible to one another from within the park. Cradled atop the Y is the most developed and visited **Island in the Sky**. Think of this as the overview section of the park, where you look down from viewpoints into the incredible canyons that make up the other sections. **Needles District** has thin hoodoos, sculpted sandstone and epic 4WD trails.

Serious skill is required to traverse the 4WD-only roads of the most inaccessible section of the park, the **Maze**.

Island in the Sky

You'll comprehend space in new ways atop the appropriately named Island in the Sky. This 6000ft-high flat-topped mesa drops precipitously on all sides, providing long and enthralling vistas. The 11,500ft Henry Mountains bookend panoramic views in the west, and the 12,700ft La Sal Mountains are to the east. Here you can stand beneath a sparkling blue sky and watch thunderheads inundating far-off regions while you contemplate applying more sunscreen. The Island sits atop a sandstone bench called the White Rim, which indeed forms a white border 1200ft below the red mesa top and 1500ft above the river canyon bottom. An impressive 4WD road descends from the overlook level.

The complimentary video at the **visitor center** (☎435-259-4712; www.nps.gov/cany; Hwy 313, 1 mile after park entrance; ☺8am-6pm Mar-Oct, 9am-4:30pm Nov-Feb) provides great insight into the nature of the park.

Overlooks and trails line each road. Most trails at least partially follow cairns over slickrock. Bring lots of water and watch for cliff edges!

Needles District

Named for the spires of orange-and-white sandstone jutting skyward from the desert floor, the Needles District's otherworldly terrain is so different from Island in the Sky that it's hard to believe they're both in the same national park.

Mesa Arch

Hike the half-mile loop to this slender, cliff-hugging span at sunrise, when the arch glows a fiery red.

The Needles district

The Needles receives only half as many visitors as the Island since it's more remote – though only 90 minutes from Moab – and there are fewer roadside attractions (but most are well worth the hike). The payoff is huge: peaceful solitude and the opportunity to participate in, not just observe, the vastness of canyon country. Morning light is best for viewing the rock spires.

Needles **visitor center** (☎435-259-4711; Hwy 211; ⏰8am-6pm Mar-Oct, 9am-4:30pm Nov-Feb) lies 2.5 miles inside park boundaries and provides drinking water.

The Maze

A 30-sq-mile jumble of high-walled canyons, the Maze is a rare preserve of true wilderness for hardy backcountry veterans.

The colorful canyons are rugged, deep and sometimes completely inaccessible. Many of them look alike and it's easy to get turned around – hence the district's name. (Think topographic maps and GPS.) Rocky roads absolutely necessitate reliable, high-clearance 4WD vehicles. Plan on spending at least three days, though a week is ideal.

If you're at all inexperienced with four-wheel driving, stay away. Be prepared to repair your jeep and, at times, the road. There may not be enough money on the planet to get you towed out of here. Most wreckers won't even try.

Don't Miss...

When driving into the Needles District, look up about 16.5 miles along Hwy 211. Even if you don't rock climb, it's fascinating to watch the experts scaling the narrow cliffside fissures near **Indian Creek** (www.friendsofindiancreek.org). There's a small parking lot from where you can cross the freely accessible Nature Conservancy and BLM grazing land.

View of Green River Canyon landscape

Sleeping

Backcountry camping in the Island is mostly open-zone (not in prescribed areas), but is still permit-limited; in Needles it's in prescribed areas only, and is quite popular, so it's hard to secure an overnight permit without advance reservation.

Willow Flat Campground (www.nps.gov/cany; tent & RV sites $15; ☺year-round) Seven miles from the Island in the Sky visitor center, this first-come, first-served, 12-site campground has vault toilets but no water, and no hookups.

Squaw Flat Campground (www.nps.gov/cany; tent & RV sites $20 ; ☺year-round) This first-come, first-served, 26-site ground, 3 miles west of the Needles visitor center, fills up every day, spring to fall. It has flush toilets and running water, but no showers or hookups.

Nearby Dead Horse Point State Park also has camping.

Monticello (34 miles from the Island) and Moab (30 miles from the Island and 75 miles from Needles) are the nearest full-service towns. Though Moab has a huge number of motels, there's often no room at the inn. Reserve as far ahead as possible in season. For a full town lodging list, see www.discovermoab.com.

Eating

There's no shortage of places to fuel up in Moab, from backpacker coffeehouses to gourmet dining rooms. Pick up the *Moab Menu Guide* (www.moabmenuguide.com) at area lodgings. Some restaurants close earlier, or on variable days, from December through March.

STATE
Utah

ENTRANCE FEE
7-day pass per vehicle $10

AREA
378 sq miles

GOOD FOR

Rappelling on rock formations

Capitol Reef National Park

Giant slabs of chocolate-red rock and sweeping yellow sandstone domes dominate the landscape of Capitol Reef, which Fremont Indians called the 'Land of the Sleeping Rainbow.'

Not as crowded as its fellow parks but equally scenic, Capitol Reef contains much of the 100-mile Waterpocket Fold, created 65 million years ago when the earth's surface buckled up and folded, exposing a cross-section of geologic history that is downright painterly in its colorful intensity. Known also for its enormous domes – one of which resembles Washington DC's Capitol Dome – the park has fantastic desert hiking trails, 800-year-old petroglyphs and a verdant 19th-century Mormon settlement with prolific fruit trees.

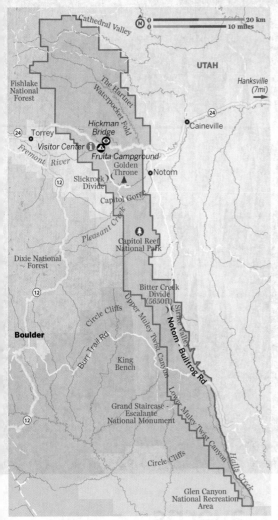

Great walks en route include the **Grand Wash** and **Capitol Gorge** trails, each following the level floor of a separate slender canyon; if you're in the mood for a more demanding hike, climb the **Golden Throne Trail** instead.

The shady, green **Fruita Campground** is a terrific 71-site camp that sits alongside the Fremont River, surrounded by orchards. There are no showers, no hookups, it's first-come, first-served and fills early spring through fall. It's 1.2 miles south of the visitor center.

Petroglyphs

East of the visitor center on Hwy 24, look for the roadside petroglyphs; these are the carvings that convinced archaeologists that the Fremont Indians were a distinct group.

Hickman Bridge Trail

A moderate 1.8-mile walk leads through both a canyon and desert wash to a natural bridge. It offers long sky views and spring wildflowers to boot. Mornings are coolest, and cairns mark some of the route. Pick up a self-guided Hickman Bridge nature trail brochure at the trailhead, about 2 miles east of the visitor center.

Hwy 24 cuts grandly through the park, but make sure to take the **scenic drive** south, a paved, dead-end 9-mile road that passes through orchards – a legacy of Mormon settlement. In season you can freely pick cherries, peaches and apples, as well as stop by the historic **Gifford Homestead** (⏰8am-5pm Mar-Oct) to see an old homestead and buy fruit-filled mini-pies.

Information

Just south of Hwy 24, the **visitor center** (☎435-425-3791; www.nps.gov/care; cnr Hwy 24 & Scenic Dr; ⏰8am-6pm Apr-Oct, to 4.30pm Nov-Mar) is also the park's headquarters. It's the only source of information in the park. All services – food, gas, medical – are based out of Torrey, 11 miles west, and Hanksville, 37 miles east.

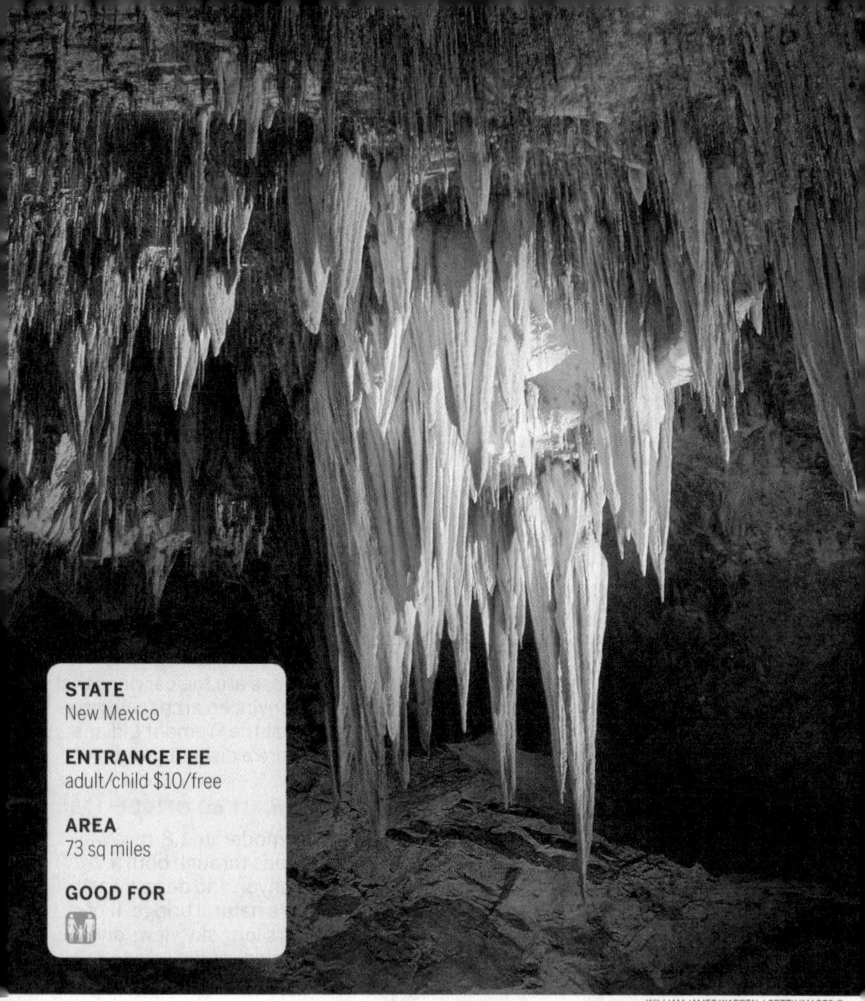

STATE
New Mexico

ENTRANCE FEE
adult/child $10/free

AREA
73 sq miles

GOOD FOR

Stalactites, Carlsbad Caverns

WILLIAM JAMES WARREN / GETTY IMAGES ©

Carlsbad Caverns National Park

Scores of wondrous caves hide under the hills at this unique national park. The cavern formations are an ethereal wonderland of stalactites and fantastical geological features.

From the visitor center you can ride an elevator, which descends the equivalent of the length of the Empire State Building in under a minute, or take a 2-mile subterranean walk from the cave mouth to the Big Room, an underground chamber 1800ft long and 255ft high.

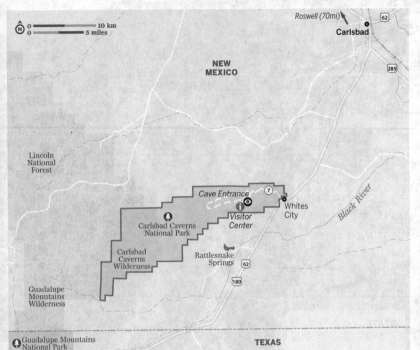

The cave's other claim to fame is the 300,000-plus Mexican free-tailed bat colony that roosts here from mid-May to mid-October. Be here by sunset, when they cyclone out for an all-evening insect feast.

Guided tours (☑877-444-6777; www.recreation.gov; adult $7-20, child $3.50-10) of additional caves are available, and should be reserved well in advance. Wear long sleeves and closed shoes; it gets chilly.

If you want to scramble to lesser-known areas further afield, ask about Wild Cave tours. Wilderness backpacking trips into the desert are allowed by permit (free); the visitor center sells topographical maps of the 50-plus miles of hiking trails. November to March is the best time

for backpacking – summer temperatures are scorching, and the countless rattlesnakes should be sleeping in winter.

Sleeping & Eating

Carlsbad, 25 miles northeast, is the closest town to the park, however, a recent boom in the oil industry means that even the most ordinary motel room in Carlsbad is liable to cost well over $200 per night, so it makes much more

sense to visit on a *long* day trip from Roswell, 95 miles north of the park.

Ho-hum chain motels line Roswell's N Main St. About 36 miles south of Roswell, the **Heritage Inn** (☑866-207-0222; www.artesiaheritageinn.com; 209 W Main St, Artesia) in Artesia offers 11 Old West–style rooms.

For simple, dependable New Mexican fare in Roswell, try **Martin's Capitol Cafe** (☑575-624-2111; 110 W 4th St, Roswell).

Lechuguilla Cave

Somewhere deep within the park's backcountry lies Lechuguilla Cave. With a depth of 1604ft and a mapped length (so far!) of some 136 miles, it's the deepest cave and third-longest limestone cave in North America. Sounds incredible – but it's only open to research and exploration teams, with special permission from the park.

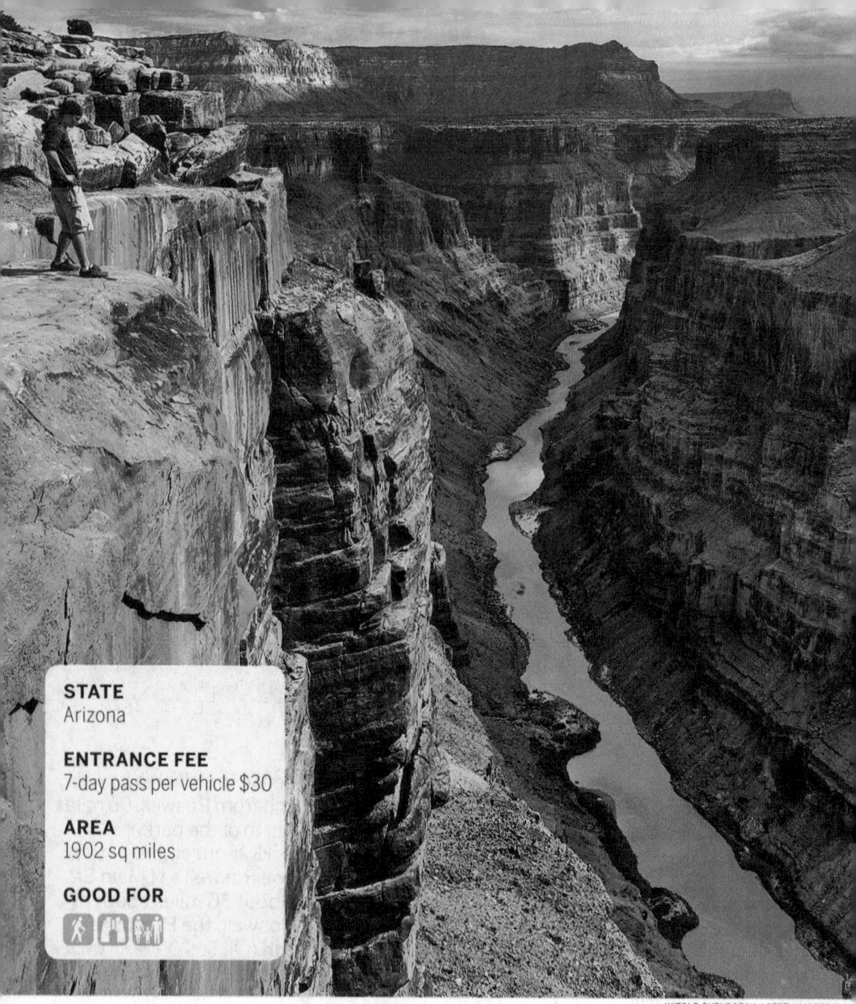

STATE
Arizona

ENTRANCE FEE
7-day pass per vehicle $30

AREA
1902 sq miles

GOOD FOR

Toroweap Overlook, North Rim

WITOLD SKRYPCZAK / GETTY IMAGES ©

Grand Canyon National Park

The Grand Canyon embodies the scale and splendor of the iconic American West, captured in its dramatic vistas, dusty inner canyon trails, and stories of exploration, preservation and exploitation.

We've all seen images of the canyon in print and on-screen, but there is nothing like arriving at the edge and taking it all in – the immensity, the depth, the light. Descend into the canyon depths, amble along the rim or simply relax at an outcrop – you'll find your own favorite Grand Canyon vista.

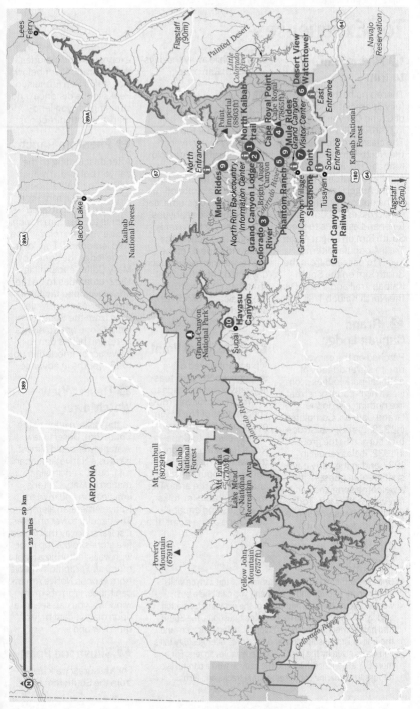

Top Experiences

❶ Hiking Rim to Rim

There's no better way to fully appreciate the grand of Grand Canyon than hiking through it, rim to rim. The classic route descends the North Rim on the North Kaibab Trail, includes a night at Phantom Ranch or Bright Angel Campground at the bottom of the canyon, crosses the Colorado River and ascends to the South Rim on Bright Angel Trail. A popular alternative is to descend from the South Rim on the South Kaibab Trail and ascend via the North Kaibab Trail.

❷ Grand Canyon Lodge

Perched on the canyon rim, this granddaddy of national-park lodges promises a high-country retreat like nothing else in the Grand Canyon. Completed in 1928, the original structure burned to the ground in 1932. It was rebuilt in 1937, and in the early days staff greeted guests with a welcome song and sang farewell as they left. Today, you'll find that same sense of camaraderie, and it's easy to while away the days at a North Rim pace.

❸ Rafting the Colorado River

Considered the trip of a lifetime by many river enthusiasts, rafting the Colorado is a wild ride down a storied river, through burly rapids, past a stratified record of geologic time, and up secretive side canyons. Though riding the river is the initial attraction, the profound appeals of the trip reveal themselves each day and night in the quiet stretches on smooth water, the musicality of ripples and birdsong, and the vast solitude of this place.

❹ Cape Royal Point

A pleasant paved drive through woods with teasing canyon views leads to the trailhead for this most spectacular of North Rim overlooks. It's an easy half-mile walk to Cape Royal Point along a paved trail with signs pointing out facts about the flora and fauna of the area. The walk is suitable for folks of all ages and capabilities. Once at the point, the expansive view includes the Colorado River below, Flagstaff's San Francisco Peaks in the distance, and stunning canyon landmarks in both directions.

❺ Phantom Ranch

After descending to the canyon bottom, it's a delight to ramble along a flat trail, past a mule corral and a few scattered cabins to Phantom Ranch, where you can relax with a cold lemonade. This lovely stone lodge, designed by Mary Colter and built in 1922, continues to be the only developed facility in the inner-canyon. Mule trips from the South Rim include one or two nights here, and hikers can reserve accommodation up to 13 months in advance.

❻ Desert View Watchtower

At the eastern edge of the South Rim, Desert View Watchtower could almost pass as a Native American ruin, but it's an amalgamation of Mary Colter's imagination and myriad Native American elements. The circular tower encases a spiral stairway that winds five stories to the top floor, with walls featuring a Hopi mural and graphic symbols from various Native American tribes. From its many windows, you can see mile upon magnificent mile of rim, river and sky.

❼ Shoshone Point

For a leisurely walk away from the South Rim circus,

Geology

One look at the reds, rusts and oranges of the canyon walls and the park's spires and buttes, and you can't help but wonder about the hows and whys of the canyon's formation. Luckily for laypeople with rock-related questions, the South Rim has answers, primarily at Yavapai Geology Museum and the Trail of Time installation, and both rims offer geology talks and walks given by the park's knowledgeable rangers. For a more DIY experience, hike into the canyon with a careful eye for fossilized marine creatures, animal tracks and ferns.

Hermit Rapids, Colorado River

hike through the ponderosa to Shoshone Point. The soundtrack to this mostly flat 1-mile walk is that of pine needles crunching underfoot and birdsong trilling overhead, and lacy shadows provide cover from the sun. Upon reaching the rim, you'll trace the edge for a short while to the stone point jutting out over the canyon depths. Shoshone Point, or the picnic area at the end of the trail, is perfect for a peaceful lunch.

⑧ Grand Canyon Railway

Things start out with a bang at the Wild West shootout in Williams, and then the 'sheriff' boards the train to make sure everything's in its place. Is it hokey? Maybe a little. Fun? Absolutely. Riding the historic rails to the South Rim takes a bit longer than if you were to drive, but you leave traffic and disembark relaxed and ready to explore the canyon.

Native American & Pioneer History

We all know about the canyon's distinct and unparalleled beauty, its awesome geologic canvas and its draw for outdoor types. Less recognized, perhaps, is the Grand Canyon's compelling human history, the drama that lies in its stories. Native Americans lived in and near the canyon for centuries, farming on its rim and in its depths. The region's national-park history is also one of intrepid pioneer scientists and artists, prospectors, railroads and tourist entrepreneurs. Ranger talks are a great way to learn the park's stories, as are historic buildings and South Rim museums.

⑨ Mule Rides

There's something classic about riding a mule into the canyon, a time-honored tradition that began with turn-of-the-20th-century pioneering tourists. While less strenuous than hiking, mule rides are a physically active experience that require a sense of adventure. Head to the South Rim for an overnight trip to Phantom Ranch and the Colorado River; or from the North Rim, you can descend into the canyon down the North Kaibab. Both rims offer jaunts above the rim.

⑩ Havasu Canyon

The 'people of the blue-green waters', as the Havasupai call themselves, take their name from the otherworldly turquoise-colored waterfalls and creek that run through the canyon. Limestone deposits on the creekbed make the water appear sky-blue, a gorgeous contrast to the deep red canyon walls. The only ways into Havasu are by foot, horse or helicopter, but those who make the 10-mile trek are richly rewarded by the magic of this place.

Mather Point, South Rim

RICHARD I'ANSON / GETTY IMAGES ©

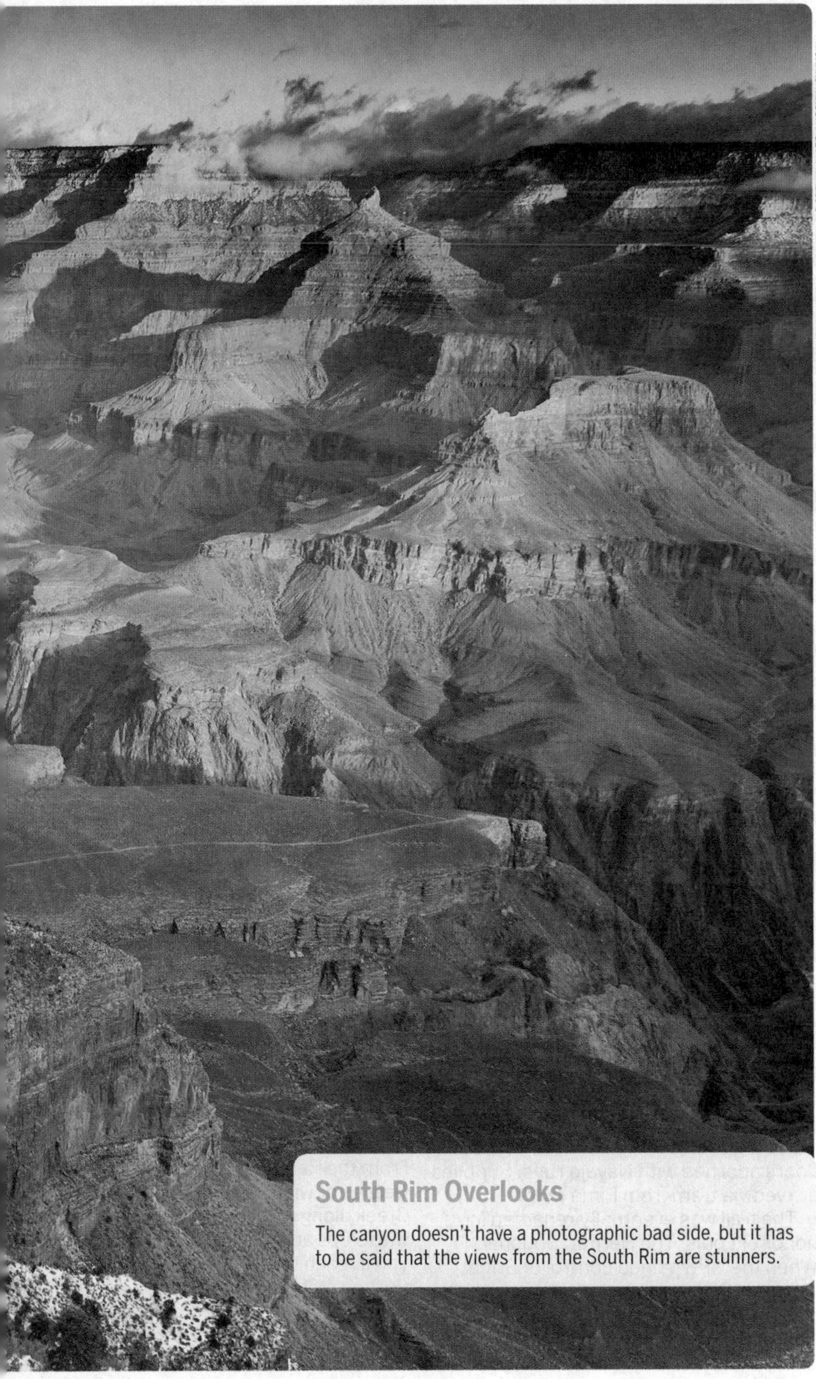

South Rim Overlooks

The canyon doesn't have a photographic bad side, but it has to be said that the views from the South Rim are stunners.

Picnickers by the Colorado River

Hike the Hermit Trail

The name seems apropos, even today, as you are unlikely to encounter many hikers and backpackers on the Hermit Trail. Though easily accessible from South Rim shuttles and the tourist hub, it feels marvelously remote. Take a moment to imagine the quiet life of Louis 'The Hermit' Boucher, the prospector who made this spot his home for many years.

In 1912 the Atchison, Topeka & Santa Fe Railway developed the trail for tourists to avoid tolls on the then privately controlled Bright Angel Trail. Mule trains ferried travelers to cushy Hermit Camp, which boasted a fancy stone cabin outfitted with a stove, glass windows, beds and wood floors adorned with Navajo rugs. Supplies arrived via tram from Pima Point.

The trail was eventually renamed in honor of Louis 'The Hermit' Boucher. When the NPS gained control of Bright Angel in 1928, luring away the mule tourism business, the Hermit was abandoned. Though officially untended since then, the trail is in remarkably good condition.

DURATION 2 days round-trip

DISTANCE 15.4 miles round-trip (to Hermit Camp), 18.4 miles round-trip (to Hermit Rapid)

DIFFICULTY Difficult

START/FINISH Hermit Trailhead

NEAREST TOWN Grand Canyon Village

TRANSPORTATION Shuttle, car

SUMMARY Tracing the path of the Hermit, this steep but rewarding out-and-back hike leads to a backcountry campground on the site of one of the park's earliest tourist accommodations.

DAY 1: HERMIT TRAILHEAD TO HERMIT CAMP (4-6 HOURS, 7.7 MILES)

From the Hermit Trailhead the rocky trail weaves down Hermit Basin toward Hermit Creek along a cobblestone route indented with steps and fraught with washouts. You'll reach the rarely used Waldron Trail (jutting off to the south) after about 1.3 miles, followed some 30 minutes later by the spur trail headed for Dripping Springs. The trail then traces over some flat rocks

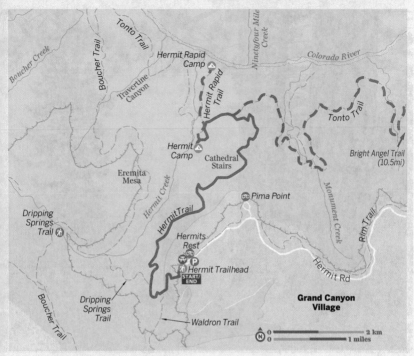

(a perfect picnic spot) before descending steeply to **Santa Maria Spring**, a cool, shady haven, marked by a pretty stone shelter and a welcome wooden bench. The lush scene belies the spring, however, which is actually more of a trickle. You can drink the water provided you treat it.

Backpackers continue past the spring as the trail levels for a mile or so before zigzagging over loose rocks. Note that the trail is showing signs of the same erosion that created the canyon. The Supai section of the trail (just below Santa Maria Spring) has deteriorated to the point where hikers will need to scramble over rocks and it can be difficult to find the trail.

Soon after descending the Redwall via a series of extremely steep, compressed switchbacks known as the **Cathedral Stairs** (keep an eye out for fossils in the bottom sections of this formation), the Hermit hits the cross-canyon Tonto Trail (6.4 miles from the trailhead, at 3210ft).

Turn left (west) to merge with the Tonto; in 1 mile you'll reach the stone remnants of the old Hermit Camp (2800ft), one of the original Fred Harvey tent accommodations.

Just beyond the ruins, the cliff-rimmed backcountry campground (with pit toilets and seasonal water) makes a glorious place to sleep.

From the campground it's another 1.5 miles to the Colorado River, which you can reach by following your nose down the creek from the campground; alternatively, the river is a bit closer if you turn down Hermit Creek just before Hermit Camp.

Down at the river, the canyon walls are exquisite black Vishnu schist shot through with veins of pink Zoroaster granite. **Hermit Rapids**, a major Colorado River rapid, marks the confluence of Hermit Creek and the Colorado. There's a backcountry campground, but no facilities.

🥾 DAY 2: HERMIT CAMP TO HERMIT TRAILHEAD (6-8 HOURS, 7.7 MILES)

To return to Hermits Rest, retrace your steps for the arduous climb back to the trailhead. For a longer wilderness excursion, with advanced backcountry permits, you can pick up the eastbound Tonto and intercept the Bright Angel.

Hiking the North Rim

🚶 Widforss Trail Day Hike

This gentle North Rim hike rises and dips along the plateau, veering towards a side canyon and meandering 5 miles to Widforss Point. It's a mild, gentle amble, with canyon views whispering rather than screaming from the edges, plenty of shade, and room for children to run among wildflowers. A picnic table at the end makes a lovely lunch spot, and at the overlook you can sit on a stone jutting over the Grand Canyon, dangling your feet above the rocky outcrop just below, listening to the silence.

DURATION 6 hours round-trip

DISTANCE 10 miles round-trip

DIFFICULTY Moderate

START/FINISH Widforss Trailhead

TRANSPORTATION Car

SUMMARY A moderate hike through woods and meadows with peeping canyon views leads to a spectacular canyon overlook.

Named after Gunnar Widforss, an early-20th-century artist who lived, worked, died and was buried at the Grand Canyon, the Widforss Trail meanders through stands of spruce, white fir, ponderosa pine and aspen to Widforss Point. Tall trees offer shade, fallen limbs provide

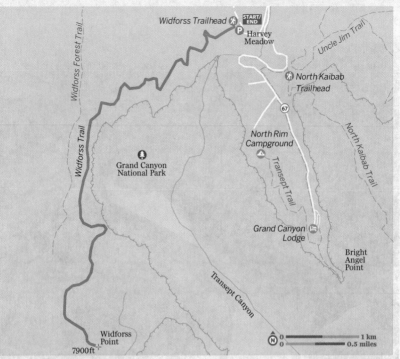

pleasant spots to relax, and you likely won't see more than a few people along the trail. To reach the trailhead, turn onto the dirt road just south of the Cape Royal Rd turnoff, continuing a mile to the Widforss Trail parking area.

After a 15-minute climb, the canyon comes into view. For the next 2 miles, the trail offers wide views of the canyon to one side and meadows and woods to the other. Halfway into the hike, the trail jags away from the rim and dips into gullies of lupines and ferns; the canyon doesn't come into view again until the end. From Widforss Point (elevation 7900ft), take the small path to the left of the picnic table to a flat rock, where you can enjoy a sandwich, the classic view and the silence. Though the total elevation change is only 350ft, rolling terrain makes the first few miles a moderate challenge. The park service offers a self-guided trail brochure for the first half of this hike; available at the trailhead and the visitor center. Follow the guided walk as listed in the brochure, then turn around, and, though you'll miss the overlook at the point, you'll have hiked the best part of the trail. This is a really pretty hike in late September or early October when the leaves are golden, and the point makes an excellent backcountry campsite.

Horseshoe Bend, Colorado River

Information

Grand Canyon Visitor Center (☎928-638-7888; www.nps.gov/grca; Visitor Center Plaza, Grand Canyon Village; ⏰8am-5pm Mar-Nov, 9am-5pm Dec-Feb; 🚌Village, 🚌Kaibab/Rim) The South Rim's main visitor center.

North Rim Visitor Center (☎928-638-7864; www.nps.gov/grca; North Rim; ⏰8am-6pm) Beside Grand Canyon Lodge.

Park Entrances

South Rim

The South Rim has two park entrances: the South Entrance, 74 miles north of Flagstaff on Hwy 180, and the East Entrance on Hwy 64, 32 miles west of Cameron and 82 miles north of Flagstaff. Most visitors enter from the South Entrance. After tackling summer queues (upwards of 45 minutes), visitors then head a few miles north to the mayhem of Grand Canyon Village – home to the park's tourist facilities, including hotels, restaurants and the visitor center.

If possible, enter the park through the East Entrance. As you drive the 25 miles to Grand Canyon Village, stopping at overlooks along the way, your first glimpses of the canyon will be more dramatic and much less hectic.

North Rim

The North Rim entrance sits 30 miles south of Jacob Lake on Hwy 67. A park pass of $30 per car (or $25 per motorcycle), good for seven days on both rims, can be purchased at the gate. Those entering on foot, by bicycle or on a shuttle bus pay $15 per person. If you arrive after-hours, a posted note will direct you – remember to pay the fee when you depart. From here, it is 14 miles to Grand Canyon Lodge.

Sleeping

South Rim

There are six lodges, two campgrounds and one RV park on the South Rim. All but Desert View Campground are located in the tourist hub around Grand Canyon Village, within walking distance of restaurants and sights and easily accessed by park shuttle transportation. El Tovar, Bright Angel, Kachina and Thunderbird lodges sit along the Rim Trail in the National Landmark Historic District, a stone's throw

from the canyon abyss. Both Maswik and Yavapai, however, sit rather depressingly in the Ponderosa forest. Maswik is a five-minute walk from the canyon and Yavapai is a mile away, across from the grocery store, bank and post office.

While convenient, don't expect the historic charm that many associate with national-park lodges. With the exception of El Tovar and rim-side cabins at Bright Angel Lodge, South Rim accommodation is not much more than a basic highway motel.

North Rim

Your best bet for exploring the North Rim is to stay at Grand Canyon Lodge or the North Rim Campground. Outside the park, the closest lodging is Kaibab Lodge, 18 miles from the rim, or Jacob Lake Inn, 44 miles from the rim. Beyond that, you'll have to drive 78 miles north to Kanab, Utah, 85 miles northeast to Marble Canyon or 125 miles northeast to Page, Arizona.

Contact the North Rim Backcountry Information Center for permits to camp at remote North Rim overlooks or at backcountry sites below the rim; you can camp for free without a permit anywhere in the bucolic North Kaibab National Forest, just outside the park gate.

Eating & Drinking

South Rim

Grand Canyon Village has all the eating options you will need, from pizza to venison, icy pints to pink cocktails. The vast majority of dining, however, is in the form of cafeterias and walk-up snack bars. The only table-service options are the El Tovar Dining Room, the Arizona Room and Bright Angel Restaurant, all in the National Historic Landmark District. There are also two grocery stores.

All South Rim bars close at 11pm, and drinks are prohibited along the rim itself. Expect slightly reduced hours September through May.

North Rim

There's only one restaurant, one cafeteria and one saloon on the North Rim – and that's part of the charm of staying up here. Luckily, the Grand Canyon Lodge's dining and drinking venues are all appealing, just steps away from sweeping vistas of the vast canyon below.

STATE
Nevada

ENTRANCE FEE
Free

AREA
120 sq miles

GOOD FOR
🚶 🔭

Wheeler Peak

PETER FRENCH / DESIGN PICS / GETTY IMAGES ©

Great Basin National Park

Rising abruptly from the desert near the Nevada–Utah border, and dominating Great Basin National Park, 13,063ft Wheeler Peak creates an awesome range of life zones and landscapes within a very compact area.

The peak's narrow, twisting scenic drive is open only during summer, usually from June through October.

Hiking trails near the summit take in superb country made up of glacial lakes, groves of ancient bristlecone pines (some over 5000 years old) and even a permanent ice field. The summit trail is an 8.2-mile round-trip trek, with a vertical ascent of nearly 3000ft.

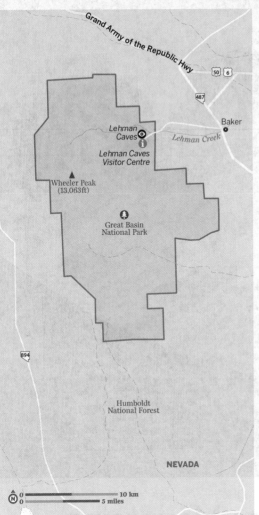

Cathedral Gorge State Park

A hundred miles south of Great Basin National Park, at **Cathedral Gorge State Park** (☎775-728-4460; http://parks.nv.gov; Hwy 93; entry per vehicle $7; ⏰visitor center 9am-4:30pm), it really does feel like you've stepped into a magnificent, many-spired cathedral, albeit one whose dome is a view of the sky. Sleep under the stars at its first-come, first-served tent & RV sites ($17), set amid badland-style cliffs.

through October. The nearby village of Baker has a gas station, a basic restaurant and sparse accommodations.

Getting There & Away

The transcontinental Hwy 50 cuts across the heart of Nevada, connecting Carson City in the west to Great Basin National Park in the east. Better known here by its nickname, 'The Loneliest Road in America,' it once formed part of the Lincoln Hwy, and follows the route of the Overland Stagecoach, the Pony Express and the first transcontinental telegraph line.

Towns are few, and the only sounds are the hum of the engine or the whisper of wind.

Lehman Caves

Back below Wheeler Peak, the main **park visitor center** (☎775-234-7331; ⏰8am-4:30pm) sells tickets for guided tours ($8 to $10) of Lehman Caves, which are brimming with limestone formations. The temperature inside is a constant 50°F (10°C), so bring a sweater.

Sleeping & Eating

The park's five developed **campgrounds** (☎775-234-7331; www.nps.gov/grba; primitive camping free, tent & RV sites $6-25) are open during summer; only Lower Lehman Creek is available year-round.

Next to the visitor center, a simple cafe stays open from May

Guadalupe Peak

WITOLD SKRYPCZAK / GETTY IMAGES ©

Guadalupe Mountains National Park

Guadalupe Mountains National Park is a Texas high spot, both literally and figuratively. At 8749ft, Guadalupe Peak is the highest point in the Lone Star State.

We won't go so far as to call it Texas' best-kept secret, but the fact is that a lot of Texans aren't even aware of the park, just on the Texas side of the Texas–New Mexico state line and a long drive from practically everywhere else in this big, sweeping state.

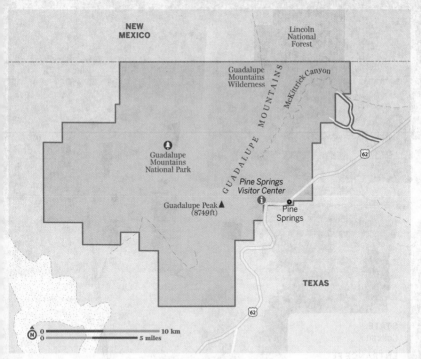

The fall foliage in McKittrick Canyon is the best in west Texas, and more than half the park is a federally designated wilderness area.

The National Park Service has deliberately curbed development to keep the park wild. There are no restaurants or indoor accommodations and only a smattering of services and programs. But if you're looking for some of the best hiking and high-country splendor Texas can muster, you should put this park on your itinerary. There are more than 80 miles of trails through the park's wilderness.

For information, exhibits and knowledgeable staff pop into the Pine Springs Visitor Center.

Fossils

The park is one of the best places in the world to see fossils from the Permian period (approximately 299 million years ago). The period ended with the most devastating mass extinction the Earth has ever experienced.

The Guadalupe Mountains were once a reef below an ancient inland sea.

Lizards

Watch for three species of horned lizards in the park: the Texas Horned lizard, Roundtail Horned lizard and the Mountain Short-horned lizard

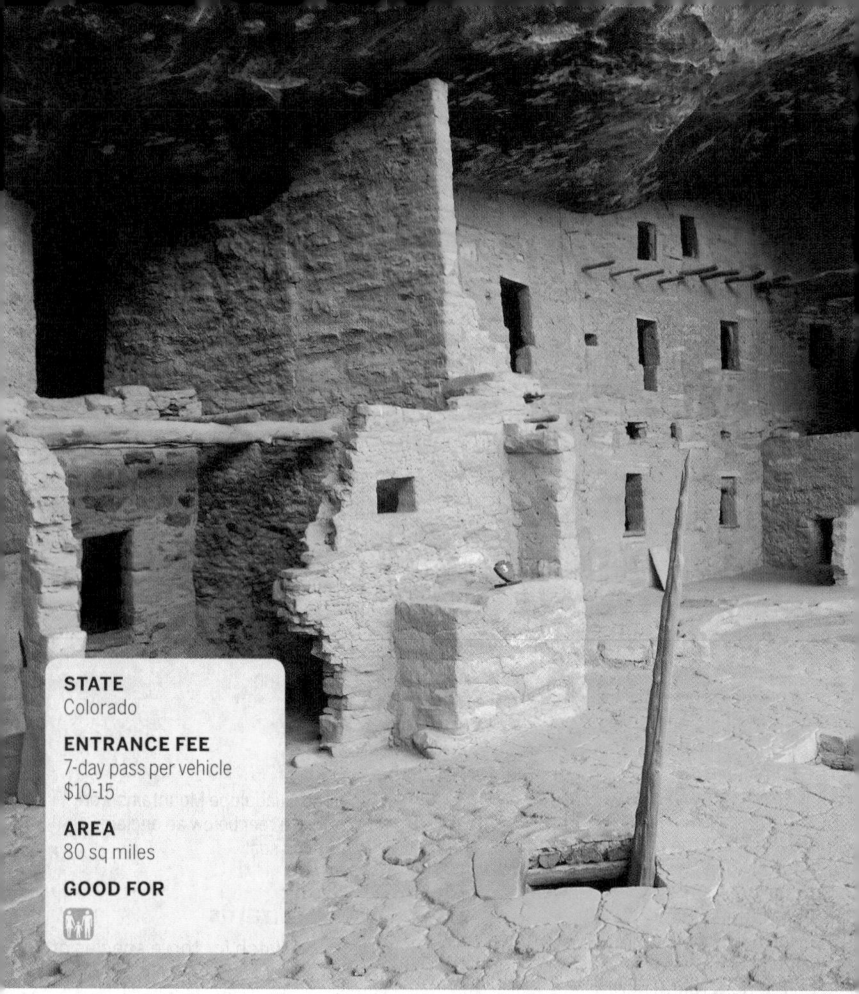
STATE
Colorado
ENTRANCE FEE
7-day pass per vehicle
$10-15
AREA
80 sq miles
GOOD FOR

Spruce Tree House

EMILY RIDDELL / GETTY IMAGES ©

Mesa Verde National Park

Shrouded in mystery, Mesa Verde is a fascinating, if slightly eerie, place. A 14th-century civilization of Ancestral Puebloans appears to have vanished from here, leaving behind a complex of cliff dwellings, some accessed by sheer climbs.

Mesa Verde is unique among parks for its focus on preserving this civilization's cultural relics. It rewards travelers who set aside a day or more to tour Cliff Palace and Balcony House, explore Wetherill Mesa or participate in one of the campfire programs. But if you only have time for a short visit, check out the Chapin Mesa Archeological Museum and walk through the Spruce Tree House, where you can climb down a wooden ladder into the cool chamber of a *kiva* (ceremonial structure, usually partly underground).

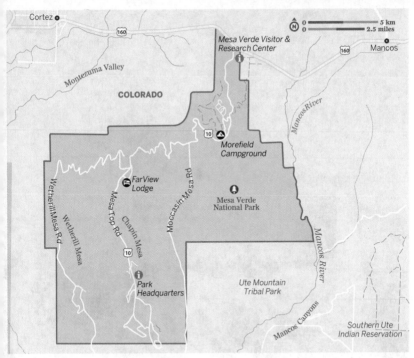

Top Experiences

❶ Chapin Mesa Museum

The **Chapin Mesa Museum** (📞970-529-4475; www.nps.gov/meve; Chapin Mesa Rd; ⊗8am-6:30pm mid-Apr–mid-Oct, 8am-5pm mid-Oct–mid-Apr) is a good first stop. Staff at the museum provide information on weekends when the park HQ is closed.

❷ Guided Tours

The park concessionaire offers **guided tours** (📞970-529-4421; www.visitmesaverde.com; adult $42-48) to excavated pit homes, cliff dwellings and the Spruce Tree House daily from May to mid-October.

Ancestral Puebloans

Ancestral Puebloans occupied the Colorado Plateau from around AD 100 to 1300, until warfare, drought and scarcity of resources likely drove them out. You can also still see their desert adobe pueblos at New Mexico's **Chaco Culture National Historic Park** (www.nps.gov/chcu; entry per vehicle $12; ⊗7am-sunset). In its prime, the community at Chaco Canyon was a major trading and ceremonial hub for the region – and the city the Puebloan people created here was masterly in its layout and design. Pueblo Bonito is four stories tall and may have had 600 to 800 rooms and kivas. The park is in a remote area approximately 80 miles south of Farmington, far beyond the reach of any public transport.

❸ Chapin Mesa

The largest concentration of Ancestral Puebloan sites is at Chapin Mesa, where you'll see the densely clustered **Far View Site** and the large **Spruce Tree House**, the most accessible of sites, with a paved half-mile round-trip path.

Long House

Cliff Palace

Information

The park entrance is off US 160, midway between Cortez and Mancos. The **Mesa Verde Visitor and Research Center** (☎800-305-6053, 970-529-5034; www. nps.gov/meve; North Rim Rd; ⊙7:30am-7pm Jun-early Sep, 8am-5pm early Sep-Oct & Apr-May, 8:30am-4:30pm Nov-Mar; 🖼), located near the entrance, has information and news on park closures (many areas are closed in winter).

④ Cliff Palace & Balcony House

If you want to see **Cliff Palace** or **Balcony House**, the only way is through an hour-long ranger-led tour booked in advance at the visitor center ($4). These tours are extremely popular; go early in the morning or a day in advance to book. Balcony House requires climbing a 32ft and 60ft ladder – those with medical problems should skip it.

⑤ Wetherill Mesa

This is the second-largest concentration of Ancestral Puebloan sites. Visitors may enter stabilized surface sites and two cliff dwellings, including the **Long House**, open from late May through late September. South from park headquarters, the 6-mile **Mesa Top Road** connects excavated mesa-top sites, accessible cliff dwellings and vantage points to view inaccessible dwellings from the mesa rim.

Ancestral Puebloan Petroglyphs

Sleeping

The nearby towns of Cortez and Mancos have plenty of midrange places to stay; inside the park there's camping and a lodge.

Morefield Campground (📞970-529-4465; www.visitmesaverde.com; North Rim Rd; tent/RV site $30/40; ⊙mid-Apr-Oct; 🎒) 🐾 The park's camping option, located 4 miles from the entrance gate, has 445 regular tent sites on grassy grounds conveniently located near Morefield Village. The village has a general store, gas station, restaurant, showers and laundry. Dry RV campsites (without hookup) cost the same as tent sites.

Far View Lodge (📞970-529-4421, toll-free 800-449-2288; www.visitmesaverde.com; North Rim Rd; r $117-177; ⊙mid-Apr-Oct; P🐕🌲📶🎒) Perched on a mesa top 15 miles inside the park entrance, this tasteful Pueblo-style lodge has 150 Southwestern-style rooms, some with kiva fireplaces. Don't miss sunset over the mesa from your private balcony. Standard rooms don't have air con (or TV) and summer daytimes can be hot. You can bring your dog for an extra $10 per night.

Eating

Far View Terrace Café (📞970-529-4421, toll-free 800-449-2288; www.visitmesaverde. com; North Rim Rd; dishes from $6; ⊙7-10am, 11am-3pm & 5-8pm May-mid-Oct; 🎒🐕) Housed in Far View Lodge immediately south of the visitor center, this self-service place offers reasonably priced meals and a convenient espresso bar. Don't miss the house special: the Navajo taco.

Metate Room (📞970-529-4421, toll-free 800-449-2288; www.visitmesaverde.com; North Rim Rd; mains $18-29; ⊙5-9:30pm mid-Apr-Oct; 🎒🐕) 🐾 With an award in culinary excellence, this upscale restaurant in the Far View Lodge offers an innovative menu inspired by Native American food and flavors. Interesting dishes include stuffed poblano chilies, cinnamon chili pork tenderloin and grilled quail with prickly pear jam.

DANITA DELIMONT / GETTY IMAGES ©

ainbow Bridge 2. Chiricahua National Monument
atural Bridges National Monument

Incredible Rock Formations

Rainbow Bridge National Monument, Arizona

Rainbow Bridge is the largest natural bridge in the world, at 290ft high and 275ft wide. A sacred Navajo site, it resembles the graceful arc of a rainbow. Most visitors arrive by boat, with a 2-mile round-trip hike. The natural monument is located on the south shore of Lake Powell, about 50 miles by water from Wahweap Marina.

Chiricahua National Monument, Arizona

A wonderfully rugged yet whimsical wonderland, Chiricahua National Monument (Hwy 181) is one of Arizona's most unique and evocative landscapes. Rain, thunder and wind have chiseled volcanic rocks into fluted pinnacles, natural bridges, gravity-defying balancing boulders and soaring spires reaching skyward like totem poles carved in stone. The remoteness made Chiricahua, which is pronounced 'cheery-cow-wha,' a favorite hiding place of Apache warrior Cochise and his men. Today it's attractive to birds and wildlife, including bobcats, bears, deer, coatis and javelinas.

Glen Canyon National Recreation Area, Arizona–Utah

In the 1960s the construction of a massive dam flooded Glen Canyon, forming Lake Powell, a recreational playground. Fifty years later this is still an environmental hot-button topic, but generations of Western families have grown up boating here. Water laps against stunning, multihued cliffs that rise hundreds of feet; narrow channels and tributary canyons twist off in every direction.

Natural Bridges National Monument, Utah

Forty miles west of Blanding via Hwy 95, this monument became Utah's first NPS land in 1908. The highlight is a dark-stained, white-sandstone canyon containing three easily accessible natural bridges. The oldest, the Owachomo Bridge, spans 180ft but is only 9ft thick. The flat 9-mile Scenic Drive loop is ideal for biking.

STATE
Arizona

ENTRANCE FEE
7-day pass per vehicle $20

AREA
42,085 sq miles

GOOD FOR

Ancient fossilized trees

Petrified Forest National Park

Home not only to an extraordinary array of fossilized ancient logs that predate the dinosaurs but this Arizona park also contains the multicolored sandscape of the Painted Desert.

This national park is an unmissable spectacle with an extraordinary landscape worn over hundreds of millions of years; a humbling timeframe, it's enough history to make even the oldest among us feel young and insignificant. There are plentiful hikes in the backcountry for quiet contemplation, and scenic drives with lots of overlooks at which to pause and take in the desert scenery.

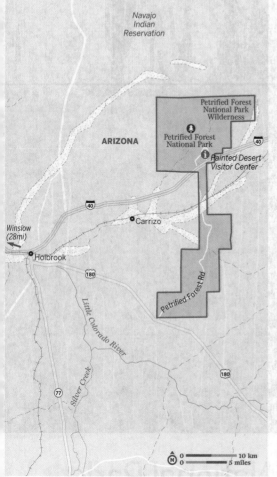

Navajo Indian Reservation

ARIZONA

Petrified Forest National Park Wilderness

Petrified Forest National Park

Painted Desert Visitor Center

Winslow (28mi)

Holbrook

Carrizo

Little Colorado River

Silver Creek

Petrified Forest Rd

0   10 km
0   5 miles

Triassic Park

Petrified Forest has plant and animal fossils from as long ago as the Late Triassic period – over 200 million years ago. Fossils can be big or small – some petrified logs here measure over 190ft – whereas a single tooth less than an inch long may very well be the first signs of a previously unknown species.

Sleeping & Eating

Just 50 miles east of Petrified Forest National Park, Winslow is a good regional base. Old motels border Route 66, and diners sprinkle downtown. The real showpiece here is the irresistible 1929 **La Posada** (☎928-289-4366; www.laposada.org; 303 E 2nd St; r $139-169; ❄❷❸), a restored hacienda with elaborate tilework and glass-and-tin chandeliers, Navajo rugs and other details accent its palatial Western-style elegance. The on-site restaurant, the much-lauded **Turquoise Room** (☎928-289-2888; www.theturquoiseroom.net; La Posada; breakfast $8-12, lunch $10-13, dinner $19-42; ⏰7am-4pm, 5-9pm), serves the best meals between Flagstaff and Albuquerque; dishes have a neo-Southwestern flair.

The park straddles I-40 at exit 311, 25 miles east of Holbrook. Its **visitor center** (☎928-524-6228; www.nps.gov/pefo; ⏰scenic drive 7am-8pm Jun & Jul, shorter hours Aug-May), just half a mile north of I-40, has maps and information on guided tours, while the 28-mile paved park road beyond offers a splendid scenic drive.

Backcountry Camping

There are no campsites, but a number of short trails, ranging from less than a mile to 2 miles, pass through the stands of petrified rock and ancient Native American dwellings. Those prepared for rugged backcountry camping need to pick up a free permit at the visitor center.

Saguaro cacti forest

STATE
Arizona

ENTRANCE FEE
7-day pass per vehicle/
bicycle $10/5

AREA
143 sq miles

GOOD FOR

Saguaro National Park

Saguaros are the most iconic symbol of the American Southwest, and an entire army of these majestic cactus plants is protected in this two-part desert playground.

The park is divided into two units, 30 miles apart to either side of the city of Tucson, and each filled with trails and desert flora.

The larger section is the Rincon Mountain District, about 15 miles east of downtown. The meandering 8-mile Cactus Forest Scenic Loop Drive, a paved road open to cars and bicycles, provides access to picnic areas, trailheads and viewpoints. Hikers pressed for time should follow the 1-mile round-trip Freeman Homestead Trail to a grove of massive saguaro.

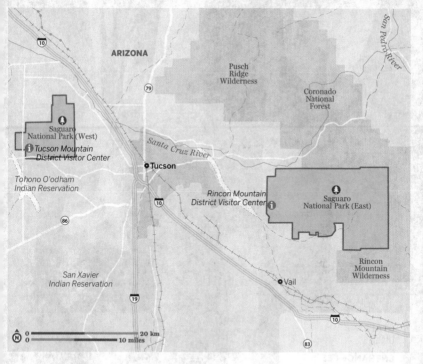

The Tucson Mountain District is located west of town. The Scenic Bajada Loop Drive is a 6-mile graded dirt road through cactus forest that begins 1.5 miles north of the visitor center. Two quick, easy and rewarding hikes are the 0.8-mile Valley View Overlook (awesome at sunset) and the half-mile Signal Hill Trail to scores of ancient petroglyphs.

Trailers longer than 35ft and vehicles wider than 8ft are not permitted on the park's narrow scenic loop roads.

Information

Each unit has its own visitor center.

Rincon Mountain District visitor center (☏520-733-5153; 3693 S Old Spanish Trail; ☺9am-5pm)

Tucson Mountain District visitor center (☏520-733-5158; 2700 N Kinney Rd; ☺9am-5pm)

Sleeping

Tucson, Arizona's second-largest city, is set in the Sonoran Desert, full of rolling, sandy hills and crowds of cacti. The vibe here is ramshackle-cool and cozy compared with the shiny vastness of Phoenix.

Lodging prices vary considerably, with lower rates in summer and fall. To sleep under stars and saguaros, try **Gilbert Ray Campground** (☏520-883-4200; www.pima.gov/nrpr; Kinney Rd; tent/RV site $10/20) near the Tucson Mountain District.

Sonoran Hot Dog

Tucson's signature 'dish' is the Sonoran hot dog, a tasty example of what happens when Mexican ingredients meet America's processed meat and penchant for excess. The ingredients? A bacon-wrapped hot dog layered with tomatillo salsa, pinto beans, shredded cheese, mayo, ketchup or mustard or both, chopped tomatoes and onions. We like 'em at **El Guero Canelo** (www.elguerocanelo.com; 5201 S 12th Ave; mains $3-8; ☺10am-11pm Mon-Thu, 8am-midnight Fri & Sat, 9am-11pm Sun).

STATE
Utah

ENTRANCE FEE
7-day pass per vehicle $30

AREA
231 sq miles

GOOD FOR

The Narrows

Zion National Park

From secret oases of trickling water to the hot-pink blooms of a prickly pear cactus, Zion's treasures turn up in the most unexpected places. That's not to say that the soaring majesty of 2000ft sandstone cliffs won't leave you awestruck, but it's the finer details that really make Zion stand apart.

You don't need to be an amateur photographer to enjoy all that Zion has to offer, however – though it is likely you'll fill up your memory card with pictures by trip's end. Whether you're capturing the play of shadows along the canyon walls, sharing the satisfaction of pulling over the final ledge of Angels Landing, admiring the echoes of water in the curves of a slot canyon or wading knee-deep in the adventure-fueled fun of the Narrows, Zion will continue to leave you breathless, every step of the way.

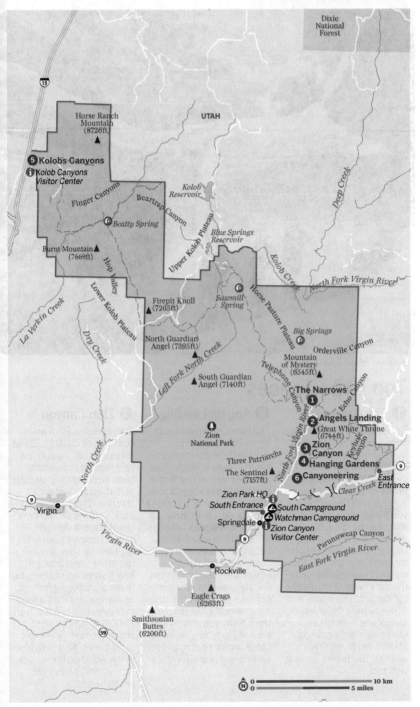

Hikers admiring a canyon cascade

Top Experiences

1 The Narrows

One of Utah's most famous backcountry routes is this remarkably fun hike down the **Virgin River**. It's deceptively easy at first, but once you hit the confluence with Deep Creek you'll be glad you brought that walking stick. By day two you'll be wading through chest-deep pools, the echoes of the rushing water growing louder and the dark canyon squeezing tighter until you reach Wall Street, where the sheer sandstone buttresses shoot up a neck-craning 1500ft. No permit? No worries: day hikers can get wet, too.

2 Angels Landing

The climb to Angels Landing in Zion Canyon is among the most memorable day hikes in Utah, if not North America. The 5-mile trail hugs the face of a towering cliff, snakes through a cool canyon and climbs up **Walter's Wiggles** (a series of 21 sharp switchbacks) before finally ascending a narrow, exposed ridge – where steel chains and the encouragement of strangers are your only friends. Your reward after reaching the 5790ft summit? A lofty view of Zion Canyon, and some unreal photos of your vertigo-defying adventure.

3 Zion Canyon

Zion National Park encompasses roughly 231 sq miles of land, though the vast majority of visitors head straight for Zion Canyon, the park's main attraction. This canyon is the park's crème de la crème: sheer sandstone cliffs, secret hanging gardens, leg-busting adventure-filled hikes and enough heart-stopping scenery to make a photographer out of anyone. In Zion Canyon, massive cliffs expose over 2000ft of Navajo sandstone, formed by ancient sand dunes. Nowhere else in the world do these rock formations reach such grand heights.

Natural pool in a slot canyon

④ Hanging Gardens

If the Utah sun has you feeling as shriveled as a raisin, you're going to find these lush desert oases all the more remarkable. Fed by mesa-top precipitation that has slowly percolated down through sandstone over the course of millennia, these vertical gardens appear where dripping seeps exit shaded canyon walls, forced outward by a layer of harder rock. Look for scarlet monkey flowers, mosses, golden columbines, maidenhair ferns and purple violets clinging marvelously to the rock face. Zion has some particularly lovely examples.

⑤ Kolob Canyons

One hour's drive from Springdale, in the park's quieter northwestern corner, you'll find dramatic finger canyons and the world's largest freestanding arch. In the park's Kolob Canyons area, sheer cliffs jut abruptly from the **Hurricane Fault** as if they rose out of the ground just yesterday. The reddish coloration of all of these cliffs is caused by iron oxides. In the more freshly exposed rocks of Kolob Canyons, the red is evenly distributed. More oxides have leached out of Zion Canyon's ancient weathered cliffs, however, leaving the uppermost layers whitish.

⑥ Canyoneering

If there's one sport that makes Zion special, it's canyoneering (also known as canyoning). It is that perfect combination of adventure, problem-solving, unsettling beauty and commitment. And indeed, it's that last element that gives the sport its particular thrill – for once you rappel into a serious canyon, there is generally only one way out.

Rappelling over the lip of a sandstone bowl, swimming icy pools, tracing a slot canyon's sculpted curves, staring up at a ragged gash of blue sky – canyoneering is beautiful, dangerous and sublime all at once. Zion's slot canyons are the park's most sought-after backcountry experience and you should reserve your permits far in advance.

Why 'Zion'?

One of the park's first Mormon settlers called the canyon 'Little Zion,' referring to it as a place of refuge. The original Paiute name was Mukuntuweap, meaning 'straight-up land.'

View from the Angels Landing trail

The Narrows

🚶 Hike the Narrows: Top Down

Soaring walls, scalloped alcoves and wading through chest-deep pools with your backpack lifted over your head make this hike truly memorable.

Overnight camping is far and away the best experience, though you can hike from the top in one very strenuous, long day (90 minutes' drive from Springdale to Chamberlain's Ranch, up to 12 hours' hiking). Remember that the most difficult sections are at the end of the hike, when you'll be the most tired; we don't recommend this unless you have ironman stamina and have done the hike before. You can also day-hike the Narrows from the bottom, the most popular approach and the only one that doesn't require a permit.

The Narrows permits are some of the most sought-after in the park and are attached to campsites, except for through-hikers. Only 40 permits per day are issued: six campsites are available online; the other six are reserved for walk-ins at the wilderness desk. Permits are not issued any time the river is flowing more than 120 cubic feet per second, so this hike may be closed at times between March and June.

DURATION	2 days
DISTANCE	16 miles one way
DIFFICULTY	Difficult
START	Chamberlain's Ranch
FINISH	Temple of Sinawava
NEAREST TOWN	Springdale
TRANSPORTATION	Shuttle, car

SUMMARY If there's one route that's made Zion famous, it's the wade down the Virgin River through a 1000ft sheer gorge known as the Narrows.

The optimum time to hike is late June through September. Flash floods are not uncommon in late summer, when, again, the park may close the route.

The trail begins at Chamberlain's Ranch, on the east side of the park, 90 minutes' drive from the south entrance. This is a one-way hike, so make reservations for a hiker shuttle, unless you have two cars and drivers. Shuttles usually leave Springdale at 6:30am; a second

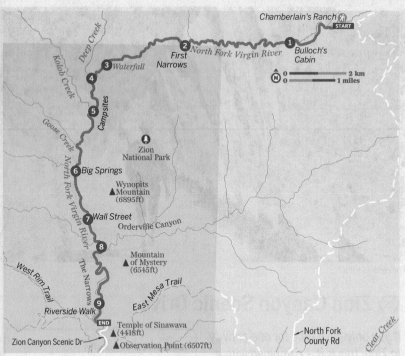

may leave around 9am if there are enough people. Past the ranch gate, a dirt road leads to the river, where you'll find an NPS trailhead marker.

The first day is the quietest, the flowing water and undulating walls casting a mesmerizing spell. The first 3 miles are out of the river and the least interesting – power through so you can spend more time with the fun stuff, exploring side canyons and taking photographs. Once you see ❶ **Bulloch's Cabin**, an old homestead about an hour from the trailhead, you'll know that soon enough, the trail becomes the river. ❷ **The Narrows**, about 3½ hours into the hike and near the park boundary, is an early highlight and provides a taste of what's to come.

From here the hike is quite photogenic, with the canyon walls gradually coming closer together. A little over four hours from the trailhead, you'll reach a log-jam ❸ **waterfall** that appears impassable. Upon closer inspection you'll soon pick out the trail that skirts around to the left. Depending on what time you started, this could be a good lunch spot.

❹ **Deep Creek** is the first major confluence, doubling the river's volume. In the subsequent 2-mile stretch, expect secretive side canyons and faster water, sometimes waist-deep and involving swims. Almost six hours from the trailhead is ❺ **Kolob Creek** (generally dry), an interesting side canyon to explore. This area is the location of the 12 overnight campsites, each on a sandy outcrop far from the others.

On day two you'll pass ❻ **Big Springs**, a good place to fill water bottles. After this are the 5 miles open to day hikers and plenty of deep pools and fast-moving water. In 2 miles you'll reach well-known ❼ **Wall Street**, certainly one of the most memorable parts of all of Zion. Save some energy for ❽ **Orderville Canyon**, a narrow side canyon that is lots of fun to explore. Orderville is about three hours downstream from Big Springs; you can follow it upstream for a half-mile. From here your company will steadily increase until you're just one of the crowd on the ❾ **Riverside Walk**.

Descending into the canyon

🚗 Zion Canyon Scenic Drive

If you only have time for one activity in Zion, this is it – combined with a few of the hikes along the way.

Note that most of the road is actually closed to private cars from March through October; you'll be traveling aboard the excellent park shuttle instead of self-driving.

Leaving from the visitor center, the first stop is the ❶ **Human History Museum**, where a 22-minute film introduces the park. The exhibits here cover the geology and human history of Zion Canyon. The building itself was erected on the site of an original Mormon homestead settled by the Crawford family. Outside the museum, interpretive signs point out the park's tallest sandstone cliffs, including the West Temple (7810ft) and the Towers of the Virgin.

Just past the museum on Hwy 9 are a few turnouts that overlook the Streaked Wall. In spring, with binoculars, scan the rim for nesting peregrine falcons. Officially, the scenic drive begins where you turn north, and cars are restricted, at ❷ **Canyon Junction**. This stop marks one end of the Pa'rus Trail, which follows the Virgin River downstream to the visitor center.

DURATION 45 minutes

DISTANCE 6.2 miles one way

START South Entrance

FINISH Temple of Sinawava

NEAREST TOWN Springdale

TRANSPORTATION Car, shuttle

SUMMARY The premier drive in the park leads between the towering redrock cliffs of Zion's main canyon and accesses all the major frontcountry trailheads.

Next, the ❸ **Court of the Patriarchs** stop fronts the shortest trail in the park, a 50yd staircase of a walk uphill to a view of the namesake peaks. Named by a Methodist minister in 1916, from left to right are Abraham, Isaac and Jacob, while crouching in front of Jacob is Mt Moroni (named for a Mormon angel). Though many people skip it, even the road-level view is nice, especially at sunset.

Ahead on your right, ❹ **Zion Lodge** houses the park's only cafe and restaurant. The lodge was first built in the 1920s, but burned down in 1966. The grassy front lawn – shaded by a cottonwood tree – is a favored place for a post-hike nap. Across the road from the lodge is the corral for horseback rides and the trailhead for the Emerald Pools.

The **❺ Grotto**, barely a half-mile north, is a large, cottonwood-shaded picnic area with tables, restrooms and drinking water. From the picnic area, the Grotto Trail leads south to Zion Lodge. Across the road from the picnic area, the West Rim Trail leads north toward Angels Landing. Those who'd rather admire Angels Landing than climb it should stroll the first flat quarter-mile of the West Rim Trail to a stone bench for the perfect vantage.

Make sure you spend some time at **❻ Weeping Rock**. There's a lot to see at this bend in the river, a great example of an 'incised meander.' Pause to admire Angels Landing, the Organ, Cable Mountain, the Great White Throne and looming Observation Point. A short detour up the bucolic Weeping Rock Trail to a sheltered alcove and hanging garden is a worthwhile diversion.

There are no trailheads at **❼ Big Bend**, but rock climbers get out here on their way to some of Zion's famous walls. Others just soak up the view, which is a different vantage of the features seen from Weeping Rock. It's a good place to bring binoculars and scan the skies for California condors.

If you're using the shuttle, the only way to the next two sights is to walk. As you continue north, on a ledge up to the right look for a reconstructed granary. Although ancient Native American in origin, it was rebuilt in the 1930s by the Boy Scouts. After about a half-mile, you get to **❽ Menu Falls**, so-named because it was pictured on Zion Lodge's first menu cover. The multilevel deck with overlook is the most popular place to get married in the park. From there it's easier to backtrack to Big Bend shuttle than to hoof it all the way up to the last stop. The canyon narrows near the cliff face that forms a natural amphitheater known as the **❾ Temple of Sinawava**, at the road's end. Across the road the rock called the Pulpit does indeed look a bit like a giant lectern. From here you can take the popular Riverside Walk to the ultimate Zion experience, the Narrows.

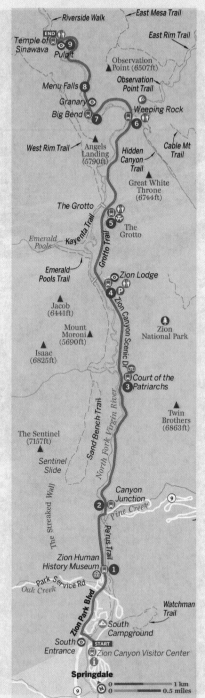

Orderville Canyon

Entrances & Access

Most visitors go straight to Zion Canyon, which is closest to the south (main) entrance, outside the town of Springdale on Hwy 9. This supremely scenic highway continues 11.5 miles east through the park and the Zion–Mt Carmel Tunnel to the east entrance. The park has two other entirely separate access points: Kolob Terrace Rd, which climbs from the town of Virgin over 4000ft up to the canyon-top area west of the main canyon, and Kolob Canyons, 40 miles (one hour) northwest of the main canyon, reached via I-15.

Zion National Park is open 24/7 year-round. Park passes can be purchased at the south (main) and east entrance stations and at Kolob Canyons visitor center. Remember to hold on to your receipt if you are traveling to both the Zion Canyon and Kolob Canyons.

Visitor Centers

In an emergency, call 🕿911 or 🕿435-772-3322 for national park rangers.

Zion Canyon Visitor Center (🕿435-772-3256; www.nps.gov/zion; Hwy 9, Zion National Park; ⏰8am-7:30pm late May–early Sep, 8am-5pm rest of year) Several rangers are on hand to answer questions at the main visitor center; ask to see the picture binder of hikes to know what you're getting into. Find out about ranger-led activities here.

Kolob Canyons Visitor Center (🕿435-586-0895; www.nps.gov/zion; Kolob Canyons Rd, Zion National Park; ⏰8am-7.30pm late May–Sep, to 5pm rest of year) A small visitor center in the Kolob Canyons section of the park.

Sleeping

Zion itself has just one lodge and a few basic campgrounds, which generally fill up from mid-March through November. The majority of visitors sleep in Springdale, just outside the park's south entrance. If you are tent camping, be forewarned that there are not a lot of great sites in the immediate area; many campsites are essentially RV parking lots.

Just inside Zion's south entrance are the park's two main campgrounds, Watchman and South. Both are adjacent to the visitor center. Neither has showers, laundry facilities or a general store; these are available in Springdale. There is a maximum stay of 14 days from March through November. Up to two vehicles and six people are allowed per site. If you show up at the end of the day and the campgrounds are marked full, it's worth asking if Watchman has any overflow sites (no-show reservations).

Watchman Campground

(🕿reservations 877-444-6777; www.recreation.gov; Hwy 9, tent sites $20, RV sites with hookups $30; ⏰year-round; 🐾) Towering cottonwoods provide fairly good shade for the 184 well-spaced sites at Watchman (95 have electricity), located south of the visitor center. Sites are by reservation (six months in advance) and you should book a minimum several months ahead, otherwise it's unlikely you'll get a spot. Fire grates, drinking water, RV hookups and flush toilets; no showers. Sites along the river cost $4 extra.

South Campground

(🕿435-772-3256; Hwy 9, tent & RV sites $20; ⏰year-round; 🐾) The South Campground sits north of the visitor center beside the busy Pa'rus Trail. The 127 campsites are entirely first-come, first-served, so show up before 9am for the best chances of finding an open site. The South Campground has no electrical hookups for RVs; generator use is allowed from 8am to 10am and 6pm to 8pm. There is a dump station, however.

Eating

Zion Lodge has the only in-park dining. Most visitors bring a picnic or eat in Springdale.

Castle Dome Café

(Zion Canyon Scenic Dr, Zion Lodge; mains $5-9; ⏰6:30am-5pm Mar-Oct) This counter-service cafe serves sandwiches, pizza, salads, Asian-ish rice bowls and ice cream. A beer garden serving local suds is located on the patio from May through mid-October.

Red Rock Grill

(🕿435-772-7760; Zion Canyon Scenic Dr, Zion Lodge; breakfast & sandwiches $6-15, dinner $16-30; ⏰6:30-10am, 11:30am-2:30pm & 5-9pm Mar-Oct, hours vary Nov-Feb) Settle into your replica log chair or relax on the big deck with magnificent canyon views. Though the dinner menu touts its sustainable-cuisine stance for dishes like roast pork loin and flat-iron steak, the results are hit-or-miss. Dinner reservations recommended. Full bar.

Pacific Northwest

Lush rainforests and volcanic peaks are the hallmarks of the Pacific Northwest. Glacial snowfields emerge from a sea of clouds, and virgin stands of massive Douglas fir and red cedar serve as reminders of what the continent's ancient forests must have once looked like. Mt Rainier steals the limelight, but North Cascades, Olympic and Crater Lake offer plenty of breathtaking scenery on their own.

Over 1500 miles to the north lies Alaska, the wildest and remotest corner of the country. The state is home to eight national parks, which together protect 54 million acres of land, or more than all the other national parks combined. If you're planning on a visit, chances are you'll be traveling by boat or plane – roads are few and far between.

Mount Rainier National Park
FENG WEI PHOTOGRAPHY/GETTY IMAGES ©

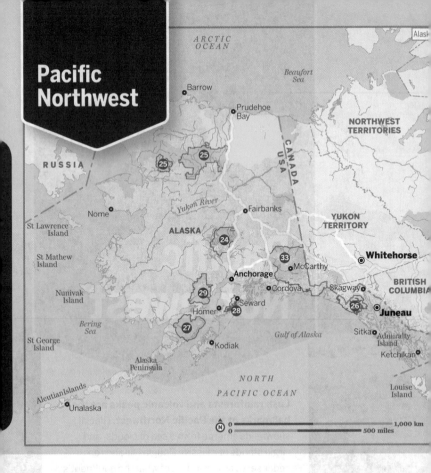

Pacific Northwest

ARCTIC OCEAN

Barrow

Prudehoe Bay

Beaufort Sea

NORTHWEST TERRITORIES

RUSSIA

CANADA
USA

Nome

Yukon River

Fairbanks

St Lawrence Island

ALASKA

YUKON TERRITORY

Whitehorse

St Mathew Island

McCarthy

Anchorage

Cordova

BRITISH COLUMBIA

Nunivak Island

Homer

Seward

Skagway

Juneau

Bering Sea

Gulf of Alaska

Sitka

Admiralty Island

St George Island

Kodiak

Ketchikan

Alaska Peninsula

NORTH PACIFIC OCEAN

Louise Island

Aleutian Islands

Unalaska

0   1,000 km
0   500 miles

☑ **DON'T MISS**

Hoh Rainforest
Moss-draped trees fill this thick, wet rainforest – the most symbolic sight of **Olympic National Park**.

Hiking in the Wild
Glaciers, jagged peaks and alpine lakes are all part of the scenery on a hike in **North Cascades National Park**.

Denali (Mt McKinley)
North America's highest mountain is a huge and hulking icy mass in **Denali National Park**.

Mt Rainier
Day hike among wildflower meadows or tramp across snow fields in **Mount Rainier National Park**.

Paddling in icy wilderness
Skip the cruise ship and paddle your way through **Glacier Bay National Park**.

㉚ Mount Rainier National Park
Flower-carpeted meadows lie at the foothills of majestic, snow-capped Mt Rainier. (p254)

㉛ North Cascades National Park
Lightly trodden wilderness for wild backcountry adventures. (p256)

㉜ Olympic National Park
Unblemished green wilderness of the highest order. (p258)

㉝ Wrangell-St Elias National Park
Get lost in the world's second-largest national park. (p260)

Inside Passage *Board a ferry and enjoy a constant visual feast*

Classic Trip

Up the Inside Passage

Set sail on an Alaska Ferry from Bellingham, Washington, tracing the lush Canadian coastline before slipping into the foggy emerald maze of Alaska's wild, remote Inside Passage.

TRIP HIGHLIGHTS

1119 mi

White Pass & Yukon Railroad
A spine-tingling ride over gorges and across trestles in vintage railcars

8 FINISH
6
5

990 mi

Lynn Canal
Dramatically carved by Mother Nature, this is North America's longest, deepest fjord

960 mi

Mendenhall Glacier
This frozen river tumbles down from the Juneau Icefield and is within easy reach

3

684 mi

Petroglyph Beach
Search for wildlife figures among the ancient rock carvings

Prince Rupert

START
● **Bellingham**

---

4 DAYS
1119 MILES/1802KM

GREAT FOR...

BEST TIME TO GO

June to September – the snow has melted and wildflowers bloom.

ESSENTIAL PHOTO

Totem poles, tall pines and soaring eagles at Chief Shakes Island.

 BEST FOR WILDLIFE

Bears, bald eagles, whales and sea lions – they're all out there waiting to be spotted.

217

Up the Inside Passage

Of the 27 All-American Roads, the Alaska Marine Hwy is the only one that takes to the water on a car ferry. Churning 3500 nautical miles from Bellingham and out to the far tendril of the Aleutian Chain, some of the highway's most dramatic scenes are pressed into the steep fjords, forests and waterlogged fishing towns of the Inside Passage. By land it takes 98 hours to reach Skagway from Bellingham, with lots of long, empty stretches where the forest seems to swallow you completely. By sea, it's a constant visual feast.

❶ Bellingham

In Bellingham, head to the brick-paved, historic **Fairhaven District**. Make sure to give yourself at least an afternoon to explore this city neighborhood, stamped onto several blocks and charmingly crammed with flower shops, cafes and bookstores. This is also where you board the **Alaska Ferry** (☏907-465-3941, 800-642-0066; www.alaska.gov/ferry; vehicle/adult/child/under 6 to Skagway US$820/363/199.50/free, to Ketchikan US$515/239/119.50/free; ♿); you can walk, bike, or drive onto the vessel. A three-day trip ends in Skagway, traveling through the US's largest national forest, the Tongass, and stopping in several ports. If you have more time, your options for taking detours are countless. A through-ticket will give you a little time to explore in each port, while point-to-point tickets let you decide how long to stay in each town.

As the ferry slides out into **Bellingham Bay**, you'll be treated to views of meringue-like Mt Baker, sienna-colored brick buildings, and Victorian homes peering from the town's hillside.

Not long after leaving port, the ferry squeezes between Canada's Vancouver Island and the mainland through the Strait of Georgia. While this isn't a cruise ship, it's comfortable and the mix of locals and travelers gives it the feeling of an authentic voyage. You'll find the solarium filled with adventurers hunkered down under heat lamps, while brightly colored tents flap in the wind on deck. The snack-bar fare is what you'd expect of public transportation, but warming up with a cup of coffee in a booth is a comfortable way to watch the coast pass by.

The Drive ›› This is like auto-pilot in the extreme. Sit back and watch the amazing scenery pass by as you travel past lighthouse stations and between islands with wild coastlines, watching for eagles and even the occasional whale.

❷ Ketchikan

Thirty-eight hours after departing Bellingham, the ferry makes its first stop

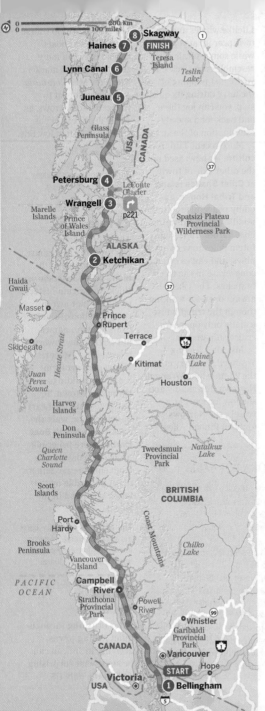

in Ketchikan. Here you'll skim along the town's thin band of colorful buildings (with equally colorful histories) before docking north of the town center. The ferry stays in port long enough for you to explore the historic, albeit touristy, **Creek Street**. Though this boardwalk is now safe for families, in Ketchikan's early boomtown years the street was a clatter of brothels and bars. Pop into **Dolly's House Museum** (www. dollyshouse.com; 24 Creek St; adult/child $5/free; ⏰8am-5pm), where you can get an insider's view of what was a working parlor. Namesake Dolly Arthur operated the brothel until prostitution was outlawed in 1953, and lived here until her death in the '70s.

For an introduction to a different kind of wildlife, head to the **Southeast Alaska Discovery Center** (www. alaskacenters.gov/ketchikan. cfm; 50 Main St; adult/child $5/free; ⏰8:30am-5pm daily; ♿). The center houses excellent exhibits on various aspects of the Southeast region (simply called 'Southeast' by locals), including ecosystems, artwork and Native Alaskan traditions, while downstairs a re-created rainforest looms. This is a great place to help you identify what you're seeing from the windows of the ferry.

The Drive » From Ketchikan, the ferry hums north through Clarence Strait to Wrangell.

Classic Trip

❸ Wrangell

Several hours after departing Ketchikan, you'll arrive at tiny, false-fronted Wrangell. You'll be greeted by the town's children, who set up folding tables (even in the rain) to sell their wares – deep-purple garnets that they've mined from the nearby Stikine River.

Wrangell practically spills over with historic, cultural and natural sights, including **Petroglyph Beach**. Less than a mile from the ferry terminal the beach is dotted with boulders depicting faces and figures that were carved thousands of years ago.

Lifelike whales and owls peer up at you, while some spirals eerily resemble crop circles. If you're just popping off the ferry during its quick stop, you can jog there and back for a speedy examination of the stones.

More recent Tlingit culture is showcased on the other side of town at **Chief Shakes Island and Tribal House**, an oddly peaceful site in the middle of the humming boat harbor. Here, six totem poles tower among pines, and eagles often congregate in the trees' branches. The island is always open for walking, though the tribal house usually only opens for cruise ship groups.

Just after leaving Wrangell, the ferry enters the 22-mile long **Wrangell Narrows**. Too skinny and shallow for most large vessels, the Narrows (dubbed Pinball Alley)

requires nearly 50 course corrections as boats thread between more than 70 channel markers. The ferry M/V *Columbia* is the largest boat to navigate the Narrows, as water depth can get as shallow as 24ft at low tide.

The Drive ❱❱ After maneuvering through the Narrows, the ferry continues northwest to Petersburg.

❹ Petersburg

At the end of the Narrows sits Petersburg, a fishing village with blond roots. Petersburg's thick Norwegian history is evident not just in the phonebook full of Scandinavian names, but also in the flowery rosemaling, a decorative Norwegian art form found on buildings throughout town. To really get into the heart of Petersburg, walk the docks of its **North Boat Harbor**. Here fisherfolk unload the day's catch from small purse seiners, distinguishable by the large nets piled in the sterns.

The Drive ❱❱ From Petersburg, the ferry heads north alongside the densely forested Admiralty Island to the port of Juneau.

❺ Juneau

After brushing through quiet fishing towns, arriving in Juneau can be somewhat surprising. This is the only US

IN SEARCH OF AURORA BOREALIS

Glowing green and red across the sky like fluorescent curtains, the Northern Lights were named after Aurora, the Roman goddess of dawn, and Boreas, the Greek name for north wind. The Native Cree call them Dance of the Spirits.

The Northern Lights can be seen to some extent anywhere above 60° north latitude, within what is known as the aurora oval. However, you can sometimes catch a glimpse as far south as Juneau.

Sightings are hindered by the perpetual twilight that dominates the night skies from late April until September. The best time to see the Northern Lights is around the 22nd of September or March, on a new moon, late at night or very early in the morning. Head to the ferry deck and await the performance.

DETOUR: LECONTE GLACIER

Start: ④ Petersburg

Complement a layover in Petersburg with a kayak tour to LeConte Glacier, at the head of serpentine LeConte Bay. Constantly calving, the glacier is somewhat infamous for icebergs that release under water and then shoot to the surface like icy torpedoes. If you're lucky you'll see one – from afar.

capital with no road access, yet it still bustles with the importance of a government center. It's also postcard perfect, with massive green cliffs rising above the city center. Be sure to stroll past the **Governor's Mansion**, its assertive columns and landscaped shrubs a contrast to the usual rainforest-rotted cabins of Southeast.

If the political climate gets to be too much, head to the laid-back **Alaskan Brewing Company** (www. alaskanbeer.com; 5429 Shuane Dr; ◷11am-6pm May-Sep, 11am-5:30pm Tue-Sat Oct-Apr) for a tour and a sample of its beers. The brewery is in the same neighborhood as the massive **Mendenhall Glacier**, which tumbles down from the Juneau Icefield and is one of the few glaciers in Southeast you can drive up to. The visitor center offers a movie about the glacier, plus hiking trails and a salmon-viewing platform.

The Drive » The route continues north, hugging the coastline into the Lynn Canal.

TRIP HIGHLIGHT

⑥ Lynn Canal

From Juneau, the ferry travels up the Lynn Canal, North America's longest (90 miles/145km) and deepest (2000ft) fjord. Glaciers and waterfalls make the canal a visual feast. It was first mapped in 1794 and was later a major route to the boomtown of Skagway during the gold rush. This was also the scene of one of the worst maritime disasters in the Pacific Northwest: in 1918 a passenger ship grounded on a reef and sunk along with all of its 343 crew and passengers.

Because of its high use, lighthouses were once scattered along the inlet; still standing are the octagonal **Eldred Rock Light** and the church-like **Sentinel Island Light**. The canal is now used less for freight and more by ferries, cruise lines and humpback whales.

The Drive » The trip north from Juneau via the Lynn Canal to Haines takes about 4½ hours.

⑦ Haines

Seventy-five miles from Juneau lies Haines, where most passengers with cars disembark as the town is the main link to the Alaska Hwy. Haines has a laid-back vibe with almost extravagant scenery. You can't miss the huge hammer outside the **Hammer Museum** (www. hammermuseum.org; 108 Main St; adult/child $3/free; ◷10am-5pm Mon-Fri May-Sep), which displays 1500 versions of humanity's first tool and chronicles history through them. Not surprisingly, this is the world's first (and only) museum dedicated solely to the humble hammer.

Between September and December, Haines' population grows by over 3500 when thousands of migrating bald eagles descend on the area. This is the largest gathering of bald eagles in the world and the town celebrates with the mid-November **Alaska Bald Eagle Festival** (www.baldeagles. org/festival). If you arrive at the same time as these white-headed guys, you'll undoubtedly be wowed.

The Drive » A short one-hour trip north along the coast brings you to Skagway.

TRIP HIGHLIGHT

⑧ Skagway

At the turn of the 20th century, Skagway boomed with the

REDFISHWEB / GETTY IMAGES ©

WHY THIS IS A CLASSIC TRIP
KORINA MILLER,
LONELY PLANET
WRITER

As the ferry enters the Inside Passage, you feel an undeniable spark of excitement. It's like following in the wake of the first European explorers. You appreciate the remoteness of it all. Catching a glimpse of a bear or a wolf on the shoreline, watching the bald eagles swoop overhead, and stopping off at communities only accessible by water – quite quickly I realized this was no ordinary trip. The word 'remarkable' came to mind.

Left: Brown bear, Chilkoot River, Haines
Top: Mendenhall Glacier
Right: Petroglyph Beach, Wrangell

gold rush, when the population went from two to 10,000 in just a few years. Sandwiched between forested slopes, it now booms with tourism; if you want to see can-can girls or pan for gold, this is the place to do it. The ferry deposits you about 100yd from **Broadway Street**, where you'll find women dressed in feathered hats and bright satiny dresses. The rest is history.

Since Skagway is likely your last ferry stop, it's worth boarding the **White Pass & Yukon Railroad** (www.wpyr.com; depot on 2nd Ave; Yukon Adventure adult/child $249/119.50 return, White Pass Summit Excursion $113/56.50), a narrated sightseeing tour aboard vintage parlor cars. This dramatic ride rumbles through Glacier Gorge and over White Pass (a 2885ft climb).

Whether you end your trip in Skagway or another port, you'll need to backtrack on the ferry, or fly south, to get home. There are few commercial flights from smaller towns, and to catch a major airline flight to Seattle you'll first need to fly to Juneau, Ketchikan or Sitka. Unless you brought your car on board, in which case you're in for a scenic road trip home.

STATE
Oregon

ENTRANCE FEE
7-day pass per vehicle
$15

AREA
287 sq miles

GOOD FOR

Crater Lake

Crater Lake National Park

The gloriously blue waters of Crater Lake reflect surrounding mountain peaks like a giant dark-blue mirror, making for spectacular photographs and breathtaking panoramas.

Crater Lake is Oregon's only national park and also the USA's deepest lake at 1943ft deep. The ancient mountain whose remains now form Crater Lake was Mt Mazama, a roughly 12,000ft volcanic peak that was heavily glaciered and inactive for many thousands of years until it came back to life 7700 years ago. A catastrophic explosion scattered ash for hundreds of miles as flows of superheated pumice solidified into massive banks. These eruptions emptied the magma chambers at the heart of the volcano, and the summit cone collapsed to form the caldera.

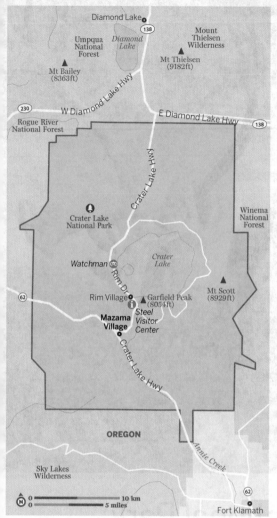

old lookout tower on the opposite side of the lake that boasts one of the park's best views.

For flower enthusiasts, there is an easy 1-mile nature trail near the Steel Visitor Center that winds through the Castle Crest Wildflower Garden Trail.

The popular and steep mile-long Cleetwood Cove Trail, at the north end of the crater, provides the only water access at the cove. Two-hour boat tours are available; book ahead.

Skiing

In winter, only the southern entrance road to Rim Village is kept plowed to provide access to several Nordic trails. Rentals are unavailable, so bring your own skis. Snowshoes are provided for free ranger-led snowshoe walks, held on weekends from Thanksgiving through March.

Information

The park's south entrance is open year-round and provides access to Rim Village, Mazama Village, and the park headquarters at the Steel Visitor Center. In winter you can only go up to the lake's rim and back down the same way; no other roads are plowed. The north entrance is only open from early June to late October, depending on snowfall.

For accommodations, try Crater Lake Lodge (the only lodging at the lake itself) or Mazama Village (7 miles from the rim). The park's eating facilities are limited – bring a picnic.

Only snowfall and rain contribute to the lake water. This purity and the lake's depth give it that famous blue color.

Hiking

Crater Lake has over 90 miles of hiking trails, though some higher ones aren't completely clear of snow until late July. From the east edge of the Rim Village parking lot, a 1.7-mile trail leads up 8054ft Garfield Peak to an expansive view of the lake; in July the slopes are covered with wildflowers. A strenuous 5-mile round-trip hike takes you to an even better lake vista atop 8929ft Mt Scott, the highest point in the park. For a steep but shorter hike, trek up 0.7 miles to the Watchman, an

MICHAEL DEYOUNG / DESIGN PICS / GETTY IMAGES ©

Caribou bull

STATE
Alaska

ENTRANCE FEE
7-day pass per adult/child
$10/free

AREA
9500 sq miles

GOOD FOR

Denali National Park

For many, Denali National Park & Preserve is the beginning and end of their Alaskan adventure. And why shouldn't it be? Here is probably your best chance in the Interior (if not in the entire state) of seeing a grizzly bear, moose or caribou.

Unlike most wilderness areas in the country, you don't have to be a hiker to view the wildlife here. The window of the park bus will do just fine for a close look at these magnificent creatures roaming free in their natural habitat.

For those with a bit more time and the desire to get further into the wild, there are vast expanses of untracked country to explore – more than 6 million acres of it, to be exact. That's more landmass than the US state of Massachusetts.

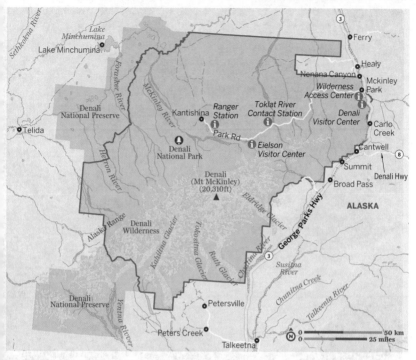

Denali

What makes 20,310ft Denali (Mt McKinley) one of the world's great scenic mountains is the sheer independent rise of its bulk. Denali begins at a base of just 2000ft, which means that on a clear day you will be transfixed by more than 18,000ft of ascending rock, ice and snow. By contrast, Mt Everest, no slouch itself when it comes to memorable vistas, only rises 12,000ft from its base on the Tibetan Plateau.

Despite its lofty heights, the mountain is not visible from the park entrance or the nearby campgrounds and hotel. Your first glimpse of it comes between Mile 9 and Mile 11 on Park Rd, if you're blessed with a clear day. The rule of thumb stressed by the National Park Service rangers is that Denali is hidden two out of every three days, but that's a random example – it could be clear for a week and then hidden for the next month. While the 'Great One' might not be visible for most of the first 15 miles of Park Rd, this is the best stretch to spot moose because of the proliferation

History

The Athabascan people used what is now Denali National Park as hunting grounds, but when gold was found near Kantishna in 1905 the area began to change. With the gold stampede came the big-game hunters, and things weren't looking very good for this amazing stretch of wilderness until a noted hunter and naturalist, Charles Sheldon, stunned by the destruction, mounted a campaign to protect the region.

From this, Mt McKinley National Park was born. Later, as a result of the 1980 Alaska National Interest Lands Conservation Act, the park was enlarged by 4 million acres, and renamed Denali National Park & Preserve. In 1923, when the railroad arrived, 36 visitors enjoyed the splendor of the new park. Nowadays some 400,000 visitors are received annually.

A number of unique visitor-management strategies have been created to deal with the masses, and generally they've been successful. The Denali National Park of today is still the great wilderness it was decades ago.

Denali (Mt McKinley) from the air

Climbing expedition, Denali (Mt McKinley)

of spruce and especially willow, the animal's favorite food. The open flats before Savage River are good for spotting caribou and sometimes brown bears.

Wildlife Watching

Because hunting has never been allowed in the park, professional photographers refer to animals in Denali as 'approachable wildlife.' That means bear, moose, Dall sheep and caribou aren't as skittish here as in other regions. For this reason, and because Park Rd was built to maximize the chances of seeing wildlife by traversing high open ground, the national park is an excellent place to view a variety of animals.

On board the park shuttle buses, your fellow passengers will be armed with binoculars and cameras to help scour the terrain for animals, most of which are so accustomed to the rambling buses that they rarely run and hide. When someone spots something and yells 'Stop!' the driver will pull over for viewing and picture-taking. The best wildlife watching is on the first morning bus.

Hiking

Even for those who have neither the desire nor the equipment for an overnight trek, hiking is still the best way to enjoy the park and to see the land and its wildlife. You can hike virtually anywhere that hasn't been closed to prevent an impact on wildlife.

There are well-maintained trails or you can get off the beaten track and explore the backcountry on your own – just get off the shuttle bus at any valley, riverbed or ridge that grabs your fancy. Thanks to its high latitude, most of the park is above the tree line, allowing hikers to enjoy broad vistas. Not only does this mean Park Rd will be rarely out of sight, it also prevents any surprise encounters with wildlife.

Check in at the Backcountry Information Center for suggestions, and remember the key to successful backcountry travel is being able to use a compass and read a topographic map.

Dall sheep

Eating & Sleeping

There are few places to stay within the park, excluding campgrounds, and only one restaurant. The majority of visitors base themselves in the nearby communities of Canyon, McKinley Village, Carlo Creek and Healy. A decent budget option in Canyon is **Denali Park Salmon Bake Restaurant & Cabins** (☏907-683-7283; www.thebakerocks.com; Mile 238.5, George Parks Hwy; cabins with/without bath $149/69; ☏), which offers no-frills cabins as well as a restaurant, shuttle service to the park, and bar with live music. Directly opposite across the George Parks Hwy is the more luxurious **Denali Princess Wilderness Lodge** (☏907-683-2282; www.princesslodges.com; Mile 238.5 George Parks Hwy; r from $269; ☏), a miniresort run by the famous cruise company.

Information

At the entrance you'll find the park headquarters, **visitor center** (☏ 907-683-2294; www.nps.gov/dena; Mile 1.5, Park Rd; ☺8am-6pm) and main campground, as well as the **Wilderness Access Center** (WAC; ☏ 907-683-9274; Mile 0.5, Park Rd; ☺5am-7pm), where you pay your park entrance fee and arrange campground and shuttle-bus bookings to take you further into the park.

In a trailer across the lot from the WAC sits the **Backcountry Information Center** (BIC; ☏ 907-683-9510; Mile 0.5, Park Rd; ☺9am-6pm), where backpackers get backcountry permits and bear-proof food containers.

Getting Around

There's only one road through the park: the 92-mile unpaved Park Rd, which is closed to private vehicles after Mile 14. The park entrance area, where most visitors congregate, extends a scant 4 miles up Park Rd.

STATE
Alaska

ENTRANCE FEE
Free

AREA
15,974 sq miles

GOOD FOR

Dogsledding near the Koyukuk River

DAVID MADISON / GETTY IMAGES ©

Gates of the Arctic & Kobuk Valley National Parks

Unchanged in four millennia, Gates of the Arctic park is part of a contiguous wilderness harboring no roads, no cell-phone coverage and a population of precisely zero. To its southwest lies desolate Kobuk Valley.

Standing in the middle of the park, 8.4 million acres of uninhabited mountains and tundra located between the Dalton Hwy and the Bering Strait, you could quite conceivably be living in the year 2016 BC, so raw is the surrounding landscape. The Kobuk Valley is known for its arctic sand dunes and migrating caribou.

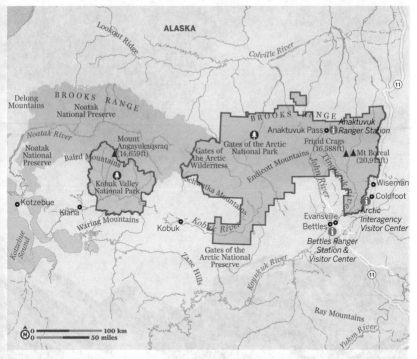

Not surprisingly, you don't come to these parks to stroll along interpretive boardwalks looking for the nearest hot-dog concession, or even follow something as rudimentary as a trail (there aren't any). Tackled alone, this is a land for burly and brave travelers with advanced outdoor experience, plenty of time on their hands and – ahem – a flexible budget (read: it's costly). If you're less intrepid, fear not. You can sign up with one of a handful of agencies and go on a guided backcountry or flightseeing tour.

Gates of the Arctic is the more accessible park as it starts just 5 miles west of the Dalton Hwy, meaning you can technically hike in, although charter flights out of Coldfoot and Bettles are

more common. Kobuk Valley is reached via charters out of the small settlement of Kotzebue.

Within the parks are dozens of rivers to run, miles of valleys and tundra slopes to hike and, of course, the 'gates' themselves: Mt Boreal and Frigid Crags, which flank the north fork of the Koyukuk River. In 1929 Robert Marshall found an unobstructed path northward to the Arctic through these landmark peaks and his name for the passage has stuck ever since.

The parks contain no visitor facilities, campgrounds or trails, and the National Park Service is intent upon maintaining its virgin quality. Unguided trekkers, paddlers and climbers entering the park

should check in at one of the ranger stations for a backcountry orientation.

Hiking

Most backpackers enter the park by way of charter air-taxis, which can land on lakes, rivers or river bars. Once on the ground they often follow the long, open valleys for extended treks or work their way to higher elevations where open tundra provides good hiking terrain.

While this appears to make planning an impossibly vague task, the landscape limits the areas that aircraft can land or pick you up, as well as where you can hike. Park staff suggest consulting flight and guide companies, as well as topographic maps, for possible routes and

Trekking on the shore of Arrigetch Creek, Gates of the Arctic National Park

Noatak River

then running it by them to make sure the area is not overused. If it is, they can suggest alternatives.

The only treks that don't require chartering a plane are those beginning from the Dalton Hwy (near Wiseman), or from the village of Anaktuvuk Pass. For hikes from the highway, which lead into several different areas along the eastern border of the park, stop at the Arctic Interagency Visitor Center in Coldfoot for advice and assistance in trip planning. Several well-known routes in this area are showing too much wear and even beginning to affect the livelihood of subsistence hunters.

Hiking into the park from Anaktuvuk Pass is surprisingly one of the more economical options, as you only need to pay for a regular scheduled flight to the village from Fairbanks. From the airstrip it's just a few miles' hike into the northern edge of the park. You can camp for free by the airstrip if needed, but elsewhere get permission until you enter the park.

Paddling

Floatable rivers in the park include the John, Alatna, Noatak, Kobuk, Koyukuk and Tinayguk. The waterways range in difficulty from Class I to III, and you should consult the park or guide companies about possible routes. Canoes can be rented in Bettles at the Bettles Lodge for around $270 per week.

Tours

Arctic Wild (☑907-479-8203; www.arcticwild.com) arranges fantastic eight-day guided backpacking trips in Gates of the Arctic National Park for $4200 per person, or a 10-day canoeing/hiking trip on the Noatak River from $5400 per person. Trips run in August.

Alternatively, you could take in the landscape from the air. **Brooks Range Aviation** (☑907-692-5444; http://brooksrange.com) runs four- to five-hour flightseeing tours of Gates of the Arctic and Kobuk Valley National Parks with a brief landing in each. You'll need to overnight in Bettles.

Mt Boreal and Frigid Crags

Getting There & Away

Bettles (population 12) is the main gateway to Gates of the Arctic, offering meals, lodging and air transport into the backcountry. Other visitors fly in from Coldfoot on the Dalton Hwy, or hike in directly from Wiseman, just north of Coldfoot. To the north, the remote Alaska Native village of Anaktuvuk Pass is another access point if traveling by foot, though you'll need to fly here first. Contact the Anaktuvuk Ranger Station for more information on visiting the park from here.

Wright Air Service (☎ 907-474-0502; www.wrightairservice.com) flies daily from Fairbanks to Bettles ($340 round-trip) and Anaktuvuk Pass ($380 round-trip). **Bettles Air Service** (☎ 907-479-7018; www.bettlesair.com) also covers these routes.

From Bettles it's necessary to charter an air-taxi to your destination within the park. Most areas can be reached in under two hours. Check with Brooks Range Aviation or Bettles Air Service for air charters.

From Coldfoot on the Dalton Hwy you can hire a charter flight with **Coyote Air Service** (☎ 907-678-5995; www.flycoyote.com).

Sleeping

Bettles Lodge (☎ 907-692-5111; www.bettleslodge.com) A 1952 vintage six-room lodge (now a National Historic Site) providing accommodations in the tiny settlement of Bettles. There's a common area with books and games, and decent meals are provided. Even better, the lodge organizes multiple trips and tours in Gates of the Arctic National Park. It's not posh but it's peaceful. Phone for packages and rates.

Information

For more information, check out the park's website. If the 'Plan Your Visit' section doesn't answer all your questions, contact the park directly.

Anaktuvuk Ranger Station (☎ 907-661-3520; www.nps.gov/gaar) Can help you plan your trip from Anaktuvuk.

Arctic Interagency Visitor Center (☎ 907-678-5209; CentralYukon@blm.gov; ☺ 11am-10pm Jun-Aug) In Coldfoot; has info for those accessing the park from the Dalton Hwy.

Bettles Ranger Station & Visitor Center (☎ 907-692-5494; www.nps.gov/gaar; ☺ 8am-5pm daily Jun-Sep, 1-5pm Mon-Fri Oct-May) In a log building less than a quarter-mile from the airstrip.

STATE
Alaska

ENTRANCE FEE
Free

AREA
5036 sq miles

GOOD FOR

Breaching humpback whale

Glacier Bay National Park

Eleven tidewater glaciers that spill out of the mountains and fill the sea with icebergs of all shapes, sizes and shades of blue have made Glacier Bay National Park an icy wilderness renowned worldwide.

When Captain George Vancouver sailed through the ice-choked waters of Icy Strait in 1794, Glacier Bay was little more than a dent in a mountain of ice. In 1879 John Muir made his legendary discovery of Glacier Bay and found that the end of the bay had retreated 20 miles from Icy Strait. Today, the glacier that bears his name is more than 60 miles from Icy Strait, and its rapid retreat has revealed plants and animals that continue to fascinate naturalists. Glacier Bay is the crowning jewel of the cruise-ship industry and the dreamy destination for anybody who has ever paddled a kayak.

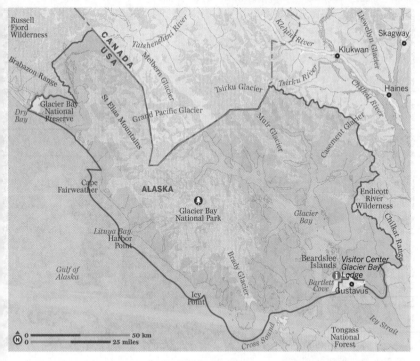

Of the more than 300,000 annual visitors to Glacier Bay, more than 90% arrive aboard a ship and never leave the boat. The rest are a mixture of tour-group members who head straight for the lodge and backpackers who wander toward the free campground.

Although the park headquarters, campground and visitor centers are located in **Bartlett Cove**, the gateway to Glacier Bay is **Gustavus**, located 9 miles away. This interesting backcountry community (population 440) is where the state ferry and Alaska Airlines land, but it has no downtown. Most of the area businesses are either spread out along the Salmon River or half-hidden in the woods. Electricity only

arrived in the early 1980s, and residents still maintain a self-sufficient lifestyle. For visitors who rush through to see the glaciers, Gustavus is little more than an airstrip left over from WWII and a road to Bartlett Cove. For those who spend a little time poking around and meeting locals, Gustavus can be an interesting place and a refreshing break from cruise-ship ports such as Skagway.

Glaciers

Glacier Bay's glaciers are 40 miles up the bay from Bartlett Cove. If you're not on a cruise ship or don't want to spend a week or two kayaking, the only way to see them is on board a tour boat.

The *Fairweather Express* operated by **Glacier Bay**

Lodge & Tours (☎888-229-8687; www.visitglacierbay.com; tours adult/child $195/97.50) is a high-speed catamaran that departs at 7:30am for an eight-hour tour into the West Arm and returns by 4pm. The tour includes lunch and narration by an onboard park naturalist.

Glacier Bay's ice, like glaciers all over Alaska, is rapidly melting. This is particularly true in Muir Inlet, or the East Arm as it's commonly called. Twenty years ago it was home to three active tidewater glaciers, but now there is only one, McBride. Only two glaciers in the park are advancing: Johns Hopkins and Lamplugh. The rest are receding and thinning.

Ranger-led forest walk near Bartlett Cove

Whale Watching

Glacier Bay is home to a variety of marine life, including whales. The humpbacks are by far the most impressive and acrobatic, as they heave their massive bodies in spectacular leaps (called 'breaching') from the water. Adult humpbacks often grow to 50ft and weigh up to 40 tons. Other marine life here includes harbor seals, porpoises, killer whales and sea otters, and other wildlife includes brown and black bears, wolves, moose, mountain goats and more than 200 bird species.

Glacier Bay is also where the cruise-ship industry and environmentalists have squared off. After the number of whales seen

in the park dropped dramatically in 1978, the National Park Service (NPS) reduced ship visits to 79 during the three-month season. But the cruise-ship industry lobbied the US Congress and the NPS in 1996 to OK a 30% increase in vessels allowed in the bay – almost 200 cruise ships a season. Environmentalists sued, and eventually a compromise of two large cruise ships per day was hammered out.

Cross Sound Express (☎888-698-2726; www.taz. gustavus.com; tours adult/child $120/60) organises whale-watching tours on the 50ft MV *Taz*, carrying up to 23 passengers. It departs the Gustavus dock daily during the summer at 8:30am and 12:30pm for a 3½-hour tour.

Paddling

Glacier Bay offers an excellent opportunity for people who have some experience on the water but not necessarily as kayakers. The **Fairweather Express** (☎907-264-4600, 888-229-8687; www.visitglacierbay.com; one way adult/child $105/52.50) drops off and picks up paddlers at two spots, usually at the entrance of the Muir Inlet (East Arm) and inside the West Arm. By using the tour boat, you can skip the long and open paddle up the bay and enjoy only the well-protected arms and inlets where the glaciers are located. The most dramatic glaciers are in the West Arm, but either one will require at least four days to paddle to glaciers if you are dropped off and picked

Sea kayaking, Muir Inlet

up. With only a drop-off, you need a week to 10 days to paddle from either arm back to Bartlett Cove.

Paddlers who want to avoid the tour-boat fares but still long for a kayak adventure should try the **Beardslee Islands**. While there are no glaciers to view, the islands are a day's paddle from Bartlett Cove and offer calm water, protected channels and pleasant beach camping. Wildlife includes black bears, seals and bald eagles, and the tidal pools burst with activity at low tide.

Hiking

Glacier Bay has few trails and in the backcountry foot travel is done along riverbanks, on ridges or across ice remnants of glaciers. The only developed trails are in Bartlett Cove.

The new **Nagoonberry Loop** is an accessible 2.2-mile trail that begins and ends at the terminus of Glen's Ditch Rd. Along the way you'll pass through all stages of a forest, from meadow to old growth, and on to the beach.

The mile-long **Forest Trail** is a nature walk that begins and ends near the Bartlett Cove dock and winds through the pond-studded spruce and hemlock forest near the campground. Rangers lead walks on this trail daily in summer; inquire at the Glacier Bay Visitor Center.

Bartlett River Trail, a 1.5-mile trail, begins just up the road to Gustavus, where there is a posted trailhead, and ends at the Bartlett River estuary.

The **Point Gustavus Beach Walk**, along the shoreline south of Bartlett Cove to Point Gustavus and Gustavus, provides the only overnight trek from the park headquarters.

Information

The best source of information is the NPS in Bartlett Cove.

Glacier Bay Visitor Center (☏907-697-2661; www.nps. gov/glba; ⊙11am-8pm) On the 2nd floor of Glacier Bay Lodge, it has exhibits, a bookshop and an information desk. There are also daily guided walks from the lodge, park films and slide presentations.

Gustavus Visitors Association (☏907-697-2454; www. gustavusak.com) Has loads of information on its website.

Visitor Information Station (☏907-697-2627; ⊙7am-7pm) Campers, kayakers and boaters can stop at the park's Visitor Information Station at the foot of the public dock for backcountry and boating permits, logistical information and a 20-minute orientation video.

Ice cave and glacial stream

Sleeping & Eating

Most of the accommodations are in Gustavus, which adds a 7% bed-and-sales tax.

Blue Heron B&B (☎907-697-2293; www.blueheronbnb.net; State Dock Rd, Gustavus; r/cottages $154/190; ☜) Surrounded by 10 acres of wildflowers and views of the Fairweather mountains. The two rooms and two cottages (with kitchenettes) are modern, bright and clean, and each has a TV/VCR and private bath. In the morning everybody meets in the sun room for a full breakfast ranging from organic rolled oats with blueberries to omelets.

Seaside Campground (☎907-697-2214; sites $20) On the edge of the Fairweather golf course, this basic campground is in a grassy field and has room for a few tents and RVs. Shower and restroom access across the road.

Gustavus Inn (☎907-697-2254, 800-649-5220; www.gustavusinn.com; Mile 1, Gustavus Rd; r $225, with shared bath $215; ☜☜) This longtime Gustavus favorite is a charming family homestead lodge mentioned in every travel book on Alaska, with good reason. It's thoroughly modern and comfortable but without being sterile or losing its folksy touch. The all-inclusive inn is well known for its gourmet dinners, which feature homegrown vegetables and fresh local seafood served family-style. Even if you can't afford to stay at the inn, book a seat at its dinner table one night.

There are also a few sleeping and eating options in Bartlett Cove.

NPS Campground This NPS facility a quarter-mile south of Glacier Bay Lodge is set in a lush forest just off the shoreline, and camping is free. There's no need for reservations; there always seems to be space. It provides a bear cache and warming shelter. Coin-operated showers are available in the park, but there's no place to buy groceries or camping supplies.

Glacier Bay Lodge (☎888-229-8687; www.visitglacierbay.com; 199 Bartlett Cove Rd; $199-224) This is the only hotel and restaurant in Bartlett Cove. The lodge has 55 rooms, a crackling fire in a huge stone fireplace, and a dining room that usually hums in the evening. Nightly slide presentations, ranger talks and movies held upstairs cover the park's natural history.

Sunnyside Market (☎907-697-3060; Dock Rd; ☺9am-6pm; ☜) This bright market and cafe is your one-stop choice for organic sundries, deli sandwiches and breakfast burritos. On Saturday there's an artsy market.

Fireweed Gallery (4 Corners, Gustavus Rd; pastries $3-6) You're there because it's the best coffee in Gustavus (and a whole lot of Alaska's Southeast) and serves freshly baked goods, but the local art is definitely easy on the eyes.

Getting There & Around

If you arrive at the Gustavus airport, you're still 9 miles from Bartlett Cove. The Glacier Bay Lodge bus meets all Alaska Airlines flights; it's free for guests and $15 for folks on Glacier Bay tours. **TLC Taxi** (☎907-697-2239) meets most ferry arrivals and also charges $15 per person for a trip to Bartlett Cove.

Air

Alaska Airlines (☎800-252-7522; www.alaskaair.com) Offers the only jet service, with a daily 25-minute trip from Juneau to Gustavus.

Alaska Seaplanes (☎907-789-3331; www.flyalaskaseaplanes.com) Has several flights per day between Gustavus and Juneau for $99 one way.

Boat

The cheapest way to reach Gustavus is via the **Alaska Marine Highway** (☎800-642-0066; www.ferryalaska.com). Several times a week the MV *LeConte* makes the round-trip run from Juneau to Gustavus (one way $35, 3½ hours) along a route that often features whale sightings.

STATE
Alaska

ENTRANCE FEE
Free

AREA
6400 sq miles

GOOD FOR

Coastal brown bear, Katmai National Park

Katmai National Park

In a national park the size of Wales, stand spine-tinglingly close to the main attraction here, 1000lb brown bears, utilizing their formidable ursine power to paw giant salmon out of the river.

Humans have lived in Katmai on the northern Alaska Peninsula for at least 9000 years, sharing the unusual volcanic landscape with wildlife including brown bears, moose, foxes, great-horned owls, bald eagles, and waterways with salmon and rainbow trout. Unconnected to the main Alaskan road network and covering an area the size of Wales, Katmai National Park is a destination for travelers seeking privacy and solitude, backcountry hiking, kayaking and paddling – plus the spectacle of salmon-trapping brown bears, epic sportfishing potential and volcanic landscapes.

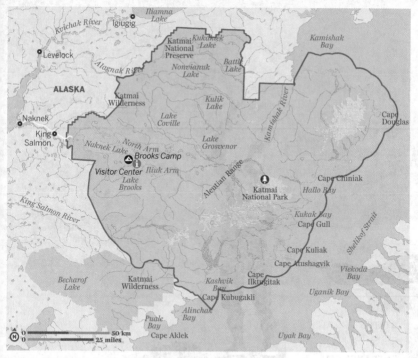

Bear Watching

Brooks Camp has three established bear-watching areas. Watch bears feeding in the mouth of the river or swimming in the bay, or photograph the salmon making spectacular leaps or a big brownie at the top of the cascade waiting with open jaws to catch a fish. At the peak of the salmon run from late June through July and September through mid-October, there might be eight to 12 bears here, two or three of them atop the falls themselves.

Hiking

Hiking and backpacking are the best ways to see the park's unusual backcountry. Like Denali National Park in Alaska's Interior, Katmai has few formal trails; backpackers follow river bars, lake shores, gravel ridges and other natural routes.

Paddling

Kayaks are the overwhelming choice for most paddlers due to high winds blowing across big lakes, and possible rough water. Accomplished paddlers should have no problem, but the conditions can sometimes get dicey for novices.

Getting There & Away

Most visitors to Katmai fly into King Salmon on **Alaska Airlines** (☎800-252-7522; www.alaskaair.com); once you're there, a number of air-taxi companies offer the 20-minute floatplane flight out to Brooks Camp.

Valley of Ten Thousand Smokes

The peculiar landscape of this trippy valley is the result of a 1912 double volcano. It covered the area in a rain of ash and opened up countless smoke vents, which jetted hot steam skyward. The post-apocalyptic spectacle served as Katmai's original raison d'être and led to the area being declared a national monument in 1918. These days, the notably less smoky valley plays second fiddle to Katmai's bear viewing, but can still be visited on a daily bus ride from Brooks Camp.

STATE
Alaska

ENTRANCE FEE
Free

AREA
1685 sq miles

GOOD FOR

Stand-up paddle boarding

Kenai Fjords National Park

Crowning this park is the massive Harding Ice Field; from it, countless tidewater glaciers pour down, carving the coast into dizzying fjords. With such a landscape – and an abundance of marine wildlife to boot – the park is a major tourist attraction.

Glorious Kenai Fjords National Park encompasses tidewater glaciers that pour down from one of the continent's largest ice fields, as well as the steep-sided fjords those glaciers have carved. Abutting the park in places, and taking in much of the most southerly part of the Kenai Peninsula, is Kachemak Bay State Park, a wondrous land of mountains, forests and fjords. Kenai is also home to boat-cruising opportunities for spectacular whale- and marine-wildlife spotting,

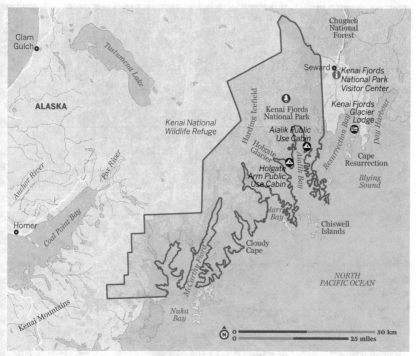

Activities

Paddle through the fjords and you might be treated to the thunder of calving tidewater glaciers, the honking and splashing of sea lions at a haul-out, or the cacophony of a kittiwake rookery. Near Peterson Glacier you might find plump harbor seals bobbing on glacier ice or breaching whales at the mouth of Resurrection Bay. Getting an orca's-eye view of this rich marine ecosystem is just one of the many rewards of propelling yourself through the rocking waters of Kenai Fjords.

Kenai National Wildlife Refuge offers excellent canoeing and hiking routes, plus some of the world's best salmon fishing. On the west side, the land flattens out into a marshy, lake-pocked region excellent for canoeing and trout fishing.

Sleeping

Public-Use Cabins (www. nps.gov/kefj/; cabins $65) There are two cabins along the fjords, as well as countless other informal campsites that line the kayak-accessible beaches of Aialik Bay and Northwestern Lagoon. Aialik Bay Cabin is on a beach that's perfect for hiking, beachcombing and whale watching; Holgate Cabin has a spectacular view of Holgate Glacier. You'll want to reserve these well in advance through the **Alaska Public Lands Information Center** (☎907-644-3661).

Alaska's Glaciers

One of the most spectacular sights is watching – and hearing – tidewater glaciers 'calve' icebergs (the act of releasing small to massive chunks of glacier). Tidewater glaciers extend from a land base into the sea (or a lake) and calve icebergs in massive explosions of water. Active tidewater glaciers can be viewed from tour boats in Glacier Bay National Park, Kenai Fjords National Park and Prince William Sound, which has the largest collection in Alaska.

1. Olympic National Park
2. Caribou near Gates of the Arctic National Park
3. Denali (Mt McKinley)

Alaska's Historical Monuments

Sitka National Historical Park

Sitka's Lincoln St ends at this 113-acre park at the site where the Tlingits were finally defeated by the Russians in 1804.

Totem Trail leads you 1 mile past 18 totems first displayed at the 1904 Louisiana Exposition in St Louis and then moved to the park. It is these intriguing totems, standing in a beautiful rainforest setting by the sea and often enveloped in mist, that have become synonymous with the national park and even the city itself.

Eventually you arrive at the site of the Tlingit fort near Indian River, where its outline can still be seen. You can either explore the trail as a self-guided tour or join a ranger-led 'Battle Walk.'

Here, the Tlingits defended their wooden fort for a week. The Russians' cannons did little damage to the walls of the Tlingit fort and, when the Russian soldiers stormed the structure with the help of Aleuts, they were repulsed in a bloody battle. It was only when the Tlingits ran out of gunpowder and flint, and slipped away at night, that the Russians were able to enter the deserted fort.

The visitor center displays Russian and indigenous artifacts, and a 12-minute video in the theater provides an overview of the Tlingit and Russian battle. You can also dial into a cell-phone tour that will guide you through the park and center.

Aleutian WWII National Historic Area, Unalaska

In 1996 Congress created this 134-acre national historic area to commemorate the bloody events of WWII that took place on the Aleutian Islands.

To learn about the 'Forgotten War,' begin at the Aleutian WWII Visitor Center, near the airport, in the original air-control tower built in 1942. Downstairs, exhibits relive the Aleutian campaign, including the bombing of Dutch Harbor by the Japanese. Upstairs is the re-created air-control tower, and in a theater you can watch documentaries about the war.

Most of the park preserves Fort Schwatka, on Mt Ballyhoo, the highest coastal battery ever constructed in the US. Looming nearly 1000ft above the storm-tossed waters of the Bering Sea, the Army fort encompassed more than 100 concrete observation posts, command stations and other structures built to withstand earthquakes and 100mph winds. The gun mounts here are still among the best preserved in the country, and include tunnels and bunkers that allowed gunners to cart ammunition from one side of the mountain to the other.

The 1634ft mountain of military artifacts is behind the airport and can be reached on foot or by vehicle via Ulakta Rd, picked up half a mile north of the ferry terminal, along Ballyhoo Rd. If on foot, the gravel road is an hour's climb to the top, but the views of Unalaska Island on the way up, and on top, are excellent. Pick up the free *Fort Schwatka Self-Guided Tour* brochure at the visitor center.

Iñupiat Heritage Center, Barrow

This 24,000-sq-ft facility houses a museum, gift shop and a large multipurpose room where short traditional dancing-and-drumming

performances take place each afternoon. Local craftspeople often assemble in the lobby to sell masks, whalebone carvings and fur garments and are happy to talk about craft and technique.

In the center's galleries, displays include everything from poster-sized, black-and-white portraits of local elders to a 35ft-long replica of a bowhead skeleton to a detailed (and artifact-rich) breakdown of traditional whaling culture and hunting practices.

Klondike Gold Rush National Historical Park, Skagway

The NPS center is in the original 1898 White Pass & Yukon Route depot. The center features displays – the most impressive being a replica of the ton of supplies every miner had to carry over the Chilkoot Pass – plus ranger programs and a small bookstore. The 25-minute film *Gold Fever: Race to the Klondike*, an excellent introduction to the gold rush, is shown on the hour.

Rangers lead a free 50-minute walking tour of the historic district from early May to late September, on the hour from 9am to 11am and at 2pm and 3pm; call to see if there are extra tours.

1. Klondike Gold Rush National Historical Park
2. Totem poles, Sitka National Historical Park

STATE
Alaska

ENTRANCE FEE
Free

AREA
5625 sq miles

GOOD FOR

Stream crossing, Lake Clark National Park

Lake Clark National Park

Lake Clark National Park and Preserve features spectacular scenery that is a composite of Alaska: an awesome array of tundra-covered hills, mountains, glaciers, coastline, the largest lakes in the state, and two active volcanoes.

Despite its overwhelming scenery and close proximity to Alaska's largest city Anchorage, fewer than 5000 visitors a year make it to this 5625-sq-mile preserve. The centrepiece of the park is spectacular Lake Clark, a 42-mile-long turquoise body of water ringed by mountains.

But the park is also where the Alaska Range merges into the Aleutian Range to form the Chigmit Mountains, and is home to two volcanoes: Mt Iliamna and Mt Redoubt. Hiking is phenomenal, but Lake Clark is best suited to the experienced backpacker.

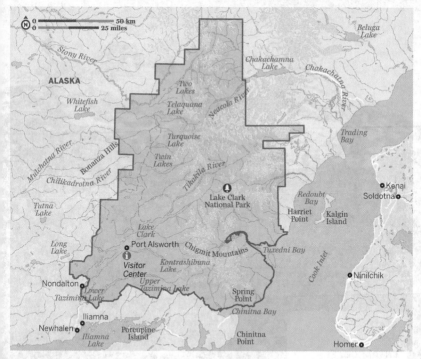

Getting Around

The **NPS Park Headquarters** (☎907-644-3626; www. nps.gov/lacl; 240 West 5th Ave, Ste 236, Anchorage; ⏱8am-5pm Mon-Fri) is the best source of information for pretrip planning.

Port Alsworth, the main entry point for the park, has a **ranger station** (☎907-781-2117; ⏱daily late May–mid-Sep) where you'll find information on both the 50-mile historic **Telaquana Trail** and **Twin Lakes**, where dry tundra slopes provide easy travel to ridges and great views.

Activities

The park is a wilderness playground for rafters, anglers and hikers. Float trips down any of the three designated wild rivers (the Chilikadrotna, Tlikakila and Mulchatna) are spectacular and exciting, with waterways rated from Class III to Class IV. The best way to handle a boat rental is through **Alaska Raft & Kayak** (☎907-561-7238, 800-606-5950; www. alaskaraftandkayak.com; 401 W Tudor Rd, Anchorage; ⏱10am-6pm Mon-Sat), which rents out inflatable sea kayaks and canoes (per day $75) and 14ft to 16ft rafts (per day $100).

Alaska Marine Highway Ferry

The easiest way to see 'Bush Alaska' without flying is to hop onto the Alaska Marine Highway ferry on its route to the eastern end of the Aleutian Islands between May and September. The scenery and wildlife on this route are spectacular. You'll pass the perfect cones of several volcanoes, the treeless but lush green mountains of the Aleutians, and distinctive rock formations and cliffs. Whales, sea lions, otters and porpoises are commonly sighted, and birdlife abounds (more than 250 species). Viewing wildlife and scenery depends, however, on the weather. It can be an extremely rough trip at times, deserving its title 'the cruise through the cradle of the storms.' The smoothest runs are from June to August, while in the fall 40ft waves and 80-knot winds are the norm.

STATE
Washington

ENTRANCE FEE
7-day pass per vehicle $25

AREA
368 sq miles

GOOD FOR

Mount Rainier

Mount Rainier National Park

Emblazoned on every Washington license plate and visible throughout much of the western state, Mt Rainier (elevation 14,411ft) is the USA's fourth-highest peak (outside Alaska) and, in the eyes of many, its most awe-inspiring.

Long home to the Puyallup and Nisqually Coast Salish tribes who exploited its rivers for fish, Mt Rainier was first spotted and named by Europeans in 1792.

Pathfinder of the modern conservationist movement, John Muir climbed Mt Rainier in 1888 and it was largely due to his efforts that it was made America's fifth national park in 1899.

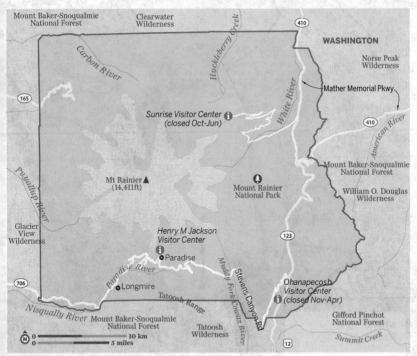

Mount Rainier National Park has four entrances. The busiest and most convenient gate, Nisqually, lies on Hwy 706 via Ashford, near the park's southwest corner. It's open year-round.

Longmire, 7 miles inside the Nisqually entrance, has a **museum and information center** (☏360-569-6575; ⏰9am-4:30pm), a number of important trailheads, and the rustic **National Park Inn** (☏360-569-2275; www.mtrainierguestservices.com; r with shared/private bath from $119/169, units $252; ⏰year-round; P❄), complete with an excellent restaurant.

More hikes and interpretive walks can be found 12 miles further east at loftier Paradise, which is served by the informative **Henry M Jackson Visitor Center** (☏360-569-6571; ⏰10am-7pm daily Jun-Sep, 10am-5pm Sat & Sun Oct-May), and the vintage **Paradise Inn** (☏360-569-2275; www.mtrainierguestservices.com; r with shared/private bath from $122/194; ⏰May-Oct), a historic 'parkitecture' inn constructed in 1916. Climbs to the top of Rainier leave from the inn.

The three other entrances are Ohanapecosh, via Hwy 123 and accessed via the town of Packwood, where lodging is available; White River, off Hwy 410, which literally takes the high road (6400ft) to the beautiful viewpoint at the **Sunrise Lodge Cafeteria** (snacks $6-9; ⏰10am-7pm Jul & Aug); and remote Carbon River in the northwest corner, which gives access to the park's inland rainforest.

Camping

Campgrounds in the park have running water and toilets, but no showers or RV hookups. Reservations at park **campgrounds** (☏877-444-6777; www.recreation.gov; campsites $20) are strongly advised during summer months. For overnight backcountry trips, you'll need a wilderness permit; check the National Park Service website for details.

The NPS website also has downloadable maps and descriptions of dozens of park trails.

STATE
Washington

ENTRANCE FEE
Free

AREA
788 sq miles

GOOD FOR

Chilliwack River Valley

North Cascades National Park

The wildest of all Pacific Northwest wildernesses, the lightly trodden North Cascades National Park has no settlements, no overnight accommodations and only one unpaved road.

The names of the dramatic mountains here pretty much set the tone: Desolation Peak, Jagged Ridge, Mt Despair and Mt Terror.

The region contains an astounding 300 glaciers and offers some of the best back-country adventures outside of Alaska.

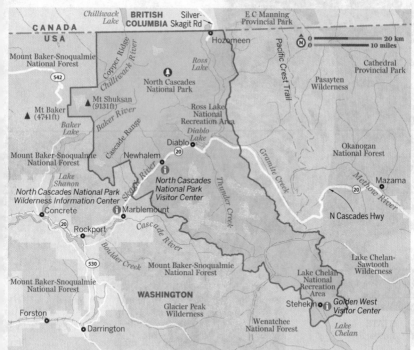

The wild and rugged North Cascades National Park is the largest of the three parks in the North Cascades National Park Service Complex.

The **North Cascades Visitor Center** (📞206-386-4495, ext 11; 502 Newhalem St, Newhalem; 🕒9am-6pm Jun-Sep, reduced hours Oct-May), in the small settlement of Newhalem on Hwy 20, is the best orientation point for visitors and is staffed by expert rangers who can enlighten you on the park's highlights. Throughout the summer, North Cascades offers ranger-led walks and talks, and interpretive programs in various locations.

Built in the 1930s for loggers working in the valley which was soon to be flooded by Ross Dam, the floating cabins at the **Ross Lake Resort** (📞206-386-4437; www.rosslakeresort.com; 503 Diablo St, Rockport; cabins $175-350; 🕒mid-Jun-late Oct) on the eponymous lake's west side are the state's most unique accommodations. There's no road in – guests can either hike the 2-mile trail from Hwy 20 or take the resort's tugboat-taxi-and-truck shuttle from the parking area near Diablo Dam.

Getting There

Primary access to the park is from the Hwy 20 corridor. The Silver-Skagit Road and State Route 542 (SR 542) are entry points for many of the park's northern regions including Hozomeen, Mount Shuksan and Copper Ridge.

Camping

Campsites are available on a first-come, first-served basis ($16 per night fee for Colonial Creek, Goodell Creek and Newhalem Creek campgrounds). Gorge Lake and Hozomeen campgrounds are free. A free permit is required for backcountry camping.

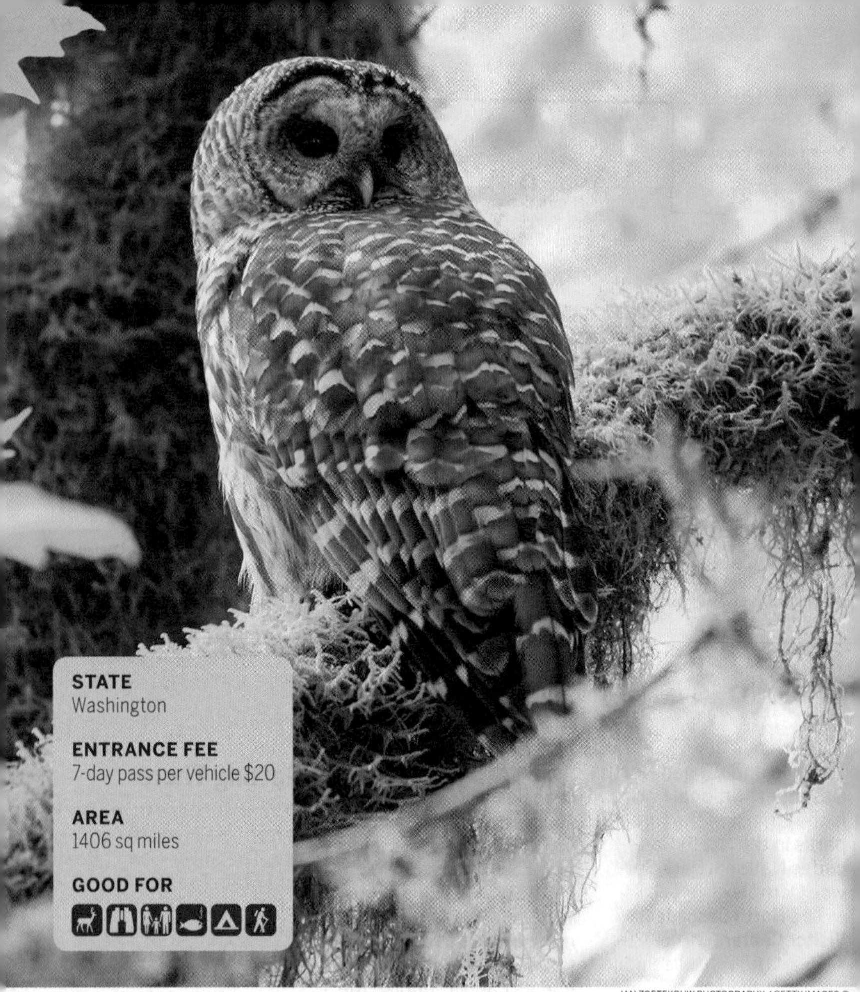

STATE
Washington

ENTRANCE FEE
7-day pass per vehicle $20

AREA
1406 sq miles

GOOD FOR

Barred owl, Olympic National Park

JAN ZOETEKOUW PHOTOGRAPHY / GETTY IMAGES ©

Olympic National Park

Home to one of the world's only temperate rainforests and a 57-mile strip of Pacific coastal wilderness, this notoriously wet national park is as 'wild' and 'west' as it gets.

Ocean and rainforest meet in aqueous harmony in Olympic National Park, which was declared a national monument in 1909 and a national park in 1938. Isolated by distance and home of one of the country's rainiest microclimates, the Pacific side of the park remains the wildest. Opportunities for independent exploration abound, with activities from hiking and fishing to kayaking and skiing.

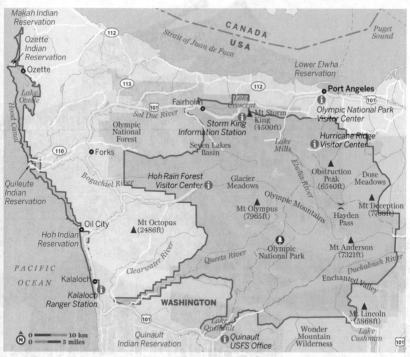

The park's easiest entry point is at Hurricane Ridge, 18 miles south of Port Angeles. At the road's end, an interpretive center gives a stupendous view of Mt Olympus (7965ft) and dozens of other peaks. The 5200ft altitude can mean you'll hit inclement weather, and the winds here can be ferocious.

The temperate rainforests and untamed coastline of the wild Pacific side of the Olympics can be accessed by the US 101. The Hoh Rainforest is a Tolkienesque maze of dripping ferns and moss-draped trees. The **Hoh Visitor Center and Campground** (☎360-374-6925; ⏰9am-5pm) has information on guided walks and longer backcountry hikes. There are no hookups or show-

ers, and it's first-come, first-served.

Lake Quinault, a beautiful glacial lake surrounded by forested peaks, lies in the park's south. It's popular for fishing, boating and swimming, and is surrounded by some of the nation's oldest trees.

Medium-grade, 13-mile Enchanted Valley Trail begins from the Graves Creek ranger station at the end of South Shore Rd and climbs up to a large meadow resplendent with wildflowers and alder trees.

Sleeping

Popular for boating and fishing, Lake Crescent is the site of the park's oldest and most reasonably priced **lodge** (☎888-896-3818; www.olympicnationalparks.com;

416 Lake Crescent Rd; lodge r/ cabins from $120/260).

Two state parks (with running water and flush toilets) along the eastern edge of the national park are popular with campers: **Dosewallips State Park** (☎888-226-7688; www.parks.wa.gov; 306996 Hwy 101; tent sites $12-35, RV sites $30-45) and **Lake Cushman State Park** (☎888-226-7688; campsites $15-66).

Information

Olympic National Park Visitor Center (☎360-565-3130; www.nps.gov/olym; 3002 Mt Angeles Rd, Port Angeles) The best overall center is situated at the Hurricane Ridge gateway, a mile off Hwy 101 in Port Angeles. Hours vary.

STATE
Alaska

ENTRANCE FEE
Free

AREA
20,625 sq miles

GOOD FOR

Mine buildings in Kennecott

CHRISBOSWELL / GETTY IMAGES ©

Wrangell-St Elias National Park

Comprising more than 20,000 sq miles of brawny ice-encrusted mountains, this is the second-largest national park in the world, meaning there's plenty of room for its 45,000-or-so annual visitors to get lost – very, very lost.

The park's vital statistics are mind-boggling. If Wrangell-St Elias were a country it would be larger than 70 of the world's independent nations. Its biggest glacier covers an area larger than the US state of Rhode Island. Plenty of its mountain peaks have never been climbed. And that's even before you've started counting the wildlife.

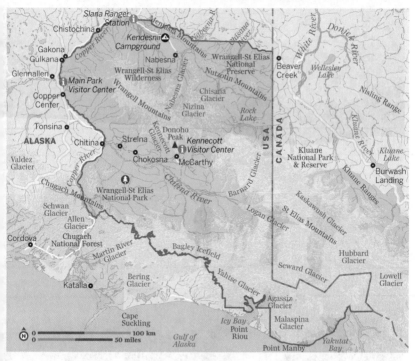

For every eight tourists who track north to Denali National Park, only one intrepid traveler tackles the little-known wilderness of Wrangell. Why? Good question. Granted, most of the park is desolate and doesn't have the infrastructure or satellite towns of Denali, though it does support one small settlement, **McCarthy** (seven hours by road from Anchorage), along with some improbable copper-mining history preserved for posterity by the National Park Service in nearby **Kennecott**.

So, how do you tackle such an immense place? Ninety-five per cent of visitors enter the park via the tiny, off-the-grid settlements of McCarthy and Kennecott, accessible by bush plane or a single unpaved road that branches off the Richardson Hwy near **Copper Center**. Between them, these hamlets have several eating establishments, a store and a hardy year-round population of around 40 people who practice subsistence hunting and grow their own vegetables. Popular activities in the area include glacier hiking, ice climbing and historical tours of Kennecott's mine buildings.

Hiking

Unlike Denali, you don't need a backcountry permit for overnight hikes, but you are encouraged to leave an itinerary at any of the ranger stations, where you can also get advice and pick up a bear canister for your trip. There's a refundable deposit required for the canister.

The visitor center in Kennecott has maps and information on day and overnight hikes.

How big?

Wrangell-St Elias is the largest national park in the US and second only in the world stakes to Northeast Greenland. It's the size of Switzerland, Yosemite and Yellowstone National Parks all in one. It stretches from one of the tallest peaks in North America, Mt St Elias, all the way to the ocean.

Hikers on Root Glacier

Nabesna Road

For connoisseurs of roads less traveled, Alaska offers few lonelier motorways than the Nabesna Rd, jutting 42 miles south from the Tok Cutoff into the northern reaches of Wrangell-St Elias National Park.

Turning onto the Nabesna Rd, you'll find yourself in a place the signs call Slana (population 124). Somewhere back through the trees there's an Alaska Natives settlement on the northern banks of the Slana River, where fish wheels still scoop salmon during the summer run. Before continuing, stop in at the NPS Slana ranger station, where you can get info about road conditions and hikes, purchase USGS maps, peruse displays and collect the free *The K'elt'aeni*, the official guide to Wrangell-St Elias National Park, which has a Nabesna Road Guide section.

In the 4 miles between the ranger station and the park entrance you'll pass a handful of accommodations. Upon entering the park proper, the Nabesna Rd turns to gravel. It's manageable in a 2WD vehicle for the first 29 miles, but after that several streams flow over it, making it impassable in high water (check at the ranger station for the latest on road conditions).

There are literally two full folders of hiking options.

If you're on the Nabesna Rd, for a relatively easy hike, try the 3-mile **Caribou Creek Trail** (Mile 19.2, Nabesna Rd), which ascends 800ft from Nabesna Rd to a dilapidated cabin with unbeatable views of the surrounding peaks.

A tougher walk is the 2.5-mile **Skookum Volcano Trail** (Mile 36.2, Nabesna Rd), which climbs 1800ft through a deeply eroded volcanic system, ending at a high alpine pass frequented by Dall sheep.

Popular overnight hikes include Donoho Peak, Erie Lake and McCarthy Creek.

Tours

Some of the best outfitters and guides in the state operate in Wrangell-St Elias.

One of the best guiding companies is **St Elias Alpine Guides** (☏ 888-933-5427; www.steliasguides.com; Motherlode Powerhouse, McCarthy). It leads great Kennecott Mill Town tours ($25), half-day hikes on Root Glacier ($75), ice climbing ($130), or a whole stash of truly adventurous stuff, including first ascents of unclimbed mountain summits. It's based in McCarthy with another office in Kennecott.

The other local guiding firm, also extremely experienced, is **Kennicott Wilderness Guides** (☏ 907-554-4444; www.kennicottguides.com; Main St, Kennecott). It offers small-group ice climbing and glacier excursions from $75, and a wide variety of multiday hiking trips.

For a full-day float along the Kennicott, Nizina and Chitina Rivers, and a trip through the vertical-walled Nizina Canyon, returning to McCarthy by bush plane, try **Copper Oar** (☏ 800-523-4453; www.copperoar.com; Motherlode Powerhouse, McCarthy). It offers this popular trip ($295 per person, two-person minimum) from June through August. The company also offers multiday paddles, glacier and alpine hikes. It's affiliated with St Elias Alpine Guides.

For scenic flights or a backcountry drop, **Wrangell Mountain Air** (☏ 907-554-4411; www.wrangellmountainair.com; Main St, McCarthy) has a fantastic reputation. Flights cost from $110 (35 minutes) to $255 (1½ hours) per person (two-person minimum).

Bush plane flying over a glacier

When to Go

The best time to visit is early June to mid-September. Winter arrives early to interior Alaska. By the end of September there is usually snow on the ground. From 15 September, services and facilities are few.

Access & Information

You can enter to park via two (dirt) roads: the Nabesna Rd and the McCarthy Rd.

There is no entrance gate to the park and technically it doesn't close, but the main visitor center (Copper Center) does close and lock its parking gates each night. No overnight parking is allowed.

There are no fuel options in the park, or along the Nabesna or McCarthy Rds. Be prepared and travel with a full tank.

Cell-phone coverage in the park is limited.

Visitor Centers

The park's main visitor information point is the **Copper Center Visitor Center Complex** (☏907 822-7250; Mile 106.8 Richardson Hwy; Mon-Fri, year-round; ⊙9am-6pm daily mid-May–mid-Sep, shorter hours Oct & Apr, closed Nov-Mar). The center is 10 miles south of Glennallen and approximately 200 miles east of Anchorage, and 250 miles south of Fairbanks. Call the visitor center for opening hours as they vary seasonally.

Slana Ranger Station (☏907-822-7401; Mile 0.5 Nabesna Rd) Located in the north of the park, two hours from the main visitor center in Copper Center.

Kennecott Visitor Center (☏907-554-1105; Kennecott Mill Town; ⊙closed in winter) Located 5 miles from McCarthy.

McCarthy Road Information Station (Mile 59 on the McCarthy Rd; ⊙closed in winter)

Sleeping

There are cabins, lodges, B&Bs, and campgrounds in and around Wrangell-St Elias. It's also possible to make camp on public land or pullouts along the Nabesna and McCarthy Rds.

At Mile 28.2, **Kendesnii Campground** (☏907-822-5234; campsites free) is the only official NPS campground in the park. It's remote and has 10 sites and vault toilets. Maintenance ends at Mile 42, though a rough track continues 4 miles to the private Nabesna Gold Mine, a national historic site.

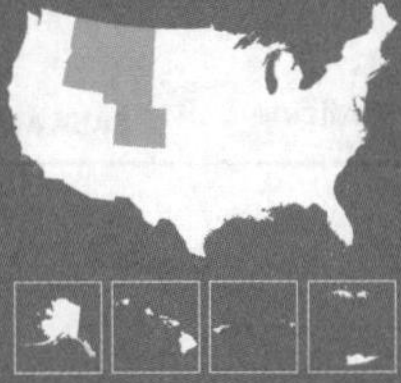

Rocky Mountains

Wildflower-strewn meadows and jagged peaks form the backbone of the continent along the Great Divide. Equally rich in wildlife, untrammeled wilderness and Wild West history, the Rockies continue to embody the spirit of the American frontier, and the range's parks remain among the country's most prized.

The parks are separated by over a thousand miles – you likely won't visit them all in a single road trip, but you can definitely pair them together. Yellowstone, the world's first national park, remains the superstar, with primordial geysers and mega wildlife sightings at every turn. Grand Teton, Glacier and Rocky Mountain reward those in search of top-of-the-world vistas and alpine adventure, while far to the south of Colorado is the region's most curious sight – the mirage-like Great Sand Dunes.

Bison, Grand Teton National Park
MARK NEWMAN / DESIGN PICS / GETTY IMAGES ©

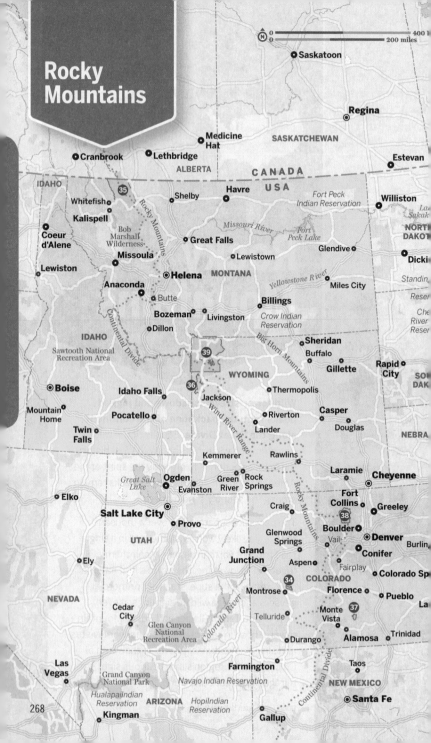

Rocky Mountains

0   400 km
0   200 miles

Saskatoon

Regina

Medicine Hat
Cranbrook
Lethbridge
SASKATCHEWAN
Estevan
ALBERTA
IDAHO
CANADA
USA
Whitefish
Shelby
Havre
Fort Peck Indian Reservation
Williston
La Sakak
Kalispell
NORTH DAKOTA
Coeur d'Alene
Bob Marshall Wilderness
Missouri River
Fort Peck Lake
Dicki
Great Falls
Glendive
Lewiston
Missoula
Lewistown
Standin
Helena
MONTANA
Yellowstone River
Rese
Anaconda
Miles City
Che River Rese
Butte
Billings
Bozeman
Livingston
Crow Indian Reservation
Dillon
Sheridan
Big Horn Mountains
Buffalo
IDAHO
Sawtooth National Recreation Area
Continental Divide
Gillette
Rapid City
SOU DAK
Boise
WYOMING
Idaho Falls
Thermopolis
Mountain Home
Jackson
Pocatello
Wind River Range
Riverton
Casper
Lander
Douglas
Twin Falls
NEBRA
Kemmerer
Rawlins
Laramie
Cheyenne
Elko
Ogden
Green River
Rock Springs
Great Salt Lake
Evanston
Fort Collins
Salt Lake City
Provo
Craig
Greeley
UTAH
Boulder
Denver
Burlin
Glenwood Springs
Vail
Ely
Conifer
Grand Junction
Aspen
Fairplay
Colorado Sp
COLORADO
Montrose
Florence
Pueblo
Cedar City
Telluride
Monte Vista
La
Nevada
Glen Canyon National Recreation Area
Colorado River
Durango
Alamosa
Trinidad
Las Vegas
Farmington
Taos
Grand Canyon National Park
Navajo Indian Reservation
NEW MEXICO
Hualapai Indian Reservation
ARIZONA
Hopi Indian Reservation
Santa Fe
Continental Divide
Kingman
Gallup

❸❹ Black Canyon of the Gunnison National Park

A dramatic volcanic chasm with almighty and fast-flowing waterways. (p280)

❸❺ Glacier National Park

Snow-blanketed ridges and glacier-sculpted horns towering over lakes and meadows blanketed in wildflowers. (p282)

❸❻ Grand Teton National Park

Picture-postcard alpine scenery and arguably the nation's most iconic mountain range. (p294)

❸❼ Great Sand Dunes National Park

An alien landscape of jagged peaks, arid scrub brush and lots and lots of sand. (p306)

❸❽ Rocky Mountain National Park

Sprawling range of snowcapped peaks, plus golden aspens, rampant rivers and inquisitive wildlife. (p312)

❸❾ Yellowstone National Park

Steaming geysers galore and surprise wildlife encounters. (p318)

DON'T MISS

Natural Wonders & Wildlife

Spot bears, bison and geysers at **Yellowstone National Park**.

Hiking

Climb the craggy wilderness of **Grand Teton National Park**.

Desertscapes

Roam the high desertscapes of **Great Sand Dunes National Park**.

Going-to-the-Sun Rd

Drive this spectacularly scenic road in **Glacier National Park**.

Longs Peak

Scale the peak or just ogle its glaciated slopes from below in **Rocky Mountain National Park**.

Grand Prismatic Spring Watch out for spurting geysers and bubbling mudpots

Classic Trip

Grand Teton to Yellowstone

Iconic Yellowstone and Grand Teton may be our closest connections to wild America. Take a hike under the sublime Teton spires and witness spurting geysers, herds of bison and howling wolves.

TRIP HIGHLIGHTS

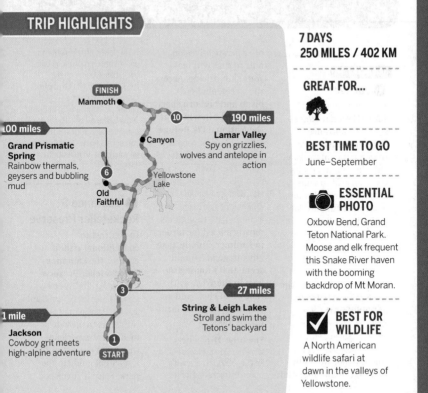

FINISH
Mammoth

10 — **190 miles**

Canyon

Lamar Valley
Spy on grizzlies, wolves and antelope in action

100 miles

Grand Prismatic Spring
Rainbow thermals, geysers and bubbling mud

6

Old Faithful

Yellowstone Lake

3 — **27 miles**

String & Leigh Lakes
Stroll and swim the Tetons' backyard

1 mile

Jackson
Cowboy grit meets high-alpine adventure

1

START

7 DAYS
250 MILES / 402 KM

GREAT FOR...

BEST TIME TO GO
June–September

ESSENTIAL PHOTO

Oxbow Bend, Grand Teton National Park. Moose and elk frequent this Snake River haven with the booming backdrop of Mt Moran.

BEST FOR WILDLIFE

A North American wildlife safari at dawn in the valleys of Yellowstone.

271

Grand Teton to Yellowstone

A life-list must, Yellowstone is nature's *tour de force*. On view are herds of bison, lumbering grizzlies and packs of wolves. Yellowstone's unique supervolcano features half the world's geysers, the country's largest high-altitude lake and a mass of blue-ribbon rivers and waterfalls. To the south, Grand Teton National Park complements with craggy peaks, peaceful waterways and sublime alpine terrain prime for exploration.

TRIP HIGHLIGHT

❶ Jackson

Just south of Grand Teton National Park's southern entrance, Jackson is much more than a park gateway. A chic destination on its own, this ski town is also a summer stunner, with plentiful outdoor activities, galleries and a shopping scene that reaches beyond trinketry, with cool boutiques and tailored outdoor gear. Don't skip the **National Museum of Wildlife Art** (☏307-733-5771; www.wildlifeart. org; 2820 Rungius Rd; adult/ child $12/6; ⊙9am-5pm), where major works by Remington and Bierstadt

offer perspectives on nature that will make your skin prickle. Across the street, elk herds, bison and bighorn sheep congregate in winter at the **National Elk Refuge** (☏307-733-9212; www.fws. gov/nationalelkrefuge; Hwy 89; horse-drawn sleigh ride adult/ child $18/14; ⊙8am-5pm Sep-May, 8am-7pm Jun-Aug, horse-drawn sleigh ride 10am-4pm mid-Dec–Mar), though it's mostly a feast for birders in summer. Finally, take advantage of a foodie scene that's among the best in the West, with renowned chefs and an emphasis on local, farm-raised food.

The Drive » From Jackson take Rte 22 to the Moose-Wilson Rd (Rte 390), so narrow it's closed to trucks and trailers.

Drive slowly; grizzly sightings are not uncommon along this back road. A booth on the roadway marks the **Granite Canyon Entrance** (⊙7-day permit per vehicle $25) to Grand Teton National Park. Pay your entry fee here. Turn into the Laurance S Rockefeller Preserve on your right, 16 miles from Jackson.

❷ Laurance S Rockefeller Preserve

In contrast to conventional visitor centers, the **Laurance S Rockefeller Preserve Center** (☏307-739-3654; Moose-Wilson Rd; ⊙8am-6pm Jun-Aug, 9am-5pm rest of year) aims to provide a meditative experience that turns out not unlike a spiritual guide to the park. Sparely furnished

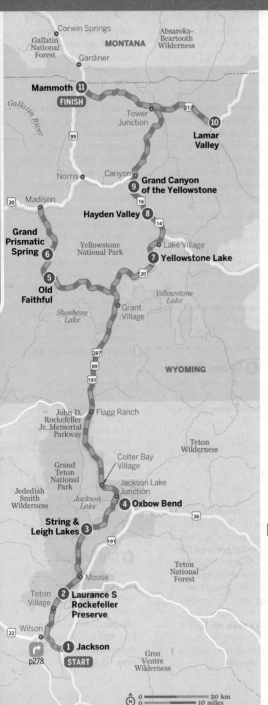

Corwin Springs

Gallatin
National
Forest

MONTANA

Absaroka-
Beartooth
Wilderness

Gardiner

Mammoth **11**
FINISH

Gallatin River

Tower
Junction

212

10
**Lamar
Valley**

Norris

Canyon

**Grand Canyon
of the Yellowstone**

89

Madison

20

16

9

Yellowstone
National
Park

Hayden Valley 8

14

Lake Village

**Grand
Prismatic
Spring 6**

5

**Old
Faithful**

Shoshone
Lake

20

7 Yellowstone Lake

Yellowstone
Lake

Grant
Village

287

89

191

WYOMING

John D.
Rockefeller
Jr. Memorial
Parkway

Flagg Ranch

Teton
Wilderness

Grand
Teton
National
Park

Jedediah
Smith
Wilderness

Colter Bay
Village

Jackson Lake
Junction

Jackson
Lake

4 Oxbow Bend

26

**String &
Leigh Lakes 3**

191

Teton
National
Forest

Moose

**2 Laurance S
Rockefeller
Preserve**

Teton
Village

Wilson

22

1 Jackson
START

p278

Gros
Ventre
Wilderness

N

0   20 km
0   10 miles

and LEED certified, it sets the scene for your foray into nature, with great quotes from naturalists etched into the walls and a gorgeous conservation library with oversized titles best enjoyed from the leather armchairs.

From here, you might take an easy stroll to **Phelps Lake**. The 7-mile loop takes about 3.5 hours. If you just have two hours, and your swimsuit, make your goal Jump Rock. A 24ft drop into clear cobalt water, it's a favorite of swimmers and picnickers, located about an hour in on the trail.

The Drive » The road ends in 4 miles at Teton Park Rd. Go left for the Moose entrance booth or go right for the Craig Thomas Visitor Center or Dornan's. Teton Park Rd runs parallel to a newly constructed cycling path that starts in Jackson (ending at Jenny Lake). Drive slowly, as wildlife are often on the road. Take advantage of the numerous scenic overlooks on the left side of the road. Turn left for Leigh and String Lake trailheads; continue on the same one-way loop for the scenic drive to Jenny Lake.

TRIP HIGHLIGHT

❸ String & Leigh Lakes

In **Grand Teton National Park** (☎307-739-3399; www. nps.gov/grte; Teton Park Rd, Grand Teton National Park; admission per vehicle $30) the drive-by views are so dramatic it's hard to keep your eyes on the road.

ROCKY MOUNTAINS **CLASSIC TRIP: GRAND TETON TO YELLOWSTONE**

Classic Trip

The adventure starts in Moose, where you can rent a canoe at **Dornan's** (☎307-733-2522; www.dornans.com; Moose Village) – ask staff for help strapping it down – and head for **String Lake & Leigh Lake** trailhead. Have your permits in hand from the visitor center. This adventure is good for the whole family. First, paddle String Lake, make a short portage and continue on Leigh Lake. Float, swim and enjoy views of the craggy peaks from your own beach. To make a night of it, you can reserve a waterfront backcountry campsite. These shores

also make for a great, gentle hike, apt for all ages. String Lake trail is 3.3 miles round-trip on foot.

While you're here, take the short loop road to Jenny Lake Lodge. If staying the night is out of your budget, it's worth stopping for a casual lunch or formal dinner – a romantic, candlelit, five-course affair.

The Drive ›\› Take a left out of the Jenny or String Lake areas to Teton Park Rd. Heading north the landscape turns from sagebrush to pine forest, climbing near densely forested Signal Mt Rd. Partial views of Jackson Lake come on the left. At the Jackson Lake Junction go right to Oxbow Bend, almost immediately after the turn on your right.

---

❹ Oxbow Bend

Families enjoy rafting the mellow section of **Snake River** that runs

through the park, with views of sharp snowbound peaks and the occasional wading moose. Contact a Jackson outfitter to book a half-day trip.

Located 2 miles east of the Jackson Lake Junction, **Oxbow Bend** is one of the most scenic and desired spots for wildlife-watching, with the stunning backdrop of Mt Moran. The oxbow was created as the river's faster water eroded the outer bank while the slower inner flow deposited the sediment.

These wet lowlands have prime wildlife-watching, so bring binoculars. Early morning and dusk are prime for spotting moose, elk, sandhill cranes, ospreys, bald eagles, trumpeter swans and other birds.

The Drive ›\› From Oxbow Bend, go right on 287/89. The road parallels Jackson Lake to the left. The last chance for camping with services on Jackson Lake is Lizard Creek. After entering Yellowstone National Park, the straight road reaches the Continental Divide (7988ft) and descends. At Yellowstone Lake, take the left-hand fork over Craig Pass (8262ft) to Old Faithful.

---

❺ Old Faithful

Heading north of the Tetons, the road climbs and pine forest stretches along the horizon. America's first national park, **Yellowstone National Park** (☎307-344-2263;

DETOUR:
WILSON, WY

Start: ❶ Jackson

Big barns and the open range make this outpost 13 miles from Jackson feel more like Marlboro country – even though the median home price averages a cool $3 million. Don't miss the **Stagecoach Bar** (☎307-733-4407; http://stagecoachbar.net; 5755 W Hwy 22, Wilson), where fun bands have ranch hands mingling with rhinestone cowgirls, hippies and hikers. Thursday is disco night and on Sundays the popular house country band croons until 10pm. Local institution **Nora's Fish Creek Inn** (☎307-733-8288; 5600 W Hwy 22, Wilson; mains $7-35; ⊗6am-2pm, 5-9:30pm) dishes up heaping country breakfasts, fresh trout and homemade cobbler.

www.nps.gov/yell; Grand Loop Rd, Mammoth, Yellowstone National Park; admission per vehicle $30; ⏱ north entrance year-round, south entrance May-Oct) covers an astounding 3472 sq miles – that's more than three times the size of Rhode Island. Entering through the South Gate, show your valid Grand Teton admission ticket so you don't pay twice, and go west on the loop road to the **Old Faithful Visitor Center** (☎307-344-2107; www.nps.gov/yell/planyourvisit/exploreoldfaithful.htm; ⏱9am-5pm) for information.

Spouting some 8000 gallons of water some 180ft high, **Old Faithful** erupts about every 90 minutes. Check for eruption estimates at the visitor center. Almost hourly throughout the day, ranger-led geology talks help explain the strange subterranean plumbing that causes geysers.

If you just missed an eruption, fill the wait with a 1.1-mile walk to **Observation Hill**, for an overview of the entire basin. Loop back via Solitary Geyser, its sudden bursts come every 4 to 8 minutes, before rejoining the boardwalk.

Another prime viewing spot is the porch of historic **Old Faithful Inn**. Even if you're not staying over, it's worth a dinner splurge.

The Drive » From Old Faithful it's only 16 miles to Madison Junction, but these are action-packed. If driving out and back (to loop back to Yellowstone Lake), you might consider taking all the easterly right-hand turnouts first, and following with the west-side turnouts the following day after camping at Madison, while driving south.

- - - - - - - - - - - - -

TRIP HIGHLIGHT

6 Grand Prismatic Spring

Exploring **Geyser Country** can take the better part of a day. If you rent or have a bicycle, you can enjoy many attractions via designated paths. Unlike the wildlife, these spurting geysers, multihued springs and bubbling mudpots are guaranteed to show up for the picture.

Leaving Madison Campground, backtrack south 2 miles and take Firehole Canyon Dr on your right. Pass the rhyolite cliffs and rapids to **Firehole Falls** and swimming area for a morning dip.

Five miles south, a pullout offers fine views of the smoking geysers and pools of **Midway Geyser Basin** to the right, and Firehole Lake Basin to the left, with bison making it a classic Yellowstone vista.

One mile on, take a right for **Fountain Paint Pot**, a huge pool of plopping goop. Next up is Midway Geyser Basin. Its main attraction is the breathtaking rainbow-hued **Grand Prismatic Spring**. Walk the boardwalk to appreciate its 370ft expanse. It drains into **Excelsior Pool**, a teal blown-out geyser that last erupted in 1985; the boiling water later fuels the Firehole River.

The Drive » From Grand Prismatic Spring, drive south toward Old Faithful. The road climbs to Craig Pass (8262ft) before descending to West Thumb, an information station on Yellowstone Lake. Go left on the shoreline road to Lake Village.

7 Yellowstone Lake

Imbibe the shimmering expanse of **Yellowstone Lake** (7733ft), one of the world's largest alpine lakes. Grand Loop Rd hugs much of the western shore. Stop to picnic at **Sand Point**, where it's worth taking a short walk to the lagoon and blacksand beach, looking beyond to the rugged Absaroka Range.

Continue north and have a look at the 1891 **Lake Yellowstone Hotel**, the park's oldest building. This buttercup yellow southern mansion has a sprawling sunroom perfect for classical concerts and cocktail hour – you may want to return at the day's end.

At the crossroads further north, take a right for **Fishing Bridge**, the springtime haunt of grizzlies scooping up fish (the lake and river have the country's highest cutthroat trout population). Don't miss the 5pm ranger talk here if your hour coincides.

A bit east, **Pelican Valley** is famed for its meadows and sagebrush, popular with moose and grizzlies. A number of great trails depart from this area. Try Storm Point, a 2.3-mile, 90-minute walk through diverse wildlife habitats.

The Drive » Drive along Yellowstone Lake to Lake Village, turning right for Fishing Bridge. Bear jams are frequent here. Drive slowly, as it gets congested with both human and animal traffic, and stop only at turnouts. A few miles on, Storm Point trail is on your right. Retrace your steps to Fishing Bridge and head north toward Hayden Valley.

8 Hayden Valley

Flowing from Yellowstone Lake, the **Yellowstone River** is broad and shallow as it meanders gently through the grasslands of Hayden Valley, the park's largest valley and one of its premier wildlife-watching spots.

A former lake bed, the valley's fine silt and clay keeps shrubs and grasses thriving, attracting bison by the herd. There's also coyotes, springtime grizzlies, and elk that turn out in great numbers for the fall rut.

MOOSE AMONG THE AUTUMN FOLIAGE IN GRAND TETON. KEN CANNING / GETTY IMAGES ©

Classic Trip

Rangers lead **wildlife-watching trips** at 7am several times weekly to pullouts 1 mile north of Sulphur Cauldron and 1.5 miles north of Trout Creek.

Also check out the mudpots and sulfur pits at **Mud Volcano**, a thermal area 6 miles north of Fishing Bridge Junction. Earthquakes in 1979 generated enough heat and gases in the mudpots to cook nearby lodgepole pines. Follow the 2.3-mile loop boardwalk to see the sights.

The Drive » The road runs parallel to the Yellowstone River to the east. It's another spot famous for bear jams (though the offender is usually bison). These buff creatures blissfully meander onto the road, so keep your distance. After the open valley changes to densely forested terrain, keep watch for the right-hand South Rim Dr with views of Yellowstone's Grand Canyon.

- - - - - - - - - - - -

❾ Grand Canyon of the Yellowstone

Here the Yellowstone River takes a dive over the Upper Falls (109ft) and Lower Falls (308ft) before raging through the thousand-foot Grand Canyon of the Yellowstone.

Heading north on Grand Loop Rd, take the right-hand turn to South Rim Dr. A steep 500ft descent, **Uncle Tom's Trail** offers the best view of both falls. Hop in the car again to continue to **Artist Point**. Canyon walls shaded salmon pink, chalk white, ochre and pale green make this a masterpiece. A short 1-mile trail continues here to Point Sublime, worth following just to bask in the landscape.

Returning to the Grand Loop, go north and turn right on North Rim Dr, a 2.5-mile one-way with overlooks. **Lookout Point** offers the best views of the Lower Falls. Hike the steep 500ft trail for closer action. This is where landscape artist Thomas Moran sketched for his famous canyon painting, supposedly weeping over his comparatively poor palette.

The Drive » Complete the South Rim Dr and return to the Grand Loop. Heading north, the second right is the one-way North Rim Dr, which loops you to the crossroads of Canyon Village. Head right here for Dunraven Pass. This section is narrow and curvy with huge drops. It descends to Tower-Roosevelt, where you can head right (east) for Lamar Valley.

- - - - - - - - - - - -

TRIP HIGHLIGHT

❿ Lamar Valley

Take the winding road to **Tower-Roosevelt** (☺ late May–mid-Oct), stopping at

Washburn Hot Springs Overlook for views of the Yellowstone Caldera. On clear days you can even see the Teton range. The road climbs Dunraven Pass (8859ft), surrounded by fir and whitebark pines.

Stop at **Antelope Creek turnouts**, with great wildlife-watching in prime grizzly habitat. It's worth hunkering down at these high vantage points with a spotting scope.

If Yellowstone was a reality show, Lamar Valley would be the set of predator-prey sparring. Wolves, bears, foxes and their prey are all commonly spotted here, although visitors are relatively few. Stop at roadside turnouts between Pebble and Slough Creek campgrounds for prime wolf-spotting.

Along this road, Buffalo Ranch hosts **Yellowstone Institute** (www.yellowstoneassociation. org) courses, with biologist-led wildlife-watching. The wolf-watching course is particularly fascinating.

The Drive » To continue to Mammoth, turn around at Pebble Creek campground and return to Tower-Roosevelt. From here it's 18 miles to Mammoth Hot Springs, with a visitor center and full services. A short section of the road around the Mammoth Hot Springs terraces is steep with hairpin turns. The Upper

YELLOWSTONE SAFARI

The Lamar Valley is dubbed the 'Serengeti of North America' for its large herds of bison, elk and the occasional grizzly or coyote. It's the best place to spot wolves, particularly in spring. Wolf-watchers should ask staff at the visitor center for the wolf-observation sheet, which differentiates the various packs and individual members.

The central Hayden Valley is the other main wildlife-watching area, where spotters crowd the pullouts around dusk. It's a good place to view large predators such as wolves and grizzlies, especially in spring when thawing winter carcasses offer almost guaranteed sightings. Coyotes, elk and bison are all common. The tree line is a good place to scan for wildlife. The more you know about animals' habitats and habits, the more likely you are to catch a glimpse of them.

In general, spring and fall are the best times to view wildlife, but each season has its own highlight. Wapati calves and baby bison are adorable in late spring, while bugling elk come out in the fall rut. In summer, observe at dawn or dusk, as most animals withdraw to forests to avoid midday heat.

It's worth having good binoculars or even renting a spotting scope. A high-end telephoto lens can also help observe wildlife at a safe distance.

Terraces are on the right coming from Tower, reached via a one-way loop not suitable for trailers and RVs.

- - - - - - - - - - - -

⑪ Mammoth Hot Springs

Go west to Mammoth Hot Springs. At over 115,000 years old, it's North America's oldest known, and most volatile, continuously active thermal area. Here the mountain is actually turning itself inside-out, depositing dissolved subterranean limestone that builds up in white sculpted layers bordering the surreal.

Take the one-way loop around the **Upper Terraces** for views, but it's best to park at the **Lower Terraces** to walk the hour's worth of boardwalks, so you can end on a descent.

End your trip with a dip in the **Boiling River**, a hot-spring swimming hole, reached via an easy half-mile footpath from a parking lot on the eastern side of the road 2.3 miles north of Mammoth. The hot springs here tumble over travertine rocks into the cool Gardner River, creating a waterfall and warm swimming hole. Though usually crowded, soaking here is still a treat.

Leave the park via the north entrance at the Montana state line.

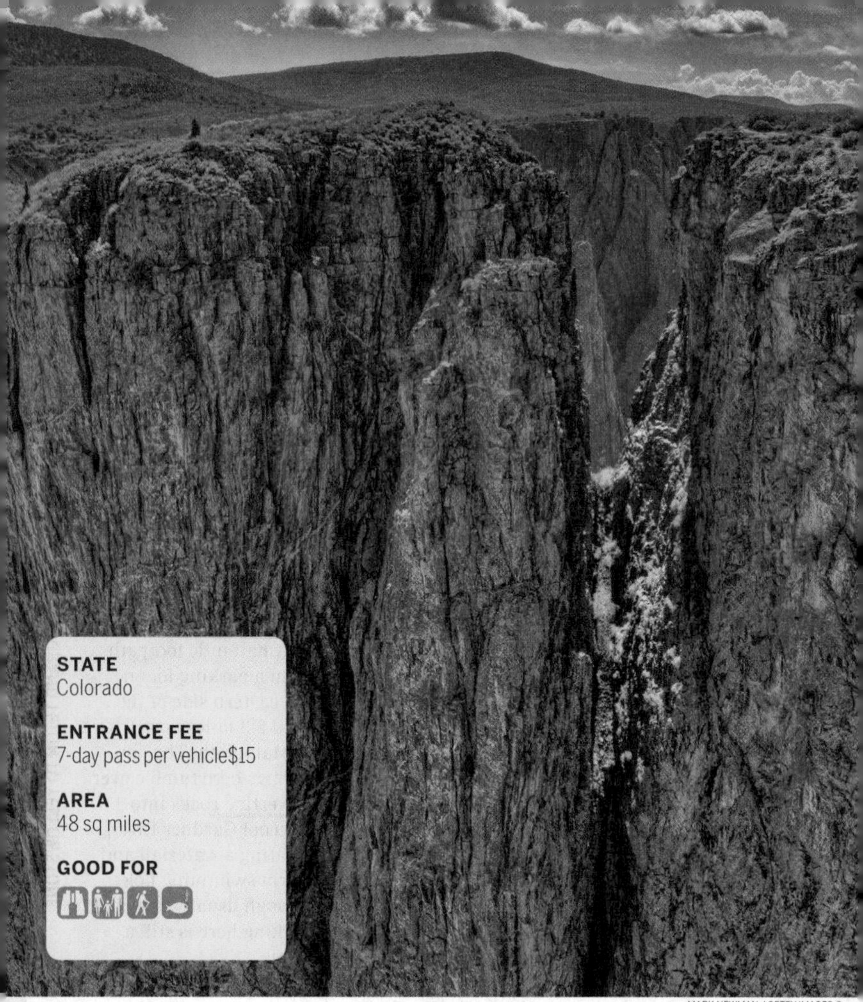

STATE
Colorado

ENTRANCE FEE
7-day pass per vehicle$15

AREA
48 sq miles

GOOD FOR

Black Canyon outlook

MARK NEWMAN / GETTY IMAGES ©

Black Canyon of the Gunnison National Park

A dark, narrow gash above the Gunnison River leads down a 2000ft chasm that's as eerie as it is spectacular. No other canyon in America combines the narrow openings, sheer walls and dizzying depths of the Black Canyon.

The Colorado Rockies are, of course, famous for their mountains, but the Black Canyon of the Gunnison National Park is the inverse of this geographic feature – a massive yawning chasm etched out over millions of years by the Gunnison River and volcanic uplift.

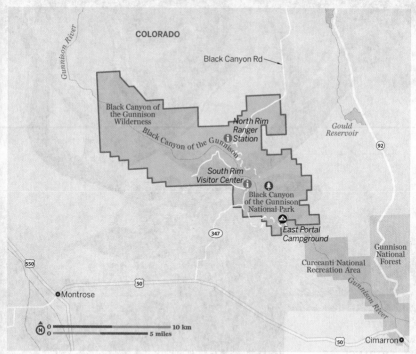

Hiking

The South Rim Visitor Center has maps and information on the park's hiking trails.

The Rim Rock Trail connects Tomichi Point with the visitor center only a quarter of a mile away. From the visitor center, the easy 1.5-mile Oak Flat Trail passes through Gambel oak, Douglas fir and aspen, and offers good views of Black Canyon. Take the Warner Point Nature Trail, a 1.5-mile round-trip beginning at the end of South Rim Rd, before watching the sunset from either High Point or Sunset View overlooks. From the remote North Rim, the SOB Draw Trail heads to the river.

Fishing

The Gunnison River offers some of the best fishing in Colorado. However, strict regulations are enforced to maintain this status. A Colorado fishing license is required and bait fishing is not allowed – only lures and flies. If caught, all rainbow trout must be released, and a limit of four brown trout per person per day applies. Fishing within 200yd of the Crystal Dam is prohibited.

Information

South Rim Visitor Center (☎800-873-0244, 970-249-1915; www.nps.gov/blca; ⏰8am-6pm summer, 8:30am-4pm fall, winter & spring)

North Rim Ranger Station (⏰8.30am-4pm, closed mid-Nov–mid-Apr)

Camping

The park has three campgrounds, although only one (South Rim Campground) is open year-round. Water is trucked into the park and only the **East Portal Campground** (☎970-249-1915; www.nps.gov/blca; campsites $12; ⏰May–mid-Oct) has river-water access. Firewood is not provided and may not be collected in the national park – campers must bring their own firewood into the campgrounds.

STATE
Montana

ENTRANCE FEE
7-day pass per vehicle $25
($15 in winter)

AREA
1584 sq miles

GOOD FOR

Bull moose

Glacier National Park

Glacier is the only place in the lower 48 states where grizzly bears still roam in abundance, and smart park management has kept the place accessible yet at the same time authentically wild.

The park was created in 1910 during the first flowering of the American conservationist movement; perennial Glacier highlights include its trio of historic 'parkitecture' lodges, the spectacular Going-to-the-Sun Rd and a rare, fully intact pre-Columbian ecosystem.

Among a slew of other outdoor attractions, the park is particularly noted for its hiking and wildlife spotting and for its fishing and boating lakes.

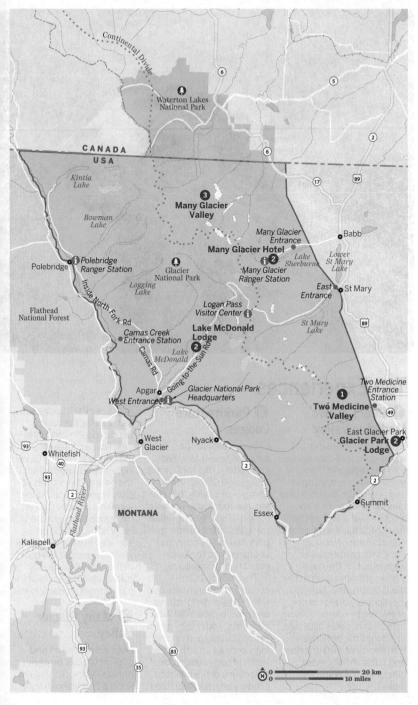

Hoary marmot

Top Experiences

❶ Bears in Two Medicine Valley

Bear sightings inspire the whole gamut of adrenaline-fuelled feelings in humans, from fascination, intrigue and reverence to shock and blind fear. You can grab a cocktail of all five in the Two Medicine Valley, once one of Glacier National Park's more accessible haunts but, in the days since car traffic diverted to the Going-to-the-Sun Rd, a deliciously quiet corner preferred by hikers, solitary fishers and – er – bears. At last count the park had in the vicinity of 400 grizzlies and substantially more black bears. Do you feel lucky?

❷ Parkitecture Lodges

Glacier's classic 'parkitecture' lodges – Many Glacier Hotel, Lake McDonald Lodge and Glacier Park Lodge – are living, breathing, functioning artifacts of a more leisurely era, when travelers to this wilderness park arrived by train and ventured into the backcountry on horseback.

These early-20th-century creations were built with Swiss-chalet features and prototypical Wild West elements. Today they seem to consciously and appealingly conjure up a romantic vision of rustic luxury, ideal reflections of the beautiful scenery on their doorsteps.

Glacier Park Lodge sits just outside the park's boundaries, in charming East Glacier. Lake McDonald Lodge and Many Glacier Hotel are situated within the park on the shores of stunning alpine lakes; the former is an easy stop on the iconic Going-to-the-Sun Rd and the latter is ensconced in what long-time visitors consider the heart of the park, with nearby trailheads for several of the park's most stunning hikes.

❸ Many Glacier Valley

Dubbed the 'heart and soul' of Glacier by park purists, Many Glacier Valley is a magical mélange of

Many Glacier Hotel

lush meadows and shimmering lakes, where the pièce de résistance is the strategically positioned Many Glacier Hotel. Known traditionally for its 'rivers of ice' – though there aren't quite so many of them these days – the valley nurtures some of the park's most accessible glaciers, including the rapidly shrinking Grinnell Glacier, spotted by conservationist and naturalist George Bird Grinnell in 1885, and the Salamander Glacier that sits tucked beneath the saw-toothed Ptarmigan Ridge, so-named for its distinctive amphibian-like shape.

❹ Hiking

You don't have to be an aspiring Everest climber to enjoy the well-tramped trails and scenic byways of Glacier National Park. Indeed, two of the park's most popular hikes are wheelchair accessible, while countless more can be easily tackled by parents with children, vacationing couch potatoes or nervous novices.

❺ White-Water Rafting & Floating

The loaded-up school buses ferrying groups from outfitters in and around West Glacier and US 2 give you an idea of rafting's popularity. All tours take place on or outside the park's boundaries, primarily on the North and Middle Forks of the Flathead River. The best water flow is from May to September, with the rapids ranking an unterrifying class I to III.

Glacier's Glaciers

Current figures suggest that, if current warming trends continue, the park could be glacier-free by as soon as 2020. Thanks to a Glacier Research Monitoring program carried out by the US Geological Survey, the Montana park's icy monoliths have been studied more than any of their counterparts. The estimates are based on research undertaken on the Sperry, Agassiz, Jackson and Grinnell Glaciers, all of which have lost approximately 35% of their volume since the mid-1960s. Many are surprised to learn that the park's current number of glaciers – 25 – is significantly less than other American national parks, including the North Cascades (with over 300) and Mt Rainier (with 25 on one mountain).

However, whatever scenario ultimately transpires, the park – contrary to popular opinion – will not have to change its name. The 'glacier' label refers as much to the dramatic ice-sculpted scenery as it does to its fast-melting rivers of ice, and these remarkable geographical features ought to be dropping jaws for a good few millennia to come.

Hidden Lake

Waterfall near Logan Pass

🚗 Driving Tour: Going-to-the-Sun Road

> **Start** West Entrance, near Apgar Village
> **End** St Mary Visitor Center
> **Length** 3 hours (with stops) / 53 miles

This is one of the most spectacular drives in the US. The Going-to-the-Sun Rd starts at the park's western entrance before tracking northeast along **Lake McDonald**. Characterized by the famous Lake McDonald Lodge, the valley here is lush and verdant, though a quick glance through the trees will highlight the graphic evidence of the 2003 Robert Fire on the opposite side of the water.

After following McDonald Creek for about 10 miles, the road begins its long, slow ascent to Logan Pass with a sharp turn to the southeast at the **Loop**, a famous hiking trailhead and the start of an increasingly precipitous climb toward the summit. Views here are unfailingly sublime as the road cuts precariously into the **Garden Wall**, a 8999ft granite ridge that delineates the west and east regions of the park along the Continental Divide. Look out for Bird Woman Falls, stunning even from a distance, and the more in-your-face **Weeping Wall**, as the gaping chasm to your right grows ever deeper.

Stop at lofty **Logan Pass** to browse the visitor center or to stretch your legs amid alpine meadows on the popular Hidden Lake Overlook Trail. Be forewarned: the Logan Pass parking lot gets very busy in July and August.

Descending eastwards, keep an eye out for majestic Going-to-the-Sun Mountain, to the north. At the 36-mile mark, you can pull over to spy one of only 25 remaining park glaciers at **Jackson Glacier Overlook**, while a few clicks further on, you can sample narrow **Sunrift Gorge** near the shores of St Mary Lake. **Wild Goose Island**, a photogenic stub of land, is situated in the center of the lake.

The St Mary Visitor Center on the lake's eastern shore is journey's end.

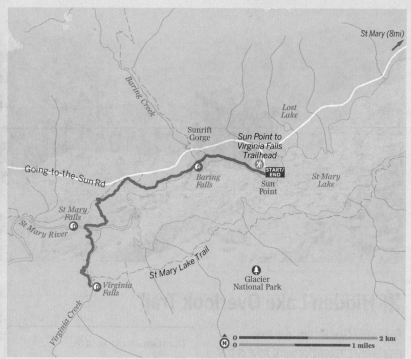

🚶 Sun Point to Virginia Falls

Handily served by the free park shuttle, the myriad trailheads along the eastern side of the Going-to-the-Sun Rd offer plenty of short interlinking hikes, a number of which can be pooled together to make up a decent ramble.

Starting at the Sun Point shuttle stop, track down a 0.25-mile trail to a rocky (and often windy) overlook perched above St Mary Lake.

Take the path west through sun-flecked forest along the lake toward shady Baring Falls, at the 0.6-mile mark, for respite from the sun and/or wind. Cross the river and continue on the opposite bank to link up with the busy St Mary Falls Trail that joins from the right. Undemanding switchbacks lead up through the trees to the valley's most picturesque falls, set amid colorful foliage on St Mary River. Beyond, the trail branches along Virginia Creek, past a narrow gorge, to mist-shrouded Virginia Falls at the foot of a hanging valley.

Retrace your steps to Sun Point for the full-length hike or shortcut to St Mary Falls or Sunrift Gorge shuttle stops.

Duration 4 hours round-trip

Distance 7 miles

Difficulty Easy

Start/Finish Sun Point shuttle stop

Elevation Change 300ft

Nearest Town St Mary

Transportation Going-to-the-Sun Rd shuttle, car

Summary Shelter from the famous St Mary Lake winds on this shady but sun-dappled trail that takes you to a trio of waterfalls.

Outhouse for Swiftcurrent Mountain lookout

🚶 Hidden Lake Overlook Trail

For many Glacier visitors this relatively straightforward hike is the one occasion in which they step out of their cars and take a sniff of the sweet-scented alpine air for which the area is famous.

Starting at Logan Pass Visitor Center, the hike ascends gradually along a raised boardwalk (with steps) through expansive alpine meadows replete with monkey-flower and pink laurel. Slippery melting snowfields add a challenge for those inadvisedly wearing flip-flops, but, rain or shine, this trail is a hit with everyone.

After about 0.6 miles, the boardwalk gives way to a gravelly dirt path. If the snow has melted, the diversity of grasses and wildflowers in the meadows around you is breathtaking. Resident trees include Engelmann spruce, subalpine fir and whitebark pine. Hoary marmots, ground squirrels and mountain goats are not shy along this trail. The elusive ptarmigan, whose brown feathers turn white in winter, also lives nearby. Up-close mountain views include Clements Mountain to the north and Reynolds Mountain in the southeast.

Duration 2 hours round-trip

Distance 3 miles

Difficulty Easy-moderate

Start/Finish Logan Pass Visitor Center

Elevation Change 494ft

Nearest Facilities Logan Pass

Transportation Going-to-the-Sun Rd shuttle, car

Summary An uberpopular hike that's part boardwalk and part path, bisecting lush meadows and melting snowfields before descending to a translucent glacial lake.

About 300yd before the overlook, you will cross the Continental Divide – probably without realizing it – before your first stunning glimpse of the otherwordly, deep-blue Hidden Lake, bordered by mountain peaks and rocky cliffs. Look out for glistening Sperry Glacier visible to the south.

Hearty souls can continue on to Hidden Lake via a 1.5-mile trail from the overlook, steeply descending 765ft.

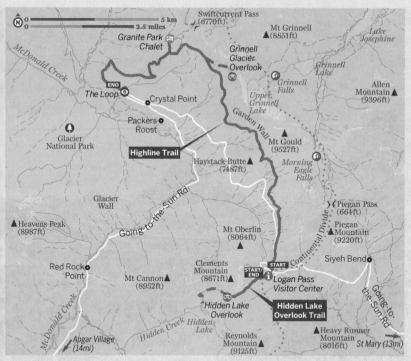

🚶 Highline Trail

A Glacier classic, the Highline Trail cuts across the famous Garden Wall, a sharp, glacier-carved ridge that forms part of the Continental Divide.

Cutting immediately into the side of the mountain (a garden-hose-like rope is tethered to the rockwall for those with vertigo), the trail presents stunning early views of the Going-to-the-Sun Rd and snowcapped Heavens Peak. Look out for the toy-sized red 'jammer' buses motoring up the valley below and the white foaming waters of 500ft Bird Woman Falls opposite.

After its vertiginous start, the trail is flat for 1.8 miles before gently ascending to a ridge that connects Haystack Butte with Mt Gould at the 3.5-mile mark. From here it's fairly flat as you bisect the mountainside on your way toward the Granite Park Chalet. After approximately 6.8 miles, with the chalet in sight, a spur path (on your right) offers the option of climbing up less than 1 mile to the Grinnell Glacier Overlook

Duration	7½ hours one way
Distance	11.6 miles
Difficulty	Moderate
Start	Logan Pass Visitor Center
Finish	The Loop
Elevation Change	830ft
Nearest Facilities	Logan Pass
Transportation	Going-to-the-Sun Rd

Summary A vista-laden extravaganza cutting underneath the Garden Wall ridge below the Continental Divide to Granite Park Chalet.

for a peek over the Continental Divide. The Granite Park Chalet appears at around 7.6 miles, providing a welcome haven for parched throats and tired feet.

From here you have three options: retrace your steps back to Logan Pass; head for Swiftcurrent Pass and the Many Glacier Valley; or descend 4 miles to the Loop, where you can pick up a shuttle bus to all points on the Going-to-the-Sun Rd.

Going-to-the-Sun Rd

Entrances

Glacier National Park has six official entrance gates. The two busiest are the West Entrance, just north of West Glacier, and the East Entrance, near St Mary at the opposite end of the iconic Going-to-the-Sun Rd. The other entrances are the Camas Creek Entrance and the Polebridge Ranger Station, both off the Outside North Fork Rd on the park's western side; and the Two Medicine Entrance (on Two Medicine Rd, west of Hwy 49) and the Many Glacier Entrance (on Many Glacier Rd, west of US 89) over on the eastern side.

Tourist Information

The park has three informative visitor centers (at Apgar, Logan Pass and St Mary) and three fully staffed ranger stations scattered within its midst (at Many Glacier, Polebridge and Two Medicine). All are overseen by knowledge-able and helpful rangers during peak season. Visitor centers usually offer other amenities such as restrooms, drinking water, bookstores, maps and interpretive displays.

Infrequently staffed ranger stations are also situated at Goat Haunt, Cut Bank, Walton, Belly River, Logging Creek and Kintla Lake.

Sleeping

In the early 1910s James Hill's Great Northern Railway built a series of grand hotels to lure rich tourists to Glacier National Park. Two of these so-called 'parkitecture' structures, Many Glacier Hotel and Lake McDonald Lodge, still stand within the park boundaries, conjuring up nostalgic memories of times gone by.

In keeping with the park's back-to-nature ethos, the lodges have been kept 'rustic,' so they are bereft of appliances such as TVs, room phones and wi-fi. All are also nonsmoking and offer at least one wheelchair-accessible room. Operated by **Glacier National Park Lodges** (☎855-733-4522; www. glaciernationalparklodges.com) and **Glacier Park, Inc** (☎406-892-2525; www. glacierparkinc.com), accommodations can be booked through their respective central reservations systems.

For comprehensive information about camping in the park, see www.nps.gov/glac/ planyourvisit/camping.htm.

Bus

Free park shuttle buses ferry visitors between spots on the Going-to-the-Sun Rd, which means all of the park's major trailheads (bar those in the remote North Fork area) are well served by public transportation from July 1 to mid-September. Service in 23-seater buses between the Apgar Visitor Center (via Apgar Village) for all westside stops leave every 30 minutes from 9am to 5:45pm. For non-stop service to Logan Pass, several smaller buses leave in the morning between 7am and 7:30am. To continue on down to the St Mary Visitor Center you have to transfer to another bus. The buses have air-conditioning, are wheelchair accessible and run on biodiesel. Most of the shuttles have bike racks. Clear route maps are provided at every shuttle stop or can be viewed on the park website at www.nps.gov/glac.

On the park's eastern side, Glacier Park Inc (www.glacierparkinc.com) runs the East Side Shuttle between Glacier Park Lodge, Two Medicine, St Mary Lodge, Many Glacier Hotel/ Swiftcurrent Motor Inn, and Prince of Wales Hotel in Waterton (Canada), from early June to mid- to late September. Journeys cost $15 per trip segment and reservations are required.

Car & Motorcycle

The only paved road to completely bisect the park is the 53-mile Going-to-the-Sun Rd. The partly unpaved Inside North Fork Rd links Apgar with Polebridge. To connect with any other roads, vehicles must briefly leave the park and re-enter via another entrance.

Train

Largely responsible for opening up the region in the 1890s, the train has been a popular method of transport to Glacier since the park's inception in 1910. Amtrak's *Empire Builder* continues to ply the Great Northern Railway's historic east–west route from Chicago to Seattle once daily (in either direction) stopping in both East Glacier (6:45pm westbound, 9:54am eastbound) and West Glacier (8:23pm westbound, 8:16am eastbound). The same train also connects with Whitefish and (by request only) Essex.

STATE
Wyoming

ENTRANCE FEE
7-day pass per vehicle $30

AREA
484 sq miles

GOOD FOR

Jackson Lake

Grand Teton National Park

Rough-cut summits rising sharply from a lush valley floor, the Tetons are a sight to behold. Simply put, this is sublime and crazy terrain, crowned by the dagger-edged Grand (13,770ft), a giant in the history of American mountaineering.

While the park is dwarfed by neighboring Yellowstone, it can offer visitors a more immediate intimacy with the landscape and more varied and scenic hiking. Climbers, boaters, anglers and other outdoor enthusiasts find plenty to do, and lovers of alpine scenery find that the Tetons' visual impact far exceeds that of Yellowstone's. Whichever way you wander, these rock spires exercise a magnetic attraction on your gaze.

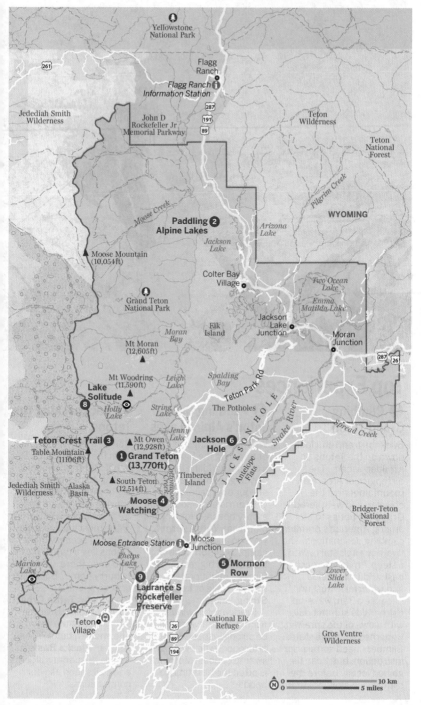

261

Yellowstone
National Park

Flagg
Ranch

Flagg Ranch
Information Station

Jedediah Smith
Wilderness

John D
Rockefeller Jr
Memorial Parkway

287
191
89

Teton
Wilderness

Teton
National
Forest

Moose Creek

Paddling 2
Alpine Lakes

Arizona
Lake

WYOMING

Jackson
Lake

▲ Moose Mountain
(10,054ft)

Pilgrim Creek

Colter Bay
Village

Two Ocean
Lake

Grand Teton
National Park

Emma
Matilda Lake

Moran
Bay

Elk
Island

Jackson
Lake
Junction

Moran
Junction

Mt Moran
(12,605ft)
▲

287 26

Mt Woodring
(11,590ft)
▲

Lake
Solitude
8

Leigh
Lake

Spalding
Bay

Holly
Lake

String
Lake

Teton Park Rd

The Potholes

J
A
C
K
S
O
N

Spread Creek

Snake River

H
O
L
E

Teton Crest Trail 3

Jenny
Lake

▲ Mt Owen
(12,928ft)

Table Mountain
(11106ft) ▲

1 **Grand Teton**
(13,770ft)

Jackson 6
Hole

Jedediah Smith
Wilderness

Alaska
Basin

▲ South Teton
(12,514ft)

Cottonwood Creek

Timbered
Island

Antelope
Flats

Bridger-Teton
National
Forest

Moose
Watching 4

Marion
Lake

Moose Entrance Station

Moose
Junction

Phelps
Lake

9 **Laurance S**
Rockefeller
Preserve

5 **Mormon**
Row

Lower
Slide
Lake

Teton
Village

26
89

National Elk
Refuge

Gros Ventre
Wilderness

194

N
0 — 10 km
0 — 5 miles

Climbing in the Tetons

Top Experiences

❶ Climbing Grand Teton

Buck the trend and look down on the Tetons on a guided ascent. The birthplace of American mountaineering, the chiseled and weathered Grand continues to be among America's premier climbing destinations. The two-day affair starts with a steep 7-mile approach past wildflower fields and waterfalls. Rest up, because a 3am wake-up call heralds summit day, with views of the sprawling wilderness of three states. Climbers need some prior instruction, but it can be gained locally before the climb.

❷ Paddling the Teton's Alpine Lakes

Whether soloing in a kayak or bundling the family into a canoe, paddling is a great way to glide into nature at your own pace. When your arms tire, shore up on empty beaches for a picnic or a swim. With a permit you can also backcountry camp. **Jackson Lake** is the Teton's biggest lake; families might prefer the smaller scale of **Leigh** and **String Lakes**.

Predominant winds from the southwest can be strong, especially in the afternoon, when waves can swamp canoes. Morning is often the best time to paddle.

❸ Backpacking the Tetons

Don't expect any breaks; from the trailhead it's all uphill. But the payback? Rolling glades that are alight with wildflowers, snow-lipped ridges and clear alpine lakes – some of the most luscious, life-affirming scenery in the Tetons lies a day's hike in. And once there, who wants to hurry home? Backpackers can spend a week on the popular **Teton Crest Trail**, rambling over the lofty spine of the Tetons. The shorter, but still challenging, **Alaska Basin** has fistfuls of summer blooms and Dall sheep as your companions.

④ Moose Watching

Majestic, massive and as gawky as overgrown teenagers, moose are a sight to behold. Bulls can weigh twice as much as a Harley-Davidson motorcycle, with massive, cupped antlers, each weighing up to 50lb, which are shed after the fall rut. You'll find moose wherever willows grow, since it's their food of choice. They can also be spotted around lakes and marshes. In the Tetons they're common around Willow Flats and Cottonwood Creek.

⑤ Mormon Row

A favorite of photographers, this gravel strip of old homesteads and wind-thrashed barns backed by the Teton's jagged panorama lies just east of Hwy 191. Sure, you could drive it, but the ultra-scenic and pancake-flat loop makes for one nice bike ride. In the 1890s, early settlers were drawn to this landscape of lush sagebrush for homesteading. The flats are also popular with bison and pronghorn, and the latter have used this corridor for seasonal migrations to the Yukon for over 6000 years.

⑥ Skiing Jackson Hole

Winter is the perfect time to combine a park visit with some serious mountain fun. The region's downhill action centers on Jackson Hole, one of the continent's best resorts. Jackson Hole offers great runs near Jackson town and the airport. However, don't limit yourself to skiing, there are back-country yurts and even heli-skiing options.

⑦ Wildflowers

Break out the hiking boots in June and you'll discover that the hillsides across the region have quietly exploded with a mosaic of wildflowers. Golden yellow balsamroots, mauve lupines, fire-red paintbrush and pink monkey flowers are just a few of the spectacular blooms competing for your attention in meadows from the Gallatins to the Tetons. Know your blooms and you might spot more wildlife – grizzlies love beargrass, while hummingbirds are drawn to fire-red Indian paintbrush. Head to higher elevations in July for even more blooms.

⑧ Lake Solitude

Rimmed by fir and pines and sporting ice until midsummer, Lake Solitude (9035ft) is a great spot to loll around (but probably not to swim). Due to the trail's popularity, this rewarding hike does however lack the elixir of its moniker, but still provides a challenge. Though it's a long hike with an elevation gain of 2240ft, it is not especially tough since the grade is quite gradual.

⑨ Laurance S Rockefeller Preserve

For solitude and stunning views, check out this newer section of Grand Teton National Park. Here, the Tetons taper to a gentle slope, and rocks from volcanic flows in Yellowstone line the Snake River. Once the JY Ranch, an exclusive Rockefeller family retreat, these 3100 acres around Phelps Lake were donated in 2001 by Laurance S Rockefeller. His grandfather John D Rockefeller had been an early park advocate, purchasing the first tracts of land to donate in 1927. Despite strong local opposition, by 1949 he had donated some 33,000 acres of former ranchland to Grand Teton National Park. It also has a contemplative visitor center and trails to the lovely Phelps Lake.

Teton Names

Impressions are everything... French Canadian fur trappers named the three Tetons – South, Middle and Grand – 'les Trois Tétons' (the three nipples), most likely in a lonely moment of Western wandering and reflection.

Trapper Osborne Russell claimed their Shoshone moniker was 'Hoary Headed Fathers.' Teewinot means 'Many Pinnacles' in Shoshone – it now describes the range as well as Teewinot Mountain.

The Snake River gets its name from the local Shoshone people, though the name Snake was mistakenly given to the Shoshone when the weaving sign for the Shoshone (who called themselves the people of the woven grass huts) was confused with the sign for a snake.

Snake River Valley

🚶 Teton Crest Trail

This classic route is one to remember. Dipping in and out of the neighboring Jedediah Smith Wilderness, the route has numerous outs – the canyons and passes that access the trail on either side. Bring plenty of sunscreen – there is almost no shade.

DURATION 4 or 5 days

DISTANCE 31.4 or 39.9 miles

DIFFICULTY Moderate-difficult

START String Lake

FINISH Granite Creek Trailhead or Teton Village

NEAREST JUNCTION North Jenny Lake Junction

SUMMARY This epic trail takes hikers rambling over the lofty spine of the Tetons for jaw-dropping views and a fair share of high exposure.

🚶 DAY 1: STRING LAKE TRAILHEAD TO HOLLY LAKE (4 HOURS, 6.2 MILES, 2540FT ASCENT)

From the String Lake parking lot take the trail that curves south around String Lake. It climbs gently until the left-hand junction with **Paintbrush Canyon**, 1.6 miles in. This steeper but moderate trail borders a stream flowing over granite boulders, passing through the Lower Paintbrush Camping Zone and some stock campsites. It reaches an upper basin surrounded by snowy peaks. The first lake isn't Holly; continue right of it to reach **Holly Lake**. There are two shady designated campsites at the lake's southeast corner. If these sites are booked, camp in the Upper Paintbrush Canyon Camping Zone.

🚶 DAY 2: HOLLY LAKE TO SOUTH FORK CASCADE CAMPING ZONE (3 HOURS, 3.2 MILES)

Ascend steeply to join the main trail; it's one hour to **Paintbrush Divide** (10,645ft). The pass may be snowy into early July – consult a ranger before going. An ice tool could come in handy here. Enjoy the outstanding views before descending along broad switchbacks to reach **Lake Solitude** after another hour or so. This route continues until the junction between the North and South Forks of Cascade Canyon, where the trail branches up the South Fork to the **South Fork Cascade Camping Zone** (19 campsites). You can start the hike from Jenny Lake and spend night one at the South Fork Camping Zone after hiking up Cascade Creek Trail; this shaves off a day.

🚶 DAY 3: SOUTH FORK CASCADE CAMPING ZONE TO ALASKA BASIN (3-3½ HOURS, 6.1 MILES, 1992FT ASCENT)

The trail climbs up to **Avalanche Divide** junction: head right (southwest) to **Hurricane Pass** (10,372ft), which has unsurpassed views of the Grand, South and Middle Tetons. (An excursion from the Avalanche Divide junction leads 1.6 miles to the divide, a scenic overlook above Snowdrift Lake.) From the pass the trail descends into the Jedediah Smith Wilderness, past Sunset Lake, into the **Basin Lakes** of the Alaska Basin, where you'll find several popular campsites. No permits are needed here since you're outside the park, but you must camp at least 300ft from lakes and 50ft from streams.

🚶 DAY 4: ALASKA BASIN TO MARION LAKE (4½ HOURS, 8.2 MILES)

The trail crosses South Fork Teton Creek on stepping stones and switchbacks up the Sheep Steps to the wide saddle of **Mt Meek Pass** (9718ft) to re-enter the park. The trail dips for the next 3 miles into the stunning plateau of **Death Canyon Shelf** and camping zone. Past the turnoff to Death Canyon, it climbs to **Fox Creek Pass** (9560ft) and continues southwest over a vague saddle to **Marion Lake** and its designated campsites.

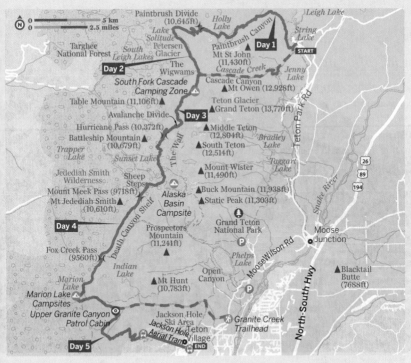

Map labels (from top): Paintbrush Divide (10,645ft), Holly Lake, Leigh Lake, Lake Solitude, Petersen Glacier, String Lake, Targhee National Forest, South Leigh Lakes, Paintbrush Canyon, **Day 1**, Mt St John (11,430ft), **START**, **Day 2**, The Wigwams, Cascade Creek, Jenny Lake, South Fork Cascade Camping Zone, Cascade Canyon, Mt Owen (12,928ft), Table Mountain (11,106ft)▲, Teton Glacier, Grand Teton (13,770ft)▲, Avalanche Divide, **Day 3**, Hurricane Pass (10,372ft), Middle Teton (12,804ft)▲, Bradley Lake, Battleship Mountain (10,679ft)▲, South Teton (12,514ft)▲, Trapper Lake, Sunset Lake, The Wall, Taggart Lake, 26, Jedediah Smith Wilderness, Sheep Steps, Mount Wister (11,490ft)▲, 89, Mount Meek Pass (9718ft), Alaska Basin Campsite, 194, Mt Jedediah Smith▲ (10,610ft), Buck Mountain (11,938ft)▲, Static Peak (11,303ft)▲, **Day 4**, Death Canyon Shelf, Prospectors Mountain (11,241ft)▲, Grand Teton National Park, Moose Junction, Fox Creek Pass (9560ft), Indian Lake, Phelps Lake, Snake River, Marion Lake, Mt Hunt (10,783ft)▲, Open Canyon, Blacktail Butte (7688ft)▲, Marion Lake Campsites, Upper Granite Canyon Patrol Cabin, Jackson Hole Ski Area, Jackson Hole Aerial Tram, Teton Village, Granite Creek Trailhead, North-South Hwy, Moose-Wilson Rd, **Day 5**, **END**

🚶 DAY 5: MARION LAKE TO TETON VILLAGE (5 HOURS, 9.7 MILES)

The trail descends into the Upper Granite Canyon Camping Zone and continues past the Upper Granite Canyon patrol cabin to the junction with the Valley Trail. From here continue south to the Granite Canyon Trailhead or straight on to Teton Village.

OTHER COMBINATIONS

The Teton Crest Trail can be accessed from the east by several steep canyons. Trailheads (south to north) are: Granite Canyon, Death Canyon, Taggart Lake, Lupine Meadows, Jenny Lake and String Lake/Leigh Lake. Hike canyon-to-canyon to make a combination hike of any length. Options include the following:

Open Canyon to Granite Canyon
One-night 19.3-mile loop from the Granite Creek Trailhead.

Granite Canyon to Death Canyon
A two- to three-night 25.7-mile loop via the Teton Crest Trail.

Death Canyon to Open Canyon A 24.7-mile loop from the Death Canyon Trailhead.

Bison grazing by Moulton Barn

🚗 Drive Hole in One

You could say Gros Ventre Butte ruined it for Jackson – there are no Teton views from the park's main hub due to the blockage created by this hump. But this driving tour, not suitable for RVs or other oversize vehicles, is just the remedy.

Head out of Jackson on Hwy 191. First stop: the ❶ **National Museum of Wildlife Art**. You may ask, why do this when you have the real thing? Just look. The way these masters envisioned this landscape will change the way you see it yourself.

    Continue north on Hwy 191. At the Gros Ventre Junction, take a right and drive along Gros Ventre Rd, skirting the ❷ **Gros Ventre River**, lined with cottonwoods, juniper, spruce and willows. The river ecology contrasts sharply with

DURATION 1 hour plus stops

DISTANCE 40-mile loop

START/FINISH Jackson

NEAREST TOWN Jackson

TRANSPORTATION Car

SPEED LIMIT 15–45mph

SUMMARY A scenic drive through sagebrush flats and forest with picturesque barns and Teton panoramas.

the dry sagebrush flats north of it, where pronghorn can often be seen, bounding at speeds up to 60mph. At the next junction, take a left to drive north on ❸ **Mormon Row**, a picturesque strip that includes a much-photographed rambling barn. At the end of the row loop left on ❹ **Antelope Flats Road**, from which you may be able to see bison and

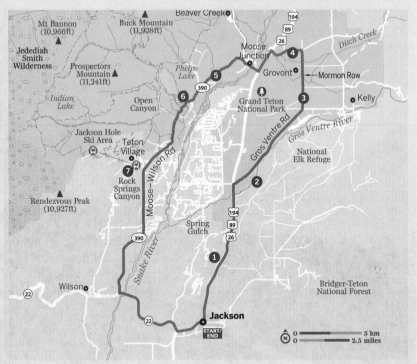

⊙⊙ Cycle Hole in One

Duration 5 hours

Distance 33-mile loop

Difficulty Moderate

Elevation Change 340ft

Start/Finish Jackson

Summary Scoot past Jackson Hole highlights on this loop with long, flat stretches.

This trail follows an abbreviated version of the Hole in One driving loop. Start in Jackson and head north on Hwy 191 to **Moose Junction**. Go left here and left again to the narrow and winding Moose–Wilson Rd. While it is paved, there are some deep potholes, so stay alert. Horned owls nest along this section. Approaching **Teton Village**, the road becomes smooth and stays that way. Continue on the flats of Moose–Wilson Rd until you hit a juncture with Hwy 22; turn left here. There will be a lot of car traffic on Hwy 22. An early start will help you avoid traffic on the narrows of Moose–Wilson Rd.

more pronghorn. It soon meets Hwy 191: go left, then right at Moose Junction.

Before the park entrance gate, take a left on the small **⑤ Moose–Wilson Road**. Squeeze to the side when you face oncoming traffic: this is why oversize vehicles are explicitly banned. Mind the blind curves, twisting through dense foliage. You will pass a dirt road to Death Canyon Trailhead and later the Granite Canyon Trailhead, both on your right.

If you're keen on a swim, detour to the latter, which will take you to **⑥ Phelps Lake** (in a few hours). This short section of the road is unpaved but even.

The road spills out near **⑦ Teton Village**, where you can take a gondola to the top for views or grab lunch at Mangy Moose Saloon. Follow the Moose–Wilson Rd south to Hwy 22. Go left to return to Jackson.

Hiking in Grand Teton

Entrances

The park has two entrance stations: Moose (south), on Teton Park Rd west of Moose Junction; and Moran (east), on US 89/191/287 north of Moran Junction. The park is open year-round, although some roads and entrances close from around November to May 1, including part of Moose–Wilson Rd, restricting access to the park from Teton Village.

Visitor Centers

Colter Bay Visitor Center
(☎307-739-3594; ◷8am-5pm early–mid-May & Sep–early Oct, 8am-7pm Jun–early Sep) On US 89/191/287, 6 miles north of Jackson Lake Lodge. Issues backcountry permits and offers crafts demonstrations and tours of its Indian Arts Museum.

Jenny Lake Visitor Center
(☎307-739-3343; ◷8am-4:30pm Sep-May, 8am-7pm Jun-Aug) On Teton Park Rd, 8 miles north of Moose Junction. Facilities include a store, lockers, geology exhibits, a relief model, restrooms and telephones.

Sleeping

Most campgrounds and accommodations are open from early May to early October, depending on the weather conditions. Camping inside the park is permitted in designated campgrounds only and is limited to 14 days (seven days at popular Jenny Lake). The **National Park Service Campgrounds** (☎800-628-9988; www.nps.gov/grte/planyourvisit/camping.htm) operates the park's six campgrounds on a first-come, first-served basis.

Jenny Lake Lodge
(☎307-733-4647; www.gtlc.com; Jenny Lake; cabins from $699; ◷Jun-Sep) Worn timbers, down comforters and colorful quilts imbue this elegant lodging off Teton Park Rd with a cozy atmosphere. It doesn't come cheap, but includes breakfast, a five-course dinner,

bicycle use and guided horseback riding. Rainy days are for hunkering down at the fireplace in the main lodge with a game or book from the stacks.

Jenny Lake Campground
(Teton Park Rd; tent sites $22; ◷mid-May–late Sep) This congenial and popular tent-only campground (51 sites) sits among the evergreens and glacial boulders 8 miles north of Moose Junction. Convenient to many trailheads, it is almost always full. Only vehicles less than 14ft long are allowed, and trailers are prohibited.

Gros Ventre Campground
(Gros Ventre Rd; sites $24; ◷late Apr–mid-Oct) Sprawling but secluded, this 372-site campground sits near the Gros Ventre River, 11.5 miles from Moose. With the tall cottonwoods for shade and a nearby river, it's very attractive. It tends to fill up later in the day, with the more private sites west of the loops going first. There's an RV dump but no hookups.

Colter Bay Campground
(www.gtlc.com; US 89/191/287; sites $22; ◷mid-May–mid-Sep) The pros and cons of this large, noisy campground (350 sites) on the east shore of Jackson Lake relate to its size. It should always have available spots and there's a separate RV park, grocery store, laundromat and hot showers available at nearby Colter Village. Propane is available, and there's a dumping station. It's 3 miles north of Jackson Lake Junction.

Eating

Visitors dine in the park for the convenience or the stunning views, but generally not for the food. The better restaurants face the challenge of getting chefs on a seasonal basis – the quality of your meal will depend largely on their success. For foodies, it's worth a trip to nearby Jackson. Other options include taking a Jackson Lake dinner and breakfast cruise or packing a picnic basket with five-star goodies. Dornan's in Moose offers an impressive selection of wines.

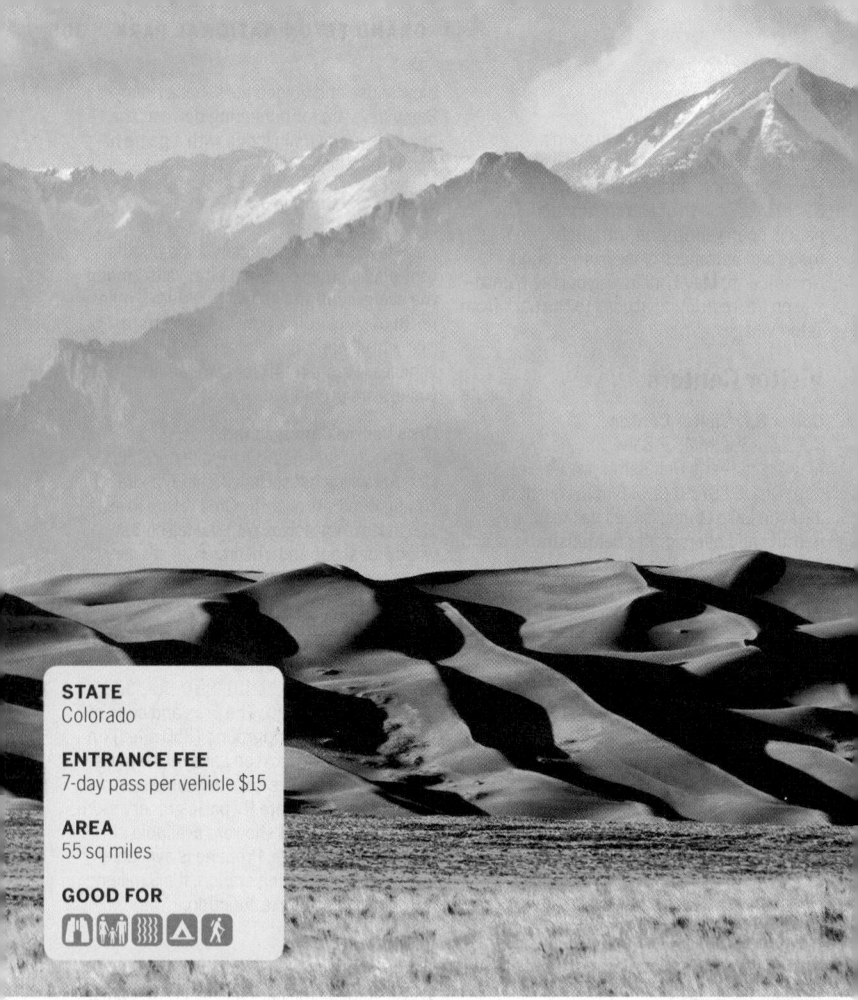

STATE
Colorado

ENTRANCE FEE
7-day pass per vehicle $15

AREA
55 sq miles

GOOD FOR

San Luis Valley

STEPHEN SAKS / GETTY IMAGES ©

Great Sand Dunes National Park

Landscapes collide in a shifting sea of sand at Great Sand Dunes National Park, making you wonder whether a spaceship has whisked you to another planet.

This 55-sq-mile dune park – with its tallest sand peak rising 700ft above the valley floor – is squeezed between the jagged 14,000ft peaks of the Sangre de Cristo and San Juan Mountains and flat, arid scrub-brush of the San Luis Valley.

Plan a visit to this national park around a full moon. Stock up on supplies, stop by the visitor center for your free backcountry camping permit, and hike into the surreal landscape to set up camp in the middle of nowhere.

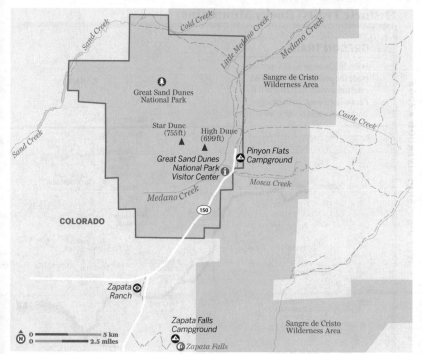

There park has numerous **hiking trails**, like the half-mile Zapata Falls (BLM Rd 5415), reached through a fun slot canyon. And there's always **sandboarding**, where you ride a snowboard down the dunes.

The most popular month to visit is June, when Medano Creek is flowing. Walking in loose sand is difficult, and summer temperatures on the dunes can exceed 130°F (54°C). Be sure to bring lots of water.

Getting There & Away

The national park is about 35 miles northeast of Alamosa and 250 miles south of Denver. From Denver, take I-25 south to Hwy 160 west and turn onto Hwy 150 north.

Sleeping

Pinyon Flats Campground (☎888-448-1474; www. recreation.gov; Great Sand Dunes National Park; tent & RV sites $20; 🐾) This is the official park campground, with a great location not far from the dune field. There are 88 sites here, but be warned: they are very popular and regularly fill up from mid-May through August. Half are available on a first-come, first-served basis (open year-round); the other 44 (open May to November 15) can be reserved online.

Zapata Falls Campground (www.fs.usda.gov; BLM Rd 5415; tent & RV sites $11; ⊙year-round; 🐾) Seven miles south of the national park, this campground offers glorious panoramas of the San Luis Valley from its 9000ft perch in the Sangre de Cristos. There are 23 first-come, first-served sites, but note that there is no water and that the 3.6-mile access road is steep and fairly washed out, making for slow going.

Zapata Ranch (☎719-378-2356; www.zranch.org; 5303 Hwy 150; per person incl full board from $360) Ideal for horseriding enthusiasts, this exclusive preserve is a working cattle and bison ranch set amid groves of cottonwood trees. Owned and operated by the Nature Conservancy, the main inn is a refurbished 19th-century log structure, with distant views of the sand dunes.

Historic Trails (Rocky Mountains)

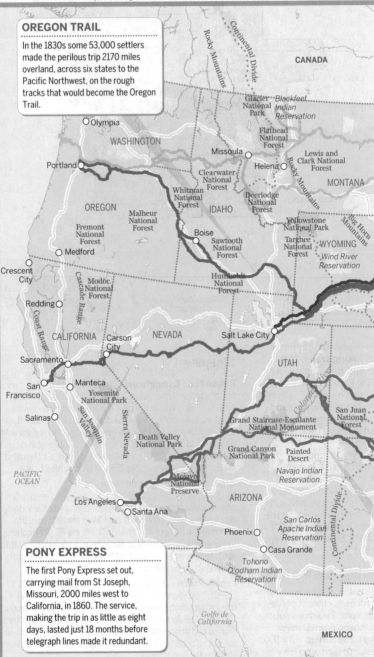

OREGON TRAIL

In the 1830s some 53,000 settlers made the perilous trip 2170 miles overland, across six states to the Pacific Northwest, on the rough tracks that would become the Oregon Trail.

PONY EXPRESS

The first Pony Express set out, carrying mail from St Joseph, Missouri, 2000 miles west to California, in 1860. The service, making the trip in as little as eight days, lasted just 18 months before telegraph lines made it redundant.

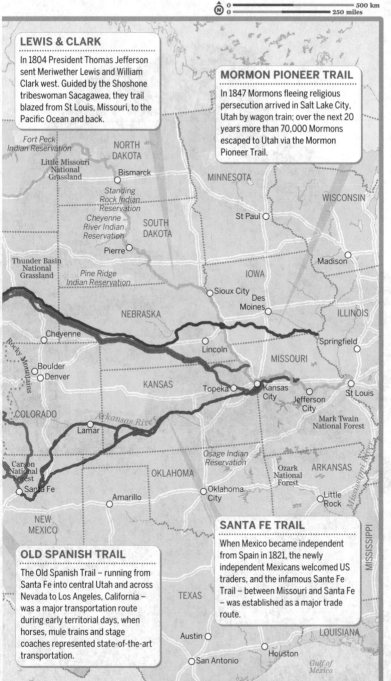

0   500 km
0   250 miles

LEWIS & CLARK

In 1804 President Thomas Jefferson sent Meriwether Lewis and William Clark west. Guided by the Shoshone tribeswoman Sacagawea, they trail blazed from St Louis, Missouri, to the Pacific Ocean and back.

MORMON PIONEER TRAIL

In 1847 Mormons fleeing religious persecution arrived in Salt Lake City, Utah by wagon train; over the next 20 years more than 70,000 Mormons escaped to Utah via the Mormon Pioneer Trail.

SANTA FE TRAIL

When Mexico became independent from Spain in 1821, the newly independent Mexicans welcomed US traders, and the infamous Sante Fe Trail – between Missouri and Santa Fe – was established as a major trade route.

OLD SPANISH TRAIL

The Old Spanish Trail – running from Santa Fe into central Utah and across Nevada to Los Angeles, California – was a major transportation route during early territorial days, when horses, mule trains and stage coaches represented state-of-the-art transportation.

DANITA DELIMONT / GETTY IMAGES ©

MICHAEL DEFREITAS / ROBERTHARDING / GETTY IMAGES ©

regon Trail
ered wagons at the Scotts Bluff
onal Monument recall those of the
nal 1830s settlers.

**2. Lewis & Clark
National Historic Trail**
Follow in the footsteps of Lewis, Clark and
their Shoshone guide Sacagawea.

**3. Santa Fe National
Historic Trail**
This trail makes its way to New Mexico, on a
route established by traders in the 1820s.

STATE
Colorado

ENTRANCE FEE
1-/7-day pass per vehicle
$20/30

AREA
415 sq miles

GOOD FOR

Loch Vale

Rocky Mountain National Park

Rocky Mountain National Park showcases classic alpine scenery, with wildflower meadows and serene mountain lakes set under snowcapped peaks.

There are over four million visitors annually to Rocky Mountain National Park, but many stay on the beaten path. Hike an extra mile and you can enjoy incredible solitude.

Elk are the park's signature mammal – you will even see them grazing hotel lawns – but also keep an eye out for bighorn sheep, moose, marmots and black bear.

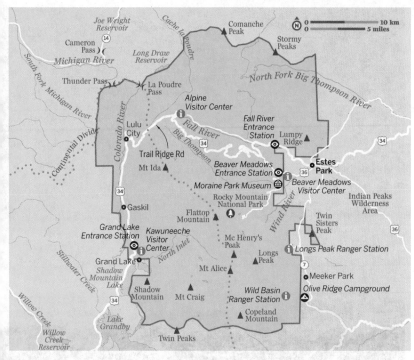

Hiking & Backpacking

With over 300 miles of trail, traversing all aspects of its terrain, the park is suited to every hiking ability.

Those with kids in tow might consider the easy hikes to Calypso Falls in the Wild Basin or Gem Lakes in the Lumpy Ridge area, or Twin Sisters Peak south of Estes Park, while those with unlimited ambition, strong legs and enough trail mix will be lured by Longs Peak.

Regardless, it's best to spend at least one night at 7000ft to 8000ft prior to setting out to allow your body to adjust to the elevation. Before July, many trails are snowbound and high water runoff makes passage difficult. Winter avalanches are a hazard.

Information

Alpine Visitor Center (www.nps.gov/romo; Fall River Pass; ⏰10:30am-4:30pm late May–mid-Jun, 9am-5pm late Jun–early Sep, 10:30am-4:30pm early Sep–mid-Oct; 👫) The views from this popular visitor center and souvenir store at 11,796ft, and right in the middle of the park, are extraordinary. You can see elk, deer and sometimes moose grazing on the hillside on the drive up Old Fall River Rd.

Beaver Meadows Visitor Center (📞970-586-1206; www. nps.gov/romo; US Hwy 36; ⏰8am-9pm late Jun–late Aug, to 4:30pm or 5pm rest of year; 👫) The primary visitor center and best stop for park information if you're approaching from Estes Park. You can see a film about the park, browse a small gift shop, and reserve backcountry campsites.

Kawuneeche Visitor Center (📞970-627-3471; 16018 US Hwy 34; ⏰8am-6pm last week May–Labor Day, 8am-5pm Labor Day–Sep, 8am-4:30pm Oct–May; 👫) This visitor center is on the west side of the park, and offers a film about the park, ranger-led walks and discussions, backcountry permits and family activities.

Standing in the Keyhole, Longs Peak

Mountain goats on Grays Peak

Getting Around

In summer a free shuttle bus operates from the Estes Park Visitor Center multiple times daily, bringing hikers to a park-and-ride location where you can pick up other shuttles. The year-round option leaves the Glacier Basin parking area toward Bear Lake, in the park's lower elevations. During the summer peak, a second shuttle operates between Moraine Park campground and the Glacier Basin parking area. Shuttles run on weekends only from mid-August through September.

Backcountry Camping

Backcountry permits ($26 for a group of up to 12 people for seven days) are required for overnight stays in the 260 designated backcountry camp sites in the park. They are free between November 1 and April 30. Phone reservations can be made only from March 1 to May 15. Reservations by snail mail or in person are accepted via the **Backcountry Office** (☎970-586-1242; www.nps.gov/romo; 1000 W Hwy 36 Estes Park CO 80517).

A bear box to store your food is required if you are staying overnight in the backcountry (established campsites already have

them). These can be rented for around $3 to $5 per day from REI in Denver or the **Estes Park Mountain Shop** (☎970-586-6548; www.estesparkmountainshop. com; 2050 Big Thompson Ave; 2-person tent $10, bear box per night $3; ⊗8am-9pm), which hires out fishing, camping and hiking gear.

Moraine Park Museum

Built by the Civilian Conservation Corps in 1923 and once the park's proud visitors lodge, this building has been renovated in recent years to host **exhibits** (☎970-586-1206; Bear Lake Rd; ⊗9am-4:30pm Jun-Oct) on geology, glaciers and wildlife.

Fall River

Eating & Sleeping

The only overnight accommodations in the park are at campgrounds. Dining options and the majority of motel or hotel accommodations are around Estes Park or Grand Lake, located on the other side of the Trail Ridge Rd Pass (open late May to October).

None of the campgrounds have showers, but they do have flush toilets in summer and outhouse facilities in winter. Sites each include fire ring, picnic table and one parking spot.

Olive Ridge Campground (☎303-541-2500; State Hwy 7; tent sites $19; ⊘mid-May–Nov) This well-kept USFS campground has access to four trailheads. In the summer it can get full; sites are mostly first-come, first-served.

Longs Peak Campground (☎970-586-1206; Longs Peak Rd, off State Hwy 7; tent sites $20; ℗) Base camp of choice for the early morning ascent of Longs Peak, one of Colorado's most easily accessible 14ers, has 26 tent-only spaces. The scenery is striking; don't expect much solitude in the peak of summer.

Getting There & Away

Trail Ridge Rd (US 34) is the only east–west route through the park and is closed in winter. The most direct route from Boulder follows US 36 through Lyons to the east entrances.

There are two entrance stations on the east side, **Fall River** (US 34) and **Beaver Meadows** (US 36). The **Grand Lake Station** (also US 34) is the only entry on the west side. Year-round access is available through **Kawuneeche Valley** along the Colorado River headwaters to Timber Creek Campground.

The main centers of visitor activity on the park's east side are the Alpine Visitor Center, high on Trail Ridge Rd, and Bear Lake Rd, which leads to campgrounds, trailheads and the Moraine Park Museum.

North of Estes Park, Devils Gulch Rd leads to several hiking trails. Further out on Devils Gulch Rd, you pass through the village of Glen Haven to reach the trailhead entry to the park along the North Fork of the Big Thompson River.

STATE
Wyoming

ENTRANCE FEE
7-day pass per vehicle $30

AREA
3472 sq miles

GOOD FOR

Old Faithful Geyser

Yellowstone National Park

In the wild, freeflowing, beating heart of the Greater Yellowstone Ecosystem, the real showstoppers are the geysers and hot springs, but at every turn this land of fire and brimstone breathes, belches and bubbles like a giant kettle on the boil.

The park's highways traverse these geysers, through meadows and forests, past roadside herds of bison and campsites aromatic with pine needles and family campfires. In between lie the country's largest collection of elk, the continent's oldest, largest wild bison herds and a pristine wilderness roamed by wolves, grizzlies, moose and antelope. Yep, it's awesome. Mountain bikers, skiiers, hardcore backpackers, boaters, kayakers and snowmobilers will all find a million adventures waiting in Yellowstone.

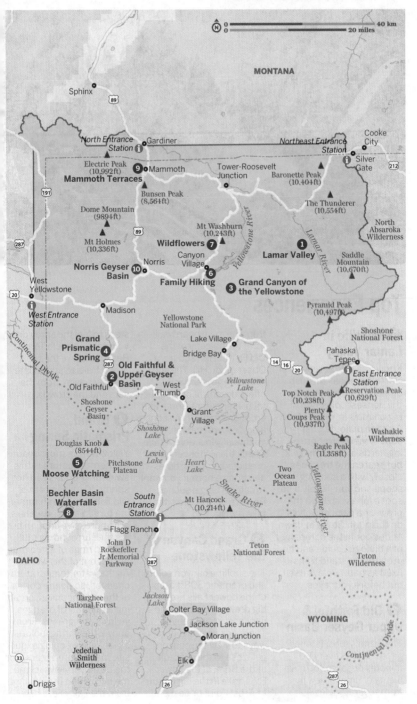

N 0 — 40 km
0 — 20 miles

MONTANA

Sphinx

89

North Entrance Station
Gardiner
Northeast Entrance Station
Cooke City
Silver Gate
212

Electric Peak (10,992ft)
9 Mammoth
Mammoth Terraces
Tower-Roosevelt Junction
Baronette Peak (10,404ft)

Bunsen Peak (8,564ft)

The Thunderer (10,554ft)

North Absaroka Wilderness

191

Dome Mountain (9894ft)
Mt Holmes (10,336ft)
89
Mt Washburn (10,243ft)
Wildflowers 7
Lamar River

1 Lamar Valley

Saddle Mountain (10,670ft)

287

Norris Geyser Basin 10
Norris
Canyon Village
6
Family Hiking
3 Grand Canyon of the Yellowstone

West Yellowstone

20

West Entrance Station

Madison

Yellowstone National River

Pyramid Peak (10,497ft)

Shoshone National Forest

Continental Divide

Grand Prismatic Spring 4

Yellowstone National Park

Lake Village
Bridge Bay

Pahaska Tepee

287

2 Old Faithful & Upper Geyser Basin

Old Faithful

West Thumb

14 16
20

East Entrance Station
Reservation Peak (10,629ft)

Shoshone Geyser Basin

Grant Village

Yellowstone Lake

Top Notch Peak (10,238ft)

Plenty Coups Peak (10,937ft)

Washakie Wilderness

Douglas Knob (8544ft)
5
Moose Watching

Shoshone Lake

Lewis Lake

Pitchstone Plateau

Heart Lake

Two Ocean Plateau

Eagle Peak (11,358ft)

Snake River

Yellowstone River

Bechler Basin Waterfalls 8

South Entrance Station

Mt Hancock (10,214ft)

IDAHO

Flagg Ranch

John D Rockefeller Jr Memorial Parkway

287

Teton National Forest

Teton Wilderness

Targhee National Forest

Jackson Lake

Colter Bay Village
Jackson Lake Junction
Moran Junction

WYOMING

33

Jedediah Smith Wilderness

Elk

Continental Divide

Driggs

26

26

287

Lower Yellowstone Falls

Top Experiences

❶ Wildlife in Lamar Valley

Known as the 'Serengeti of North America,' the lush Lamar Valley is home to the densest collection of big animals in Yellowstone. A dozen pullouts offer superb views over grazing herds of bison and elk, but search the tree lines closely with a spotting scope and you'll likely also spot a lone grizzly on the prowl or a pack of wolves on the hunt. Come at dawn or dusk or in the company of a biologist guide and be prepared to stand transfixed as nature plays itself out before your eyes.

❷ Old Faithful & Upper Geyser Basin

The world's most famous geyser erupts every 90 minutes or so, so you have plenty of time to view it from several angles –

from the main boardwalk, from the balcony of the Old Faithful Inn and from Observation Hill. The surrounding geyser basin offers dozens of other spectacular spouters; some that erupt dramatically just once a day, others that thrash continually in a violent rage. Check the visitor center for predicted eruption times and bring a book if you want to catch a biggie such as Beehive or Grand, as it may take a while.

❸ Grand Canyon of the Yellowstone

The sublime canyon colors and dramatic 308ft drop of the Lower Falls are the big draws of Yellowstone's very own grand canyon. There are several different ways to view the canyon: get close to the drop-off at the Brink of the Lower Falls, take in the big picture at Artist Point or descend

steps to feel the spray on your face at Uncle Tom's. Best of all, take the rim's hiking trails to appreciate the views away from the cars and the crowds.

❹ Grand Prismatic Spring

Yellowstone's most beautiful thermal feature is this swimming-pool-sized hot spring, 10 miles north of Old Faithful. The shimmering turquoise-blue waters are impressive enough but it's the surrounding multicolored rings of algae that push it out of this world. As the water temperature changes, so do the colors of the thermophiles, creating a rainbow of oranges, yellows and greens. From above, the spring looks like a giant eye weeping exquisite multicolored tears. For the best overviews, climb the hill behind the springs from the Fairy Falls hike.

⑤ Moose Watching

The largest of the world's deer species, moose are a sight to behold. Bulls can weigh twice as much as a Harley-Davidson motorcycle, with massive, cupped antlers, each weighing up to 50lb, which are shed after the fall rut. Moose are common in Yellowstone, and you'll find them wherever willows grow, since it's their food of choice. They can also be spotted around lakes and marshes. Look for them in the Bechler region and the Gallatin River drainages.

⑥ Family Hiking

Nature trails, hikes to beaches, lookout points, lakes and geysers... adventure just comes naturally to kids, who will be thrilled by their first sighting of a backcountry bison or belching mud pots. Yellowstone's Young Scientist Program ups the ante by helping kids explore the park with a specialized toolkit in hand.

⑦ Wildflowers

Trek into the wilderness in June and you'll find that the hillsides have erupted with a mosaic of stunning wildflowers. Golden yellow balsamroots, mauve lupines, fire-red paintbrush and pink monkey flowers are just a few of the spectacular blooms that dot the countryside, competing for your attention. Watch out for wildlife among the flowers – grizzlies love beargrass, while hummingbirds are drawn to Indian paintbrush. Head to higher elevations in July for even more blooms.

⑧ Bechler Basin Waterfalls

Hidden in the remote southwest corner of Yellowstone, close to nowhere and accessed by a single bone-crunching dirt road, Bechler hides the park's most spectacular collection of waterfalls. Union, Dunanda, Colonnade and Cave Falls are the better-known destinations but there are dozens of other thundering falls, feathery cascades and hidden hot springs that entice hardy backpackers and day hikers to brave the fearsome mosquitoes and boggy trails. Come in August and September for the best conditions.

⑨ Mammoth Terraces

Northern Yellowstone's major thermal feature is a graceful collection of travertine terraces and cascading hot pools. Some terraces are bone dry, while others sparkle with hundreds of minuscule pools, coral-like formations and a fabulous palette of colors that could come from an impressionist painting. The miniature mountain of thermal action is in constant flux. Get bonus views of several terraces by taking the little-trod Howard Eaton Trail, or ski it in winter, when you'll likely share the terraces with elk.

⑩ Norris Geyser Basin

Yellowstone's hottest and most active geyser basin and its tallest geyser (in fact the world's tallest, at 400ft) are not at Old Faithful but further north. Boardwalks lead around the bone-white plain, past hissing fumaroles, blue pools, colorful runoffs and rare acidic geysers. The Yellowstone hot spot is so close to the surface here that the land actually pulsates. Stay at the nearby campground and you can stroll over from your campsite at sunset while looking out for elk along the Gibbon River.

Meet the Rangers

One of the best free services offered by the park service is its series of ranger-led activities. From boardwalk strolls explaining the interior plumbing of a geyser, to guided wildlife watching at dawn and short, guided hikes, the commentary given by the park's affable rangers will really add to your understanding of the park. Check times in the park newspaper, *Yellowstone Today*, and time your itinerary around a couple of these presentations. At the very least, catch the nightly campfire talks given at most park campgrounds, some of which are aimed specifically at young families.

If you're nervous about hiking by yourself and would prefer to hike in a group, rangers also lead guided walks to several places in the park. Destinations vary year to year, but may include short hikes to Mystic Falls, Beaver Ponds, Lake Overlook, Storm Point, the southern rim of the Grand Canyon of the Yellowstone and around the Upper Geyser Basin. Walks are limited to a couple of hours, are free, and include some of the most interesting strolls in the park.

Grand Prismatic Spring

Trail to Mt Washburn

🚶 Hike Mt Washburn

This popular return hike climbs gradually to the fire-lookout tower on the summit of 10,243ft Mt Washburn for some of the park's best views.

Over 10,000 hikers do this trail annually, so leave early to get trailhead parking. Older teenagers should be able to do the hike.

Mt Washburn is all that remains of a volcano that erupted around 640,000 years ago, forming the vast Yellowstone caldera. Interpretive displays in the lookout tower point out the caldera extents, making this a memorable place to get a sense of the awesome scale of the Yellowstone super-volcano. The peak is named after Montana surveyor-general Henry Washburn, who rode up the peak to see the view during the Washburn, Langford and Doane expedition of 1870.

The suggested route starts from Dunraven Pass (8859ft) on the Grand Loop Rd, 4.8 miles north of Canyon and 14.2 miles south of Tower. An alternative route begins from the larger Chittenden parking area (5 miles north of the pass) for a marginally shorter but less interesting hike (but good bike trail) to the summit.

DURATION 4 hours

DISTANCE 6.4 miles round-trip

DIFFICULTY Moderate

ELEVATION CHANGE 1400ft

START/FINISH Dunraven Pass trailhead (4K9)

NEAREST TOWN/JUNCTION Canyon Village

SUMMARY Yellowstone's most popular day hike offers unsurpassed 360-degree mountaintop views, with the chance of spotting bighorn sheep and black bears.

Use Trails Illustrated's 1:70,000 map No 304 Tower/Canyon.

Snow often obstructs the Dunraven Pass approach through the end of June and can block the trail into July. Wildflower displays in July and August are legendary. Frequent afternoon thunderstorms bring fierce winds and lightning, so pack a windbreaker even if the weather looks clear and be ready to make a quick descent if a storm rolls in.

Keep in mind that grizzlies flock to Mt Washburn's east slopes in large numbers

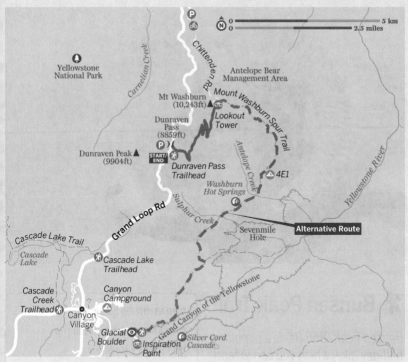

during August and September in search of ripening whitebark pine nuts.

The wide trail follows a rough, disused road (dating from 1905) and so makes for a comfortable, steady ascent, following a series of long ribbon-like loops through a forest of subalpine firs. After 20 minutes the views start to open up. The fire tower appears dauntingly distant, but the climb really isn't as painful as it looks. Continue northeast up broad switchbacks, then follow a narrow ridge past a few stunted whitebark pines (look out for bears) to the gravel Chittenden Rd at the Mt Washburn Trail junction. At the junction the road left leads up to the three-story fire-lookout tower, about two hours from the trailhead. The side trail right at the junction leads down the Washburn Spur Trail to Canyon Junction.

The viewing platform and ground-level public observation room has restrooms (but no water), a public 20x Zeiss telescope, displays on the Yellowstone caldera and graphics to help you identify the surrounding peaks and valleys. The fire tower was built in the 1930s and is one of three in the park still staffed from June to October. The majestic panoramas (when the weather is clear) stretch over three-quarters of the park, across the Yellowstone caldera south to Yellowstone Lake, Canyon and the Hayden Valley and north to the Beartooth and Absaroka Ranges. Below you are the smoking Washburn Hot Springs. Keep your eyes peeled for bighorn sheep basking near the summit. If the crowds get too much, you can always head five minutes down the Washburn Spur Trail for some peace and quiet. From the summit, return the way you came.

🏃 ALTERNATIVE ROUTE: MT WASHBURN SPUR TRAIL TO CANYON

6 hours / 11.2 miles / 2340ft descent
If you can arrange a shuttle, or hitch a lift to Dunraven Pass, consider hiking from Mt Washburn along the 5.4-mile Mt Washburn Spur Trail to the junction with the Sevenmile Hole Trail and on another 2.7 miles to the Glacial Boulder trailhead in Canyon, a total 11.2-mile hike through the heart of grizzly country. This hike can be done in reverse, but this adds 850ft of ascent.

Bighorn sheep

🚶 Bunsen Peak Trail

Bunsen Peak (8564ft) is a popular half-day hike, which you can extend to a more demanding day hike by continuing down the mountain's gentler eastern slope to the Bunsen Peak Rd and then waaay down (800ft) to the base of seldom-visited Osprey Falls (the side trip is not covered here).

The initial Bunsen Peak Trail climbs east out of Gardner's Hole to the exposed summit of Bunsen Peak, offering outstanding panoramas of Mammoth, the Gallatin Range, Swan Lake Flat and the Blacktail Deer Plateau. Even if you just make it halfway up the hill you'll be rewarded with superb views.

Bunsen Peak's trails (especially along the south slope) are free of snow much earlier than those on most other peaks in the park and thus can be negotiated as early as May with some mild glissading. Be prepared for frequent afternoon thunderstorms, which bring fierce winds and lightning year-round.

DURATION 2½ hours

DISTANCE 4.2-mile round-trip

DIFFICULTY Moderate

ELEVATION CHANGE 1300ft

START/FINISH Bunsen Peak trailhead (1K4)

NEAREST TOWN/JUNCTION Mammoth

SUMMARY A short but steep hike up the side of an ancient lava plug for superb views.

Bunsen Peak was named by the 1872 Hayden Survey for German scientist Robert Wilhelm Eberhard von Bunsen (after whom the Bunsen burner was also named), whose pioneering theories about the inner workings of Icelandic geysers influenced early Yellowstone hydrothermal research. The mountain is actually an ancient lava plug, the surrounding volcanic walls of which have partially eroded away. So, yes, you are effectively climbing up the inside of a former volcano!

From the Mammoth Visitor Center, drive 4.5 miles south on Grand Loop Rd, cross the Golden Gate Bridge and

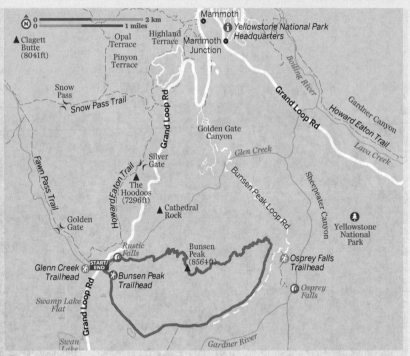

turn left into the unpaved parking area on the east side of the road, just beyond the Rustic Falls turnout. The parking lot is small and fills up quickly, so get here early or try the overflow a little further on at Swan Lake Flats.

From 7250ft, the well-trodden single-track dirt trail begins just beyond a barricade on the left (north) side of unpaved Bunsen Peak Rd. The trail climbs immediately through sagebrush interspersed with wildflowers, then enters a young Douglas fir and lodgepole pine mosaic. You'll get early views of the Golden Gate below and to the left, and the ash-colored jumble of the hoodoos to the north. About half an hour from the trailhead a series of meadows offer views southwest to Swan Lake Flat, Antler Peak (10,023ft), Mt Holmes (10,336ft), Terraced Mountain and Electric Peak (10,992ft). Five minutes later, at one of the many switchbacks, you'll gain a great view of the eroded sandstone cliffs and spire of Cathedral Rock, with views down to the red roofs and bleached traver-

tine mounds of Mammoth. The layered sandstone-and-shale mountain of Mt Everts (7841ft), to the north, offers proof that the area was underwater 70 to 140 million years ago. Beyond the Cathedral Rock outcrop, the switchbacks get steeper on the north side of the mountain and the exposed dome-shaped peak comes into view. Keep your eyes peeled for bighorn sheep.

The trail passes under electricity wires before communications equipment marks the first of three small summits, 2.1 miles from the trailhead. Continue east along the loose talus ridge to the exposed easternmost summit for the best southern panoramas. Electric Peak, one of the highest in the Gallatin Range, looms largest to the northwest, marking the park's northern boundary, with the Absaroka Range to the northeast. Either retrace your steps down the west slope or wind around the peak to descend the east slope to the Osprey Falls Trail.

White-water rafters on Gallatin River

Entrances

The following entrances are open to vehicles 24 hours a day during open months:

North At Gardiner, Montana; open year-round.

Northeast Near Cooke City, Montana; open year-round.

East On US 14/16/20, from Cody, Wyoming; open early May to early November.

South On US 89/191/287, north of Grand Teton National Park; open early May to early November.

West On US 20/191/287 near West Yellowstone, Montana; open mid-to-late April to early November.

Sleeping

Although competition for campsites and lodging may be fierce, there's nothing quite like falling asleep to the eerie sounds of bugling elk and howling wolves and waking to the sulfur smell of the earth erupting and bubbling in the area.

You can make reservations for park accommodations and five of the park's 12 campgrounds through the park concessionaire, **Xanterra** (☎866-439-7375, 307-344-7311; www.yellowstonenationalparklodges.com). Online bookings are now possible for both hotels and campgrounds.

Camping

There are around 2200 formal campsites in the park, plus well over 100 backcountry sites. Aside from backcountry campsites (which require a hike to reach), camping inside the park is allowed only in 12 designated campgrounds and it is limited to 14 consecutive days from July 1 to Labor Day, and 30 days for the rest of the year. Check-out time is 11am.

The National Park Service has seven campgrounds available on a first-come, first-served basis only. Call ☎307-344-2114 for recorded NPS campsite information.

Xanterra runs the Canyon, Madison, Fishing Bridge, Bridge Bay and Grant Village campgrounds and these are a few dollars pricier than the national-park campgrounds. They feature flush toilets, cold running water and vending machines and a couple have showers (included in the price).

A few sites are reserved for backpackers and cyclists at all campgrounds except Slough Creek and Canyon. Slough Creek fills early, due to popularity with anglers and wolf-watchers. Canyon is popular because of its central location. Boaters favor Grant Village and Bridge Bay; canoeists and anglers often base themselves at Lewis Lake. The Madison Campground is closest to Old Faithful, though Grant Village isn't far off. Fishing Bridge is always full of RVs in midsummer, and reservations are essential.

Lodging

Today's cabins and campgrounds are direct descendants of classy turn-of-the-20th-century hotels and Wylie tent camps, the latter an affordable early option that opened up the park to budget-minded auto tours. Of the cabin options, rustic Lake Lodge is the most peaceful, and Roosevelt Lodge offers the most authentic Western experience. Lake Yellowstone Hotel and Old Faithful Inn provide the park's most atmospheric and upscale accommodations. For reservations and information call Xanterra.

Rooms are priced at double occupancy, but most lodges have rooms that sleep up to six for an extra $16 per person. All Yellowstone hotel rooms are non-smoking and none have TVs.

Eating & Drinking

Food in the park is split between campfire cuisine, cafeteria food, a couple of fast-food choices, and the more pleasant dining rooms of the park's historic inns. The park concessionaire, Xanterra, runs most dining options; most are pretty good value considering the prime real estate and there have been moves in recent years to add a range of healthy and gluten-free options. You can preview park menus at the Xanterra website.

The park's cafeterias are bland but convenient, and reasonably economical for families. All serve breakfast and most offer an all-you-can-eat buffet. Kids' menus are available almost everywhere. Almost all offer sandwiches for lunch and heavier, pricier and more interesting fare for dinner.

There's also fast food at major junctions, plus snack shops and grocery supplies in the Yellowstone General Stores. The Grant Village, Old Faithful Inn and Lake Yellowstone Hotel dining rooms all require dinner reservations.

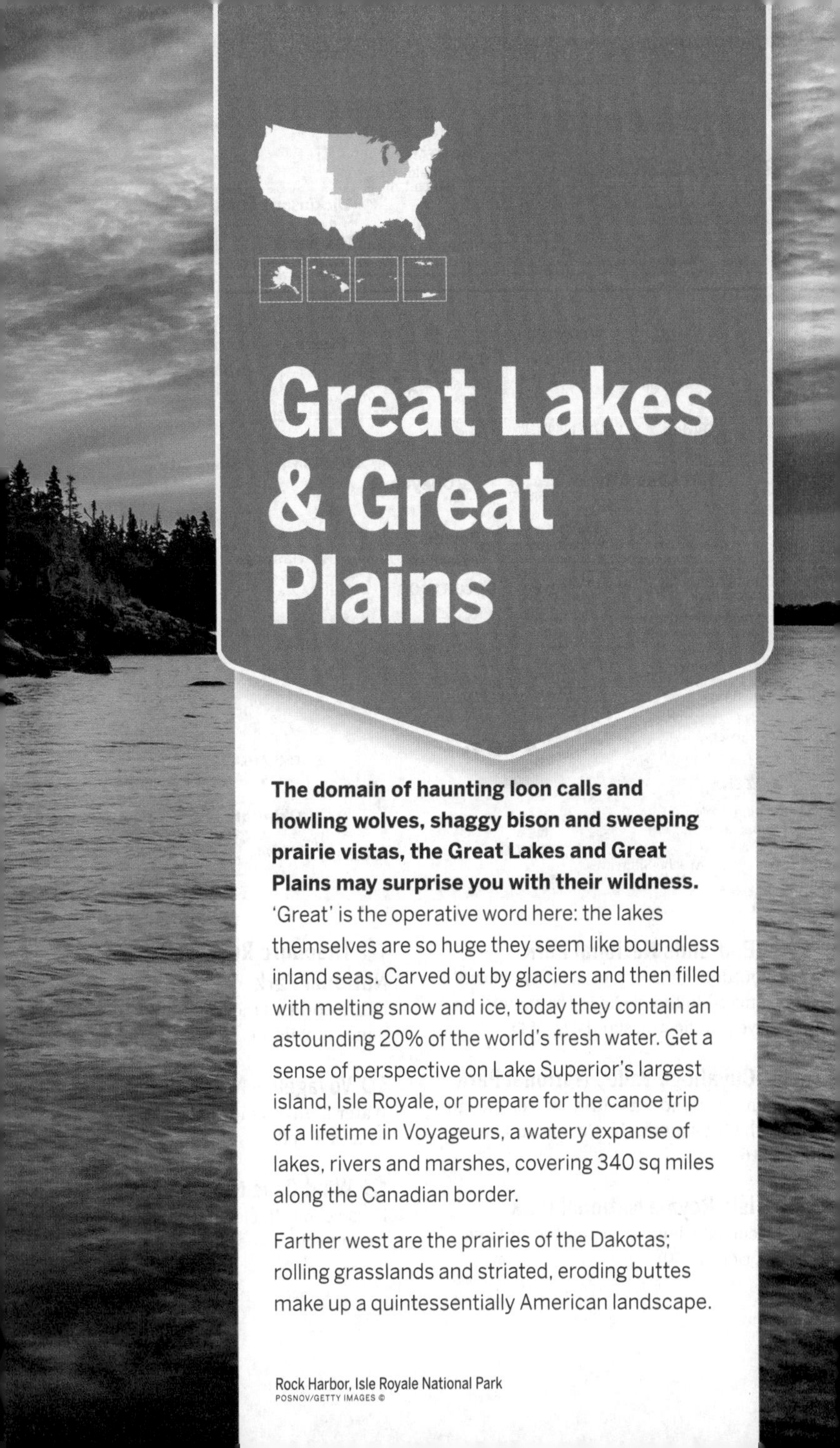

Great Lakes & Great Plains

The domain of haunting loon calls and howling wolves, shaggy bison and sweeping prairie vistas, the Great Lakes and Great Plains may surprise you with their wildness.

'Great' is the operative word here: the lakes themselves are so huge they seem like boundless inland seas. Carved out by glaciers and then filled with melting snow and ice, today they contain an astounding 20% of the world's fresh water. Get a sense of perspective on Lake Superior's largest island, Isle Royale, or prepare for the canoe trip of a lifetime in Voyageurs, a watery expanse of lakes, rivers and marshes, covering 340 sq miles along the Canadian border.

Farther west are the prairies of the Dakotas; rolling grasslands and striated, eroding buttes make up a quintessentially American landscape.

Rock Harbor, Isle Royale National Park
POSNOV/GETTY IMAGES ©

Great Lakes & Great Plains

40 Badlands National Park
An outdoor museum of geology, where bison and bighorn sheep roam amid native prairie grasslands. (p344)

41 Cuyahoga Valley National Park
Open farmland, cascading waterfalls and rolling hills along the Cuyahoga River. (p346)

42 Isle Royale National Park
A secluded island in the middle of Lake Superior. (p350)

43 Theodore Roosevelt National Park
Otherworldly landscapes and an abundance of wildlife. (p352)

44 Voyageurs National Park
Water highways in the heart of North America. (p356)

45 Wind Cave National Park
Honeycomb-like calcite formations in a passage-riddled cave. (p358)

DON'T MISS ✓

Rainbow Rocks
Gape at the rock
formations streaked
red, brown, black and
silver, and framed
by green prairie in
**Theodore Roosevelt
National Park**.

Badlands Loop Rd
Drive the stunning
Hwy 240 in **Badlands
National Park**.

Isle Royale
Journey across Lake
Superior to the wilds of
**Isle Royale National
Park**.

Wind Cave
Tour one of the world's
longest caves in **Wind
Cave National Park**.

Touring the waterways
Experience the
waterways like a 17th-
century voyageur in
**Voyageurs National
Park**.

Mt Rushmore Meet the giants of American history

Black Hills Loop

Shaggy bison lumber across the plains. Giant monuments praise great men. Windswept prairies unfurl below towering mountains. This drive embraces the region's heritage in all its messy glory.

TRIP HIGHLIGHTS

1 mile

Rapid City
A surprising city with great food and drink

Spearfish

Lead

192 miles

Deadwood
Relive the Wild West in this gold rush town

START/ FINISH

Hill City

Jewel Cave National Monument

Wind Cave National Park

Mt Rushmore National Memorial
The familiar icon is stunning in person

24 miles

Peter Norbeck Scenic Byway
A roller-coaster ride through beautiful scenery

27 miles

2–3 DAYS
265 MILES / 426KM

GREAT FOR...

BEST TIME TO GO
May to September, when all sights are open.

ESSENTIAL PHOTO
Any angle that puts a new angle on the four mugs at Mt Rushmore.

BEST FOR OUTDOORS
Where the buffalo roam is just the start of critter-filled days amid beautiful scenery.

Classic Trip

Black Hills Loop

In the early 1800s, 60 million buffalo roamed the plains. Rampant overhunting decimated their ranks and by 1889 fewer than 1000 remained. Today, their numbers have climbed to 250,000; several Black Hills parks manage healthy herds. On this tour you'll see the iconic buffalo and other legendary sights, including the Badlands, Mt Rushmore, the Crazy Horse Memorial, sprawling parks and the town made famous for having no law at all: Deadwood.

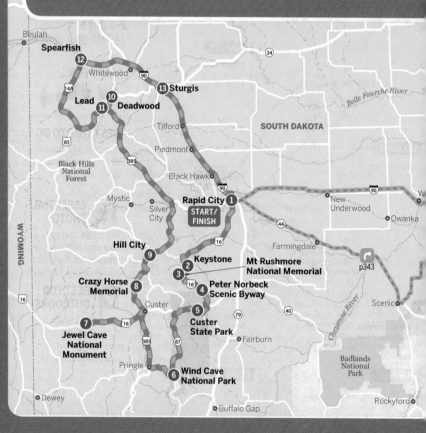

❶ Rapid City

A worthy capital to the region, 'Rapid' has an intriguing, lively and walkable downtown. Well-preserved brick buildings, filled with quality shops and places to dine, make it a good urban base and hub for your looping tour. Get a walking-tour brochure of Rapid's historic buildings and public art from the visitor center. Check out the watery fun on **Main St Square**.

Wall

Cottonwood

Buffalo Gap
National
Grassland

Cedar
Pass

White River

Pine Ridge Indian
Reservation

Beyenne River

While strolling, don't miss the **Statues of Presidents** (www.cityofpresidents.com; 631 Main St; ⊙ info center noon-9pm Mon-Sat Jun-Sep) on downtown street corners. From a shifty-eyed Nixon in repose to a triumphant Harry Truman, lifelike statues dot corners throughout the center. Collect all 42.

Learn about how dramatic natural underground events over the eons have produced some spectacular rocks. See these plus dinosaur bones and some stellar fossils at the **Museum of Geology** (www.museum.sdsmt.edu; 501 E St Joseph St, O'Harra Bldg; ⊙9am-5pm Mon-Fri, to 6pm Sat, noon-5pm Sun summer, 9am-4pm Mon-Fri, 10am-4pm Sat rest of year), located at the South Dakota School of Mines & Technology.

The Drive » Choose from the commercial charms on Hwys 16 and 16A on the 21-mile drive to Keystone.

❷ Keystone

One indisputable fact about the Black Hills? It will always, always, always take longer than you think to reach a key attraction. Trust us. Slow-moving Winnebagos, serpentine byways and kitschy roadside distractions will deaden your pace. And the distractions start early on Hwy 16

where family-friendly and delightfully hokey tourist attractions vie for dollars on the way to Mt Rushmore, including the animal-happy **Bear Country USA** (www.bearcountryusa.com; Hwy 16; adult/child $16/10; ⊙8am-6pm summer, reduced hours rest of year, closed winter; 🚗) and **Reptile Gardens** (www.reptilegardens.com; Hwy 16; adult/child $16/11; ⊙8am-6pm summer, reduced hours rest of year, closed winter; 🚗).

Kitsch reigns supreme in Keystone, a gaudy town bursting with rah-rah patriotism, Old West spirit and too many fudgeries. The fuss is directly attributable to its proximity to Mt Rushmore 2 miles west.

The Drive » It's a mere 3-mile jaunt uphill to Mt Rushmore. Keep yours eyes peeled for the first glimpse of a prez.

❸ Mt Rushmore National Memorial

Glimpses of Washington's nose from the roads leading to this hugely popular monument never cease to surprise and are but harbingers of the full impact of this mountainside sculpture once you're up close (and past the less impressive parking area and entrance walk). George Washington, Thomas Jefferson, Abraham Lincoln and Theodore

Roosevelt each iconically stare into the distance in 60ft-tall granite glory.

It's hugely popular, but you can easily escape the crowds and fully appreciate **Mt Rushmore** (www.nps.gov/moru; off Hwy 244; parking $11; ☺8am-10pm summer, 8am-5pm rest of year) while marveling at the artistry of sculptor Gutzon Borglum and the immense labor of the workers who created the memorial between 1927 and 1941.

The **Presidential Trail** loop passes right below the monument for some fine nostril views and gives you access to the worthwhile Sculptor's Studio. Start clockwise and you're right under Washington's nose in under five minutes. The **nature trail** to the right as you face the entrance connects the viewing and parking areas, passing through a pine forest and avoiding the crowds and commercialism.

The official Park Service information centers have excellent bookstores with proceeds going to the park. Avoid the schlocky Xanterra gift shop and the disappointing Carvers Cafe, which looked much better in the scene where Cary Grant gets plugged

in *North by Northwest*. The main **museum** is far from comprehensive but the fascinating **Sculptor's Studio** conveys the drama of how the monument came to be.

The Drive ›› Backtrack slightly from Mt Rushmore and head southwest for the 16 miles of thrills on the Iron Mountain Rd.

TRIP HIGHLIGHT

④ Peter Norbeck Scenic Byway

Driving the 66-mile Peter Norbeck Scenic Byway is like flirting with a brand-new crush: always exhilarating, occasionally challenging and sometimes you get a few butterflies. Named for the South Dakota Senator who pushed for its creation in 1919, the oval-shaped byway is broken into four roads linking the most memorable destinations in the Black Hills (drivers of large RVs should call Custer State Park for tunnel measurements).

Iron Mountain Road (Hwy 16A) is the real star, beloved for its pigtailing loops, Mt Rushmore–framing tunnels and one gorgeous glide through sun-dappled pines. It's a 16-mile roller coaster of wooden bridges, virtual loop-the-loops, narrow tunnels and stunning vistas. Expect lots of drivers going even slower than you are.

The 14-mile **Needles Highway** (Hwy 87) swoops below granite spires, careens past rocky overlooks and slings though a super-narrow tunnel.

The Drive ›› Once past the Iron Mountain Rd, other Peter Norbeck Scenic Byway options aside, it is only 3 miles along Hwy 16 west to the Custer State Park visitor center.

---

⑤ Custer State Park

The only reason 111-sq-mile **Custer State Park** (www.custerstatepark.info; 7-day pass per vehicle $15) isn't a national park is that the state grabbed it first. It boasts one of the largest free-roaming bison herds in the world (about 1500), the famous 'begging burros' (donkeys seeking handouts) and more than 200 bird species. Other wildlife include elk, pronghorns, mountain goats, bighorn sheep, coyotes, prairie dogs, mountain lions and bobcats. Meandering over awesome stone bridges and across sublime alpine meadows, the 18-mile **Wildlife Loop Road** allows plenty of spotting.

The **Peter Norbeck Visitor Center** (☎605-255-4464; www. custerstatepark.info; US 16A; ☺8am-8pm summer, 9am-5pm rest of year), situated on the eastern side of the park, contains good exhibits and offers gold-

DETOUR:
BADLANDS NATIONAL PARK & MORE

Start: ❶ Rapid City

More than 600 buffalo, also known as North American bison, roam **Badlands National Park** (☎605-433-5361; www.nps.gov/badl; Hwy 240; 7-day pass per person/carload $7/15; ⊙Ben Reifel Visitor Center 7am-7pm summer, 8am-5pm spring & fall, 9am-4pm winter; 🚻). The name originated with French trappers and the Lakota Sioux, who described the park's jagged spires and crumbling buttes as 'bad lands'. Today, this crumbling former floodplain is visually compelling, its corrugated hillsides enlivened by a palette of reds and pinks.

You can see the eroding rocks up close on the **Notch Trail**, a 1.5-mile (round-trip) leg stretcher that twists through a canyon, scampers up a wooden ladder then curves along a crumbly ridgeline to an expansive view of grasslands and more serrated walls. At the **Ben Reifel Visitor Center** just down the road, a visually stunning film captures the park's natural diversity with jaw-dropping close-ups of the plants and animals that thrive in the mixed-grass prairie.

From Rapid City, head about 50 miles east on I-90, where **Badlands Loop Road** (Hwy 240) links with I-90 at exits 131 and 110. The loop stretches west from the visitor center into the park's north unit, curving along a narrow ridge of buttes known as the Badlands Wall. It can be driven in an hour, but stopping at the numerous overlooks can easily fill a morning. Exit 110 off I-90 also serves Wall, home to the eponymous **Wall Drug** (www.walldrug.com; 510 Main St; ⊙6:30am-6pm, extended hours in summer; 🚻), one of the world's great – and unmissable – tourist traps.

To avoid I-90 back to Rapid City, pick up Hwy 44. Jagged bluffs give way to rolling prairie on this made-for-convertibles byway that swings through the **Buffalo Gap National Grassland** (www.fs.fed.us/grasslands; 798 Main St, Wall; ⊙8am-4:30pm Mon-Fri) on its way west.

---

panning demonstrations and guided nature walks. The nearby **Black Hills Playhouse** (www.blackhillsplayhouse.com; adult/child $32/15; ⊙schedule varies Jun–mid-Aug) hosts summer theater.

Hiking through the pine-covered hills and prairie grassland is a great way to see wildlife and rock formations. **Trails** through Sylvan Lake Shore, Sunday Gulch, Cathedral Spires and French Creek

Natural Area are all highly recommended.

The park is named for the notorious George A Custer, who led a scientific expedition into the Black Hills in 1874. The expedition's discovery of gold drew so many new settlers that an 1868 treaty granting the Sioux a 60-million-acre reservation in the area was eventually broken. Crazy Horse and the Lakotas retaliated, killing Custer and 265 of his men at Montana's

Battle of the Little Big Horn in 1876.

The Drive » Near the western edge of Custer State Park, head due south on Hwy 87 for 19 miles from US 16. It's beautiful ride through a long swath of wilderness and park.

- - - - - - - - - -

❻ Wind Cave National Park

This park, protecting 44 sq miles of grassland and forest, sits just south of Custer State Park. The central feature is, of

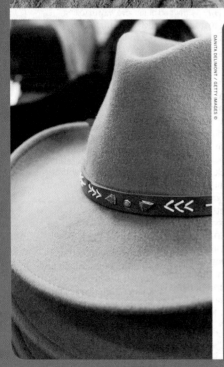

WHY THIS IS A CLASSIC TRIP
RYAN VER BERKMOES, LONELY PLANET WRITER

From the moment you catch a glimpse of George Washington's nose poking out between a couple of pine trees, you are in for one surprise after another in South Dakota's beautiful Black Hills. There are thrills: the drive through the twists and turns of the Iron Mountain Road are like a Disney ride; and there's the wild and woolly: the Deadwood cemetery's graves of notorious characters including Calamity Jane.

Top: Badlands National Park
Left: Cowboy hats for sale
Right: Prairie dog

DANITA DELIMONT / GETTY IMAGES ©

FRILET PATRICK / HEMIS FR / GETTY IMAGES ©

FRILET PATRICK / HEMIS FR / GETTY IMAGES ©

course, the cave, which contains 132 miles of mapped passages. The cave's foremost feature is its 'boxwork' calcite formations (95% of all that are known exist here), which look like honeycomb and date back 60 to 100 million years. The strong gusts of wind that are felt at the entrance, but not inside, give the cave its name. For an introduction to the cave's history and geology, wander the exhibits at the **visitor center** (www. nps.gov/wica; ⊘9am-6pm summer, reduced hours rest of year) prior to one of the ranger-led cave **tours** (☏reservations 605-745-4600; adult $7-23, child $3.50-4.50) (most are one to 1½ hours; the four-hour Wild Cave Tour offers an orgy of spelunking).

Not all of the park's treasures are underground. Wind Cave's above-ground acres abound with bison and prairie dogs.

The Drive ⟫ Scenic drives continue as you go from one big hole in the ground to another. Jewel Cave is 38 miles northwest on US 385 and US 16.

- - - - - - - - - - - - -

❼ Jewel Cave National Monument

Another of the Black Hills' many fascinating caves is Jewel Cave, 13 miles west of Custer on US 16, so named because calcite crystals line

nearly all of its walls. Currently 168 miles have been surveyed, making it the third-longest known cave in the world, but it is presumed to be the longest. **Tours** (adult $4-27, child free-$4) range in length and difficulty and are offered on a first-come basis. Make arrangements at the **visitor center** (www.nps. gov/jeca; ⊙8am-5:30pm summer, to 4:30pm rest of year).

The Drive » Retrace your route for 13 miles until US 385 joins US 16 and then go north for 5 miles.

❽ Crazy Horse Memorial

The world's largest monument, the **Crazy Horse Memorial** (www. crazyhorsememorial.org; US 385; per person/car $10/27; ⊙8am-dusk summer, to 5pm rest of year) is a 563ft-tall work-in-progress. When finished it will depict the Sioux leader astride his horse, pointing to the horizon saying, 'My lands are where my dead lie buried.'

Never photographed or persuaded to sign a meaningless treaty, Crazy Horse was chosen for a monument that Lakota Sioux elders

hoped would balance the presidential focus of Mt Rushmore. In 1948 a Boston-born sculptor, the indefatigable Korczak Ziolkowski, started blasting granite. His family have continued the work since his death in 1982. (It should be noted that many Native Americans oppose the monument as desecration of sacred land.)

No one is predicting when the sculpture will be complete (the face was dedicated in 1998). A rather thrilling laser-light show tells the tales of the monument on summer evenings.

The visitor center complex includes a Native American museum, a cultural center, cafes and Ziolkowski's studio.

The Drive » It's a short 10-mile drive north on US 16/385 to the refreshments of Hill City.

❾ Hill City

One of the most appealing towns up in the hills, **Hill City** (www. hillcitysd.com) is less frenzied than places such as Keystone. Its main drag has cafes and galleries.

The **1880 Train** (www.1880train.com; 222 Railroad Ave; adult/child round-trip $28/12; ⊙early May–mid-Oct) is a classic steam train running through rugged country to and from Keystone.

An interesting little train museum is next door.

The Drive » Lakes, rivers, meadows and a few low-key tourist traps enliven the 42 miles on US 385 to Deadwood through the heart of the Black Hills.

TRIP HIGHLIGHT

❿ Deadwood

'No law at all in Deadwood, is that true?' So began the iconic HBO TV series. Today things have changed, although the 80 gambling halls, big and small, would no doubt put a sly grin on the faces of the hard characters who founded the town.

Deadwood's atmospheric streets are lined with gold-rush-era buildings lavishly restored with gambling dollars. Its storied past is easy to find at its museums and cemeteries. There's eternal devotion to Wild Bill Hickok, who was shot in the back of the head here in 1876 while gambling.

Actors reenact famous **shootouts** (⊙2pm, 4pm & 6pm Jun-Aug) on Main St during summer. **Hickok's murder** (657 Main St; ⊙1pm, 3pm, 5pm & 7pm Jun–mid-Sep) is acted out in Saloon No 10. A trial of the killer takes place in the **Masonic Temple** (cnr Main & Pine Sts).

The Drive » Lead is just 4 miles uphill from Deadwood, through land scarred by generations hunting for gold.

Pronghorn antelope, Wind Cave National Park

⑪ Lead

Lead (pronounced *leed*) has an unrestored charm and still bears plenty of scars from the mining era. Gape at the 1250ft-deep **Homestake gold mine** (☎605-584-3110; www.homestaketour.com; 160 W Main St; viewing area free, tours adult/child $7.50/6.50; ⊗tours 9am-4pm May-Sep) to see what open-pit mining can do to a mountain. Nearby are the same mine's shafts, which plunge more than 1.5 miles below the surface and are now being used for physics research.

The Drive » Climb out of steep canyons for 11 miles on US 14A until you plunge back down into Spearfish Canyon.

⑫ Spearfish

Spearfish Canyon Scenic Byway (www.byways.org; US 14A) is a waterfall-lined, curvaceous 20-mile road that cleaves from the heart of the hills into Spearfish. There's a sight worth stopping for around every bend; pause for longer than a minute and you'll hear beavers hard at work.

The Drive » It's a quick 22 miles east on I-90 to Sturgis. That solitary headlight in the rearview mirror is a hog hoping to blow past. From Sturgis back to Rapid City is only 36 miles.

⑬ Sturgis

Fast food, Christian iconography and billboards for glitzy biker bars featuring dolled-up models unlikely to ever be found on the back of a hog are just some of the cacophony of images of this tacky small town on I-90 (exits 30 and 32). Things get even louder for the annual **Sturgis Motorcycle Rally** (www.sturgismotorcyclerally.com; ⊗early Aug), when around 500,000 riders, fans and curious onlookers take over the town.

343

STATE
South Dakota

ENTRANCE FEE
7-day pass per vehicle $15

AREA
379 sq miles

GOOD FOR

Badlands National Park

EDDIE BRADY / GETTY IMAGES ©

Badlands National Park

This otherworldly landscape, oddly softened by its fantastic rainbow hues, is a spectacle of sheer walls and spikes stabbing the dry air. It was understandably named mako sica (badland) *by Native Americans.*

Looking over the bizarre formations from the corrugated walls surrounding Badlands is like seeing an ocean someone boiled dry. Take Hwy 44 for a scenic alternative between the Badlands and Rapid City as well as down to Pine Ridge Indian Reservation. Rangers can map out back-road routes that will let you do looping tours of Badlands National Park and the grasslands without ever touching I-90.

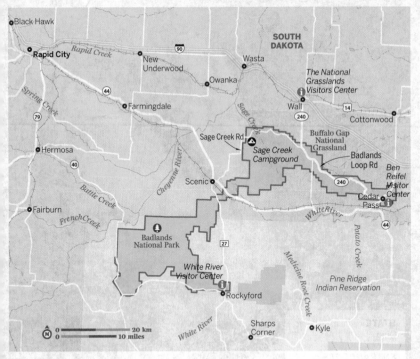

Highway 240 Badlands Loop Road

The park's north unit gets the most visitors. The stunning Hwy 240 Badlands Loop Rd is easily reached from I-90 (exits 110 and 131) and you can drive it in an hour if you're in a hurry (and not stuck behind an RV). Lookouts and vistas abound.

Sage Creek Rim Road

The portion of the Badlands west of Hwy 240 along this gravel road is much less visited. There are stops at prairie-dog towns; and this is where most backcountry hikers and campers go. As there is almost no water or shade here, don't strike out unprepared. The even less-accessible south units are in the Pine Ridge Indian Reservation and see few visitors.

Buffalo Gap National Grassland Nature Reserve

The Badlands, along with the surrounding Buffalo Gap National Grassland Nature Reserve, protects the country's largest prairie grasslands, several species of Great Plains mammal (including bison and black-footed ferret), prairie falcons and lots of snakes.

Sleeping

The primitive **Sage Creek Campground** (campsites free) is first-come, first-served. The developed **Cedar Pass Campground** (www.cedarpasslodge.com; sites $20-35) takes reservations. Hotels can be found on I-90 in Kadoka and Wall, or stay at a cozy cabin inside the park at the renovated **Cedar Pass Lodge** (☑605-433-5460; www.cedarpasslodge.com; Hwy 240; cabins $160; ☺ mid-Apr–mid-Oct), which has a restaurant and shops.

Information

The main visitor center for the park, **Ben Reifel Visitor Center** (☑605-433-5361; www.nps.gov/badl; Hwy 240; ☺8am-7pm Jun-Aug, to 5pm Apr, May, Sep & Oct, to 4pm Nov-Mar) has good exhibits and advice for ways to ditch your car to appreciate the park's geologic wonders.

Brandywine Falls

STATE
Ohio

ENTRANCE FEE
Free

AREA
51 sq miles

GOOD FOR

Cuyahoga Valley National Park

Along the winding Cuyahoga River, between Cleveland and Akron, this park is one of Ohio's nicest surprises.

A landscape of secluded trails, waterfalls, rolling hills, a scenic railroad and open farmland, Cuyahoga Valley National Park is a short trip, but worlds away from the once-gritty city of Cleveland. It was designated national park status in 2000 and is Ohio's only national park.

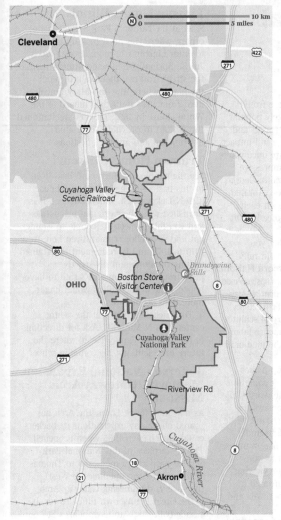

brings you to the waterfall's gorge where you can inspect the high-quality Berea Sandstone (which accumulated some 320 million years ago).

Ohio & Erie Canal Towpath Trail

The Towpath Trail runs nearly 20 miles through the park, It follows the route of the historic Ohio and Erie Canal, once a successful transportation route between Cleveland and Portsmouth on the Ohio River. It intersects with a number of the park's other trails and historic sites.

Scenic Train Ride

Wave down the train at stations throughout the park and jump on board the Cuyahoga Valley Scenic Railroad. It runs through the park, linking Canton, Akron and Cleveland. Take a round-trip or get on and off to explore the park at your leisure. Buy your tickets from the station just before you board or from www.cvsr.com.

Camping & Lodging

There are a number of B&B-style lodgings, as well as several campgrounds in and around the park.

Boston Store Visitor Center

Start your visit to the park at the Boston Store. Built around 1836, it was originally a place to store goods and with boarding rooms for workers from the surrounding area. It went on to become a post office and private residence, before becoming the **visitor center** (☐330-657-2752;

1550 Boston Mills Rd, east of Riverview Road Peninsula; ☉ 8am-6pm May-Aug, reduced hours rest of the year).

Brandywine Falls

These 65ft cascading falls are among the park's top attractions. Carved by Brandywine Creek, the falls once powered mills built by the area's early settlers. A boardwalk

Throughout spring, fall and especially in summer, weekends can be busy along the the Towpath Trail. Come in spring for the wildflowers or fall when the foliage is extra pretty. Skiing, snowshoeing and sledding are popular in the winter months.

Presidential Memorials

Mount Rushmore, South Dakota

Glimpses of Washington's nose from the roads leading to this hugely popular monument never cease to surprise, and they are but harbingers of the full impact of this mountainside sculpture once you're up close (and past the less impressive parking area and entrance walk). George Washington, Thomas Jefferson, Abraham Lincoln and Theodore Roosevelt each iconically stare into the distance in 60ft-tall granite glory.

Although it's hugely popular, you can easily escape the crowds and fully appreciate the **Mount Rushmore National Memorial** (☎605-574-2523; www.nps.gov/moru; off Hwy 244; parking $11; ⊙8am-10pm late May–mid-Aug, to 9pm mid-Aug–Sep, to 5pm Oct-May) while marveling at the artistry of sculptor Gutzon Borglum and the immense labor of the workers who created the memorial between 1927 and 1941.

The **Presidential Trail** loop passes right below the monument for some fine nostril views and accesses the worthwhile **Sculptor's Studio**, which conveys the drama of how the monument came to be. Start clockwise and you're right under Washington's nose in under five minutes. The **nature trail** to the right as you face the entrance connects the viewing and parking areas, passing through a pine forest and avoiding the crowds and commercialism.

The official Park Service **information centers** have excellent bookstores with proceeds going to the park. Avoid the schlocky Xanterra gift shop and the ho-hum Carvers Cafe, which looked much better in the scene where Cary Grant gets plugged in *North by Northwest*. The main **museum** is underwhelming.

The nearest lodging and restaurants to Mt Rushmore are in Hill City or Keystone, a one-time mining town now devoted to milking the monument.

1. Mount Rushmore National Monument 2. Gateway Arch

Lincoln Home, Illinois

Start at the National Park Service visitor center, where you must pick up a ticket to enter Lincoln's 12-room abode (426 S 7th St, Springfield), located directly across the street. You can then walk through the house where Abe and Mary Lincoln lived from 1844 until they moved to the White House in 1861; rangers are stationed throughout to provide background information and answer questions.

Truman Home, Missouri

See the simple life Harry and Bess lived in this basic but charming wood house (219 N Delaware St, Independence). It is furnished with their original belongings and you fully expect the couple to wander out and say hello. Truman lived here from 1919 to 1972 and in retirement entertained visiting dignitaries in his strictly pedestrian front room – he's said to have hoped none of the callers would linger more than 30 minutes.

Tour tickets are sold at the visitor center (223 N Main St). Ask for directions to the Truman Family Farm, where the future president 'got his common sense.'

Jefferson National Expansion Memorial/Gateway Arch, Missouri

As a symbol for St Louis, the Arch has soared above any expectations its backers could have had in 1965 when it opened. The centerpiece of this National Park Service property (a memorial to Thomas Jefferson's role in opening the West), the silvery, shimmering Gateway Arch is the Great Plains' own Eiffel Tower. It stands 630ft high and symbolizes St Louis' historical role as 'Gateway to the West.' A tram ride takes you to the tight confines at the top.

A massive project has transformed the area around the Arch in time for its 50th birthday. A large plaza now covers I-70 and connects the Arch and its park directly to the Old Courthouse and the rest of downtown. It's a huge and welcome improvement. Note that some portions of the upgrade, which includes all of the parks, won't be complete until 2017. Find out more at www.cityarchriver.org. Book tickets in advance on the NPS website.

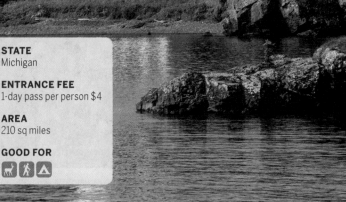

STATE
Michigan

ENTRANCE FEE
1-day pass per person $4

AREA
210 sq miles

GOOD FOR

Rock Harbor Lighthouse

STEVENSCHREMP / GETTY IMAGES ©

Isle Royale National Park

Totally free of vehicles and roads, this is certainly the place to go for peace and quiet. It gets fewer visitors in a year than Yellowstone National Park gets in a day, which means the 1200 moose creeping through the forest are all yours.

This 210-sq-mile island in Lake Superior is laced with 165 miles of hiking trails that connect dozens of campgrounds along Superior and inland lakes. And getting to the isle is half the fun. Once you've made the journey across the lake, explore coves and bays by boat and backpack your way through the wilderness.

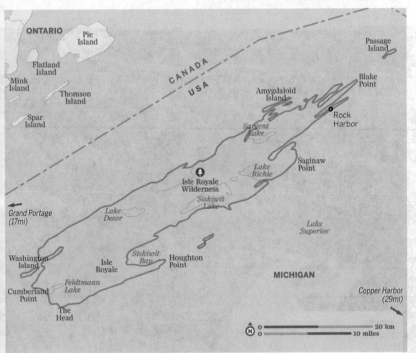

For this adventure you'll need to come prepared with a tent, camping stove, sleeping bag, food and water filter...or you can be a softie and bunk at the **Rock Harbor Lodge** (☎906-337-4993; www. isleroyaleresort.com; r & cottages $224-256; ☺late May–early Sep).

From the dock outside the **park headquarters** (800 E Lakeshore Dr) in Houghton, the **Ranger III** (☎906-482-0984) departs for the six-hour boat trip (round-trip adult/child $126/46) to Rock Harbor, at the east end of the island.

Isle Royale Seaplanes (☎877-359-4753; www.isle royaleseaplanes.com) offers a quicker trip, flying from Houghton County Airport to Rock Harbor in 30 minutes (round-trip $310).

Or head 50 miles up the Keweenaw Peninsula to Copper Harbor (a beautiful drive) for the **Isle Royale Queen** (☎906-289-4437;

Entry Points & Visitor Centers

Houghton (Michigan)
The isle's mainland headquarters, located along the Portage Canal.

Rock Harbor Located on the northeast end of the isle.

Windigo Located on the southwest end of the isle.

When to Go

Late June to September is the best time to visit the park, It's closed from November to mid-April. Watch for the mosquitoes, blackflies and gnats in June and July. Summer nights can be cool.

www.isleroyale.com) three-hour crossing (round-trip adult/child $130/65).

Bringing a kayak or canoe on the ferries costs an additional $50 round-trip; ensure you make reservations well in advance. You can also access Isle Royale from Grand Portage, Minnesota.

STATE
North Dakota

ENTRANCE FEE
7-day pass per vehicle $20

AREA
110 sq miles

GOOD FOR

Little Missouri River

Theodore Roosevelt National Park

A tortured region known as the 'badlands' whose colors seem to change with the moods of nature, Theodore Roosevelt National Park is North Dakota's natural highlight.

Bizarre rainbow-streaked rock formations are framed by green prairie in this vast park where only the rush of rivers and the distant hoof-beat of animals interrupts the silence. Wildlife abounds: mule deer, wild horses, bighorn sheep, elk, bison, around 200 bird species, and sprawling subterranean prairie-dog towns.

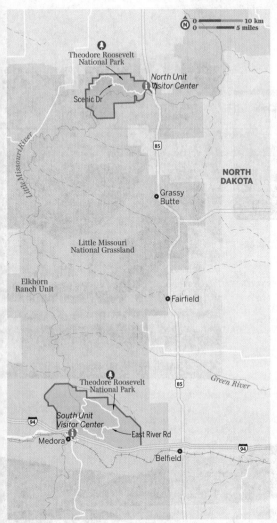

Theodore Roosevelt

Young Theodore Roosevelt came to North Dakota to ditch his city-slicker image. As president, inspired by his time in North Dakota, he earned the title 'The Father of Conservation' for his work creating national forests and parks.

Information

The park has three visitor centers, including the **South Unit Visitor Center** (off I-94 exits 24 & 27, Medora; ☺8am-6pm Jun-Sep, 8am-4:30pm Sep-May), with Theodore Roosevelt's old cabin out back.

Sleeping

The park has two simple campgrounds (sites $7 to $14) and free backcountry camping (permit required).

Getting There & Away

Arrowing across North Dakota, I-94 provides easy access to most of the state's top attractions, although it would not be the road of scenic choice (US 2 is more atmospheric).

Mountain Time

The southwest quarter of North Dakota, including Medora, uses Mountain Time, which is one hour earlier than the rest of the state's Central Time.

The park is divided into two sections. Most visitors to the South Unit opt for the 36-mile scenic drive that begins in Medora, an enjoyable town with motels just off I-94; prairie dogs are a highlight.

The North Unit (68 miles north of I-94 on US 85) gets few visitors, but is well worth the journey for the 14-mile drive to the Oxbow Overlook, with its wide views into the vast and colorfully striated river canyon. The verdant surrounds are protected as the Little Missouri National Grassland, and are full of bison.

Hikers can explore 85 miles of backcountry trails. For a good adventure, hike or cycle the 96-mile Maah Daah Hey Trail between the park units.

EDWARD KINSMAN / GETTY IMAGES ©

1. Isle Royale National Park
This peaceful island is the ideal place to see moose in their natural habitat.

2. Badlands National Park
Rainbow-hued rock formations protect the country's largest prairie grasslands.

3. Cuyahoga National Park
Waterfalls, rolling hills, a scenic railroad and open farmland.

4. Wind Cave National Park
One of the largest free-roaming bison herds in the world inhabit this park.

STATE
Minnesota

ENTRANCE FEE
Free

AREA
340 sq miles

GOOD FOR

Backcountry campsite

STEVENSCHREMP / GETTY IMAGES ©

Voyageurs National Park

Lying close to the geographic heart of the North American continent, Voyageurs National Park is an outstanding mix of land and waterways formed from ancient earthquakes, volcanoes and glaciers.

In the 17th century, French-Canadian fur traders, or voyageurs, began exploring and traveling on the Great Lakes and northern rivers by canoe. What is now Voyageurs National Park covers part of their customary waterway, and has given rise to the park's name.

And it really is all about water up here. With water forming 40% of the park's area, most of the park is accessible only by hiking or motorboat in summer, and snowmobiles, skiing or snowshoes in winter.

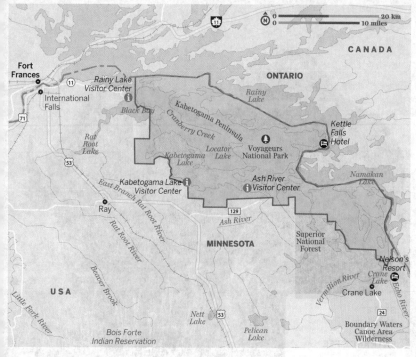

Sights & Activities

There are several visitor centers in the park, all of which are accessible by car and good places to begin your visit.

Twelve miles east of International Falls on Hwy 11 is **Rainy Lake Visitors Center** (☎218-286-5258; ⏰9:30am-5pm late May–mid-Oct, reduced hours rest of the year), the main park office. Ranger-guided walks and boat and canoe tours are available here during the summer months. Seasonal visitor centers are at **Ash River** (☎218-374-3221; ⏰9:30am-5pm late May–late Sep) and **Kabetogama Lake** (☎218-875-2111; ⏰9:30am-5pm late May–late Sep), and offer a range of boat, canoe and ranger-led tours.

The areas also have outfitters, rentals, guided tours and services, plus some smaller bays for canoeing.

Sleeping

The park has more than 270 campsites, houseboat sites and day-use sites within its boundaries, and visitors are required to organise permits for overnight camping or houseboat stays (fees apply).

Houseboating is obviously a very popular choice in the region. Outfitters such as **Ebel's** (☎888-883-2357; www.ebels.com; 10326 Ash River Trail) and **Voyagaire House-boats** (☎800-882-6287; www.voyagaire.com; 7576 Gold Coast Rd) can set you up.

Rentals range from $275 to $700 per day, depending on boat size. Novice boaters are welcome and receive instruction on how to operate the vessels.

Otherwise, your choices are pretty much camping or resorts. The 12-room, shared-bath **Kettle Falls Hotel** (☎218-240-1724; www.kettlefallshotel.com; r/cottage $80/180; ⏰May–late Oct) is an exception, located inside the park and accessible only by boat; make arrangements with the owners for pick-up (per person round-trip $45). **Nelson's Resort** (☎800-433-0743; www.nelsonsresort.com; 7632 Nelson Rd; cabins from $205) at Crane Lake is a winner for hiking, fishing and relaxing under blue skies.

STATE
South Dakota

ENTRANCE FEE
Free

AREA
44 sq miles

GOOD FOR

Bison on the prairie

Wind Cave National Park

Beneath the mixed-grass prairie and pine forest lies one of the world's longest, most complex cave systems. In 1903, Wind Cave was the first cave in the world to be designated a national park.

The central draw of the park is the cave, which contains 132 miles of mapped passages, although experts believe they have found less than 10% of the overall number. The strong wind gusts that are felt at the entrance, but not inside and which give the cave its name, relate to the difference in atmospheric pressure between the cave and the land surface.

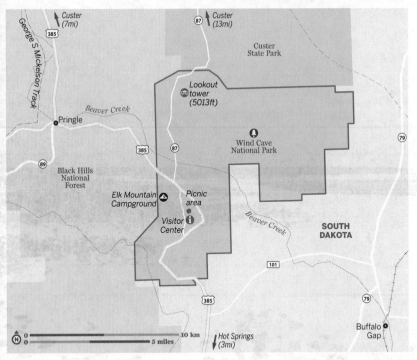

The cave's foremost feature is its 'boxwork' calcite formations (95% of all that are known exist here), which look like honeycomb and date back 60 to 100 million years. Continuing exploration is finding further cave formations, such as popcorn, frostwork and flowstone displays.

The **visitor center** (📞605-745-4600; www.nps.gov/wica; off US 385; ⏰8am-6pm Jun-Aug, reduced hours Sep-May) has details on cave tours, which leave from the visitor center, and are ranger-guided. Tickets (from $10) are sold on a first-come, first-served basis.

Activities

Hiking is a popular activity in the park, and you'll find 30 miles of hiking trails, three nature trails and plenty of cross-country walks to enjoy,

Horseback riding is another popular activity, but riders must obtain a permit (free) from the visitor center, which are for one-day use only. You will also find an abundance of native wildlife, including elk, prairie dogs and free-roaming bison herds.

Sleeping

The year-round campground usually has space ($18 per site when water and toilet facilities are available, $9 from late fall to early spring when the water is turned off). Backcountry camping (free with permit) is also offered in the northwest area of the park. All drinking water must be carried in to this area, and open fires are prohibited at all times.

Custer State Park

The only reason 111-sq-mile **Custer State Park** (📞605-255-4515; www.custerstatepark.info; 7-day pass per vehicle $15; ⏰24hr; 🚗) isn't a national park is that the state grabbed it first. Just north of the Wind Cave, it boasts one of the largest free-roaming bison herds in the world (about 1300), the 'begging burros' (donkeys seeking handouts) and more than 200 bird species. Other wildlife include elk, pronghorns, mountain goats, bighorn sheep, coyotes, prairie dogs, mountain lions and bobcats.

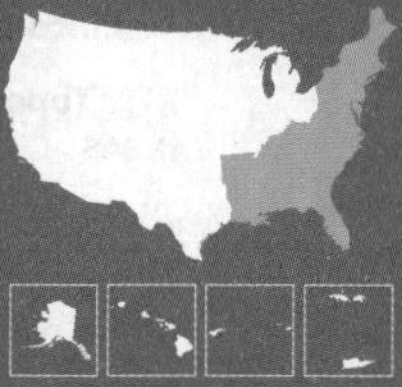

The East

From Maine's rocky, weather-beaten shores to Florida's tropical birds and endless shades of blues and greens, the Atlantic and Appalachia defy expectations. Often overshadowed by the mighty vistas out West – even Congress didn't set about designating parks here until the 1920s – this massive swath of land is nonetheless home to some of the continent's most diverse ecosystems.

Alligators, manatees, panthers and flamingos populate the Everglades, while Biscayne and the Dry Tortugas shelter vibrant coral reefs. Over 100 species of trees can be found in the old-growth stands of the Great Smoky Mountains, which are often visited in combination with Shenandoah, linked via the scenic Blue Ridge Parkway and the Appalachian Trail. Near the country's northeasternmost tip is Acadia, a parcel of untamed, rugged New England coastline.

Sunset, Everglades
TIM KIUSALAAS/GETTY IMAGES ©

The East

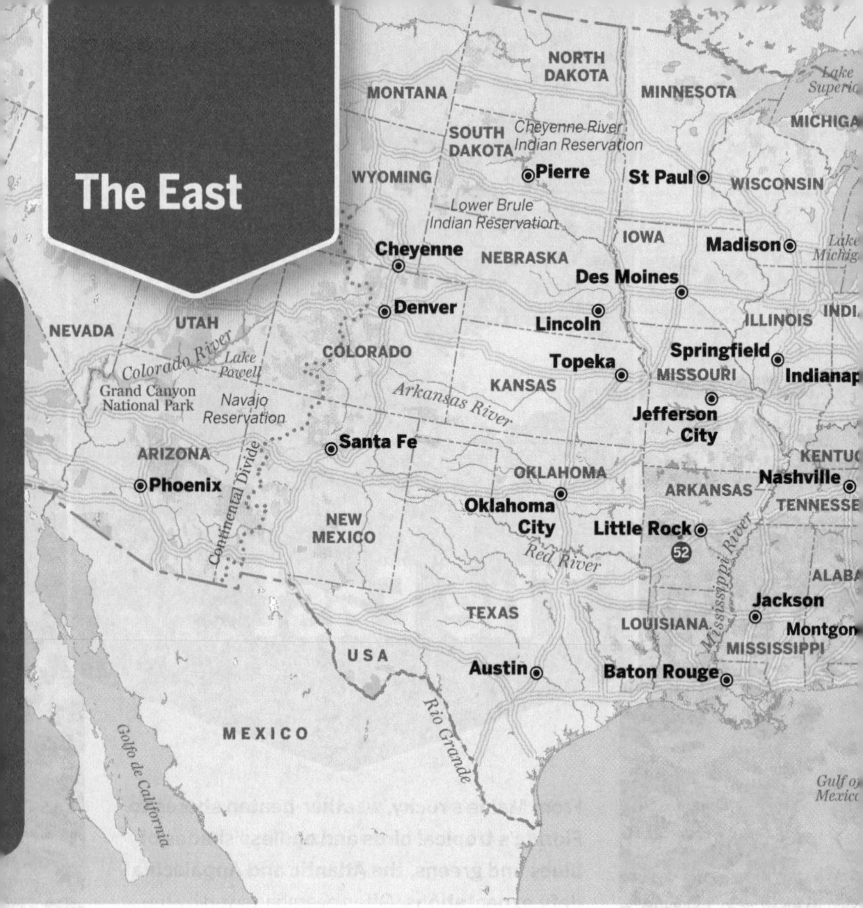
NORTH DAKOTA
MONTANA
MINNESOTA
Lake Superior
MICHIGAN
SOUTH DAKOTA
Cheyenne River Indian Reservation
WYOMING
Pierre
St Paul
WISCONSIN
Lower Brule Indian Reservation
IOWA
Madison
Lake Michigan
Cheyenne
NEBRASKA
Des Moines
Denver
Lincoln
ILLINOIS
NEVADA
UTAH
Colorado River
Lake Powell
COLORADO
Topeka
Springfield
Indianapolis
Grand Canyon National Park
Navajo Reservation
KANSAS
Arkansas River
MISSOURI
Jefferson City
ARIZONA
Santa Fe
Phoenix
Continental Divide
OKLAHOMA
KENTUCKY
Nashville
ARKANSAS
TENNESSEE
NEW MEXICO
Oklahoma City
Little Rock
52
Red River
Mississippi River
ALABAMA
TEXAS
Jackson
LOUISIANA
Montgomery
MISSISSIPPI
USA
Austin
Baton Rouge
Rio Grande
MEXICO
Golfo de California
Gulf of Mexico

㊻ Acadia National Park

Surf beaches, coastal mountains and quiet lakes make for an unspoiled wilderness. (p374)

㊼ Biscayne National Park

Home of the world's third-largest coral reef. (p380)

㊽ Congaree National Park

Extraordinary biodiversity and some of the tallest trees in eastern USA. (p386)

㊾ Dry Tortugas National Park

Coral reefs, marine life and a striking fort. (p388)

㊿ Everglades National Park

The largest subtropical wilderness in North America. (p396)

(51) Great Smoky Mountains National Park

America's favorite, beloved for its waterfalls, scaleable peaks and photogenic mountain villages. (p398)

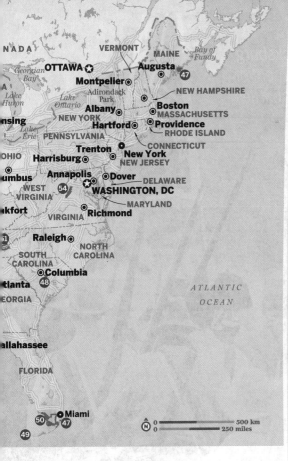

DON'T MISS

Sunrise, Cadillac Mountain
Watch the first sunrise over America in **Acadia National Park**.

Park Loop Road
Stop at Thunder Hole to watch (and hear) the surf crash on this 27-mile loop through **Acadia National Park**.

Hiking
Take to the trailheads to experience the magic of the **Great Smoky Mountains**.

Wildlife
Watch for birds, reptiles and an array of plant life in the mangroves and forests of **Everglades National Park**.

Blue Ridge Parkway
Road trip through the Appalachians on this drive that connects **Shenandoah National Park** with **Great Smoky Mountains National Park**.

52 Hot Springs National Park
Nicknamed the 'American Spa' for its mineral-rich waters. (p404)

53 Mammoth Cave National Park
Stalactites, stalagmites and vast underground cathedrals inside the world's longest cave system. (p410)

54 Shenandoah National Park
Miles of the Appalachian Trail and a backdrop of vibrant seasonal colors. (p412)

Fredericksburg
Reenactment of
Civil War battles

The Civil War Tour

Virginia and Maryland pack many of the seminal sites of America's bloodiest war into a space that includes some of the Eastern seaboard's most attractive countryside.

TRIP HIGHLIGHTS

Antietam
START
● Frederick

105 miles

Manassas National Battlefield Park
Wander Bull Run's bucolic fields

⓷

★ WASHINGTON, DC

153 miles

Fredericksburg
Deep-forest parks hide this battlefield

⓸

230 miles

Richmond
Enjoy historic hotels, great eats and magnificent museums

FINISH
⓽

⓻

Petersburg ●

320 miles

Appomattox Court House National Park
Where the war, and your trip, ends

**3 DAYS
320 MILES / 515KM**

GREAT FOR...

📖

BEST TIME TO GO
September to November for sunny skies and autumnal color shows at preserved battlefields.

ESSENTIAL PHOTO
The fences and fields of Antietam at sunset.

BEST FOR FOODIES
Lamb burgers at Richmond's Burger Bach.

The Civil War Tour

The Civil War was fought from 1861 to 1865 in the nation's backyards, and many of those backyards are between Washington, DC and Richmond. On this trip you will cross battlefields where over 100,000 Americans perished and are buried, foe next to foe. Amid rolling farmlands, sunny hills and deep forests, you'll discover a jarring juxtaposition of bloody legacy and bucolic scenery, and along the way, the places where America forged its identity.

1 Antietam

While most of this trip takes place in Virginia, there is Civil War ground to be covered in neighboring Maryland, a border state officially allied with the Union yet close enough to the South to have Southern sympathies. Confederate General Robert E Lee, hoping to capitalize on a friendly populace, tried to invade Maryland early in the conflict. The subsequent Battle of Antietam, fought in Sharpsburg, MD, on September 17, 1862, has the dubious distinction of marking the bloodiest day in American history. The battle site is preserved at **Antietam National Battlefield** (☏301-432-5124; www.nps.gov/anti; 5831 Dunker Church Rd, Sharpsburg; ☺8:30am–around 6pm) in the corn-and-hill country of north-central Maryland.

As befits an engagement that claimed 22,000 casualties in the course of a single, nightmarish day, even the local geographic nomenclature

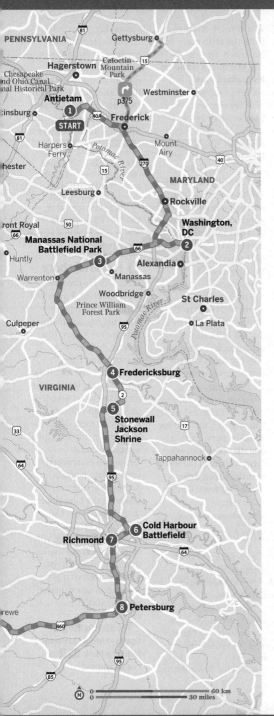

has become violent. An area known as the Sunken Road turned into 'Bloody Lane' after bodies were stacked there. In the park's cemetery, many of the Union gravestones bear the names of Irish and German immigrants who died in a country they had only recently adopted.

The Drive » Take MD-65 south out of Antietam to the town of Sharpsburg. From here, take MD-34 east for 6 miles, then turn right onto US 40A (eastbound). Take US 40A for 11 miles, then merge onto US 70 south, followed 3 miles later by US 270 (bypassing Frederick). Take 270 south to the Beltway (I-495); access exit 45B to get to I-66 east, which will eventually lead you to the National Mall, where the next stops are located.

- - - - - - - - - - - - -

❷ Washington, DC

Washington, DC, was the capital of the Union during the Civil War, just as it is the capital of the country today. While the city was never invaded by the Confederacy, thousands of Union soldiers passed through, trained and drilled inside of the city; indeed, the official name of the North's main fighting force was the Army of the Potomac.

The **National Museum of American History** (www.americanhistory.si.edu; cnr 14th St & Constitution Ave NW; ⊙10am-5:30pm, to 7:30pm Jun-Aug; 🚻), located directly on the National Mall, has good permanent exhibitions on the Civil

Classic Trip

War. Perhaps more importantly, it provides visitors with the context for understanding why the war happened.

Following the war, a grateful nation erected many monuments to Union generals. A statue worth visiting is the **African American Civil War Memorial** (www.afroamcivilwar.org; cnr U St & Vermont Ave NW; underground rail U St-Cardozo), next to the eastern exit of the U St metro stop, inscribed with the names of soldiers of color who served in the Union army.

The Drive » From Washington, DC, it takes about an hour driving along I-66W to reach Manassas.

- - - - - - - - - - -

TRIP HIGHLIGHT

❸ Manassas National Battlefield Park (Bull Run)

The site of the first major pitched battle of the Civil War is mere minutes from the strip malls of Northern Virginia. NPS-run **Manassas National Battlefield Park** (☏703-361-1339; www.nps.gov/mana; 12521 Lee Hwy; adult/child $3/free, film $3; ⏰8:30am-5pm, tours 11:15am, 12:15pm, 2:15pm Jun-Aug) occupies the site where, in 1861, 35,000 Union soldiers and 32,500 Confederates saw the view you have today: a stretch of gorgeous countryside that has miraculously survived the predations of the Army of Northern Virginia real-estate developers.

This is as close as many will come to 19th-century rural America; distant hills, dark, brooding tree lines, low curving fields and the soft hump of overgrown trench works.

Following the battle, both sides realized a long war was at hand. Europe watched nervously; in a matter of weeks, the largest army in the world was the Union Army of the Potomac. The second biggest was the Confederate States of America Army. A year later, at the Battle of Shiloh, 24,000 men were listed as casualties – more than all the accumulated casualties of every previous American war combined.

The Drive » In Manassas, take US 29N for 13 miles and then turn left onto US 17S (Marsh Rd). Follow it south for about 35 miles to get to downtown Fredericksburg.

- - - - - - - - - - -

TRIP HIGHLIGHT

❹ Fredericksburg

If battlefields preserve rural America, Fredericksburg is an example of what the nation's main streets once looked like: orderly grids, touches of green, and friendly storefronts. But for all its cuteness, this is the site of one of the worst blunders in American military history. In 1862, when the Northern Army attempted a massed charge against an entrenched Confederate position, a Southern artilleryman looked at the bare slope that Union forces had to cross and told a commanding officer, 'A chicken could not live on that field when we open on it.' Sixteen charges resulted in an estimated 6000 to 8000 Union casualties.

Fredericksburg & Spotsylvania National Military Park FREE is not as immediately

---

WHAT'S IN A NAME, PART 1?

Although the Civil War is the widely accepted label for the conflict covered in this trip, you'll still hear die-hard Southern boosters refer to the period as the 'War Between the States.' What's the difference? Well, a Civil War implies an armed insurrection against a ruling power that never lost its privilege to govern, whereas the name 'War Between the States' suggests said states always had (and still have) a right to secession from the Republic.

DETOUR:
GETTYSBURG NATIONAL MILITARY PARK

Start: ❶ Antietam

The Battle of Gettysburg, fought in Gettysburg, PA, in July of 1863, marked the turning point of the war and the high-water mark of the Confederacy's attempted rebellion. Lee never made a gambit as bold as this invasion of the North, and his army (arguably) never recovered from the defeat it suffered here.

Gettysburg National Military Park (☏717-334-1124; www.nps.gov/gett; incl museum & visitor center, adult/child/senior $12.50/8.50/11.50; ⊙park 6am-10pm Apr-Oct, to 7pm Nov-Mar, museum 8am-6pm Apr-Oct, to 5pm Nov-Mar) does an excellent job of explaining the course and context of the combat. Look for Little Round Top Hill, where a Union unit checked a Southern flanking maneuver, and the field of Pickett's Charge, where the Confederacy suffered its most crushing defeat up to that point. Following the battle Abraham Lincoln gave his Gettysburg Address here to mark the victory and the 'new birth of the nation' on said country's birthday: July 4.

You can easily lose a day here just soaking up the scenery – a gorgeous swath of rolling hills and lush forest interspersed with hollows, rock formations and farmland. To get here, jump on US 15 northbound in Frederick, MD during the drive between Antietam and Washington, DC. Follow 15 north for 35 miles to Gettysburg.

compelling as Manassas because of the thick forest that still covers the battlefields, but the woods themselves are a sylvan wonder. Again, the pretty nature of... well, nature, grows over graves; the nearby Battle of the Wilderness was named for these thick woods, which caught fire and killed hundreds of wounded soldiers after the shooting was finished.

The Drive » From Fredericksburg, take US 17 south for 5 miles, after which 17 becomes VA-2 (also known as Sandy Lane Dr and Fredericksburg Turnpike). Follow this road for 5 more miles, then turn right onto Stonewall Jackson Rd (State Rd 606).

- - - - - - - - - - - - -

❺ Stonewall Jackson Shrine

In Chancellorsville, Robert E Lee, outnumbered two to one, split his forces and attacked both flanks of the Union army. The audacity of the move caused the Northern force to crumble and flee across the Potomac River, but the victory was costly; in the course of the fighting, Lee's ablest general, Stonewall Jackson, had his arm shot off by a nervous Confederate sentry (the arm is buried near the Fredericksburg National Park visitor center; ask a ranger for directions there).

The wound was patched, but Jackson went on to contract a fatal dose of pneumonia. He was taken to what is now the next stop on this tour: the **Stonewall Jackson Shrine** (☏804-633-6076; 12019 Stonewall Jackson Rd, Woodford; ⊙9am-5pm) in nearby Guinea Station. In a small white cabin set against attractive Virginia horse-country, overrun with sprays of purple flowers and daisy fields, Jackson uttered a series of prolonged ramblings. Then he fell silent, whispered, 'Let us cross over the river and rest in the shade of the trees,' and died.

The Drive » You can get here via I-95, which you take to I-295S (then take exit 34A), which

Classic Trip

WHY THIS IS A CLASSIC TRIP
ADAM KARLIN, AUTHOR

Want to see some of the finest countryside left in the Eastern seaboard, while simultaneously exploring the contradictions, struggles and triumphs at the root of the American experiment? Yeah, we thought so. The Civil War Tour allows travelers to access the formative spaces of the nation, all set against a backdrop of lush fields, dark forests, dirt-rutted country lanes and the immense weight of history.

Top: Visitors at Manassas National Battlefield Park
Left: Cold Harbor Battlefield
Right: Appomattox Court House National Park

MIZCMORE / GETTY IMAGES ©

takes 50 minutes. Or, for a back road experience (one hour, 10 minutes), take VA-2S south for 35 miles until it connects to VA-643/Rural Point Rd. Stay on VA-643 until it becomes VA-156/Cold Harbor Rd, which leads to the battlefield.

----

❻ Cold Harbor Battlefield

By 1864, Union General Ulysses Grant was ready to take the battle into Virginia. His subsequent invasion, dubbed the Overland (or Wilderness) Campaign, was one of the bloodiest of the war. It reached a violent climax at Cold Harbor, just north of Richmond.

At the site now known as **Cold Harbor Battlefield** (☎804-226-1981; www.nps. gov/rich; 5515 Anderson-Wright Dr, Mechanicsville, VA; ☺sunrise-sunset, visitor center 9am-4:30pm), Grant threw his men into a full frontal assault; the resultant casualties were horrendous, and a precursor to WWI trench warfare.

The area has reverted to a forest and field checkerboard overseen by the National Park Service. Ask a ranger to direct you to the third turnout, a series of Union earthworks from where you can look out at the most preserved section of the battlefield: the long, low field Northern soldiers charged across. This landscape has essentially not changed in over 150 years.

The Drive » From Cold Harbor, head north on VA-156/Cold Harbor Rd for about 3 miles until it intersects Creighton Rd. Turn left on Creighton and follow it for 6 miles into Richmond.

TRIP HIGHLIGHT

7 Richmond

There are two Civil War museums in the former capital of the Confederacy, and they make for an interesting study in contrasts. The **Museum of the Confederacy** (MOC; ☏804-649-1861; www.moc.org; 1201 E Clay St; admission $8; ☺10am-5pm Mon-Sat, from noon Sun) was once a shrine to the Southern 'Lost Cause,' and still attracts a fair degree of neo-Confederate types. But the MOC has also graduated into a respected educational institution, and its collection of Confederate artifacts is probably the best in the country. The optional tour of the Confederate White House is recommended for its quirky insights (did you know the second-most powerful man in the Confederacy may have been a gay Jew?).

On the other hand, the **American Civil War Center** (☏804-780-1865; www.tredegar.org; 490 Tredegar St; adult/student/child 7-12 $8/6/2; ☺9am-5pm; 👶), located in the old Tredegar ironworks (the main armament producer for the Confederacy), presents the war from three perspectives: Northern, Southern and African American. Exhibits are well presented and insightful. The effect is clearly powerful and occasionally divisive, a testament to the conflict's lasting impact.

The Drive » Take Rte 95 southbound for about 23 miles and get on exit 52. Get onto 301 (Wythe St) and follow until it becomes Washington St, and eventually VA-35/Oaklawn Dr.

Look for signs to the battlefield park from here.

---

8 Petersburg

Petersburg, just south of Richmond, is the blue-collar sibling city to the Virginia capital, its center gutted by white flight following desegregation. **Petersburg National Battlefield Park** (US 36; vehicle/pedestrian $5/3; ☺9am-5pm) marks the spot where Northern and Southern soldiers spent almost a quarter of the war in a protracted, trench-induced stand-off. The Battle of the Crater, made well-known in Charles Frazier's *Cold Mountain*, was an attempt by Union soldiers to break this stalemate by tunneling under the Confederate lines and blowing up their fortifications; the end result was Union soldiers caught in the hole wrought by their own sabotage, killed like fish in a barrel.

The Drive » Drive south of Petersburg, then west through back roads to follow Lee's last retreat. There's an excellent map available at www.civilwartraveler.com; we prefer taking VA-460 west from Petersburg, then connecting to VA-635, which leads to Appomattox via VA-24, near Farmville.

WHAT'S IN A NAME, PART 2?

One of the more annoying naming conventions of the war goes thus: while the North preferred to name battles for defining geographic terms (Bull Run, Antietam), Southern officers named them for nearby towns (Manassas, Sharpsburg). Although most Americans refer to battles by their Northern names, in some areas folks simply know Manassas as the Battle Of, not as the strip mall with a good Waffle House.

9 Appomattox Court House National Park

About 92 miles west of Petersburg is **Appomattox Court House National Park** (📞434-352-8987; www.nps.gov/apco; vehicle $10; ⏰8:30am-5pm), where the Confederacy finally surrendered. The park itself is wide and lovely, and the ranger staff are extremely helpful.

There are several marker stones dedicated to the surrendering Confederates; the most touching one marks the spot where Robert E Lee rode back from Appomattox after surrendering to Union General Ulysses Grant. Lee's soldiers stood on either side of the field waiting for the return of their commander. When Lee rode into sight he doffed his hat; the troops surged toward him, some saying goodbye while others, too overcome to speak, passed their hands over the flanks of Lee's horse. The spot's dedicated to defeat, humility and reconciliation, and the imperfect realization of all those qualities is the character of the America you've been driving through.

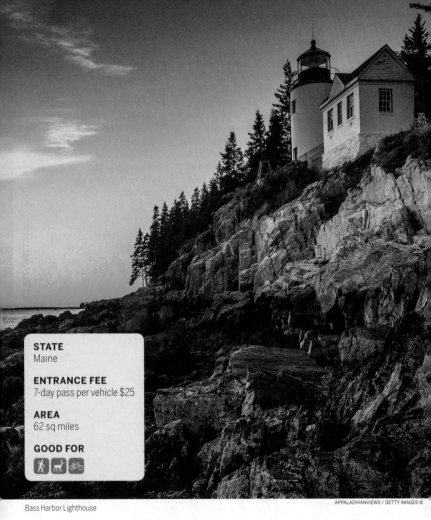

STATE
Maine

ENTRANCE FEE
7-day pass per vehicle $25

AREA
62 sq miles

GOOD FOR

Bass Harbor Lighthouse

Acadia National Park

The only national park in New England encompasses an unspoiled wilderness of undulating coastal mountains, towering sea cliffs, surf-pounded beaches and quiet ponds.

Acadia was established on land that John D Rockefeller donated to the national-parks system to save from encroaching lumber interests.

Today you can hike and bike along the same carriage roads that Rockefeller once rode his horse and buggy on.

The park includes most of Mt Desert Island and tracts of land on the Schoodic Peninsula and Isle au Haut, and holds a wide diversity of wildlife including moose, puffins and bald eagles. The dramatic landscape offers a plethora of both leisurely and adrenaline-filled activities.

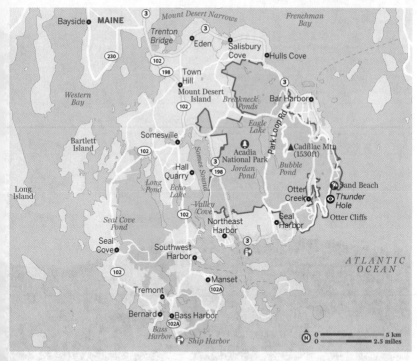

Top Experiences

❶ Park Loop Road

Unfurling for 27 gorgeous miles, Park Loop Rd is the main sightseeing jaunt through the park (mid-April–November). If you're up for a bracing swim or just want to stroll Acadia's longest beach, stop at **Sand Beach**. About a mile beyond Sand Beach you'll come to **Thunder Hole**, where wild Atlantic waves crash into a deep, narrow chasm with such force that it creates a thundering boom, loudest during incoming tides. Look to the south to see **Otter Cliffs**, a favorite rock-climbing spot that rises vertically from the sea. At **Jordan Pond** choose from a 1-mile nature trail loop around the south side of the pond or a 3.2-mile trail that skirts the entire pond perimeter. After you've worked up an appetite, reward yourself with a relaxing afternoon tea on the lawn of Jordan Pond House. Near the end of Park Loop Rd a side road leads up to Cadillac Mountain.

❷ Cadillac Mountain

The majestic centerpiece of Acadia National Park is Cadillac Mountain, the highest coastal peak in the eastern US, reached by a 3.5-mile spur road off Park Loop Rd. Four trails lead to the summit from four directions should you prefer hiking boots to rubber tires. The panoramic 360-degree view of ocean, islands and mountains is a winner any time of the day, but it's truly magical at dawn when hardy souls flock to the top to watch the sun rise over Frenchman Bay.

❸ Hiking

Some 125 miles of hiking trails crisscross the park, from easy half-mile nature walks and level rambles to mountain treks up steep and rocky terrain. A standout is the 3-mile round-trip **Ocean Trail**, which runs between Sand Beach and Otter Cliffs and takes in the most interesting coastal scenery in the park.

Fall foliage

Thunder Hole

④ Ranger Programs

Scores of ranger-led programs, including nature walks, birding talks and kids' field trips, are available in the park. Check out the stars from the sand during the Stars over Sand Beach program. Check the schedule online or at the visitor center.

⑤ Cycling the Carriage Roads

Acadia has 45 miles of carriage roads that are ideal for cycling.

The carriage roads were built by national-parks philanthropist John D Rockefeller, who was an accomplished equestrian with a love of auto-free wilderness and wanted a way to get into the heart of Mount Desert Island solely by horse and buggy.

The hand-hewn stonework, made of locally quarried granite, also includes 17 handsome stone bridges and two gate lodges. The roads are a generous 16ft in width and include unique features like roughly cut granite coping stones, dubbed Rockefeller's Teeth, that serve as guardrails.

Information

Acadia National Park is open year-round, though Park Loop Rd and most facilities are closed in winter. An admission fee is charged from May 1 to October 31. The fee, which is valid for seven consecutive days, is $25 per vehicle, $20 per motorcycle and $12 on bike or foot.

Start your exploration at **Hulls Cove Visitor Center** (☑ 20 7-288-3338; ME 3; ⊙ 8:30am-4:30pm mid-Apr–Jun, Sep & Oct, 8am-6pm Jul & Aug), from where the 27-mile Park Loop Rd circumnavigates the eastern portion of the park.

Sleeping & Eating

The park has three campgrounds and there are scores of restaurants, inns and hotels in Bar Harbor, just a mile beyond the park.

Acadia National Park Campgrounds (☎877-444-6777; www.nps.gov/acad; campsites $22-30) Four miles south of Southwest Harbor, **Seawall** has both by-reservation and walk-up sites. Five miles south of Bar Harbor on ME 3, year-round **Blackwoods** fills quickly in summer, when reservations are strongly recommended. Both sites have restrooms and pay showers. Both are also densely wooded but only a few minutes' walk to the ocean. A third campground with 92 campsites, **Schoodic Woods** opened in September 2015 on the Schoodic Peninsula; for its first season it was first-come, first-served, but reservations are recommended thereafter.

Jordan Pond House (☎207-276-3316; www.acaciajordanpondhouse.com; afternoon tea $10.50, mains $9-24; ⊙11am-8pm mid-May–Oct) Afternoon tea at this lodge-like teahouse has been an Acadia tradition since the late 1800s. Steaming pots of Earl Grey come with hot popovers (hollow rolls made with egg batter) and strawberry jam. Eat outside on the broad lawn overlooking the lake. The park's only restaurant, Jordan Pond also does fancy but often mediocre lunches and dinners.

Getting There & Around

The convenient **Island Explorer** (www.exploreacadia.com; ⊙late Jun–early Oct) runs eight shuttle-bus routes throughout Acadia National Park and to adjacent Bar Harbor, linking trailheads, campgrounds and accommodations.

STATE
Florida

ENTRANCE FEE
Free

AREA
270 sq miles

GOOD FOR

Sealife on the reef

Biscayne National Park

Just to the east of the Everglades is Biscayne National Park, or the 5% of it that isn't underwater. Let us explain: a portion of the world's third-largest reef sits here off the coast of Florida, along with mangrove forests and the northernmost Florida Keys.

A bit overshadowed by the Everglades, Biscayne is unique as national parks go, requiring both a little extra planning and a lot more reward for your effort. The offshore keys, accessible only by boat, offer pristine opportunities for camping.

Generally, summer and fall are the best times to visit the park; you'll want to snorkel when the water is calm. This is some of the best reef-viewing and snorkeling you'll find in the US, outside Hawaii and nearby Key Largo.

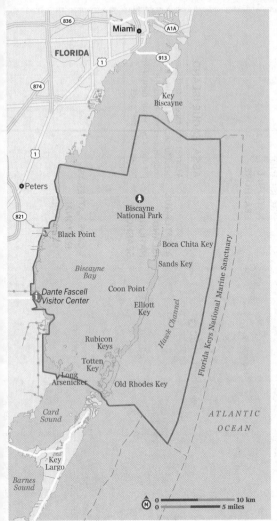

Camping

It costs $25 to moor your boat overnight at Elliott or Boca Chita harbors, but that fee covers the use of one campsite for up to six people and two tents. Bring all supplies, including water, and carry everything out. There's no water on Boca Chita, only saltwater toilets, and since it has a deeper port it tends to attract bigger (and louder) boats (and boaters). Bring your own water to both islands; while there is potable water on Elliot Key, it's best to be prepared.

arrange a private charter boat tour around the park for $300.

Activities

Boating and **fishing** are naturally very popular here, but to do either you'll need to get some paperwork in order. You will also want to make sure you comply with local slow-speed zones, designed to protect the endangered manatee. Maps of all the slow zones can be obtained from rangers, and are needed for navigation purposes in any case.

Although Biscayne is a national park, it is governed by state law when it comes to fishing, so if you want to cast a line, you'll need a state license.

For information, contact **Biscayne Underwater** (www.biscayneunderwater. com) or **Dante Fascell Visitor Center** (📞305-230-7275; www.nps.gov/bisc; 9700 SW 328th St; 🕐9am-5pm Nov-Apr, 10am-5pm May-Oct).

Tours & Rentals

The park itself offers canoe rentals, transportation to the offshore keys, snorkeling and scuba-diving trips, and glass-bottom boat viewing of the exceptional reefs. All tours require a minimum of six people, so call to make reservations. Three-hour glass-bottom boat trips ($45) depart at 10am and are very popular; if you're lucky you may spot some dolphins or manatees. Canoe rentals cost $12 per hour and kayaks $16; they're rented from 9am to 3pm. Three-hour snorkeling trips ($45) depart at 1:15pm daily; you'll have about 1½ hours in the water. Scuba trips ($99) depart at 8:30am Friday to Sunday. You can also

National Seashores (Eastern USA)

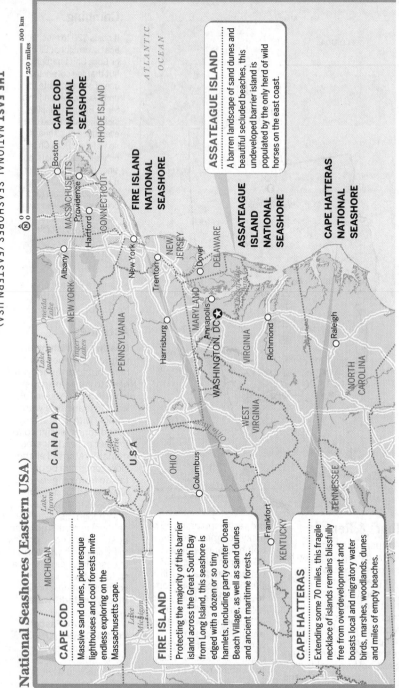

CAPE COD

Massive sand dunes, picturesque lighthouses and cool forests invite endless exploring on the Massachusetts cape.

FIRE ISLAND

Protecting the majority of this barrier island across the Great South Bay from Long Island, this seashore is edged with a dozen or so tiny hamlets, including party center Ocean Beach Village, as well as sand dunes and ancient maritime forests.

CAPE HATTERAS

Extending some 70 miles, this fragile necklace of islands remains blissfully free from overdevelopment and boasts local and migratory water birds, marshes, woodlands, dunes and miles of empty beaches.

ASSATEAGUE ISLAND

A barren landscape of sand dunes and beautiful secluded beaches, this undeveloped barrier island is populated by the only herd of wild horses on the east coast.

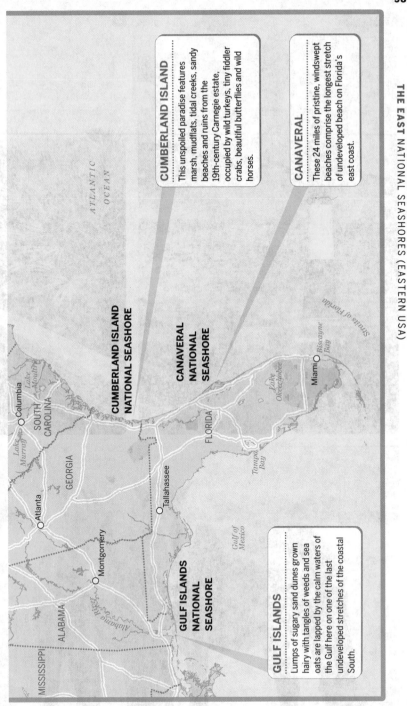

CUMBERLAND ISLAND

This unspoiled paradise features marsh, mudflats, tidal creeks, sandy beaches and ruins from the 19th-century Carnegie estate, occupied by wild turkeys, tiny fiddler crabs, beautiful butterflies and wild horses.

CANAVERAL

These 24 miles of pristine, windswept beaches comprise the longest stretch of undeveloped beach on Florida's east coast.

GULF ISLANDS

Lumps of sugary sand dunes grown hairy with tangles of weeds and sea oats are lapped by the calm waters of the Gulf here on one of the last undeveloped stretches of the coastal South.

CUMBERLAND ISLAND NATIONAL SEASHORE

CANAVERAL NATIONAL SEASHORE

GULF ISLANDS NATIONAL SEASHORE

ATLANTIC OCEAN

Straits of Florida

Columbia

SOUTH CAROLINA

Lake Moultrie

Lake Murray

Atlanta

GEORGIA

Tallahassee

FLORIDA

Lake Okeechobee

Miami

Biscayne Bay

Tampa Bay

Gulf of Mexico

Montgomery

ALABAMA

MISSISSIPPI

Alabama River

MIKEREGA / GETTY IMAGES ©

MICHAELWARRENPIX / GETTY IMAGES ©

Fire Island Lighthouse
e Island is ringed with charming hamlets, sand
nes and forests.

Canaveral National Seashore
e longest stretch of undeveloped beach in
rida's east.

Cumberland Island
touched tidal creeks, marshes, mudflats and
aches.

Wild ponies
ld horses roam secluded Assateague Island.

SILVRSHOOTR / GETTY IMAGES ©

STATE
South Carolina

ENTRANCE FEE
Free

AREA
35 sq miles

GOOD FOR

The Boardwalk Trail

Congaree National Park

America's largest intact, old-growth floodplain forest can be found in this park. The lush trees growing here are some of the tallest in the eastern USA, forming one of the highest temperate deciduous forest canopies left in the world.

Waters from the Congaree and Wateree Rivers pass through this park's floodplain, carrying nutrients and sediments that nourish and regenerate the ecosystem and support the growth of national and state champion trees. As a result, extraordinary biodiversity exists here. This is what draws people to the park, as well as the Congaree Swamp. However, Congaree is actually not a swamp, because it does not contain standing water throughout most of the year. What it does contain, though, is a variety of rare and endangered species of plants and animals.

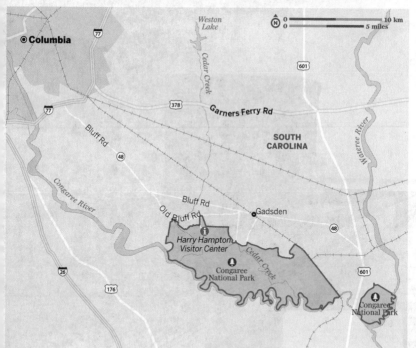

Hiking

Hiking the park's many trails allows you to get more closely acquainted with Congaree National Park. Whether you are looking for a short hike on the **Boardwalk Trail**, or desire a longer trek into the backcountry, there are options available for hikers of all skills and abilities. Depending on what you want to see, trails can lead you to oxbow lakes, the Congaree River, or stands of impressive old-growth trees that help make up the tallest deciduous forest in the USA.

Because most of the park lies within a floodplain, the terrain is generally flat with only slight elevation changes. All trails begin from the **Harry Hampton Visitor Center** and vary in length.

Canoeing & Kayaking

Traveling on **Cedar Creek** by canoe or kayak is a great way to experience the park. This creek passes through a primeval old-growth forest which contains some of the tallest trees in eastern North America. Opportunities are abundant for viewing various types of wildlife such as river otter, deer, turtles, wading birds, and even alligators. Paddling the creek requires visitors to bring their own canoe or kayak with them, unless taking part in a guided tour. Outfitters in the city of **Columbia** have gear for rent if you do not have your own. The park does not rent out kayaks or canoes.

Eating & Sleeping

There are no food services within the park. Limited food options are available in the town of Gadsden, about 10 minutes from the park. A variety of restaurants are available in the city of Columbia, about 20 minutes from the park. Camping is the only form of overnight lodging that is available at the park. There are no lodges, hotels or cabins located here. Note that backcountry camping is free.

Longleaf Campground (100 National Park Rd, Hopkins; campsite $10)

Bluff Campground (100 National Park Rd, Hopkins; campsite $5)

STATE
Florida

ENTRANCE FEE
7-day pass per adult/
child $10/free

AREA
100 sq miles

GOOD FOR

Fort Jefferson

Dry Tortugas National Park

Floating in the middle of the Gulf of Mexico, this is America's most inaccessible national park. Your efforts to get here (by boat or plane only) will be rewarded with amazing snorkeling, diving, bird-watching and stargazing.

Ponce de León christened the area Tortugas (pronounced tor-*too*-guzz) after the sea turtles he found here, and the 'Dry' part was added later to warn about the absence of fresh water on the island.

But this is more than just a pretty cluster of islands with no drinking water. Come for spectacular coral reefs, an abundance of marine life and a good dose of history.

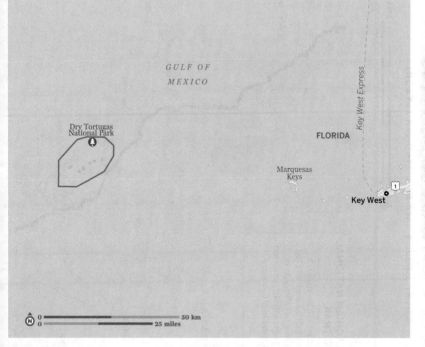

Fort Jefferson

The never-completed Civil War–era **Fort Jefferson** provides a striking hexagonal centerpiece of red brick rising up from the emerald waters on **Garden Key**. The founding legislation of the park mandates that the National Park Service protects, stablilizes, restores and interprets the fort for future generations. It's an imposing example of 19th-century masonry fortification – bring your camera.

Swimming & Snorkeling

Dry Tortugas is in the southwest corner of the Florida Keys reef system, the third largest in the world (after Australia and Belize). And with only 1% of the park on dry ground, getting in the water is the best way to see the park's marine life.

Getting There

Yankee Freedom (☎800-634-0939; www.drytortugas. com; Historic Seaport; day trip adult/child $170/125) is a fast ferry that leaves from the north end of Grinnell St in Key West; the fare includes breakfast, a picnic lunch, snorkeling gear and tour of the fort. Or, you can hop on a **Key West Seaplane** (☎305-293-9300; www.key westseaplanecharters.com; half-day trip adult/child 3-12yr $300/239) for a half-day or full-day trip. Whichever you choose, reserve at least a week ahead.

Camping

If you really want to enjoy the park's isolation, stay overnight at one of Garden Key's 10 campsites (site $15). Reserve early through the park office, and bring everything you need, because once that boat leaves, you're on your own.

Bird-Watching Season

Between the months of March and September, some 100,000 sooty terns come to nest on the islands of the Dry Tortugas. They are joined by brown noddies, roseate terns, double-crested cormorants and brown pelicans.

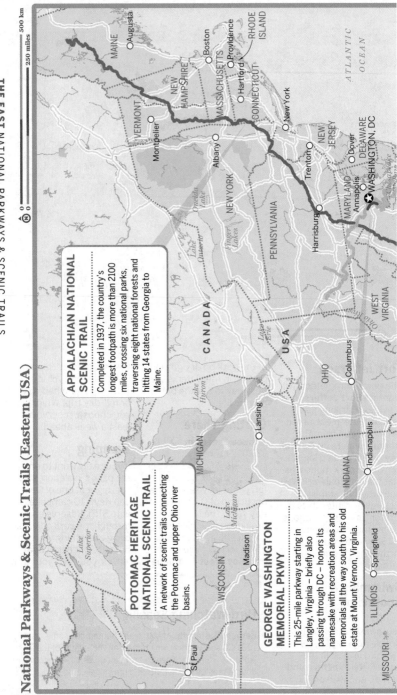

National Parkways & Scenic Trails (Eastern USA)

APPALACHIAN NATIONAL SCENIC TRAIL

Completed in 1937, the country's longest footpath is more than 2100 miles, crossing six national parks, traversing eight national forests and hitting 14 states from Georgia to Maine.

POTOMAC HERITAGE NATIONAL SCENIC TRAIL

A network of scenic trails connecting the Potomac and upper Ohio river basins.

GEORGE WASHINGTON MEMORIAL PKWY

This 25-mile parkway starting in Langley, Virginia – briefly also passing through DC – honors its namesake with recreation areas and memorials all the way south to his old estate at Mount Vernon, Virginia.

0   250 miles
0   500 km

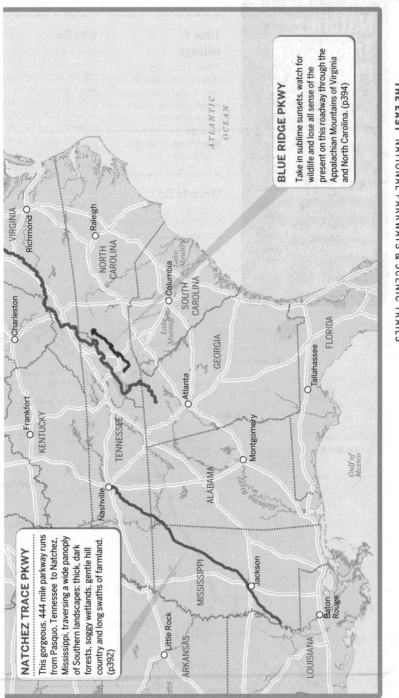

BLUE RIDGE PKWY

Take in sublime sunsets, watch for wildlife and lose all sense of the present on this roadway through the Appalachian Mountains of Virginia and North Carolina. (p394)

NATCHEZ TRACE PKWY

This gorgeous, 444 mile parkway runs from Pasquo, Tennessee to Natchez, Mississippi, traversing a wide panoply of Southern landscapes: thick, dark forests, soggy wetlands, gentle hill country and long swaths of farmland. (p392)

Natchez Trace Parkway

With emerald mounds, jade swamps, hiking trails, opulent mansions, riverside saloons and layer upon layer of American history, the Natchez Trace Parkway is the richest drive in the South.

Time & Mileage

Time: Three days, though you could do it in two. Travel times aren't exactly speedy on the two-lane road.
Mileage: 444 miles.
Start/End: Nashville, TN/Natchez, MS.

When to Go

April to June and September to November are best. Summer can be hotter than hot.

Why Go

Think about this as you set out: you'll be following the same path as a who's who of historic figures, including Andrew Jackson (7th president of the US and face of the $20 bill), Jefferson Davis (president of the Confederacy), James Audubon (naturalist and painter), Meriwether Lewis (famous explorer who died on the Trace in 1809), Ulysses S Grant (18th president of the US) and – wait for it – a

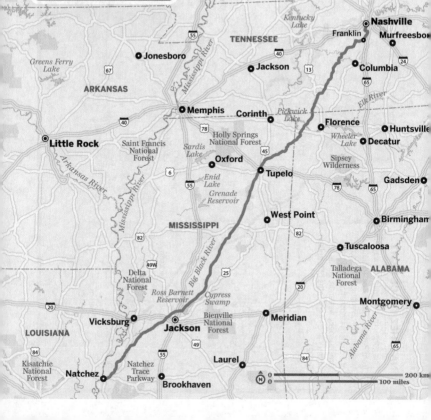

Cypress Swamp

young Elvis Presley. The drive meanders by various cultural and historic sites that let you learn more about each man.

The Route

Nashville is the easiest place to access the parkway, and for country-music fans and wannabe songwriters all over the world, a trip to the city is the ultimate pilgrimage, with boot-stomping honky-tonks, the Country Music Hall of Fame and a sweet historic district to explore. There's also good eatin' at local cafeterias, the ultimate way to indulge in everything from barbecue chicken and pig's feet to turnip greens and baked apples.

About 10 miles beyond Nashville, the road swings by one of the Civil War's bloodiest battlefields at Franklin, where 20,000 Confederates and 17,000 Union soldiers fought on November 30, 1864. Further along are Confederate grave sites for unknown soldiers. Several centuries-old indigenous burial mounds likewise rise up along the way. Emerald Mound, near Natchez, is one of the nation's largest, and the massive grassy pyramid still buzzes with ancient energy.

Other highlights en route include the town of Tupelo – where you can visit the humble house where Elvis grew up, learned to play the guitar and dreamed big – and tree-shaded, milky-green Cypress Swamp, filled with alligators. Natchez itself is a living antebellum museum, all sweeping spiral staircases, chandeliers and thick column houses.

Resources

Natchez Trace Parkway (www.nps.gov/natr) Park-service website that provides road construction updates, plus information on local activities and historic sites.

Natchez Trace Compact (www.scenic trace.com) State tourism bureaus of Tennessee, Alabama and Mississippi band together to offer route itineraries, maps and event info.

Blue Ridge Parkway

Snaking through the Appalachian Mountains of Virginia and North Carolina, the parkway immerses road trippers in glorious highlands scenery, with plenty of pull-offs for vista-gaping, hiking and Southern hospitality.

Time & Mileage

Time: At least two days, but allow five days to do it right. It's slow going on the steep, curvy roads, plus you'll want to pit-stop for hiking, eating and sightseeing.
Mileage: 469 miles.
Start/End: Front Royal, VA/Cherokee, NC.

When to Go

April through October, when visitor facilities are open (many close during winter) is best. May is best for wildflowers.

Leaf-peepers pour in during October. Expect big crowds if you go during the summer or early autumn.

Why Go

Although it skirts dozens of small towns and a few metropolitan areas, the Blue Ridge Pkwy feels far removed from modern-day America. Here, rustic log cabins with creaky rocking chairs on the front porches still dot the hillsides, while signs for folk-art shops and live-bluegrass-music joints

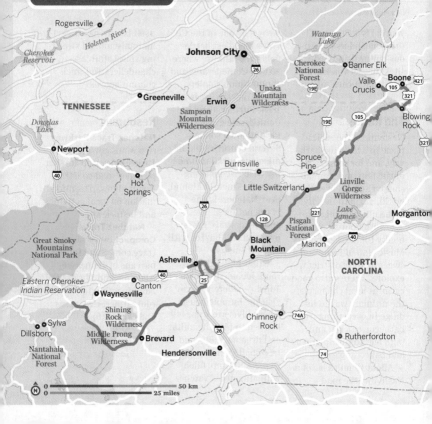

Blue Ridge Mountains and Blue Ridge Parkway

entice travelers onto meandering side roads. Log-cabin diners dish up heaping piles of buckwheat pancakes with blackberry preserves and a side of country ham.

When you need to work off all that good Southern cooking, over 100 hiking trails can be accessed along the Blue Ridge Pkwy, from gentle nature walks to rough-and-ready tramps along the legendary Appalachian Trail. Go canoeing, kayaking or inner-tubing along rushing rivers, or dangle a fishing line over the side of a rowboat on petite lakes.

The Route

The bucolic byway connects Virginia's Shenandoah National Park with Great Smoky Mountains National Park, straddling the North Carolina–Tennessee border. Towns along the way include Boone and Asheville in North Carolina and Galax and Roanoke in Virginia, with Charlottesville, VA, also a short drive away. Bigger cities within range of the parkway include Washington, DC (140 miles), and Richmond, VA (95 miles).

Many road trippers also add Skyline Drive (p413) onto their Blue Ridge route. The bendy, 105-mile Skyline connects to the parkway's northern end and ups the scenic ante by doling out mind-blowing mountain vistas on its ramble through Shenandoah National Park. One caveat: you will have to pay a $20 fee to travel the road – this is not a toll, but rather the park's admission charge.

- - - - - - - - - -

Resources

Blue Ridge Parkway (www.blueridgeparkway. org) Maps, activities and places to stay along the way. Also offers the free *Blue Ridge Parkway Travel Planner* to download.

Hiking the Blue Ridge Parkway (Randy Johnson; 2010) This book offers in-depth trail descriptions, topographic maps and other essential info for hikes both short and long.

Skyline Drive (www. visitskylinedrive.org) Lodging, hiking and wildlife along the picturesque addendum to the parkway.

STATE
Florida

ENTRANCE FEE
7-day pass per vehicle $20

AREA
2344 sq miles

GOOD FOR

Mangrove estuary system

Everglades National Park

More than Miami, the Everglades make South Florida truly unique. Called the 'River of Grass' by Native Americans, this is not just a wetland, or a swamp, or a lake, or a river, or a prairie, or a grassland – it is all of the above.

When you watch anhinga flex their wings before breaking into corkscrew dives, or the slow, Jurassic flap of a great blue heron gliding over its domain, or the sun kissing miles of unbroken sawgrass as it sets behind humps of skeletal cypress domes, you'll start to have an idea of what we're speaking of. Forget what you've heard about airboats and swamp buggies – the Everglades should be approached with the same silence and gentle persuasion it shows its animal inhabitants.

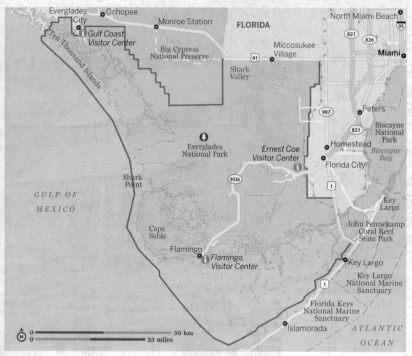

When to Go

The busy dry season, December through March, brings optimum wildlife viewing along watercourses. However, some kayak routes will be difficult during this time.

The weather heats up from April through June, but there's a good mix of water and wildlife. July through November means heat, bugs and (except October and November) chances of hurricanes.

When you arrive, be sure to pick up brochures, which detail hiking trails, paddling routes, campgrounds, business hours and other useful information, from the Ernest Coe, Shark Valley or Gulf Coast information centers.

Sleeping

The park's two developed campgrounds have water, toilets and grills. The best are the first-come, first-served sites at **Long Pine Key** (☎305-242-7745; www.nps.gov/ever/; campsite $20), just west of Royal Palm Visitor Center.

Reserve ahead for campsites at **Flamingo** (☎877-444-6777; www.nps.gov/ever/planyourvisit/; campsite $20), which have cold-water showers and electricity.

There is **backcountry camping** (☎239-695-2945, 239-695-3311; www.nps.gov/ever/; permit $15, plus per person per night $2) throughout the park, which includes beach sites, ground sites and chickees (covered wooden platforms above the water). A permit from the visitor center is required from November to April.

There are good hotels in Everglades City and Homestead.

Getting There & Around

The Glades comprise the 80 southernmost miles of Florida, and are easily accessible from Miami. They are bound by the Atlantic Ocean to the east and the Gulf of Mexico to the west.

You need a car to properly enter, and a good pair of walking boots is essential to penetrate the interior.

Canoes and kayaks can be rented from outfits inside and outside of the park, or else you can seek out guided canoe and kayak tours. Bicycles are well suited to the flat roads.

STATES
North Carolina &
Tennessee

ENTRANCE FEE
Free

AREA
815 sq miles

GOOD FOR

Log cabin with split rail fence

Great Smoky Mountains National Park

Running down the spine of the ancient Appalachian Mountains, the iconic Great Smoky Mountains National Park offers visitors a chance to experience deep, mossy, mysterious old-growth forests.

A magic place for hikers, bikers, wildlife-watchers and lovers of scenic drives, this park is the country's most popular, attracting nearly 10 million visitors a year. Studies have shown, though, that 95% of visitors never venture further than 100yd from their cars, so it's easy to leave the teeming masses behind – you'll be glad you did.

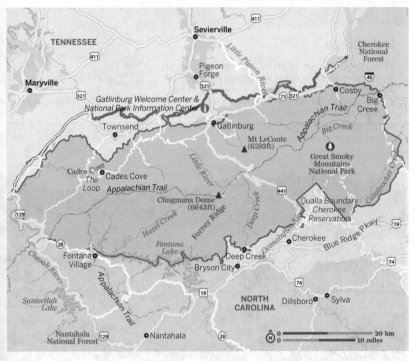

History

For millennia, these misty mountains were the primary domain of the Cherokee people. The Native Americans were later supplanted by Scotch-Irish, French and German settlers, a conglomeration that one early settler characterized as 'a heady brew.' In Cades Cove and Cataloochee the historic log homes, churches, mills and schoolhouses of these mountain people still stand with doors wide open.

The park was founded in 1934, and much of its infrastructure was built by Civilian Conservation Corps workers during the Great Depression. Unlike most other national parks, Great Smoky charges no admission fee, nor will it ever; this proviso was written into the park's original charter as a stipulation for a $5 million Rockefeller family grant.

Orientation

Great Smoky Mountains National Park straddles the North Carolina and Tennessee border, which runs diagonally through the heart of the park, shadowed by the Appalachian Trail (AT). The park encompasses some 521,000 acres and more than 800 sq miles. As the crow flies, it is roughly 65 miles wide and 25 miles long.

The north–south Newfound Gap Rd/Hwy 441 spans the park from one end to the other, connecting the gateway towns of Gatlinburg, Tennessee on the north–central border and Cherokee, North Carolina on the south–central border.

Cades Cove Area

Many consider this special place to be a national treasure, thanks to its poignant cultural legacy, telling pioneer architecture and plentiful wildlife. An 11-mile loop road encircles the cove, with parking areas at the base of the various sights. The loop is open to traffic from dawn to dusk except on summer Wednesdays and Saturdays, when bikers and hikers rule the road. Pick up the self-guided auto tour booklet ($1) from any visitor center or at the entrance to Cades Cove itself.

Mt LeConte

Mt LeConte (6593ft) is the park's third-highest peak, and one of its most familiar sights, visible from practically every viewpoint. The only way to get to the top is on foot. It is accessible by six trails, which range from 5 to 10 miles in length. At the summit, LeConte Lodge is the park's only non-camping lodging, but you better book ahead – it's often full up to a year in advance.

Great Smoky Mountains National Park

Great Smoky's most-used entrances lie just outside the gateway towns of Gatlinburg and Cherokee, at opposite ends of Newfound Gap Rd/Hwy 441.

Also heavily used is the Hwy 73 entrance near Townsend, Tennessee, which offers a straight shot to Cades Cove.

Hiking

Whether you have an irrepressible urge to climb a mountain or just want to get some fresh air, hiking in Great Smoky Mountains National Park is the single best way to experience the sublime beauty of this singular place. Even if you're only here for a short visit, be sure to include at least one hike in your itinerary. Trails range from flat, easy and short paths to longer, more strenuous endeavors. Many are excellent for families, some are wheelchair accessible, and the majority of trailheads begin from major sights. No matter what your physical ability or endurance level, there's a hike out there for you.

Backpacking

More than 800 miles of well-marked backcountry trails crisscross these mountains, including 70 miles of the 2,181-mile Appalachian Trail. Popular hikes include the 11.4-mile Gregory Bald at Cades Cove, the 13.4-mile Trillium Gap trail to the summit of Mt LeConte, and the 31.2-mile stretch of the Appalachian Trail East (you must make reservations to sleep in the AT's hiking shelters). Backcountry camping is free, but you must obtain a permit at one of the ranger stations or visitor centers.

Cycling

Bicycles are welcome on most park roads, with the exception of the Roaring Fork Motor Nature Trail. However, it is important that you choose your road wisely. Due to steep terrain, narrow byways and heavy car traffic, many park roads are not well suited for safe or enjoyable riding. Great Smoky has no mountain-biking trails. Bicycles are allowed only on the Gatlinburg Trail, the Oconaluftee River Trail and the Lower Deep Creek Trail. They are prohibited on all other park trails.

By far the best place for a carefree cycling tour is Cades Cove, particularly when the road is closed to cars (Wednesday and Sunday before 10am from mid-May to late September). In summer and fall, rent cycles from **Cades Cove Campground Store** (☎865-448-9034; www.cadescovetrading.com; bike rental adult/child per hr $7.50/4.50).

Driving Tours

Many visitors to Great Smoky never leave their cars, and while we don't recommend that, it's understandable – this park has some of the loveliest scenic drives around. Most of the drives have *Auto Tour* brochures ($1) available at the visitor centers.

Horseback Riding

A staggering – or should we say galloping – 550 miles of the park's hiking trails are open to horses and their humans. Assuming you're not towing your own horse, sign on for a trail ride at one of the park's three stables, all open between mid-March and mid-November. Trail rides are about $30 per person.

Cades Cove Riding Stables (☎865-448-9009; www.cadescovestables.com)

Smokemont Riding Stable (☎828-497-2373; www.smokemontridingstable.com)

Smoky Mountain Riding Stables (☎865-436-5634; www.smokymountainriding stables.com)

Smoky Mountains Day Hikes

These are a few of our favorite short hikes on, or bordering, the North Carolina side of the park.

Charlie's Bunion Follow the Appalachian Trail 4 miles from the Newfound Gap overlook to a rocky outcrop for sweeping mountain-and-valley views.

Big Creek Trail Hike an easy 2 miles to Mouse Creek Falls or go another 3 miles to a backcountry campground; the trailhead is near I-40 on the park's northeastern edge.

Boogerman Trail Moderate 7-mile loop passing old farmsteads; accessible via Cove Creek Rd.

Chasteen Creek Falls From Smokemont campground, this 4-mile round-trip passes a small waterfall.

Eating

Nuts and berries notwithstanding, there's nothing to eat in Great Smoky Mountains National Park, save for guests-only fare at LeConte Lodge, vending machines at Sugarlands Visitor Center, and the meager offerings sold at the Cades Cove Campground Store. Luckily, there are lots of restaurant options in the surrounding towns.

Sleeping

Great Smoky Mountains National Park provides varied camping options, but only one place where you can get a room, and you have to hike to the top of a mountain to enjoy this privilege. Gatlinburg has by far the most sleeping options of any gateway town.

Camping

The National Park Service maintains developed campgrounds at 10 locations in the park. Each campground has restrooms with cold running water and flush toilets, but there are no showers or electrical or water hookups in the park. Each individual campsite has a fire grate and picnic table.

Campsites at Cades Cove, Cataloochee, Cosby, Elkmont, and Smokemont may accept **reservations** (☏800-365-2267; www. recreation.gov), but only between May 15 and October 31. Sites may be reserved up to six months in advance. All other campgrounds are first-come, first-served. There are a number of options for group camping for groups of eight or more – check out the park website for more info. Backcountry camping is allowed by permit only – pick one up at any one of the visitor centers.

Park Policies & Regulations

Campers must store all food in bear-proof containers or on storage poles. Backcountry campfires are forbidden. If you plan to fish, you need either a North Carolina or Tennessee fishing license, which are sold at sporting goods stores and gas stations outside the park.

Information

The National Parks Services' **Great Smoky Mountains National Park website** (www. nps.gov/grsm) has comprehensive and extremely valuable information about campgrounds, hiking trails, activities, visitor center hours and more.

Maps

A variety of useful maps, hiking guides and driving tours are available for sale at all the visitor centers.

Dangers & Annoyances

Black bears are active throughout the park, and can be dangerous. Campers should keep all food in their cars or tied to cables, and hikers should never approach or feed bears. If a bear approaches you, back away slowly. If the bear continues to approach, shout or wave your arms to intimidate it. As a last resort, throw rocks or other objects, or try to deter the bear with a large stick. Never try to run.

When to Go

The park is open year-round, but summer and fall are the most popular seasons. Some facilities are closed late fall through early spring, and roads may be closed in winter due to inclement weather.

When You Arrive

Great Smoky Mountains National Park is open every day, year-round. However, Newfound Gap Rd often closes during winter storms, and several others, including Clingmans Dome Rd, close during the winter months. As there are no fee stations, you will have to stop by a visitor center to pick up a park map.

Getting There & Around

The closest major airport is Knoxville's McGhee Tyson Airport, 45 miles from the Gatlinburg entrance.

STATE
Arkansas

ENTRANCE FEE
Free

AREA
8.67 sq miles

GOOD FOR

Geothermal springs

Hot Springs National Park

Most national parks are far from bustling cities and keep natural resources away from commercial users, but not Hot Springs. The smallest of the national parks, Hot Springs borders a city of the same name that has made an industry out of tapping and sharing the park's major resource: mineral-rich waters of hot springs.

The purpose of Hot Springs National Park is to protect its exceptional geothermal spring water and associated lands for public health, wellness, and enjoyment. The park is popular with visitors for the 47 hot springs that emerge from the Hot Springs Mountain at an average 143°F (62°C). It is also the only unit of the national-park system that is administered to give away its primary natural resource to the general public, and as such it has become known as the 'American Spa.'

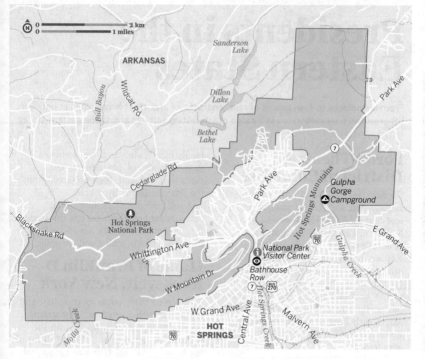

A promenade runs through the park around the hillside behind **Bathhouse Row**, where some springs survive intact, and a network of trails covers Hot Springs' mountains. Many of the old bathhouses have been converted into art galleries affiliated with the National Parks Service (NPS).

Hot Springs

The springs are all grouped near the base of Hot Springs Mountain. Each day about 700,000 gallons of water flow from the springs into an intricate piping and reservoir system. This supplies water to commercial baths, such as the popular **Buckstaff Bath House** (501-623-2308; www.buckstaffbaths.com; 509 Central Ave; thermal bath $33, with massage $71; 8-11:45am & 1:30-3pm Mon-Sat Mar-Nov, closed Sat afternoon Dec-Feb) and to free 'jug fountains,' where people can fill containers with the fresh-tasting, chemical-free water.

For more information on the park and its hot springs, head to the **NPS Visitor Center** (Fordyce Bath House; 501-620-6715; www.nps.gov/hosp; 369 Central Ave; 9am-5pm) on Bathhouse Row.

Hiking

Walking paths have been a part of Hot Springs National Park for over a century. The park has 26 miles of trails where you can spot wildflowers, rock formations and, of course, stunning scenery. The trails are of varying length and difficulty, and hikers should always stay on the trails and avoid shortcuts so as not to damage the surrounding environment.

Sleeping

There is no park-owned lodging except the **Gulpha Gorge Campground** (www.nps.gov/hosp/planyourvisit/campground.htm; 305 Gorge Rd, Hot Springs; campsites $10, with hookups $30). Sites are first-come, first-served. You cannot make a reservation. The city of Hot Springs nearby offers many lodging facilities.

Presidents in the Eastern States

From birthplaces to final places of rest, and sites of important happenings in between, US presidents are celebrated in a range of interesting settings across the eastern states.

Ford's Theatre, District of Columbia

On April 14, 1865, John Wilkes Booth assassinated Abraham Lincoln in his box seat here (☏202-426-6924; www.fords.org; 511 10th St NW, Washington, DC; ◷9am-4:30pm; ⓂMetro Center) FREE. Timed-entry tickets let you see the flag-draped site. They also provide entry to the basement museum (displaying Booth's .44-caliber pistol, his muddy boot etc) and to Petersen House (across the street), where Lincoln died. Arrive early because tickets do run out. Reserve online ($6.25 fee) to ensure admittance.

The play the president and Mrs Lincoln watched was *Our American Cousin*. Booth knew the farce and knew at what line the audience would laugh most. He shot Lincoln at that moment to muffle the sound. Park Service rangers tell the full story.

The theater still holds performances, and sometimes the venue is closed to the public. It's always smart to check the schedule before heading out. Ford's posts it online, or you can call the box office to make sure the site is open.

John F Kennedy National Historic Site, Massachusetts

Four of the nine Kennedy children were born and raised in this modest house (www.nps.gov/jofi; 83 Beals St, Brookline; ◷9:30am-5pm Wed-Sun May-Oct; ⓣCoolidge Corner) FREE, including Jack, who was born in the master bedroom in 1917. Matriarch Rose Kennedy oversaw the restoration of the house in the late 1960s; today her narrative sheds light on the Kennedys' family life. Guided tours allow visitors to see furnishings, photographs and mementos that have been preserved from the time the family lived here.

A self-guided walking tour of the surrounding neighborhood sets the scene for the Kennedy family's day-to-day life, including church, school and shopping.

Home of Franklin D Roosevelt, New York

FDR served three terms as president and instituted lasting progressive programs; he also made the decision to drop the A-bomb on Japan to end WWII. A tour of his home (☏845-486-7770; www.nps.gov/hofr; 4097 Albany Post Rd, Hyde Park; adult/child $18/ free, museum only adult/child $9/free; ◷9am-5pm), relatively modest considering his family wealth, is interesting, but it can be unpleasantly crowded in summer.

In this case, better to focus on the excellent museum, built around FDR's own library, where he recorded his groundbreaking radio program of 'fireside chats.

Sagamore Hill, New York

Theodore Roosevelt's Long Island home (☏516-922-4788; www.nps.gov/sahi; 20 Sagamore Hill Rd, Oyster Bay; museum & grounds free, house tour adult/child $10/ free; ◷9am-5pm Wed-Sun) FREE, often called the 'summer White House,' is open to visitors by guided tour. There's also an excellent museum (free), and the surrounding land is a nature preserve.

....

1. Reenactment at Petersen House, where Abraham Lincoln was assassinated
2. Home of Franklin D Roosevelt

Abraham Lincoln Birthplace

Theodore Roosevelt Inaugural, New York

Guided tours of the Ansley-Wilcox House (☑716-884-0095; www.nps.gov/thri; 641 Delaware Ave, Buffalo; adult/child $10/5; ⊘tours hourly 9:30am-3:30pm Mon-Fri, from 12:30pm Sat & Sun) tell the dramatic tale of Teddy's emergency swearing-in here in 1901, after President William McKinley was assassinated while attending Buffalo's Pan American Exposition.

Theodore Roosevelt Birthplace, New York

This National Historic Site (☑212-260-1616; www.nps.gov/thrb; 28 E 20th St, btwn Park Ave S & Broadway, New York; adult/child $3/free; ⊘guided tours 10am, 11am, 1pm, 2pm, 3pm & 4pm Tue-Sat; ⑤N/R/W, 6 to 23rd St) is a bit of a cheat, since the physical house where the 26th president was actually born was demolished in his own lifetime. But this building is a worthy reconstruction by his relatives, who joined it with another family residence next door.

If you're interested in Roosevelt's extraordinary life, which has been somewhat overshadowed by the enduring legacy of his younger cousin Franklin D, visit here – especially if you don't have the time to see his spectacular summer home, Sagamore Hill, in Long Island's Oyster Bay. Guided tours of the property last 30 minutes.

Abraham Lincoln Birthplace, Kentucky

The Abraham Lincoln Birthplace (www.nps. gov/abli; 2995 Lincoln Farm Road, Hodgenville; ⊘8am-4:45pm, to 6:45pm summer) FREE is a faux-Greek temple constructed around an old log cabin. Ten minutes away is Honest Abe's boyhood home at Knob Creek, with access to hiking trails.

Adams National Historic Park, Massachusetts

The Adams family sights are accessible by guided tours departing from the Adams National Historic Park Visitor Center (www. nps.gov/adam; 1250 Hancock St, Quincy; adult/child $5/free; ⊘9am-5pm mid-Apr–mid-Nov; Ⓣ Quincy Center). Every half-hour (until 3:15pm), trolleys travel to the **John Adams and John Quincy Adams Birthplaces**, the oldest presidential birthplaces in the USA. These two 17th-century saltbox houses stand side by side along the old Coast Rd, which connected Plymouth to Boston.

The houses are furnished as they would have been in the 18th century, so visitors can see where John Adams started his law career, started his family and wrote the Massachusetts Constitution (which was later used as the basis for the US Constitution).

General Ulysses S Grant National Memorial

From here, the trolley continues to the **Old House**, also called Peacefields, which was the residence of four generations of the Adams family from 1788 to 1927. The house contains original furnishings and decorations from the Adams family, including the chair in which John Adams died on July 4, 1826, the 50th anniversary of the Declaration of Independence (and, spookily, the same day that Thomas Jefferson died on his estate in Virginia). On the grounds, the spectacular two-story library and the lovely formal gardens are highlights.

General Ulysses S Grant National Memorial, New York

Popularly known as Grant's Tomb ('Who's buried in Grant's Tomb?' 'Who?' 'Grant, stupid!' goes a classic joke), this landmark (www.nps.gov/gegr; Riverside Dr at 122nd St, New York; ☺9am-5pm Wed-Sun; ⑤1 to 125th St) FREE holds the remains of Civil War hero and 18th president Ulysses S Grant and his wife, Julia. Completed in 1897 – 12 years after his death – the imposing granite structure is the largest mausoleum in America.

Seventeen Gaudi-inspired mosaic benches, designed by Chilean artist Pedro Silva in the 1970s, surround the mausoleum. It's a downright hallucinatory installation – and a good spot to contemplate the musings of the late, great comedian George Carlin, who was known to light up here back in the day.

George Washington Birthplace, Virginia

Eleven miles southeast of Colonial Beach, at the point where Pope's Creek flows into the Potomac River, is a rustic patchwork of tobacco fields, wheat plots, broadleaf forest and waterfront views over the bluffs of the Northern Neck. It's a gorgeous spot, and the site where John Washington – great-grandfather of the first president – settled in 1657. Washington carved out a plantation here, where his most famed descendant was born in 1732.

An obelisk fashioned from Vermont marble, a one-tenth replica of the Washington Monument in Washington DC, greets visitors to the George Washington Birthplace National Monument, run by the National Park Service. The site is interesting as George Washington's birthplace (☎804-224-1732; www.nps.gov/gewa; 1732 Popes Creek Road, Colonial Beach; ☺9am-5pm) FREE, of course, but it's more engaging as a peek into the lifestyle of the plantation owners who formed Virginia's original aristocracy, a class of essentially large land-owning gentry, which stood in contrast to the small-plot farmers and mercantile class of Northern colonies like New York and Massachusetts.

STATE
Kentucky

ENTRANCE FEE
Free

AREA
83 sq miles

GOOD FOR

Stalactites and stalagmites

Mammoth Cave National Park

With hidden underground rivers and more than 400 miles of explored terrain, the world's longest cave system shows off sci-fi-looking stalactites and stalagmites up close.

Mammoth Cave National Park's cave system is at least three times longer than any other known cave, with vast interior cathedrals, bottomless pits and strange, undulating rock formations. The caves have been used for prehistoric mineral-gathering, as a source of saltpeter for gunpowder, and as a tuberculosis hospital.

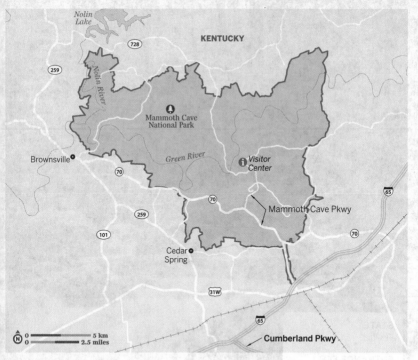

Sights & Activities

The only way to see the caves is on the excellent **ranger-guided tours** (☎800-967-2283; adult $7-55, child $5-20) and it is wise to book ahead, especially during the summer. Tours range from subterranean strolls to strenuous, day-long spelunking adventures (for adults only). The historic tour is especially interesting.

In addition to the caves, the park also contains 85 miles of trails – hiking is allowed on all of them, plus 60 miles are designated for horseback riding and 25 miles for mountain biking.

Sleeping

There are three **campgrounds** (sites $12 to $50), with restrooms within the park, though only a few sites have electricity or water hookups; there are also 13 free backcountry campsites. Get your backcountry permit at the park **visitor center** (Mammoth Cave Parkway). **Mammoth Cave Hotel** (☎270-758-2225; mammothcavehotel.com) has a number of rooms and cottages and is nearby the entrance to the caves and visitor center.

Getting There & Away

If you're coming from the north, take Exit 53 (Cave City Exit) off I-65. From the south, take Exit 48 (Park City Exit) off I-65.

History

Guided tours of the cave system have been offered since 1816. By the early 20th century Mammoth Cave had become such a popular attraction that owners of smaller local caves began diverting travelers heading to Mammoth by claiming it was flooded or quarantined. The inevitable conflicts became known as the 'Cave Wars.' Today you'll still see plenty of billboards beseeching you to visit other caves around Mammoth. The area became a national park in 1941 and now attracts 600,000 visitors each year.

STATE
Virginia

ENTRANCE FEE
7-day pass per vehicle $20

AREA
310 sq miles

GOOD FOR

Waterfall, Shenandoah National Park

Shenandoah National Park

Shenandoah is one of the most colorful national parks in the country. In spring and summer the wildflowers explode; in fall the leaves burn bright red and orange; and in winter a cold, starkly beautiful hibernation period sets in.

White-tailed deer are a common sight in Shenandoah and, if you're lucky, you might spot a black bear, bobcat or wild turkey. There are more than 500 miles of hiking trails, including 101 miles of the Appalachian Trail. Hikes range from tough rocky scrambles to the summits of Old Rag and Bearfence Mountains (with some of the best views in Virginia), to easier trails that run by spectacular waterfalls.

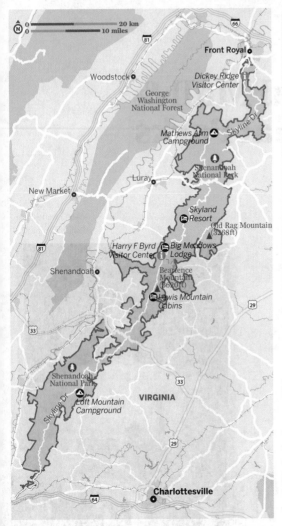

Skyline Drive

A 105-mile-long road running down the spine of the Blue Ridge Mountains, Shenandoah National Park's Skyline Drive redefines the definition of 'Scenic Route.' You're constantly treated to an impressive view, but keep in mind the road is bendy, slow-going (35mph limit) and is congested in peak season. It's best to start this drive just south of Front Royal; from here you'll snake over Virginia wine and hill country. Numbered mileposts mark the way; there are lots of pull-offs. Our favorite is around Mile 51.2, where you can take a moderately difficult 3.6-mile-loop hike to Lewis Spring Falls.

you're going camping or on extended hikes.

Information

The park lies just 75 miles west of Washington, DC, and can be easily accessed from several exits off I-81.

There are two visitor centers, **Dickey Ridge** (☎540-635-3566; Skyline Dr, Mile 4.6; ☺9am-5pm Apr-Nov) in the north and **Harry F Byrd** (☎540-999-3283; Skyline Dr, Mile 51; ☺9am-5pm Apr-Nov) in the south. Both can provide maps and backcountry permits, as well as information on horseback riding, hang gliding, cycling (only on public roads) and other outdoor activities.

Sleeping & Eating

There are four National Park Service campgrounds within the park (Mathews Arm, Big Meadows, Lewis Mountain and Loft Mountain). Camping elsewhere requires a backcountry permit, available for free from visitor centers.

There are also some not-so-rough lodges (Skyland Resort, Big Meadows Lodge and Lewis Mountain Cabins), all bookable online at www.goshenandoah. com.

Skyland and Big Meadows have restaurants and taverns with occasional live music. Big Meadows offers the most services, including gas, laundry and camp store.

It's best to bring your own food into the park if

National Mall & Memorial Parks

Left: Lincoln Memorial
Right: The White House

A nation is many things: her people, her history, her politics and her amassed knowledge. Somehow, every item listed above is given architectural life on the National Mall, the center of iconography of the most iconic city in America. This is where the nation's ideals are expressed in stone, landscaping, educational institutions, monuments and memorials.

The Mall is also, for you first-timers, a big old lawn. Really, that's the gist of it – a couple miles of scrubby grass sandwiched between the Capitol and Lincoln Memorial, pinned down by the Washington Monument, flanked by hot-dog vendors and T-shirt stands, and containing therein the American experience. This communal space is where Americans come to protest, to rally, to watch presidents get inaugurated. It's also where locals come to jog, dog-walk and toss a Frisbee.

With all the monuments and museums to see (for free!), you could spend your entire trip here. It's easy to get lost in the National Gallery of Art or the Air and Space Museum for half a day. Whatever places you decide to explore, be prepared to walk. The main row of sights, from the Smithsonian museums west to the Lincoln Memorial, is about 2 miles tip to tip. The new DC Circulator bus route stops by many of the hot spots, but you'll still end up hoofing it quite a bit. Eating and drinking options are thin on the ground beyond the museum cafes. And while the monuments are beautiful at night, there's not much going on after hours.

DOUG McKINLAY / GETTY IMAGES ©

SEAN PAVONE / GETTY IMAGES ©

Washington Monument

1 Just peaking at 555ft (and 5in), the Washington Monument (☉9am-5pm, 10pm Jun-Aug) is the tallest building in the district. It took two phases of construction to complete; note the different ues of the stone. A 70-second elevator de whisks you to the observation deck or the city's best views. Same-day tickets or a timed entrance are available at the osk by the monument. Arrive early. During peak season it's a good idea to reserve ckets in advance (www.recreation.gov).

Lincoln Memorial

2 Anchoring the Mall's west end is the hallowed shrine to Abraham Lincoln, who gazes peacefully across the reflecting pool beneath his neoclassical Doric-columned abode. To the left of Lincoln you can read the words of the Gettysburg Address, and the hall below highlights other great Lincoln-isms; on the steps, Martin Luther King Jr delivered his famed 'I Have a Dream' speech.

World War II Memorial

3 Dedicated in 2004, the WWII memorial honors the 400,000 Americans who died in the conflict, along with the 16 million US soldiers who served between 1941 and 1945. The plaza's dual arches symbolize victory in the Atlantic and Pacific theaters. The 56 surrounding pillars represent each US state and territory. Stirring quotes speckle the monument. You'll often see groups of veterans paying their respects here.

Vietnam Veterans Memorial

4 The opposite of DC's white, gleaming marble is this black, low-lying 'V,' an expression of the psychic scar wrought by the Vietnam War. The monument follows a descent deeper into the earth, with the names of the 58,272 dead soldiers – listed in the order in which they died – chiseled into the dark wall. It's a subtle, but profound monument – and all the more surprising as it was designed by 21-year-old undergraduate student Maya Lin in 1981. **Three Soldiers by Frederick Hart**

Thomas Jefferson Memorial

5 Set on the south bank of the Tidal Basin amid the cherry trees, this memorial honors the third US president, political philosopher, drafter of the Declaration of Independence and founder of the University of Virginia. Designed by John Russell Pope to resemble Jefferson's library at the university, the rounded monument was initially derided by critics as 'the Jefferson Muffin.' Inside is a 19ft bronze likeness, and excerpts from Jefferson's writings are etched into the walls. Historians criticize some of the textual alterations (edited, allegedly, for space considerations). Regardless, there are wonderful views across the waterfront onto the Mall.

Korean War Veterans Memorial

6 Nineteen steel soldiers wander through clumps of juniper past a wall bearing images of the 'Forgotten War' that assemble, in the distance, into a panorama of the Korean mountains. It's best visited at night, when the sculpted patrol – representing all races and combat branches that served in the war – takes on a phantom cast. In winter, when snow folds over the infantry's field coats, the impact is especially powerful.

Martin Luther King Jr Memorial

7 Opened in 2011, this is the Mall's first memorial dedicated to a non-president, as well as to an African American. Sculptor Lei Yixin carved the piece. Besides Dr King's image, known as the Stone of Hope, there are two blocks behind him that represent the Mountain of Despair. A wall inscribed with King's stirring quotes flanks the statues. It sits in a lovely spot on the banks of the Tidal Basin. **Martin Luther King Jr. Memorial, designed by Lei Yixin**

DC War Memorial

8 This small Greek-style temple commemorates local soldiers killed in WWI, making it the only local District memorial on the Mall. Twelve Doric 22ft-high marble columns support the circular structure inside are the names of the 26,000 Washingtonians who served in the war and the 499 DC soldiers killed in action. Various parties have tried to expand the site into a national WWI memorial. Congressional representatives have introduced bills to this effect, but to date nothing has been enacted.

National Mall

Folks often call the Mall 'America's Front Yard,' and that's a pretty good analogy. It is indeed a lawn, unfurling scrubby green grass from the Capitol west to the Lincoln Memorial. It's also America's great public space, where citizens come to protest their government, go for scenic runs and connect with the nation's most cherished ideals writ large in stone, landscaping, monuments and memorials.

You can sample quite a bit in a day, though it'll be a full one that requires roughly 4 miles of walking. Start at the **Vietnam Veterans Memorial ❶**, then head counterclockwise around the Mall, swooping in on the **Lincoln Memorial ❷**, **Martin Luther King Jr Memorial ❸** and **Washington Monument ❹**. You can also pause for the cause of the Korean War and WWII, among other monuments that dot the Mall's western portion.

Martin Luther King Jr Memorial

Walk all the way around the towering statue of Dr King by Lei Yixin and read the quotes. His likeness, incidentally, is 11ft taller than Lincoln and Jefferson in their memorials.

Tidal Basin

Smithsonian Castle

Seek out the tomb of James Smithson, the eccentric Englishman whose 1826 financial gift launched the Smithsonian Institution. His crypt is in a room by the Mall entrance.

Department of Agriculture

❺

❻

West Building

East Building

❼

National Air & Space Museum

Simply step inside and look up, and you'll be impressed. Lindbergh's *Spirit of St Louis* and Chuck Yeager's sound barrier–breaking Bell X-1 are among the machines hanging from the ceiling.

National Museum of the American Indian

US Capitol

Then it's onward to the museums, all fabulous and all free. Begin at the **Smithsonian Castle ⑤** to get your bearings – and to say thanks to the guy making all this awesomeness possible – and commence browsing through the **National Air & Space Museum ⑥**, **National Gallery of Art & National Sculpture Garden ⑦** and **National Museum of Natural History ⑧**.

TOP TIPS

Start early, especially in summer. You'll avoid the crowds, but more importantly you'll avoid the blazing heat. Try to finish with the monuments and be in the air-conditioned museums by 10:30am. Also, consider bringing snacks, since the only food available is from scattered cart vendors and museum cafes.

Lincoln Memorial

Commune with Abe in his chair, then head down the steps to the marker where Martin Luther King Jr gave his 'Dream' speech. The view of the Reflecting Pool and Washington Monument is one of DC's best.

STEVEN GREAVES /GETTY IMAGES ©

Korean War Veterans Memorial

National WWII Memorial

National Museum of African American History & Culture

National Museum of American History

National Sculpture Garden

Vietnam Veterans Memorial

Check the symbol that's beside each name. A diamond indicates 'killed, body recovered.' A plus sign indicates 'missing and unaccounted for.' There are approximately 1200 of the latter.

Washington Monument

As you approach the obelisk, look a third of the way up. See how it's slightly lighter in color at the bottom? Builders had to use different marble after the first source dried up.

National Museum of Natural History

Wave to Henry, the elephant who guards the rotunda, then zip to the 2nd floor's Hope Diamond. The 45.52-carat bauble has cursed its owners, including Marie Antoinette, or so the story goes.

National Gallery of Art & National Sculpture Garden

Beeline to Gallery 6 (West Building) and ogle the Western Hemisphere's only Leonardo da Vinci painting. Outdoors, amble amid whimsical sculptures by Miró, Calder and Lichtenstein. Also check out IM Pei's design of the East Building.

EDDIE BRADY / GETTY IMAGES ©

White House

The most striking thing about the White House is how much it feels like a house. A 55,000-sq-ft house, but still a real one where a family lives. If you're lucky enough to get inside on a public tour, you'll see several rooms in the main residence, each rich in presidential lore: this is where Thomas Jefferson ate; Abe Lincoln's coffin stood over there...

The walk-through is self-guided and starts at the visitor entrance by the White House's southeast gate. From there you pass by the **Library ❶**, Vermeil Room and China Room, all on the ground floor (they're roped off, so you don't actually go in). Next you go up a flight of stairs to the State Floor and continue on through the **East Room ❷**, Green Room, **Blue Room ❸**, Red Room and **State Dining Room ❹**. Unlike the floor below, you can enter these rooms. The Secret Service guys standing guard everywhere are ace at answering questions – really.

The White House's 2nd and 3rd floors, as well as the east and west wings, are off-limits. So you won't get to see two of the most famous rooms – the **Lincoln Bedroom ❺** and the **Oval Office ❻** – but you'll feel their aura.

You depart from the building's front (north) side. Before leaving the neighborhood, swing over to 15th St NW and stroll south to E St NW. Turn right and walk along the South Lawn, and you'll have a picture-perfect **view ❼** of the house you just visited.

State Dining Room
Residence, State Floor
Imagine inviting over 130 of your closest kings, prime ministers and movie stars for a little poached lobster. The fireplace mantel's quote is from a letter John Adams wrote in 1800.

DANITA DELIMONT / GETTY IMAGES ©

West Wing

State Floor

Oval Office
West Wing, Ground Floor
Suppose you were allowed into the west wing. You'd see the Oval Office, the president's official workspace. Each president has changed it to suit his taste, even designing his own carpet.

BARRY WINIKER / GETTY IMAGES ©

East Room
Residence, State Floor
Admire the White House's largest room, used for ceremonies and press conferences. Lincoln, Kennedy and five other presidents have lain in state here. Note how gilded eagles hold up the piano.

Blue Room
Residence, State Floor

Pretend the president is receiving you here, as he does other guests. Fifth prez James Monroe bought the gilded French Empire decor. Eighth prez Martin Van Buren painted the room blue.

BARRY WINIKER / GETTY IMAGES ©

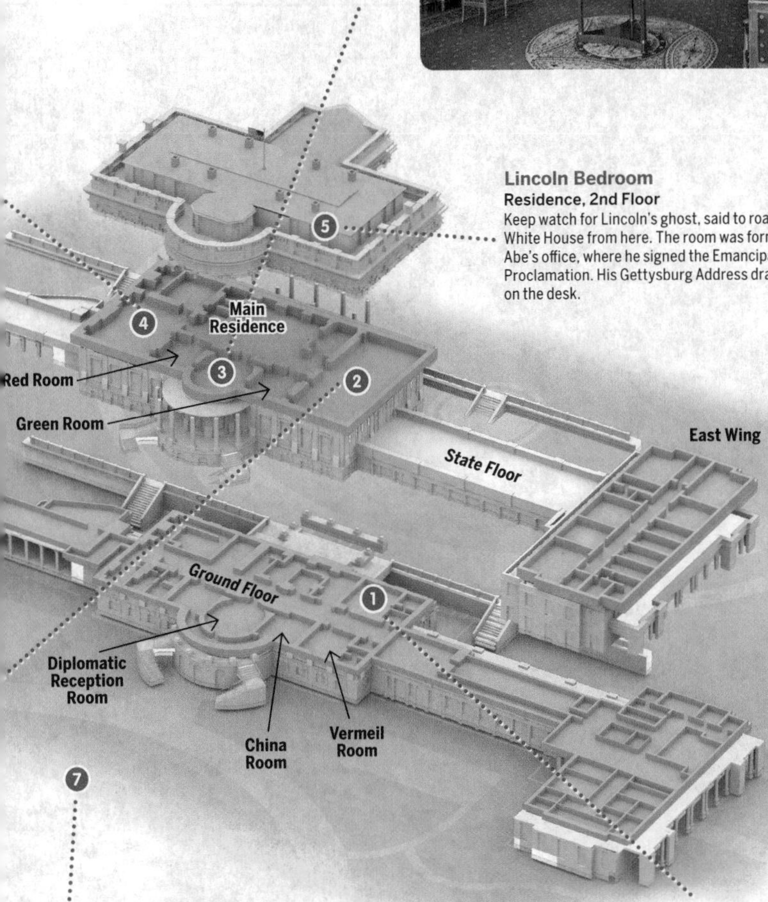

Lincoln Bedroom
Residence, 2nd Floor

Keep watch for Lincoln's ghost, said to roam the White House from here. The room was formerly Abe's office, where he signed the Emancipation Proclamation. His Gettysburg Address draft sits on the desk.

(5)

Main Residence

(4)

(3)

(2)

Red Room

Green Room

State Floor

East Wing

Ground Floor

(1)

Diplomatic Reception Room

China Room

Vermeil Room

(7)

View from E St NW

Snap your keepsake pictures across the South Lawn (taking photographs inside the White House is forbidden). Recognize the view? It's commonly used as the backdrop to TV news reports.

STEPHEN BOTANO / GETTY IMAGES ©

Library
Residence, Ground Floor

Scan the shelves of history, fiction and biography, and check out that chandelier. It belonged to the family of James Fenimore Cooper (author of *Last of the Mohicans*, 1826).

Hawaii & US Territories

Hawaii may evoke visions of surfboards, palm-fringed beaches, hulas and leis, but the state's national parks reveal a very different side. On Hawaii's Big Island, you can observe creation itself at Hawaiʻi Volcanoes National Park, home to the world's longest continuous volcanic eruption and the unforgettable sight of molten lava flowing into the sea. On Maui's Haleakalā, a giant shield volcano, you can sleep inside the crater and swim in stream-fed pools in subtropical forest.

In the Caribbean, the US Virgin Islands offer 20 sq miles of paradise on St John, with coral reefs, sugar-sand beaches and over 800 species of plants. Some 2600 miles southwest of Hawaii are the Polynesian islands of American Samoa, renowned for coral reefs and rainforests.

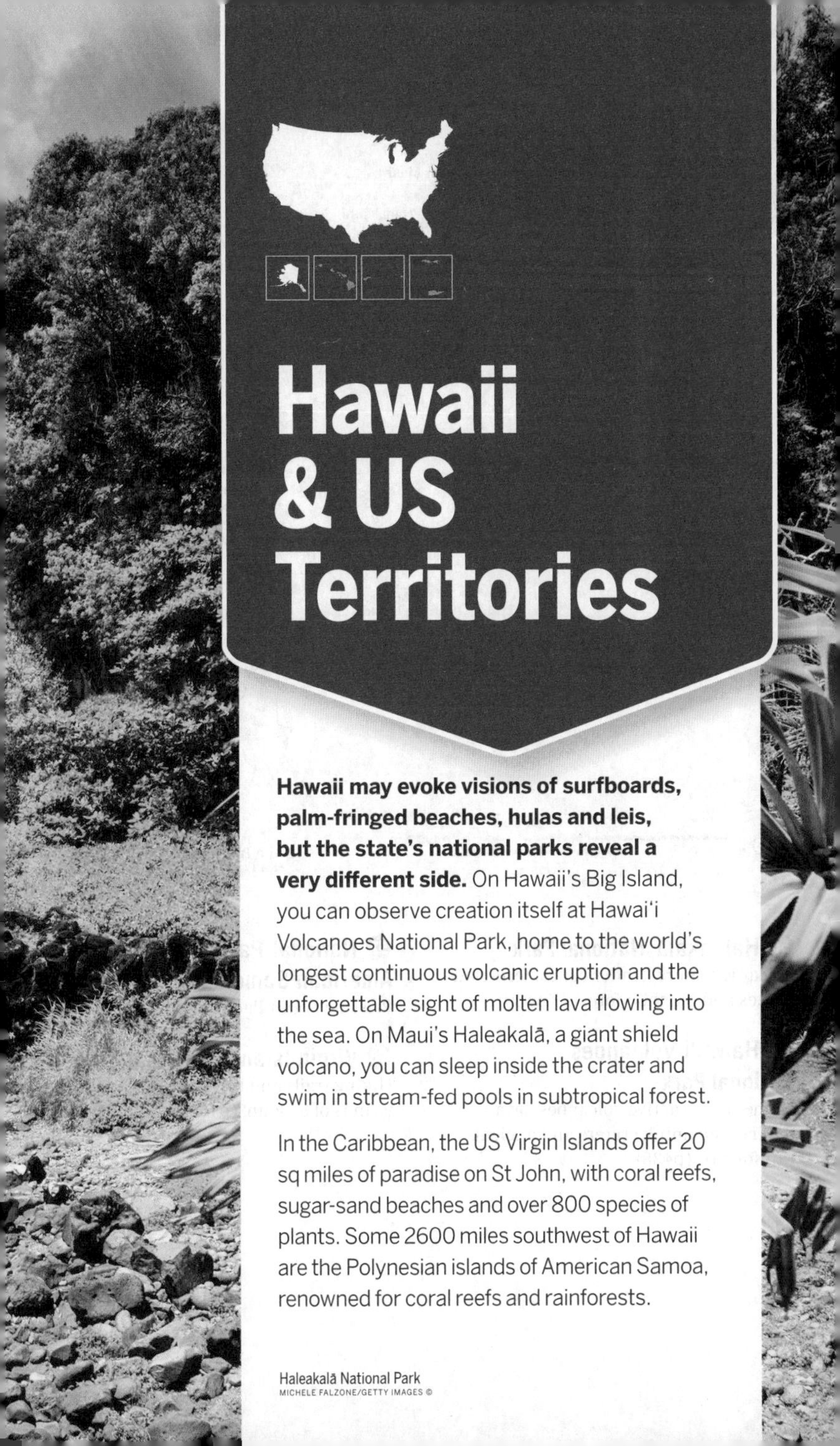

Haleakalā National Park
MICHELE FALZONE/GETTY IMAGES ©

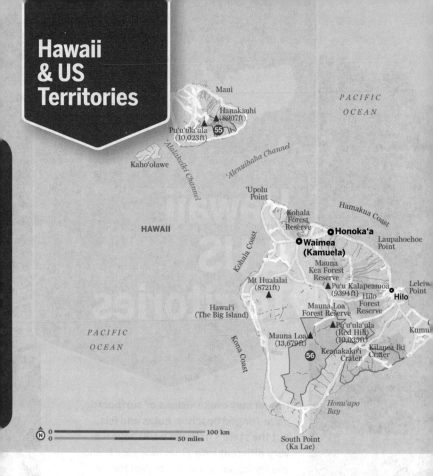

Hawaii & US Territories

Maui

Hanakauhi (8007ft)

Pu'u'ula'ula (10,023ft) 55

'Alalakeiki Channel

Kaho'olawe

'Alenuihaha Channel

PACIFIC OCEAN

'Upolu Point

Hamakua Coast

Kohala Forest Reserve

HAWAII

● Honoka'a

Kohala Coast

● Waimea (Kamuela)

Laupahoehoe Point

Mauna Kea Forest Reserve

Mt Hualalai (8721ft) ▲

▲ Pu'u Kalapeamoa (9394ft)

Hilo Forest Reserve

Leleiw Point

● Hilo

Hawai'i (The Big Island)

Mauna Loa Forest Reserve

Kona Coast

Pu'u'ula'ula (Red Hill) (10,035ft)

Kumu

PACIFIC OCEAN

Mauna Loa ▲ (13,679ft)

56

Keanakako'i Crater

Kilauea Iki Crater

Honu'apo Bay

N 0 _____ 100 km
0 _____ 50 miles

South Point (Ka Lae)

55 Haleakalā National Park
Volcanic craters, cinder cones, fern-clad gorges and bamboo forests. (p430)

56 Hawai'i Volcanoes National Park
Home to two active volcanoes, lava deserts, steaming craters and ancient rainforests. (p438)

57 National Park of American Samoa
Pristine South Pacific landscapes. (p450)

58 Virgin Islands National Park
Hiking trails and historic ruins across the islands of St John. (p452)

✓ DON'T
MISS

Chain of Craters Rd
Motor through ever-changing tropical scenery on your way down Kilauea Volcano in **Hawai'i Volcanoes National Park**.

Sunrise
Get up early to watch the sun rise in **Haleakalā National Park**.

Kilauea Iki Trail
Hike through ohia forest and across a volcanic crater in **Hawai'i Volcanoes National Park**.

Sliding Sands
Take the path into an unearthly world of stark lava sights and ever-changing clouds in **Haleakalā National Park**.

Island Hikes
Hike along a coral-fringed bay in the **National Park of American Samoa** or take one of the 20 trails through **Virgin Islands National Park**.

STATE
Hawaii

ENTRANCE FEE
3-day pass per vehicle $15

AREA
60 sq miles

GOOD FOR

Volcanic landscapes, Haleakalā National Park

Haleakalā National Park

As you hike down into the belly of Haleakalā, the first thing you notice is the crumbly, lunar-like landscape. It's impossible not to be awed by the raw beauty of this ancient place, now a haven for wildlife and surefooted hikers.

To fully experience Maui make your way to the summit of Haleakalā. Like a yawning mouth, the huge crater opens beneath you, in all its raw volcanic glory, caressed by mist and, in the experience of a lifetime, bathed in the early light of sunrise. Lookouts on the crater's rim provide breath-taking views of the moonscape below, and the many cinder cones marching across it.

The rest of this amazing park, which is divided into two distinct sections, is all about interacting with this mountain of solid lava, and the rare life-forms that live upon it, some of them found only here.

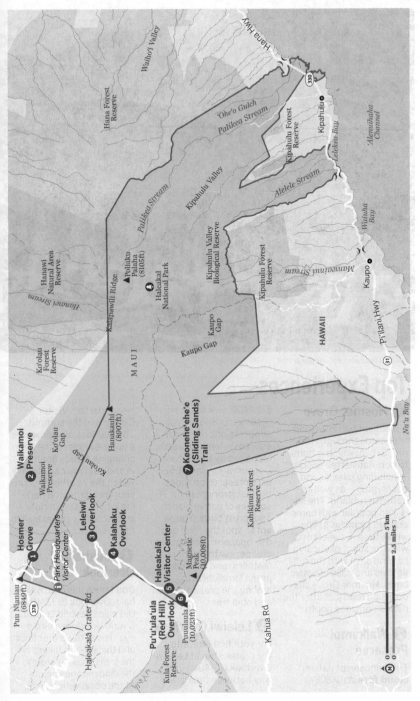

Haleakalā silversword, native to Hawaii

Top Experiences

❶ Hosmer Grove

A pleasant half-mile loop trail winds through Hosmer Grove, which is home to non-native tree species – including pine, fir and eucalyptus – as well as native scrubland. The site is also popular with campers and picnickers. The whole area is sweetened with the scent of eucalyptus and alive with the red flashes and calls of native birds. Hosmer Grove sits on a side road just after the park's entrance booth.

❷ Waikamoi Preserve

This windswept native **cloud forest** (☎808-572-4400; www.nature.org; ⊙hiking tour 8:45am Thu) supports one of the rarest ecosystems on earth. Managed by the Nature Conservancy, the 8951-acre preserve provides the last stronghold for 76 species of native plants and forest birds. You're apt to spot the 'i'iwi and the 'apapane (both honeycreepers with bright red feathers) and the yellow-green 'amakihi flying among the preserve's koa and ohia trees.

❸ Leleiwi Overlook

For your first look into the crater, stop at Leleiwi Overlook (8840ft), midway between the Park Headquarters Visitor Center and the summit. The overlook also provides a unique angle on the ever-changing clouds floating in and out. You can literally watch the weather form at your feet. From the parking lot, it's a five-minute walk across a gravel trail to the overlook.

❹ Kalahaku Overlook

Don't miss this one. Kalahaku Overlook (9324ft), 0.8 miles beyond Leleiwi Overlook, offers a bird's-eye view of the crater floor and the ant-size hikers on the trails snaking around the cinder cones below. At the observation deck,

Waikamoi Preserve

plaques provide information on each of the volcanic formations that punctuate the crater floor. From the deck you'll also get a perfect angle for viewing both the Koʻolau Gap and the Kaupo Gap on the rim of Haleakalā.

Between May and October the *ʻuaʻu* (Hawaiian dark-rumped petrel) nests in burrows in the cliff face at the left side of the observation deck. Even if you don't spot the birds, you can often hear the parents and chicks making clucking sounds. Of about 20,000 *ʻuaʻu* remaining today, most nest right here at Haleakalā. These seabirds were thought to be extinct until sighted in the crater during the 1970s.

❺ Haleakalā Visitor Center

Perched on the rim of the crater at 9745ft, this **visitor center** (www.nps.gov/hale; ☺sunrise-3pm) is the park's main viewing spot. And what a magical sight awaits. The ever-changing interplay of sun, shadow and clouds reflecting on the crater floor creates a mesmerizing dance of light and color. The center has displays on Haleakalā's volcanic origins and details on what you're seeing on the crater floor 3000ft below.

The Sunrise Experience

Haleakalā means 'House of the Sun.' So it's no surprise that since the time of the first Hawaiians people have been making pilgrimages up to Haleakalā to watch the sunrise. It's an experience that borders on the mystical. Mark Twain called it 'the sublimest spectacle' he'd ever witnessed.

Plan to arrive at the summit 90 minutes before the sunrise to guarantee a parking spot. Park at the summit or beside the crater at the Haleakalā Visitor Center. About 30 minutes later the night sky lightens and turns purple-blue, and the stars fade away. Ethereal silhouettes of the mountain ridges appear. The undersides of the clouds lighten first, accenting the night sky with pale silvery slivers and streaks of pink.

About 20 minutes before sunrise, the light intensifies on the horizon in bright oranges and reds. Turn around for a look at Science City, whose domes turn a blazing pink. For the grand finale, when the the sun appears, all of Haleakalā takes on a fiery glow. It feels like you're watching the earth awaken.

The best photo opportunities occur before the sun rises. Every morning is different, but once the sun is up, the silvery lines and the subtleties disappear.

The start of the Keonehe'ehe'e (Sliding Sands) Trail

Waterfalls in the Kipahulu Area

⑥ Pu'u'ula'ula (Red Hill) Overlook

You may find yourself standing above the clouds while exploring Pu'u'ula'ula (10,023ft), Maui's highest point. On a clear day you can see the Big Island and O'ahu. When the light's right, the colors of the crater are spectacular. An *'ahinahina* garden has been planted at the overlook, making this the best place to see these luminous silver-leafed plants.

⑦ Keonehe'ehe'e (Sliding Sands) Trail

Make time for this stunner, starting at the southern side of the Haleakalā Visitor Center and winding down to the crater floor. If you take this hike after catching the sunrise, you'll walk directly into a gentle warmish wind and rays of sunshine. There's no shade, so bring water and a hat.

The path descends into an unearthly world of stark lava sights and ever-changing clouds. The first thing you'll notice is how quiet everything is. The only sound is the crunching of volcanic cinders beneath your feet.

The full trail leads 9.2 miles to the Paliku cabin and campground. There are great views, but virtually no vegetation. As you head across the crater floor to Kapalaoa, verdant ridges rise on your right, giving way to ropy pahoehoe (smooth-flowing lava). From Kapalaoa cabin to Paliku, the descent is gentle and, in contrast to the crater's barren western end, the Paliku area receives heavy rainfall, with ohia forests climbing the slopes.

Plan Ahead

Haleakalā National Park has two different sections: the ethereal Summit Area and the coastal Kipahulu Area. There is no direct road connection between them. Thus travelers typically visit the summit on one day, and the Kipahulu Area on another (usually heading to or from Hana).

Sleeping

Maui's best campgrounds are in Haleakalā National Park. All of the camping options are primitive; none have electricity or showers. Backcountry campgrounds have pit toilets and limited nonpotable water supplies that are shared with the crater cabins. Water needs to be filtered or chemically treated before drinking; conserve it, as water tanks occasionally run dry. Fires are allowed only in grills and in times of drought are prohibited entirely. You must pack in all your food and supplies, and pack out all your trash. Also be aware that during periods of drought you'll be required to carry in your own water.

Keep in mind that for sleeping at an elevation of 7000ft, you'll need to be well equipped – without a waterproof tent and a winter-rated sleeping bag, forget it.

Hosmer Grove Campground (campsite free) Wake up to birdsong at Hosmer Grove, the only drive-up campground in the Summit Area section of Haleakalā National Park. On the slopes of the volcano, surrounded by towering trees and adjacent to one of Maui's best birding trails, this campground at an elevation of 6800ft tends to be a bit cloudy, but a covered picnic pavilion offers shelter if it starts to rain. Camping is free on a first-come, first-served basis, with a limit of 50 people. No permit is required, though there's a three-day camping limit per month. The campground is just after the park entrance booth, and has grills, toilets and running water.

Backcountry Campgrounds (campsite free) For hikers, two backcountry campgrounds lie in the belly of Haleakalā Crater. They are collectively called the Wilderness Campgrounds. The easiest to reach is at Holua, 3.7 miles down the Halemau'u Trail. The other is at Paliku, below a rainforest ridge at the end of Halemau'u Trail. Weather can be unpredictable at both. Permits are required. These are free and issued at the Park Headquarters Visitor Center on a first-come, first-served basis between 8am and 3pm up to one day in advance. Photo identification and a 10-minute orientation video are required. Because only 25 campers are allowed at each site, permits can go quickly when larger parties show up.

Haleakalā Wilderness Cabins (☎808-572-4400, reservations 877-444-5777; www.recreation.gov; per cabin with 1-12 people $75) Three rustic cabins dating from the 1930s lie along trails on the crater floor at Holua, Kapalaoa and Paliku. Each has a wood-burning stove, a propane burner, 12 bunks with sleeping pads (but no bedding), pit toilets and a limited supply of water and firewood. There is no electricity. Hiking distances to the cabins from the crater rim range from 4 to just over 9 miles. The driest conditions are at Kapalaoa. Those craving lush rainforest will find Paliku serene. Holua has unparalleled sunrise views. The cabins can be reserved online up to six months in advance. A photo ID is required for the permittee, and all of those staying in the cabin must watch a 10-minute wilderness orientation video.

Entrance Fees & Passes

Haleakalā National Park (☎808-572-4400; www.nps.gov/hale; 3-day pass per vehicle/motorbike/individual on foot or bicycle $15/10/8; ♿) never closes, and the pay booth at the park entrance opens before dawn to welcome the sunrise crowd. The fee covers both sections of the park. If you're planning several trips, or are going on to Hawai'i (Big Island), consider buying an annual pass ($25), which covers all of Hawaii's national parks.

Getting There & Around

Haleakalā Crater Rd (Hwy 378) twists and turns for 11 miles from Hwy 377 near Kula up to the park entrance, then another 10 miles to Haleakalā summit. It's a good paved road, but it's steep and winding. You don't want to rush, especially when it's dark or foggy. Watch out for cattle wandering across the road. The drive to the summit takes about 1½ hours from Pa'ia or Kahului, two hours from Kihei and a bit longer from Lahaina. If you need gas, fill up the night before, as there are no services on Haleakalā Crater Rd.

STATE
Hawaii

ENTRANCE FEE
7-day pass per vehicle $15

AREA
328 sq miles

GOOD FOR

Volcanic terrain, Hawai'i Volcanoes National Park

Hawai'i Volcanoes National Park

Set on the sloping hillside of the world's most active volcano, this fantastic park dramatically reminds you that nature is very much alive and in perpetual motion.

An incredible network of hiking trails encompasses lava flows and tubes, steam vents and wild beaches. Alternatively, take in many of the major sights by car in one long, winding downhill drive. Don't miss the otherworldly overlook of Halema'uma'u, an enormous fiery crater that spews tons of ash into the sky.

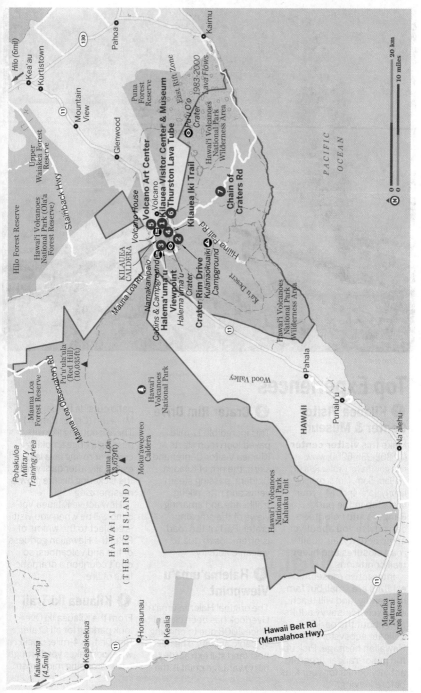

Volcanic vents, Kilauea Crater

Top Experiences

❶ Kilauea Visitor Center & Museum

Make this **visitor center** (☎808-985-6000; www. nps.gov/havo; Crater Rim Dr; ⏰9am-5pm, film screenings hourly 9am-4pm; 👪) your first stop in the park. Rangers and volunteers can advise you about volcanic activity, air quality, road closures and hiking-trail conditions.

Interactive museum exhibits are small but family friendly, and will teach even science-savvy adults a lot about the park's delicate ecosystem and Hawaiian heritage. Pick up fun junior-ranger program activity books for your kids before leaving.

❷ Crater Rim Drive

This incredible 11-mile paved loop road starts at Kilauea Visitor Center and skirts the rim of Kilauea Caldera, passing steam vents and rifts, hiking trailheads and amazing views of the smoking crater. Part of the road is often closed due to volcanic activity.

❸ Halema'uma'u Viewpoint

The original Halema'uma'u Overlook has been closed since 2008 due to ongoing volcanic activity. The next best (and still extraordinary) vantage point is the patio outside the Jaggar Museum (Crater Rim Dr). There's nothing like witnessing a huge smoking crater or roiling lava lake, especially after dark when the flickering hellfire glow is mesmerizing.

How active Kilauea Volcano will be when you visit is subject to the whims of Pele, the Hawaiian goddess of fire and volcanoes, so don't count on a dramatic lake of fire.

❹ Kilauea Iki Trail

From the Kilauea Iki Overlook parking lot off Crater Rim Dr, this 4-mile, clockwise loop takes you through a jaw-dropping microcosm

Thurston Lava Tube

of the park. It quickly descends 400ft through fairytale ohia forest, then cuts across mile-wide Kilauea Iki crater. Scattered vents lace the crater's surface with steam plumes, while the wrinkly, often iridescent lava surface is peppered with *ohelo* shrubs, ohia trees and ferns.

Hit the trail before 8am to beat the day-tripping crowds. The faint footpath across the crater floor is marked by *ahu* (stone cairns) to aid navigation. Don't wander off-trail to explore any steaming vents, lava tubes or caves without an experienced guide.

❺ Volcano Art Center

Near the visitor center, this innovative local gallery spotlights museum-quality pottery, paintings, sculpture, jewelry, Hawaiian quilts and more. The nonprofit shop, housed in historic Volcano House

hotel, is worth a visit just to admire its solid artisanship.

❻ Thurston Lava Tube

On Kilauea's eastern side, Crater Rim Dr passes through rainforest *kipuka* thick with tree ferns and ohia trees. An often overflowing parking lot is the access point for the everpopular Thurston Lava Tube. A 528yd loop walk starts in ohia forest filled with birdsong before heading underground through a gigantic lava tube that's artificially lit.

Lava tubes form when the outer crust of a lava river starts to harden but the liquid lava underneath continues to flow through. After the flow drains out, the hard shell remains.

Viewing the Lava Up Close

Lucky travelers can view live lava making the 64-mile journey from the Pu'u 'O'o Vent to the ocean. Where the lava will be flowing when you visit and whether or not you can reach it are impossible to predict. Sometimes it's an arduous 13-mile round-trip hike from the end of Chain of Craters Road. Ask at the Kilauea Visitor Center for updates.

It's usually a much easier hike to the flow from the free, county-run lava-viewing area outside the park at the end of Hwy 130 in Puna. If the show is really on, there will be surface flows, lava 'skylights' and flaming trees. When the flow mellows or changes course, you'll be able to see a steam plume during the day, and an unearthly red glow after dark. Bring a flashlight and water, and plan to stick around after sunset.

Chain of Craters Road

❼ Chain of Craters Road

Possibly the most scenic road trip on an island packed with really scenic road trips, this paved road winds almost 20 miles and 3700ft down the southern slopes of Kilauea, ending abruptly at the volcano's East Rift Zone on the coast. You'll have striking vistas of the coastline far below, but for miles the predominant view is of hardened lava; you can sometimes find thin filaments of volcanic glass, known as Pele's hair, in the cracks and crevices. The best time for photos is early morning and late afternoon, when sunlight slants off the lava.

PHILIP ROSENBERG / GETTY IMAGES ©

Petroglyphs, Chain of Craters Road

Sleeping & Eating

The park's two drive-up campgrounds are relatively uncrowded outside summer. Nights can be crisp and cool, however; you should bring rainproof gear. Campsites operate on a first-come, first-served basis (and with a seven-night limit).

There are also several great backcountry sites, which require permits.

Kulanaokuaiki Campground (www.nps.gov/ havo; Hilina Pali Rd; campsites free) About 5 miles down Hilina Pali Rd, this minimally developed campground has eight campsites, pit toilets and picnic tables, but no water. Campfires are prohibited.

Namakanipaio Cabins & Campground (📞info 808-756-9625, reservations 866-536-7972; www.hawaiivolcanohouse.com; campsites/cabins $15/80) The park's busiest campground is off Hwy 11, about 3 miles west of the visitor center. Tent camping is in a small, unshaded meadow with little privacy. Facilities include restrooms, drinking water, picnic tables and BBQ grills. Book ahead for simple, A-frame wooden cabins with shared communal bathrooms and hot showers; check-in at Volcano House.

Volcano House (📞866-536-7972, 808-756-9625; www.hawaiivolcanohouse.com; Crater Rim Dr; r $185-385; 🐾) 🏃 With an unforgettable location perched on the rim of Kilauea Caldera, the reborn Volcano House has long enjoyed its unique status as the park's only hotel. Eco-conscious renovations have brought long-overdue upgrades to the restaurant, bar, fireplace lobby areas, gift shops and 33 spacious, if quite plain and thin-walled, guest rooms. Reserve well in advance.

Both the refurbished **Rim Restaurant** (www. hawaiivolcanohouse.com/dining; Crater Rim Dr, Volcano House; breakfast buffet adult/ child $18/9, lunch mains $11-19, dinner mains $19-39; 🕐7-10am, 11am-2pm & 5-9pm), serving better-than-average Hawaii Regional cuisine crafted from local ingredients, and **Uncle George's Lounge** (Crater Rim Dr, Volcano House; mains $11-19; 🕐11am-9pm), a pint-size bar with live music and food, have enormous windows that afford absolutely staggering volcano views (as do certain guest rooms). If you can't spring for the room, just sip a beer. Slowly.

Getting There & Around

The park is 30 miles (45 minutes) from Hilo and 95 miles (2¼ hours) from Kailua-Kona via Hwy 11. The turnoffs for Volcano village are a couple of miles east of the main park entrance. Hwy 11 is prone to flooding, washouts and closures during rainstorms. Periods of drought may close Mauna Loa Rd and Hilina Pali Rd due to wildfire hazards.

The public **Hele-On Bus** (📞808-961-8744; www.heleonbus.org; adult one-way $2) departs fives times daily (except Sunday) from Hilo, arriving at the park visitor center about 1¼ hours later, with one bus continuing to Ka'u.

In the park, cyclists are permitted only on paved Crater Rim Dr, Chain of Craters Road, Hilina Pali Rd and Mauna Loa Rd.

Information

The park is open 24 hours a day, except when eruption activity and volcanic gases necessitate temporary closures. For current lava flows, and trail, road and campground status, check the website or call ahead.

The park's main entrance sits at almost 4000ft, with varying elevation and climates inside the park boundaries. Chilly rain, wind, fog and vog typify the fickle weather, which can go from hot and dry to a soaking downpour in a flash. Near Kilauea Caldera, temperatures average 15°F (8°C) cooler than in Kona, so bring a rain jacket and pants, just in case.

Vog & Sulfuric Fumes

Halema'uma'u Crater and Pu'u 'O'o vent belch thousands of tons of sulfur dioxide daily. Where lava meets the sea it creates a 'steam plume,' where sulfuric and hydrochloric acid mix with airborne silica (or glass particles): all this combines to create 'vog' which, depending on the winds, can settle over the park. People with respiratory and heart conditions, pregnant women, infants and young children should take care when visiting.

Hawaii's Other Protected Areas

In addition to its two national parks, Hawaii also has seven national historical parks, sites, trails and memorials, most of which help to preserve Hawaiian culture. Hawaii also has nine national wildlife refuges (www.fws.gov/pacific/refuges) on the main islands that protect endangered waterbirds and plants.

Pu'uhonua o Honaunau National Historical Park

Standing at the end of a long semi-desert of thorny scrub and lava plains, the park fronting Honaunau Bay provides one of the state's most evocative experiences of ancient Hawai'i, and easy access to some of the best snorkeling anywhere.

In ancient Hawai'i the *kapu* (taboo) system regulated every waking moment. A maka'aina (commoner) could not look at *ali'i* (chiefs) or walk in their footsteps. Women couldn't cook for men, nor eat with them. Fishing, hunting and gathering timber were restricted to certain seasons. And on and on.

Violators of *kapu* were hunted down and killed. After all, according to the Hawaiian belief system, breaking *kapu* infuriated the gods. And gods wrought volcanic eruptions, tidal waves, famine and earthquakes, which could be devastating to the entire community.

There was one loophole, however. Commoners who broke *kapu* could stave off death if they reached the sacred ground of a *pu'uhonua* (place of refuge). A *pu'uhonua* also gave sanctuary to defeated warriors and wartime noncombatants (men who were too old, too young or unable to fight).

To reach the *pu'uhonua* was no small feat. Since royals and their warriors lived on the grounds surrounding the refuge, *kapu* breakers had to swim through violent, open ocean, braving currents and sharks, to safety. Once inside the sanctuary, priests performed ceremonies of absolution to placate the gods. *Kapu* breakers could then return home to start afresh.

The *pu'uhonua* at Honaunau was used for several centuries until 1819, when Hawai'i's old religious ways were abandoned after King Kamehameha II and regent Queen Ka'ahumanu ate together in public, overthrowing the ancient *kapu* system forever.

Kalaupapa National Historical Park

The spectacularly beautiful **Kalaupapa Peninsula** is the most remote part of Hawaii's most isolated island. The only way to reach this lush green peninsula edged with long, white-sand beaches is on a twisting trail down the steep *pali*, the world's highest sea cliffs, or by plane. This remoteness is the reason it was, for more than a century, where Hansen's disease patients were forced into isolation. From its inception until separation ended in

Right: Green sea turtle at Kaloko-Honokohau National Historical Park

1969, 8000 patients were forced to come to Kalaupapa. Less than a dozen patients (respectively called 'residents') remain. They have chosen to stay in the only home they have ever known and have resisted efforts to move them away. The peninsula has been designated a national historical park and is managed by the Hawaii Department of Health and the National Park Service.

While the state of Hawaii officially uses the term 'Hansen's disease' for leprosy, many Kalaupapa residents consider that to be a euphemism that fails to reflect the stigma they have suffered, and continue to use the old term 'leprosy.' The degrading appellation 'leper,' however, is offensive to all. 'Resident' is preferred.

State laws dating back to when the settlement was a quarantine zone require everyone who enters the settlement to have a 'permit.' The law is no longer necessary for health reasons but is enforced in order to protect the privacy of the residents. For this reason, all visitors must have a guide. Permits are issued by the tour operators. Because the exiled

patients were not allowed to keep children if they had them, the residents made a rule that no one under the age of 16 is allowed in the settlement – this is strictly enforced, as are the permit requirements. Only guests of Kalaupapa residents are allowed to stay overnight.

The guided tour is Moloka'i's most well-known attraction but, interesting as it is, the tour itself is not the highlight: this is one case where getting there truly is half the fun. Riding a mule or hiking down the steep trail, winding through lush green tropical forest, catching glimpses of the sea far below, is unforgettable.

Kaloko-Honokohau National Historical Park

Though it may appear to be desolate lava rock, this national park is worth exploring. It covers 1160 acres of oceanfront and includes fishponds, ancient heiau (stone temples) and house sites, burial caves, petroglyphs, *holua* (sled courses), and a

1. Tiki carving 2. Shores of Kalaupapa National Historical Park

restored 1-mile segment of the ancient King's Trail footpath. Visit in the early morning or late afternoon (or when it's overcast), as midday temperatures can be unbearable. Trails cross rough chunks of 'a'a lava, so wear good shoes.

WWII Valor in the Pacific National Monument

One of the USA's most significant WWII sites, this National Park Service monument narrates the history of the Pearl Harbor attack and commemorates fallen service members. The monument is entirely wheelchair accessible. The main entrance also leads to Pearl Harbor's other parks and museums.

The monument grounds are much more than just a boat dock for the USS Arizona Memorial. Be sure to stop at the two museums, where multimedia and interactive displays bring to life the Road to War and the Attack & Aftermath through historic photos, films, illustrated graphics and taped oral histories. A shore-side walk passes signs illustrating how the attack unfolded in the now-peaceful harbor.

The bookstore sells just about every book and movie ever produced on the Pearl Harbor attack and WWII's Pacific theater, as well as informative illustrated maps of the battle. If you're lucky, the few remaining, 90-plus-year-old Pearl Harbor veterans who volunteer might be out front signing autographs and answering questions.

Various ticket packages are available for the three attractions that have admission fees. The best deal is a seven-day pass that includes admission to all. Tickets are sold online at www.pearlharborhistoricsites.org, at the main monument ticket counter, and at each attraction.

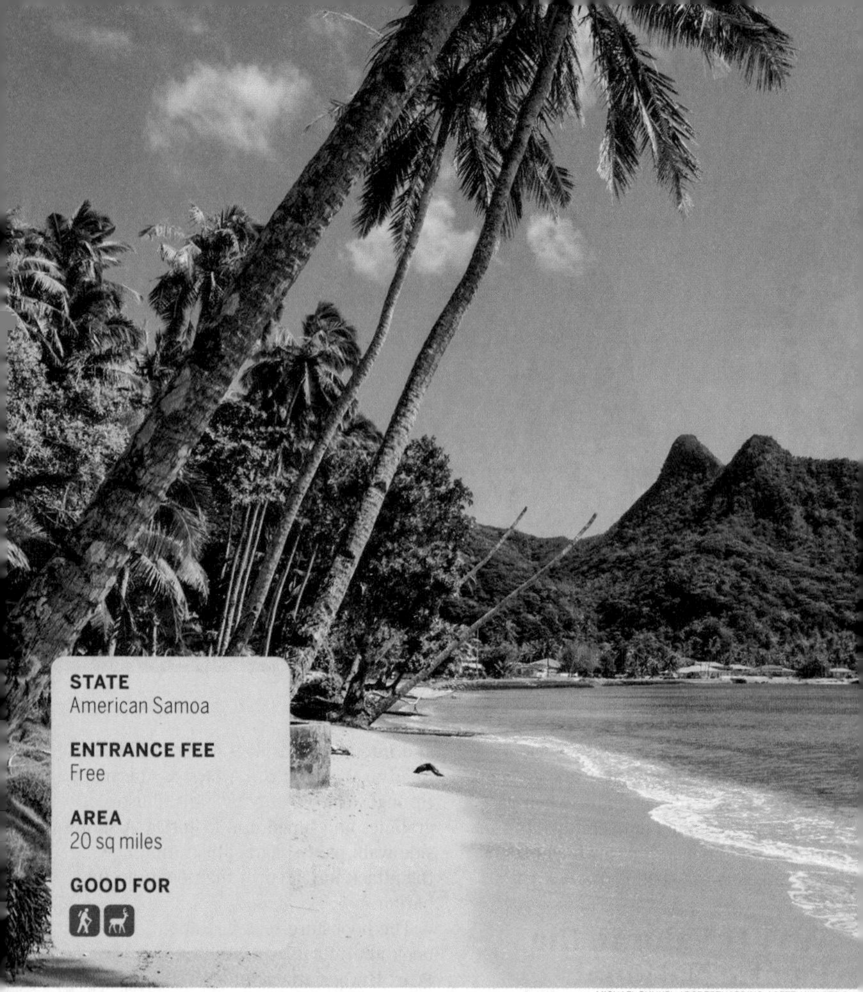
STATE
American Samoa
ENTRANCE FEE
Free
AREA
20 sq miles
GOOD FOR

Tutuila Island

MICHAEL RUNKEL / ROBERTHARDING / GETTY IMAGES ©

National Park of American Samoa

The only US territory south of the equator, the National Park of American Samoa is unlike any other, spreading itself across three rainforest-clad South Pacific islands.

Created in 1988, the territory's sole national park protects huge swaths of pristine landscapes, coral reefs, tropical rainforests, marine environments, and the Samoan culture. (Samoa means 'sacred earth' in the local language.) The park's territory includes the islands of Tutuila, Ofu and Ta'u. There are a number of good hiking options in the park. The best of them, in order of difficulty (easy

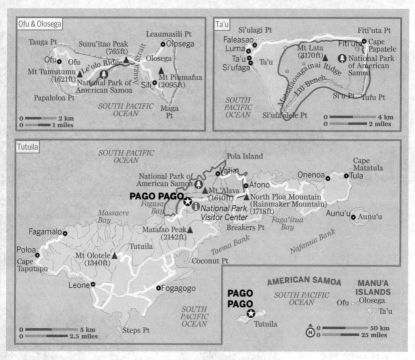

to challenging) include the following:

Pola Island Trail

Vatia is a peaceful village situated on a lovely, coral-fringed bay. Guarding the mouth of the bay, tiny Pola Island has sheer, 394ft-high cliffs populated by seabirds. For a close-up of soaring rocks and birds, head through the village and park at the school, then walk 0.2 miles to the isolated beach at the base of the cliffs.

Amalau Valley

From Aua, a surfaced road switchbacks steeply up over Rainmaker Pass and down to Afono and Vatia. Between these two villages is the beautiful, secluded Amalau Valley, home to many forest bird species and two rare species of fly-

ing fox. Stop at the lookout point just past the western side of Amalau Bay for some wonderful views.

Mt Alava

The National Park Service hiking trail that leads up Mt Alava (1611ft) and then down to the coast presents a wonderful way to experience the park's lowland and montane rainforests, its thriving birdlife, and the peacefulness that permeates it. On Mt Alava,

a stairway leads up to a TV transmission tower and the rusted remains of a cable-car terminal that once ran 1.1ft across Pago Pago Harbor to Solo Hill. The 3.4-mile ridge trail (1½ to two hours one way) starts from Fagasa Pass. Behind the rest *fale* at the end of this section, a very steep trail (including ladders in places) leads 1.2 miles down to Vatia; allow an additional two hours for the descent.

Visitor Information

Check out the **National Park Visitor Information Center** (☎633 7082; www.nps.gov/npsa; Pago Pago; ⊗8am-4.30pm Mon-Fri) for tourist info, a (free) map, plus a day-hikes pamphlet, information on WWII sites and a homestay program with choices on Tutuila and Ta'u. It also has updates on coral reef health, water quality and more.

STATE
US Virgin Islands

ENTRANCE FEE
Free

AREA
20 sq miles

GOOD FOR

Trunk Bay

Virgin Islands National Park

Virgin Islands National Park covers two-thirds of the islands of St John, plus 5650 acres underwater. It's a tremendous resource, offering miles of shoreline, pristine reefs and hiking trails.

In 1493, Columbus spotted the islands, naming them after St Ursula's legendary 11,000 virgins. Since then, Spain, France, Holland, England, Denmark and the US have controlled various parts of the islands. A haven for wildlife and outdoor activities, the park is also home to historic sites and ruins, preserving the complex history of this unique landscape.

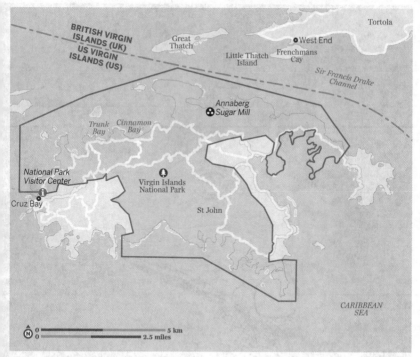

The park's **visitor center** (⏱ 8am-4.30pm) is in Cruz Bay, on the dock across from the Mongoose Junction shopping arcade. It's an essential first stop to obtain free guides on hiking trails, snorkeling spots, bird-watching lists, petroglyph sites and daily ranger-led activities.

Trunk Bay

Trunk Bay is arguably one of the most beautiful beaches in the world. The 225yd-long long snorkel trail here is perfect for beginner snorkelers, with descriptive plaques along the trail describing the coral reefs and fish species to keep an eye out for. The bay is patrolled by lifeguards and there's a day fee ($4) to access the beach. You'll also find a bathhouse, snack bar, souvenir shop and snorkeling gear available to rent.

Cinnamon Bay

Just east of Trunk Bay are the shallow, clear waters of Cinnamon Bay. Adjacent to the beach is the Cinnamon Bay **campground**, offering bare tent sites, furnished canvas tents and screened cottages. The campground also has a restaurant and store. Sailing, snorkeling and scuba-diving lessons can be arranged from the sport center here; snorkeling and windsurfing gear is also available for rent.

Hiking

There are more than 20 hiking trails across the park, accessible boardwalk meanders through historic ruins, to more strenuous, backcountry trails to see petroglyphs. Pick up a copy of *The Hiker's Guide to the Virgin Islands National Park* from the visitor center's bookstore.

Annaberg Historic Trail

In 1796, when the sugar boom was under-way in the Virgin Islands, Irish-born merchant and slave trader James Murphy established a large-scale processing facility, known as the Annaberg Sugar Mill. Today, visitors can follow the Annaberg Historic Trail through the ruins of what was once St John's most prosperous sugar factory.

1. Iguana
Diverse wildlife inhabits the Salt River Bay National Historic Park.

2. Christiansted
Downtown Christiansted features colorful colonial buildings.

t Croix

ick Island Reef National onument, St Croix

such a small land mass – 1 mile long 0.5 miles wide – Buck Island draws big wds. It's not so much what's on top t what's underneath that fascinates: an 800-acre fish-frenzied coral reef system rounding the island, protected as Buck and Reef National Monument. The sea rdens and a marked underwater trail ate captivating snorkeling on the island's st side. Most visitors glide here aboard r boats departing from Christiansted, 5 les to the west.

hristiansted ational Historic Site

is historic site includes several structures. e most impressive is Fort Christiansvaern 49), a four-point citadel occupying the

deep-yellow buildings on the town's east side. Built out of Danish bricks (brought over as ships' ballast), the fort protected citizens from the onslaught of pirates, hurricanes and slave revolts. Cannons on the ramparts, an echoey claustrophobic dungeon and latrines with top-notch sea views await inside. Nearby, the three-story neoclassical Danish West India and Guinea Company Warehouse served as company headquarters; slaves were auctioned in its central courtyard.

Salt River Bay National Historic Park

About 4 miles west of Christiansted via Rte 80, Salt River Bay is the only documented place where Christopher Columbus landed on US soil. Don't expect bells and whistles; the site remains undeveloped beach. The 700 acres surrounding the Salt River estuary is an ecological reserve filled with mangroves, egrets and bioluminescent life come nighttime.

Understand
USA's National
Parks

History

Few things are as quintessentially American as national parks. As writer Wallace Stegner famously put it, they are 'the best idea we ever had. Absolutely American, absolutely democratic.' A handful of people once had the foresight to pull in the reins on rampant hunting, logging, mining and tourist development, so that we might save at least some of our most magnificent treasures for future generations – their actions constitute one of the greatest chapters in US history.

A Magnificent Park

American portrait artist George Catlin (1796–1872) is credited with being the first person to conceptualize a 'nation's park.' He envisioned a 'magnificent park' to protect the country's remaining indigenous people, buffalo and wilderness from the onslaught of western expansion. But more than three decades would pass before anything remotely resembling that vision existed.

In 1851, members of an armed militia accidentally rode into a massive granite valley in the Sierra Nevada and decided to call it 'Yosemity,' possibly a corruption of the Miwok word *Oo-hoo'-ma-te* or *uzumatel*, meaning 'grizzly bear.' The name stuck, and soon word of the valley and its waterfalls got out. Within no time, entrepreneurs were divvying up the land in hopes of profiting from tourists.

Thanks to a handful of outspoken writers, artists, naturalists and – most importantly – the efforts of the great landscape architect Frederick Law Olmsted, Yosemite Valley was spared privatization. In 1864 President Abraham Lincoln signed a bill into law that put Yosemite Valley, and the nearby Mariposa Grove of giant sequoias, under the control of California. Although it wasn't a national park, it was the first time *any* government had mandated the protection of a natural area for public use.

Birth of a National Park

Four years later, a group of men bankrolled by Northern Pacific Railroad headed into the Wyoming wilderness to investigate reports of thermal pools and geysers. Among their discoveries were the Great Fountain

TIMELINE	1864	1872	1890
	President Lincoln designates Yosemite Valley and the Mariposa Grove a protected state park.	President Ulysses S Grant designates Yellowstone the world's first national park.	Yosemite National Park is established, but the state of California retains control of Yosemite Valley and Mariposa Grove.

Geyser and another geyser they would name Old Faithful. Soon, lobbyists at Northern Pacific, with their eyes on tourist dollars, rallied alongside conservationists for a public park like Yosemite. In 1872 President Ulysses S Grant signed the landmark Yellowstone National Park Act, creating the country's first national park.

Meanwhile, in Yosemite, the famed naturalist John Muir lamented the destruction that logging companies, miners and sheep – which he famously deemed 'hoofed locusts' – were wreaking upon the park. In 1890 Yosemite became the country's second national park, but it wasn't until 1905 that Muir convinced Congress to expand the boundaries to include all of Yosemite Valley and the Mariposa Grove.

Over the next 25 years, presidents signed off on six more national parks, including Mt Rainier (1899), Crater Lake (1902), Mesa Verde (1906) and Glacier (1910).

Mather & the National Park Service

Still, there existed no effective protection or management of the new parks until the creation of the National Park Service (NPS) in 1916. The NPS was the brainchild of an industrialist and conservationist named Stephen Mather, who convinced the Department of the Interior that a single governing body was precisely what the parks needed. When President Woodrow Wilson signed the National Park Service Act into law, Mather became the first director.

Mather believed that the best way to promote and improve the parks was to get people into them. A public relations guru, Mather encouraged park superintendents to run publicity campaigns, created the park ranger system, initiated campfire talks and opened the first park museums. His efforts – always coupled with media outreach – were so successful that by 1928 he had tripled the number of park visitors to three million.

While Mather was extremely successful in developing the parks, some felt he'd gone too far. Conservation groups such as the National Parks

THE FATHER OF OUR NATIONAL PARKS

A self-described 'poetico-trampo-geologist-botanist,' Scottish-born John Muir (1838–1914) was an eloquent writer, naturalist and arguably the greatest defender of our early national parks. His writings were pivotal in the creation not just of Yosemite, but of Sequoia, Mt Rainier, Petrified Forest, and Grand Canyon National Parks. Famously – but unsuccessfully – Muir fought to save Yosemite's Hetch Hetchy Valley, which he believed rivaled Yosemite Valley in beauty and grandeur. Although he couldn't stop the damming of the river, his writings on the issue cemented the now widely held belief that our national parks should remain as close as possible to their natural state.

1894	1906	1916	1923
After a poacher is caught killing bison in Yellowstone, Congress grants the park the power to enforce conservation laws, carried out by the US Army.	Mesa Verde becomes the seventh national park and the first dedicated to protecting cultural heritage.	Stephen Mather convinces the Department of the Interior to create the National Park Service.	Yosemite's Hetch Hetchy Valley is dammed to provide water for San Francisco, the first shot in a continuing battle between conservationists and developers.

Association and the Sierra Club felt that Mather's emphasis on development came at the expense of the parks themselves. Mather's successor and protégé, Horace Albright, partially addressed these concerns by creating a national wildlife division within the NPS.

FDR & the CCC

With the Great Depression of the 1930s, the parks went through significant changes. President Franklin Delano Roosevelt created the Civilian Conservation Corps (CCC) and put thousands of young men to work improving national-park roads, visitors' shelters, campsites and trails. During his presidency, FDR also created Joshua Tree, Capitol Reef, and Channel Islands National Monuments (all of which would become national parks), and Olympic and Kings Canyon National Parks.

With the beginning of WWII, the country's greatest public relief program came to an end, CCC workers went off to war, and the national-park budget was slashed. Simultaneously, postwar prosperity allowed more Americans to travel – and hordes of them headed to the parks. By 1950 some 32 million people visited America's national parks. Within five years the number topped 60 million.

Mission 66

The number of travelers descending on the parks put tremendous pressure on them. In 1956 NPS Director Conrad Wirth created Mission 66, a 10-year plan to improve park infrastructure and dramatically increase visitors' services. The plan established the first park visitor centers, more staff and improved facilities. Over the course of Mission 66, Congress also added more than 50 new protected areas to the national-park system.

In 1964 George Hartzog succeeded Wirth as director of the NPS and continued to add new acquisitions. During his tenure nearly 70 new parks would come under the jurisdiction of the NPS. In 1972 President Nixon replaced Hartzog with his own appointee, and expansions to the park service were halted.

Doubling Down

Little was added to the national-parks system until 1980, when President Carter signed the Alaska National Interest Lands Conservation Act into law. The landmark legislation instantly protected over 80 million acres and doubled the amount of land under control of the national parks. Ten new national parks and monuments were created in the process. Although controversial in Alaska, the move has been widely heralded as one of the greatest conservation measures in US history.

In 1908 Theodore Roosevelt declared the Grand Canyon a national monument. The act was met with utter outrage from Arizona politicians, mining claim holders and ranchers, who believed he overstepped his bounds as president – a theme that continues to this day concerning the designation of federal lands.

1926	1933	1941–49	1956–66
The last wolves in Yellowstone are killed as a result of the federal predator control program, which also targets mountain lions, bears and coyotes.	FDR creates the Civilian Conservation Corps; CCC workers improve infrastructure in national parks and plant over 3 billion trees throughout the US.	Ansel Adams photographs every national park in the US, bar the Everglades, for the NPS.	Mission 66 improves park facilities and creates the first national park visitor centers.

THEODORE ROOSEVELT: THE CONSERVATION PRESIDENT

In 1903, President Theodore Roosevelt undertook a two-month-long campaign tour of the USA. In between giving 263 speeches in 25 states, he still managed to spend two weeks exploring Yellowstone and three nights camping out with John Muir in Yosemite. But the greatest legacy of that trip – which was to have a lasting impact on the degree of protection afforded to national parks – arose from time spent at the Grand Canyon. Upon seeing the canyon for the first time, Roosevelt famously declared, 'Leave it as it is. You cannot improve on it. The ages have been at work on it, and man can only mar it.'

Muir may have provided the philosophical underpinnings of the national parks, but it was Roosevelt who transformed the vision into reality. An avid hunter, birder, far-sighted thinker and lover of the outdoors, Roosevelt's time out West – before he became president – profoundly shaped his life and legacy. By the time he left office in 1909, he had signed off on five national parks, 18 national monuments, 51 federal bird sanctuaries and 100 million acres of national forest.

The Parks Today

Since Yellowstone was created in 1872, the national-park system has grown to encompass over 400 sites and 84 million acres. The parks today protect many of the continent's most sensitive ecosystems, some of the world's most remarkable landscapes, and America's most important historical and cultural landmarks. Over the years, more than 11 billion people from the US and around the world have visited them. They are the country's greatest treasure.

Despite a steady increase in visitation, however, the parks still face a variety of threats and obstacles, including loss of biodiversity, declining air and water quality, climate disruption and insufficient funding. In 2011, the NPS released a Call to Action: an initiative to help the service prepare for its second century, with aims such as reducing greenhouse gas emissions by 20%, increasing community involvement and continuing to raise awareness for the parks among all Americans.

The National Park adopted its official logo in 1951. Shaped like an arrowhead, it features a bison and sequoia tree set against a snowcapped peak in the background.

Hot Topics

While conservationists, policy makers and the NPS debate how to best protect the parks, nearly everyone agrees the parks need money – except, it seems, for Congress. With budget cuts and obstructionist gridlock becoming increasingly the norm in Washington, the NPS has begun to turn to private donors and corporate sponsorships in order to make up for the federal shortfall. With the suggestion of sponsors' 'naming rights to any unit of the National Park System or a National Park System facility' in

1980	1995	2011	2011
The Alaska National Interest Lands Conservation Act doubles the amount of land under control of the NPS.	Fourteen gray wolves are reintroduced to Yellowstone nearly 70 years after they disappeared from the park ecosystem.	The NPS releases a Call to Action to prepare for the 2016 centennial, with the aim of reaching new audiences and cutting greenhouse gas emissions, among other initiatives.	A proposed ban on the sale of plastic water bottles in the Grand Canyon is blocked after Coca-Cola, an NPS donor, expresses displeasure. Public outcry allows the NPS to finally implement the ban.

THE ANTIQUITIES ACT, NATIONAL MONUMENTS & OTHER NPS SITES

In 1906 Congress passed the Antiquities Act, which gives the president the authority to protect public land by designating it a **National Monument**. It was originally designed to protect Native American archaeological sites out West, but Theodore Roosevelt quickly realized that he could use the Act to protect any tract of land for any reason – and without opposition from lobbyists or political opponents in Congress. The Grand Canyon was the most famous example of Roosevelt's decisive stroke.

In 2015 there were 117 national monuments. More are designated every year, while others change status. Most are administered by the NPS. Other sites that come under NPS jurisdiction include **National Historic Sites** and **Parks** (eg Independence Hall), **National Memorials** (eg Lincoln Memorial), **National Parkways**, **National Seashores**, **National Recreation Areas** and **National Preserves**, which are like parks, except that fossil fuel extraction and sport hunting are permitted (many Alaskan parks hold a dual park–preserve status). In total the NPS currently administers over 400 natural and historic sites, including 59 national parks.

the 2015 National Defense Authorization Act, the future of NPS funding is on a slippery slope indeed.

System-wide challenges are not the only matters garnering national attention. Congestion, crowds and cars remain a constant source of concern, and more and more parks are introducing free shuttles to combat traffic and reduce air pollution. And from the ongoing debate about snowmobiles in Yellowstone to the concern about melting glaciers in Glacier National Park, there are plenty of other park-specific issues fueling debate beyond the doors of local diners.

Want to join the 221,000 people already volunteering in the national parks? To date, more than 97 million volunteer hours have been logged to make these places better. To learn more about opportunities near you, visit www. volunteer.gov.

2013	2014	2015	2016
Congressional gridlock shuts down the federal government; all national parks are forced to close for a 16-day period. Six states reopen their parks using state money.	Park visitation reaches an all-time high with 292.8 million visitors over the course of the year.	The NPS estimates the backlog of deferred maintenance in national parks – the upkeep of roads, trails, buildings, campgrounds and so on – at $11.5 billion.	The National Park Service celebrates the 100th anniversary of its founding.

Conservation

Protecting the national parks has been a challenge since the day Yellowstone was created in 1872. Thanks to the efforts of passionate individuals, the parks now safeguard some of the greatest natural treasures on the planet. But they face new, often concurrent, threats. Climate change, invasive species, overuse and irresponsible land use on park peripheries all jeopardize the national parks today.

Climate Change

According to National Park Service Director Jon Jarvis, climate change is 'the greatest threat to the integrity of our national parks that we have ever experienced.' Although park biologists are only just beginning to understand its impact, nearly all agree that it's taking a toll.

Scientists worry, for example, that due to rising temperatures in the Mojave Desert, Joshua trees may disappear almost entirely from Joshua

Above Kayaker, Glacier Bay National Park

Tree National Park within the next 60 to 90 years. Glacier National Park may be devoid of glaciers by 2020 if melting continues at current rates (in 1850 the park contained 150 glaciers; today there are 25). And in Sequoia and Kings Canyon National Parks, there is concern that changing temperatures and rainfall patterns may threaten the park's giant sequoias.

Invasive Species

Invasive species pose a severe threat to the national parks. In the Southern Appalachians, a non-native insect called the hemlock woolly adelgid is decimating eastern hemlock forests. In Great Smoky Mountains National Park, where the insect was discovered in 2003, trees are already beginning to die. In Shenandoah, where the insect has been present since 1980, nearly 95% of the hemlocks have perished.

In Glacier National Park, botanists have identified over 125 non-native plants that are reducing food sources for local wildlife. In Sequoia and Kings Canyon National Parks, non-native trout have practically wiped out the mountain yellow-legged frog population, landing the frog on the candidate list for endangered species. In Hawai'i Volcanoes National Park, invasive species, including feral animals, mongooses and numerous plant species, pose tremendous threats to native flora and fauna.

Of course, we can hardly remove ourselves from the list of invasive species. Each year, nearly 300 million visitors clock up more than a billion cumulative hours in the parks. Traffic, auto emissions, roads and the simple fact of human presence in sensitive wildlife areas all take their toll on park ecosystems.

Over 200 national parks and monuments contain at least one endangered species.

Park Peripheries

Aside from the impact visitors make on the parks, humans are putting immense pressure on many locations by operating high-impact businesses outside park boundaries. Conservationists battled for more than two decades to prevent Kaiser Ventures from creating the nation's largest landfill on the edge of Joshua Tree National Park. In Alaska mining companies attempted to create the continent's largest open-pit gold and copper mine only miles from Clark Lake National Park. Great Smoky Mountains, Grand Canyon and Big Bend National Parks are all affected by emissions from coal-fired power plants, which drift over the parks and contaminate the air. Sensitive riparian areas along the Grand Canyon's Colorado River have long been impacted by upriver damming and water holding. And on Washington's Olympic Peninsula, logging companies have clear-cut forests right up to the borders of the park, which has displaced the northern spotted owl from the region.

Sustainable Visitation

According to Jim Nations, former vice president for park research at the National Parks Conservation Association, 'less than one-fourteenth of 1% of the national budget goes to the national parks.' Despite this, park visitors can make a positive impact by traveling sustainably and getting involved with park associations. Whenever you can, ride park shuttles instead of driving your car. Skip high-impact park activities such as snowmobiling in Yellowstone and flight-seeing trips over the Grand Canyon. Conserve water in the desert parks and prevent erosion by always staying on trails. If you're backpacking, use biodegradable soaps (or skip them altogether) and follow the principles of Leave No Trace (www.lnt.org).

Nearly every national park has an associated foundation or other nonprofit that supports its parent park. These organizations, which include Yellowstone Park Foundation (www.ypf.org), the Yosemite Conservancy (www.yosemiteconservancy.org) and Friends of the Smokies (www.friendsofthesmokies.org), conduct everything from trail maintenance to

Lava flows, Hawai'i Volcanoes National Park

habitat restoration. Members can volunteer or donate to programs that are critical to the parks' well-being.

The National Parks Conservation Association (www.npca.org) covers all of the parks. Since 1919, this nonprofit organization has been protecting and preserving America's national parks through research, advocacy and education.

Outdoor Activities

We've yet to meet someone visiting a national park so they can hang around inside. The outdoors is what the parks are all about, and getting out usually means getting active. With environments ranging from the subtropics of the Everglades to the Alaskan tundra, the possibilities are endless.

Hiking

Above Fiery Furnace, Arches National Park

Nothing encapsulates the spirit of the national parks like hiking. Thousands of miles of trails crisscross the parks, offering access to their most scenic mountain passes, highest waterfalls, deepest canyons and quietest corners. Trails run the gamut of accessibility, from the flat, paved paths of Yosemite's **Loop Trails** to the thrilling exposed ascent of **Longs Peak** in Rocky Mountain.

Regardless of the style of the trail, you'll find that exploring on foot generally offers the best park experience. The relatively slow pace of walking brings you into closer contact with the wildlife, and allows you to appreciate the way different perspectives and the day's shifting light can alter the scenery. The satisfaction gained from completing a hike is also a worthy reward; it's one thing to look over the rim of the Grand Canyon, it's another to work up a sweat hiking back up from the canyon floor.

Backpacking

There are hundreds of amazing day hikes to choose from in the park system, but if you want the full experience, head out into the wilderness on an overnight trip. The claim that 99% of park visitors never make it into the backcountry may not be true everywhere, but you will unquestionably see far fewer people and witness exponentially more magic the farther from a road you go. Backcountry campsites are also much more likely to have openings than park lodges and car campsites (which fill up months in advance), making accommodations less of a headache.

Even if you have no backpacking experience, don't consider it out of reach. Most national parks have at least a few backcountry campsites within a couple of hours' walk of a trailhead, making them excellent options for first-time backpackers. You will need gear, however: an appropriate backpack, tent, sleeping bag and pad, stove, headlamp and food are all essential.

Familiarize yourself with the park rules and backcountry ethics before heading out. You will need a permit; if you have your heart set on a famous excursion, apply well in advance online. Most park visitor centers have a backcountry desk, where you can apply for walk-in permits, get trail information, learn about wildlife (bear canisters are generally required in bear country) and check conditions. Before hitting the trail, learn about low-impact camping principles at Leave No Trace (lnt.org).

Preparation & Safety

Walks can be as short or long as you like, but remember this when planning: be prepared. The wilderness may be unlike anything you have ever experienced, and designating certain parcels as 'national parks' has not tamed it.

The weather, particularly out West, can be extraordinary in its unpredictability and sheer force. The summer sun is blazing hot, sudden thunderstorms can drop enough water in 10 minutes to create deadly flash floods, snow can fall at any time of year above tree line, while ferocious windstorms can rip or blow away your poorly staked tent.

No matter where you are, water should be the number one item on your packing checklist – always carry more than you think you'll need. If you're doing any backpacking, make sure you have a way to purify water, and check with rangers ahead of time about the availability of water along the trail.

If your trip involves any elevation change, take the time to acclimatize before tackling a long hike, to avoid altitude sickness. Sunblock, a hat, ibuprofen and warm wind- and waterproof layers are all non-negotiable at high altitudes. Snow cover can last through the end of June above 11,000ft feet; check with rangers to see if you'll need gaiters and snowshoes.

After the elements, getting lost is the next major concern. Most day hikes are well signed and visitors are numerous, but you should always take some sort of map. If you plan on going into the backcountry, definitely take a topographic (topo) map and a compass. You can pick up

OUTDOOR ACTIVITIES HIKING

Classic Day Hikes

....
Iceberg Lake (Glacier)
....
Hoh River Trail (Olympic)
....
Angels Landing (Zion)
....
Harding Icefield Trail (Kenai Fjords)
....
Sky Pond (Rocky Mountain)

Canyonlands National Park

detailed maps in most visitor centers; National Geographic's *Trails Illustrated* series is generally excellent.

At lower elevations and in desert parks, always inquire about ticks, poison oak, poison ivy and rattlesnakes before heading out. Most day hikes are on well-maintained trails, but it's good to know what's out there.

And all hikers, solo or not, should always remember the golden rule: let someone know where you are going and how long you plan to be gone.

Rafting, Kayaking & Canoeing

John Wesley Powell led the first recorded descent of the Colorado River in 1869 – with only one arm. The 10-man survey team took four 21ft boats from Wyoming to Nevada in three months, passing through the Grand Canyon. One boat, many supplies and three men were lost along the way.

Rafts, kayaks, canoes and larger boats are a wonderful way to get to parts of the parks that landlubbers can't reach. River-running opportunities abound in the parks, but none stand out quite like the **Colorado River**. The most famous trip along the Colorado is a three-week odyssey through the Grand Canyon – arguably the best possible way to visit – though you can also take a heart-thumping multi-day excursion further upstream through the desert wilds of Canyonlands. The **Snake River** in Grand Teton National Park has rafting for all skill levels, as does the **Pigeon River**.

If larger bodies of water are more your speed, one of the best parks to explore in a canoe or kayak is **Voyageurs** on the Minnesota–Canada border, which consists of over 30 lakes and 900 islands. Another northern park offering kayaking trips is **Isle Royale**, the largest island in Lake Superior. Many of the campgrounds in both of these parks are only accessible by boat.

In Glacier National Park, the lake paddling is excellent and accessible, thanks to boat ramps and rentals on several lakes. In Grand Teton, **String** and **Leigh Lakes** are great for family and novice paddlers, and you can rent boats at Colter Bay. In Yosemite, **Tenaya Lake** makes for spectacular paddling. Yellowstone's **Shoshone Lake** is the largest back-country lake in the Lower 48, and offers boat-in access to some of the remotest areas of the park.

Boat Tours & Snorkeling

Both the Atlantic and the Pacific have a handful of marine-based parks – many accessible only by boat, and several perfect for underwater adventures. Boat trips exploring the vast **Everglades** are de rigueur in the dry season, while only 5% of **Biscayne**, Florida's largest stretch of undeveloped Atlantic coastline, is land – glass-bottom boats and snorkeling tours are obligatory to check out the coral reefs offshore. Southern California's **Channel Islands** are another prime destination for snorkeling, diving and boat tours.

If you're prepared to leave the continental US, the **Dry Tortugas**, **Virgin Islands** and **American Samoa** are certainly the best options for snorkeling and diving in sapphire-blue waters.

And of course, at the other end of the spectrum, there's Alaska: **Glacier Bay's** calving icebergs and humpback whales are generally visited on a cruise (though you can kayak if you prefer), while volcanic **Katmai** offers innumerable river-running, lake-paddling and sea-kayaking options. Daily boat tours also explore the inlets and islands at **Kenai Fjords**, Alaska's 'smallest' park.

Rock Climbing & Mountaineering

There's no sport quite like rock climbing. From a distance it appears to be a feat of sheer strength, but balance, creativity, technical know-how and a Zen-like sangfroid are all parts of the game. Clinging by your fingertips 2000ft up on one of Yosemite's renowned big walls? Not the place to lose your cool. Thankfully, there are plenty of options for climbers of all ages and levels that don't require the mind control of a Jedi. Sign up for a day of guided climbing – the **Yosemite Mountaineering School** is a great place to start. Other world-renowned destinations include Joshua Tree, Zion, Acadia and the Black Canyon of the Gunnison.

Closely related to rock climbing is mountaineering: the technical ascent of a summit, involving ropes, climbing equipment, and, when there are glaciers, ice axes and crampons. Mountaineering routes are a dime a dozen out West; some of the most famous summits include **Longs Peak** (Rocky Mountain), **Grand Teton**, **Mt Ranier**, and, of course, **Denali**. Other incredible locales to rope up include the awe-inspiring peaks of the **North Cascades** and **Glacier National Park**. Because of the exposure and high altitude on these routes, the risks can be high. Like rock climbing, you'll want to hire a guide if you don't already have significant experience.

Cycling & Mountain Biking

As a general rule, expect more options for two-wheeled fun just outside park boundaries. There are, however, some exceptions: in Yosemite the 12 miles of paved pathways along the **Loop Trails** make for incredibly scenic and leisurely pedaling. In Zion, you can rent a bike and ride the 6.2-mile **Zion Canyon Scenic Drive** (closed to cars most of the year), which connects with the paved Pa'rus Trail. In Bryce, the 34-mile **Bryce Canyon Scenic Drive** makes for an excellent longer ride. Many parks have bicycle rental shops close to the main entrance.

On the down side, cycling within national parks can sometimes be challenging due to heavy traffic and steep grades. Anyone who's been grazed by an RV mirror can attest to that.

Mountain biking on trails is largely prohibited in the national parks, but some parks have dirt roads that substitute. **Canyonlands National Park** is particularly full of them, and there are several gravel roads in

OUTDOOR ACTIVITIES BOAT TOURS & SNORKELING

In January 2015, climbers Tommy Caldwell and Kevin Jorgeson became the first to free climb El Capitan's 3000ft Dawn Wall in Yosemite, a feat long thought impossible. The pair spent 19 days on the cliff face, sleeping on portaledges and documenting their progress with their phones.

Great Smoky. In Utah, you won't have to stray very far for some of the best mountain biking in the world, found on the desert slickrock outside **Arches** and **Zion**.

Winter Sports

Cross-Country Skiing & Snowshoeing

Come winter, trails and roads in many parks get blanketed with snow and the crowds disappear. It's a magical time to visit, and those willing to step into skis or snowshoes and brave the elements will be rewarded. The best parks for both activities are Glacier, Yellowstone, Grand Teton, Rocky Mountain, Yosemite, Voyageurs, Olympic, Mt Rainier and Denali, though this is far from a comprehensive list. Surprisingly, there's even cross-country skiing at the Grand Canyon.

In most of these parks, rangers lead snowshoe hikes, which can be an excellent entry to the sport and a great way to learn about the winter environment. Visitor centers are the best place to check for information.

In 2014 the Spaniard Kilian Jornet summitted Denali's West Buttress route in an incredible nine hours and 45 minutes, climbing 13,000ft over 16 miles of glacial terrain. He then skied down to base camp in two hours.

Downhill Skiing & Snowboarding

Most of the best downhill skiing takes place outside the parks. Three parks, however, do have downhill ski resorts. **Badger Pass** in Yosemite National Park is an affordable, family-friendly resort. Just inside the border of Olympic National Park, **Hurricane Ridge** has only three lifts and is the westernmost ski resort in the Lower 48. At Ohio's Cuyahoga Valley, the **Boston Mills/Brandywine Ski Resort** offers about a dozen short trails. The most notable skiing adjacent to parks covered in this guide is **Jackson Hole**, Wyoming, which has long runs, deep powder and a screeching 4139ft vertical drop.

Swimming

With the exception of the higher-elevation parks (like Glacier and Rocky Mountain) and northern parks like Denali, summer means heat, and heat means swimming. Alpine lakes make for wonderful but often frigid swimming, and many of the larger lakes have beaches and designated swimming areas.

As river rats the world over will attest, nothing beats dipping into a swimming hole and drip-drying on a rock in the sun. But be careful – every year, swimmers drown in national-park rivers. Always check with visitor centers about trouble spots and the safest places to swim. Unless you're certain about the currents, swim only where others are swimming.

SO MUCH TO DO...

For those who want to try it all, here's some more fodder for fun:

Stargazing It's outstanding in Capitol Reef and Bryce. Also check park newspapers for nightly astronomy walks.

Soaking Submerge your sore muscles in thermal hot springs at Yellowstone, Olympic or Hot Springs.

Canyoneering Rope up and descend into Utah's mesmerizing slot canyons; with a guide, no experience is necessary.

Glissading Take your ice axe and slide down the snowfields on Mt Ranier.

Tide pooling Olympic, Acadia and the Channel Islands are tide-pool heaven.

Sand surfing Rent a board or simply slide on your butt in Colorado's Great Sand Dunes.

Caving Join a subterranean tour at Mammoth Cave, Wind Cave or Carlsbad Caverns.

Canoeing, Voyageurs National Park,

Midnight Hole, Great Smoky Mountains National Park

Top places to get wet are Zion's **Virgin River**, the **Merced River** in Yosemite Valley, **Sedge Bay** in Yellowstone, **Leigh Lake** in Grand Teton, **Midnight Hole** in Great Smoky and **Sol Duc Hot Springs** in Olympic.

Fishing

For many, the idea of heading to the national parks without a fishing rod is ludicrous. Yellowstone offers some of the best fly-fishing in the country. Olympic's **Hoh** and **Sol Duc Rivers** are famous for their runs of salmon and winter steelhead. Waters in Yosemite's high country, particularly the **Tuolumne River**, can be great for small, feisty trout. **Glacier**, **Grand Teton** and, of course, most of Alaska's parks all offer outstanding fishing. **Great Smoky** has exceptional fishing for trout and bass.

Wherever you fish, read up on local regulations. Fishing permits are always required, and those caught fishing without one will be fined. (Children under 15 are generally not required to have a license.) Some waters, including many streams and rivers, are catch-and-release only, and sometimes bait-fishing is prohibited. Certain native fish, such as bull trout, kokanee salmon and wild steelhead, are often protected, and anglers in possession of these can be heavily fined. The best place to check regulations is online. For details on regulations, check the park's NPS website (www.nps.gov) and refer to the respective state's department of fish and game website. Find the latter by searching for the state plus 'fish and game.'

Horseback & Mule Riding

Our most time-tested form of transport still makes for a wonderful way to experience the great outdoors. Horseback riding is possible in many of the parks, and outfitters within or immediately outside the parks offer everything from two-hour rides to full- and multiday pack trips. Rides run around $40 per hour or $80 per half-day.

In **Great Smoky**, over 550 miles of trails are open to horses, and outfitters abound. Popular horseback excursions such as the descent into the **Grand Canyon** or the **High Sierra Camps** in Yosemite require reservations far in advance.

Classic Back-Country Trips

Nankoweap Trail (Grand Canyon)

High Sierra Camps Loop (Yosemite)

Redwood Creek Trail (Redwood)

Teton Crest Trail (Grand Teton)

Bechler River (Yellowstone)

OUTDOOR ACTIVITIES FISHING

Wildlife

It's no coincidence that the establishment of many of the earliest national parks co-incided with a wave of near mass extinctions in the United States: by the 1890s the passenger pigeon, bison, eastern elk, wolf, mountain lion and grizzly bear – along with their habitats and numerous less heralded species – were all on the verge of disappearing forever. Today, some of these animals have made a comeback, thanks in large part to the protection afforded by the national parks.

Bison, Moose & Other Grazers

The continent's largest land mammal is the **American bison** (or buffalo). Some 60 million bison once roamed North America, but Euro-American settlers, in one of the saddest chapters of American history, reduced their numbers to about 300. Beginning in the 1860s, the US government and army encouraged the slaughter in order to deprive the

Plains Indians of their primary means of survival. But for many Americans traveling West, killing bison was done for the sheer pleasure of sport – as evidenced by the 'hunting by rail' trips organized by railroads, which left untold thousands of rotting buffalo corpses in their wake. By the 1890s, Yellowstone's bison herd was the only one remaining in the country, with poachers successfully reducing its numbers one by one.

What could have been a disaster instead became a turning point. Thanks to the determined intervention of George Bird Grinnell, editor of *Forest & Stream* and founder of the Audubon Society, and a young politician by the name of Theodore Roosevelt, Congress passed an 1894 law granting national parks the power to protect all wildlife within their boundaries. Previous to this, poachers were simply expelled from park lands; now they could be arrested. Yellowstone's bison were gradually bred back from the brink of extinction, and today an estimated 4900 roam the park.

Other large grazers are commonplace throughout many parks. **Moose**, the largest of the world's deer species, stand 5ft to 7ft at the shoulder and can weigh up to 1000lb. They're common in Yellowstone, Glacier, Rocky Mountain, Grand Teton, Voyageurs and Denali. The same parks are home to **elk**, which grow antlers up to 5ft long and weigh up to 700lb. These majestic herbivores graze along forest edges and are commonly sighted. They were reintroduced to Great Smoky in 2001.

Bighorn sheep are synonymous with the Rocky Mountains, and have made a slow but steady comeback after nearing extinction in the 1800s. Today they are sighted throughout the Rockies, and in Joshua Tree, Zion and Bryce Canyon. During late-fall and early-winter breeding seasons, males charge each other at 20mph and clash their horns so powerfully that the sound can be heard for miles.

The fuzzy, sure-footed **mountain goat**, actually a species of antelope, lives at high altitudes throughout the year and has a habitat spread across the Rockies, Cascades and parts of Alaska. On the Western plains, the **pronghorn antelope** is North America's fastest land animal, capable of reaching speeds of 55mph.

WILDLIFE BEARS

Explore.org has some fabulous live animal webcams from around the world, including four grizzly cams in Alaska's Katmai National Park.

Bears

If you see a bear on your trip to a national park, odds are it will be a **black bear**. These mostly vegetarian foragers are much more common than their larger, more elusive cousins, grizzly bears. Black bears are very adaptable and in some places, such as Yosemite, have become so accustomed to humans that they regularly roam campsites and break into cars at night for food.

Black bears, which are sometimes brown or cinnamon colored, roam montane and subalpine forests throughout the country and are surprisingly common. The Rockies and the Sierras have the highest populations, but it's also possible to spot them in the Great Smoky Mountains, Shenandoah, Voyageurs and even parts of Florida. Black bears are usually not aggressive unless there are cubs nearby, but they will go after food or food odors. Make sure to store your food and trash properly, and use a bear canister if you plan on backpacking.

The **grizzly bear** once ranged across the western US, but today its population in the Lower 48 is estimated to be around 1500 to 1800. In the continental US, grizzlies are only found in the mountainous regions of Montana, Idaho, Wyoming and Washington. In Alaska, of course, they are much more common – Katmai's Brooks Falls is an iconic bear fishing hole. Of the national parks within the Lower 48, Yellowstone has the most grizzlies, with a population of around 750 bears; you can sometimes spot them at dawn in the Lamar Valley (take a telescope or binoculars).

Adult grizzly bears in Alaska can catch and eat over 30 fish in a single day. The bears need to cram a year's worth of food into a mere six months of eating.

Grizzlies can reach up to 800lb and can be distinguished from black bears by their concave snout, rounded ears and prominent shoulder hump.

Grizzly attacks are rare, but they do happen. Most occur because people surprise them or inadvertently come between a mother and her cub. The National Park Service (www.nps.gov) has excellent information on bears and how to handle encounters.

Wolves & Coyotes

The **gray wolf** was once the Rocky Mountains' main predator, but relentless persecution reduced its territory to a narrow belt stretching from Canada to the Northern Rockies. The last wolves in Yellowstone were killed in 1926, but wolves were successfully reintroduced to the park beginning in 1995. The last official count in 2013 showed 95 wolves, though there are an estimated 400 in the Greater Yellowstone ecosystem. The Lamar Valley is your best chance for a wolf sighting, and you can sign up for a wolf-watching excursion with the Yellowstone Institute (www.yellowstoneassociation.org).

Coyotes and **foxes** are common in many of the parks. When it comes to coyotes, you're far more likely to hear them than see them. Listening to them howl at night as you doze off to sleep is an eerie yet wonderful experience.

Cats

North America's largest cat is the **mountain lion** (also known as a puma or cougar), an elusive and powerful predator. Highly adaptable, mountain lions are present in many parks, including Yellowstone, Grand Teton, Glacier, Yosemite, Joshua Tree and Grand Canyon. It's highly unlikely you'll spot one, as they avoid human contact. If you're camping, however, you may hear one scream – it's an utterly terrifying sound in the darkness and a virtual guarantee that you won't fall back asleep until dawn. Adult males can measure over 7ft nose to tail and weigh up to 220lb, though they are usually smaller. Though they rarely trouble

RETURN OF THE WOLF

The wolf is a potent symbol of America's wilderness. This smart, social predator is the largest species of canine – averaging more than 100lb and reaching nearly 3ft at the shoulder. An estimated 400,000 once roamed the continent from coast to coast, from Alaska to Mexico.

Wolves were not regarded warmly by European settlers. The first wildlife legislation in the British colonies was a wolf bounty. And as 19th-century Americans moved West, they replaced the native herds of bison, elk, deer and moose with domestic cattle and sheep, which wolves found equally tasty.

To stop wolves from devouring the livestock, extermination soon became official government policy. Up until 1965, for $20 to $50 an animal, wolves were shot, poisoned, trapped and dragged from dens, until in the Lower 48 states only a few hundred gray wolves remained, in northern Minnesota and Michigan.

In 1944 naturalist Aldo Leopold called for the return of the wolf. His argument was ecology, not nostalgia. His studies showed that wild ecosystems need their top predators to maintain healthy biodiversity; in complex interdependence, all animals and plants suffered with the wolf gone.

Protected and encouraged, wolf populations made a remarkable recovery, and there are now more than 6000 counted in the continental US and over 8000 in Alaska. However, heavy pressure from ranchers has resulted in gray wolves having their protected status removed in almost all states over the past few years. According to the Wolf Conservation Center, some 1700 wolves have since been killed.

Grey wolf

humans, there are sporadic attacks every couple of years, usually involving children or joggers.

Bobcats and **lynx** are also present in most of these parks and are equally hard to spot.

Small Mammals

Small mammals often get short shrift on people's watch lists, but animals like beavers, pikas, marmots and river otters are a delight to see. **Beavers** (and their dams) are found in Rocky Mountain, Yellowstone, Grand Teton, Voyageurs and Glacier National Parks, and are particularly fun to watch. **Marmots**, despite being little more than glorified ground squirrels, are enjoyable to watch hopping around on rocks in the high country. They are found in the subalpine regions of both the Rockies and the Sierras. Other critters you might come across include bats, squirrels, voles, mice, chipmunks, raccoons, badgers, skunks, shrews and martens.

Birds

Everglades is the national park most famous for its birds. Over 350 species have been spotted there, including 16 different wading birds and dozens of terns, gulls and other shorebirds. Acadia National Park is close behind with 338 species on record. Needless to say, bird-watching in both parks is outstanding. But don't rule out the inland parks. In Yellowstone, 316 bird species have been sighted. Most of the NPS park websites (www.nps.gov) have complete bird lists – bring binoculars for the best experience.

Birds of prey – including eagles, falcons, hawks, owls and harriers – are common in the parks, especially the western ones. **Osprey**, which nest and hunt around rivers and lakes, are a commonly spotted raptor. Keep your eyes peeled for **bald eagles**, which can be seen throughout

Best Wildlife Sightings

Wolves, black bears and grizzlies – Yellowstone

Elk and bighorn sheep – Rocky Mountain

Bison and moose – Grand Teton

Manatee – Biscayne

Bald eagles and osprey – North Cascades

Humpback whales – Glacier Bay

Craig Childs' *The Animal Dialogues* is a must-read for anyone interested in wildlife. The insatiably curious Childs interweaves superb research with hair-raising stories of his own nose-to-nose encounters with animals of all kinds, from the lowly mosquito all the way up to the awesome mountain lion.

Black-tailed prairie dog, Wind Cave National Park

Voyageurs and the Rockies, as well as in Mt Rainier, Olympic and the North Cascades. Extremely rare, **California condors** are sometimes spotted in Pinnacles, Grand Canyon and Zion. There are 225 known wild California condors, spread throughout California, Utah and Arizona.

Amphibians & Reptiles

Frogs, toads and salamanders thrive in and around streams, rivers and lakes in several of the parks. With 24 species of **salamanders**, Great Smoky Mountains is often deemed the salamander capital of the world. The creepy-looking Pacific giant salamander, which can reach up to 12in in length, is found in Olympic and Mt Rainier. The incredible tiger salamander has adapted to life in the barren Great Sand Dunes.

When it comes to reptiles, Everglades National Park reigns supreme. Not only is it home to **crocodiles**, **alligators** and **caiman**, but also over 20 species of snakes, including the eastern coral snake, diamondback rattlers and boa constrictors. Everglades is also home to 16 **turtle** and **tortoise** species.

Love 'em or hate 'em, **snakes** are here to stay in most of the parks – but snakebites are rare (in Yellowstone, the NPS reports two in the history of the park). Western and prairie rattlesnakes are common, but they are generally docile and would rather rattle and scram than bite. Gopher and garter snakes are the most common of all.

Trees & Plants

If you were to travel to every national park in this guide, you'd experience a vast array of plant life, from the salty mangroves of the Everglades to the bizarre Joshua trees of the Mojave Desert, and the rich volcanic soil of Hawaii to the arctic tundra in Alaska.

Top Great gray owl,
Yosemite National Park
Bottom Humpback
whale

Mariposa Grove, Yosemite National Park

IN THE REALM OF GIANTS

Yosemite, and Sequoia and Kings Canyon are home to the world's largest living things: giant sequoias. Although they aren't the tallest trees, nor the thickest, they are the biggest in terms of sheer mass. Living up to 3000 years, giant sequoias are also among the oldest living organisms. The General Sherman tree, in Sequoia, stands 275ft tall and measures 100ft around, making it the largest living single-specimen organism on earth. Think of it this way: according to the National Park Service, its trunk alone is equivalent to 15 blue whales or 25 military battle tanks. Now that's a big tree.

Trees

The national parks protect some of the greatest forests in the world. Redwood has the planet's tallest trees; Yosemite's Mariposa Grove of giant sequoias is home to some of the planet's largest trees, while the park's high country holds subalpine forests that are nothing short of high-altitude fairylands. North of the Sierra Nevada, in the Cascade Range, Mount Rainier National Park protects thick forests of western hemlock, Douglas fir, cedar, true firs, and western white pine. West of the Cascades, Olympic National Park is home to some of the greatest stands of temperate rainforest and old-growth forest.

In the Rockies, sparse piñon-juniper forests cover the drier, lower elevations, while the sweet-scented ponderosa pines dominate the montane zone. One of the Rockies' most striking trees is the quaking aspen, whose leaves flutter and shimmer in the mountain breeze and turn entire hillsides golden yellow in fall. The stunted, gnarled bristlecone pine, the oldest living life form on the planet, grows throughout the West in stands just below tree line. Many are thousands of years old.

In the drier, hotter climates of Zion, Bryce Canyon and Grand Canyon, trees are fewer, but still common. Many Zion visitors are surprised to find a lush riparian zone along the Virgin River that supports beautiful stands of cottonwoods and gorgeous bigtoothed maples. In the Mojave Desert is the strange Joshua tree, actually a giant yucca.

As far as biological diversity goes, however, the Great Smoky Mountains are king. The old-growth forests of the Smokies are home to more native tree and plant species than anywhere else in the USA. Drive 900 miles south from Great Smoky and you end up in Everglades National Park, home to vast mangroves forests and tropical hardwoods.

Smaller Plants

When it comes to the smaller plants of the national parks, none seem to make an impression like wildflowers do. If you're traveling in spring or summer, it's always worth doing a little research on your park of choice to find out what's blooming when. For example, wildflowers put on a spectacular show in Death Valley every spring, usually in late February and March, and on good years it's worth planning a trip around them. Throughout the Rockies, June and July are prime wildflower months. In the Sierras, wildflowers bloom in spring at lower elevations, in early summer up around Tuolumne Meadows, and as late as mid-July at the highest elevations.

On the Colorado Plateau (Zion, Bryce, Grand Canyon), wildflowers such as desert marigolds and slickrock paintbrush bloom for a short period in early spring. The plateau's most interesting plants are arguably the cacti and desert succulents that make this mostly desert region so unique. Although many plants are specific to the plateau, others are drawn from adjacent biological zones such as the Great Basin, Mojave Desert and Rocky Mountains.

In the Southern Appalachians, the Great Smoky Mountains boast an incredible 1500 flowering plants, including nine native species of rhododendron and azalea (blooming late May through June).

WILDLIFE TREES & PLANTS

The oldest known tree on the planet is a bristlecone pine growing in the White Mountains of California. Known as Gargi, it is 5065 years old!

The Great Smoky Mountains are home to over 17,000 identified plant and animal species. This ancient eco-region shares a surprisingly similar taxonomic makeup with southwestern China – including such plant genera as magnolia, hickory, sassafras and ginseng.

Geology

Tectonic collisions, glaciation, volcanic eruptions, erosion – the forces of nature and time have worked wonders on the continent, and nowhere is that geological history more beautifully evident than in the national parks. Each park tells its own ancient story through landscapes that are as unique as they are complex.

The East

The eastern United States is defined by the Atlantic Ocean and the Appalachian Mountains, which run parallel to the coastline from Maine to Alabama. The sedimentary Appalachians are the continent's oldest mountains, dating back some 300 million years, a time when North America was part of the supercontinent Pangaea.

Above Kenai Fjords National Park

The northern Appalachians, with numerous peaks over 5000ft, were further sculpted by the last ice age: **Acadia's** Mt Desert Island, for example, was created some 20,000 years ago, when glacial ice sheets sheared it from the mainland. Peaks in the central Appalachian region (home to **Shenandoah**) top out around 4000ft, while those in the southern part of the range (including **Great Smoky**) extend over 6000ft. Steep elevation gradients, deep V-shaped valleys, ridges, abundant rainfall and high summertime humidity make the Appalachians one of the most diverse ecosystems in all of North America.

Heading south, things get wetter and warmer, passing through the floodplain forests in South Carolina's **Congaree**, until you reach the swamps of southern Florida, where the **Everglades** are located. Today, the park protects the largest subtropical wilderness in North America. With an average elevation of only 6ft, the park is an expansive wetland atop an ancient seabed, with a tremendous variety of coastal and marine ecosystems.

Great Lakes & Plains

In geological terms, the Great Lakes area represents the southern part of what is known as the Canadian Shield. Consisting mainly of igneous (volcanic) and metamorphic rock 2.5 to 3.5 billion years old (by comparison, the Jurassic dinosaurs were lumbering about only 200 million years ago), this region was profoundly shaped during the last ice age. The most obvious remnants of the massive glaciers here are the five Great Lakes, which represent the greatest expanse of fresh water on the continent, consisting of 20% of the world's supply. Both **Isle Royale** and **Voyageurs** are defined by their lakes, marshes and boreal forest – a mix of conifers and hardwoods adapted to the short growing season of the far north.

The Great Plains is the relatively flat prairie that extends over much of the central United States. Once an inland sea, it eventually became fertile grassland, which was most recently developed for agriculture. It was originally home to millions of bison, and you can get some sense of what parts of the prairie looked like in the **Badlands**, **Theodore Roosevelt** and **Wind Cave**, all in the Dakotas.

Rocky Mountains

Nearly 1000 miles west of the Appalachians, the Rocky Mountains begin their dramatic ascent from the western reaches of the Great Plains and climb to over 14,000ft. Much younger than the Appalachians, the Rockies were created by tectonic uplift between 70 million and two million years ago. The mountains were carved and eroded by water and wind and finally, during the Pleistocene ice age of two million years ago, hewn by glaciers into the landscapes we see today.

Colorado's Great Sand Dunes are composed of 29 different rocks and minerals – from obsidian and sulfur to amethyst and turquoise – and cover an incredible 30 sq miles of land, with dunes as tall as 700ft.

SUBTERRANEAN WONDERS

The national parks' caves are often overlooked by road-tripping families on summer vacations. After all, is walking around in a chilly, pitch-black tunnel really as appealing as spotting bears in Yellowstone or hugging giant trees in Sequoia? Maybe not on the surface, but the thrill of exploring the underworld's bizarre formations should not be overlooked. Three enormous cave systems in the US have been protected as national parks: **Mammoth Cave** (Kentucky), **Carlsbad Caverns** (New Mexico), and **Wind Cave** (South Dakota). Rangers lead tours of all three, plus you can hike down into Carlsbad's Big Room on your own. Mammoth is the world's largest known cave system, with over 400 miles of labyrinths. Interested in spelunking? Sign up for mammoth's challenging Wild Cave Tour. Other parks with smaller caves to explore include **Pinnacles**, **Kings Canyon** and **Sequoia** in California.

Black Canyon of the Gunnison National Park

National Park Extremes

Highest point
Denali, 20,310ft

Lowest point
Death Valley, -282ft

Tallest tree
Redwood, 379ft

Biggest tree
Sequoia, 52,500 cubic ft

Wettest region
Olympic, annual rainfall 11.25ft

Largest park
Wrangell-St Elias, total area 20,625 sq miles

Yellowstone was shaped by the same ice age, but what really differentiates it from other parks in the range is its volcanic activity. Yellowstone sits on a geological 'hot spot,' a thin piece of the earth's crust that is essentially floating atop a massive, 125-mile-deep plume of molten rock. Fueled by this underground furnace, Yellowstone bubbles like a pot on a hot stove to produce over 10,000 geothermal features – more than all other geothermal areas on the planet combined.

Yellowstone, **Grand Teton**, **Glacier**, **Rocky Mountain**, **Black Canyon** and the **Great Sand Dunes** together protect some 3 million acres of the Rockies. Rocky Mountain has the highest point in these parks, its iconic Longs Peak punching 14,259ft into the sky.

Southwest

At the southwest end of the Rockies, the mountains descend to the Colorado Plateau, a 130,000-sq-mile region centered on the arid Four Corners area of the United States. Home to **Grand Canyon**, **Zion** and **Bryce Canyon** – among numerous other parks – the Colorado Plateau is one of the world's densest concentrations of exposed rock. Arizona's **Petrified Forest** is a trove of Late Triassic-era fossils, which date back 225 million years.

Unlike the Rocky Mountains to the east and the Sierras to the west, the plateau has remained stable for millions of years, during which water and wind slowly eroded the landscape, forming the spectacular canyons, arches, hoodoos and other rock formations you see today. From an aerial perspective, the plateaus and cliffs form a remarkable staircase that steps downward from the pink cliffs of Bryce Canyon, to the white and red cliffs of Zion, and finally to the chocolate cliffs abutting the Grand Canyon – each color represents a different geological era. This so-called **Grand Staircase** exposes the hundreds of millions of years of layered rock that make the region so visually awesome.

Death Valley National Park

California

South of Zion, the Colorado Plateau meets the Mojave Desert, which is home to the hottest, driest places in North America. Here you'll find **Death Valley**, which protects over 5000 sq miles of what is no less than a crazy quilted geological playground. Encompassing far more than Death Valley itself, the park contains giant sand dunes, marbled canyons, extinct volcanic craters and palm-shaded oases.

At the southernmost edge of the Mojave lies **Joshua Tree**, which straddles both the Mojave and the Sonoran Deserts. The Mojave section of the park is home to a particularly striking member of the yucca family, the namesake Joshua tree.

Northwest of the California deserts, the Sierra Nevada is a 400-mile-long mountain range with tremendous biological and geological diversity. The Sierras are an uplifted, westward-tilting slab of granite that broke off from the earth's crust and thrust upward roughly 10 million years ago.

Between two million and 10,000 years ago, glaciers 'flowed' from high-elevation ice fields, scouring out canyons and valleys and sculpting the range into a granite masterpiece. In Yosemite, evidence of glaciation is everywhere and is what makes the park so spectacular.

The Sierras' highest peaks stand within the areas protected by **Yosemite**, and **Sequoia** and **Kings Canyon**, with Mt Whitney (14,505ft; in Sequoia), standing taller than any other peak in the Lower 48.

Although located in northern California, the coastal **Redwoods** and **Lassen Volcanic National Parks** are more closely related to the temperate rainforests and fiery peaks of the Pacific Northwest.

Rock-star Vistas
....

Olmsted Point, Yosemite
....
The Narrows, Zion
....
Bryce Canyon Amphitheater, Bryce Canyon
....
Bright Angel Point, Grand Canyon
....
Hidden Valley, Joshua Tree

Petrified wood, Petrified Forest National Park

Pacific Northwest

North of the Sierra Nevada stands the Cascade Range, a volcanic mountain range stretching from northern California into British Columbia (Canada). The range's highest peak is 14,411ft **Mt Rainier**, a massive stratovolcano protected by Mount Rainier National Park. The volcano is 'episodically active' and is considered the most hazardous volcano in the Cascades. The mountain is covered in snow for much of the year and contains expansive ice fields and 25 glaciers. It last erupted in 1854. Other major parks in the range include Oregon's **Crater Lake** – an extinct volcano whose caldera filled with water 7700 years ago and is today the deepest (and clearest) lake in the US – and the **North Cascades**, a rugged swathe of glacier-bound jagged peaks, featuring both temperate rainforest on the west side of the range and drier ponderosa forests on the east.

West of the Cascades, on Washington's Olympic Peninsula, the Olympic Mountains plunge dramatically into the Pacific Ocean. They are a separate range entirely and, unlike the volcanic Cascades, were formed five to 15 million years ago during convergence of the Juan de Fuca and North American plates. Between the Olympic's highest peaks, which top out at 7965ft, and the ocean below, **Olympic National Park** protects a landscape drenched in rain, hammered by wind and pounded by waves.

The 2663-mile Pacific Crest Trail, which extends from Canada to Mexico, passes through seven national parks. Similar in nature, the Appalachian (2160 miles) and Continental Divide (3100 miles) Trails follow the country's other main north–south mountain ranges, passing through an additional five national parks.

Alaska

Dramatic mountain ranges arch across the landmass of Alaska. The **Pacific Mountain System**, which includes the Alaska, Aleutian and St Elias Ranges, as well as the Chugach and Kenai Mountains, sweeps along the south before dipping into the sea southwest of Kodiak Island. Most of Alaska's eight national parks are located here, including the granddaddy of them all, **Denali** – its namesake mountain is North America's tallest peak (20,310ft). Further north looms the imposing and little-visited Brooks Range, skirting the Arctic Circle, where you'll find the wild and remote **Gates of the Arctic**.

In between the Alaska and Brooks Ranges is interior Alaska, an immense plateau rippled by foothills, low mountains and magnificent rivers; among them the third longest in the US, the mighty Yukon River, which runs for 2300 miles. At the state's far southeastern corner is **Glacier Bay** – the perfect place to observe glacial retreat in action.

In geological terms Alaska is relatively young and still very active. The state represents the northern boundary of the chain of Pacific Ocean volcanoes known as the Ring of Fire and is the most seismically active region of North America. In fact, Alaska claims 52% of the earthquakes that occur in the country and averages more than 13 each day. Most are mild shakes, but some are deadly. Three of the six largest earthquakes in the world – and seven of the 10 largest in the US – have occurred in Alaska.

GEOLOGY HAWAII

The largest national park is Alaska's Wrangell-St Elias. Bigger than Switzerland, it's also home to the second-tallest peak in the US, Mt St Elias (18,008ft), whose dizzying climb from sea level occurs in just 10 miles.

Hawaii

The Hawaiian archipelago embraces more than 50 volcanoes (and 137 islands and atolls), part of the larger, mostly submerged Hawaiian–Emperor Seamount chain that extends 3600 miles across the ocean. Hawaii's volcanoes are created by a rising column of molten rock – a hot spot – under the Pacific Plate. As the plate moves northwest a few inches each year, magma pierces upward through the crust, creating volcanoes.

Each new volcano slowly creeps northwest past the hot spot that created it. As each volcanic island moves off the hot spot, it stops erupting and instead of adding more new land, starts eroding. Wind, rain and waves add geologic character to the newly emerged islands, cutting deep valleys, creating sandy beaches and turning a mound of lava into a tropical paradise. For a first-hand look at the different ecosystems that a volcano's slopes harbor, explore **Haleakalā**, which rises over 10,000ft up from near sea level.

Straddling the hot spot today, the **Hawaii Volcanoes**' Kilauea, on the Big Island, is the world's most active volcano. All Hawaiian volcanoes are shield volcanoes that erupt with effusive lava to create gently sloped, dome-shaped mountains, but they can also have a more explosive side, as Kilauea dramatically reminded onlookers and scientists in 2008.

Index

OUR STORY

A beat-up old car, a few dollars in the pocket and a sense of adventure. In 1972 that's all Tony and Maureen Wheeler needed for the trip of a lifetime – across Europe and Asia overland to Australia. It took several months, and at the end – broke but inspired – they sat at their kitchen table writing and stapling together their first travel guide, *Across Asia on the Cheap*. Within a week they'd sold 1500 copies. Lonely Planet was born.

Today, Lonely Planet has offices in Franklin, London, Melbourne, Oakland, Beijing and Delhi, with more than 600 staff and writers. We share Tony's belief that 'a great guidebook should do three things: inform, educate and amuse'.

5/26/16

THIS BOOK

This is the first edition of Lonely Planet's *USA's National Parks*. This guidebook was produced in Lonely Planet's Melbourne office.

Writer
Christopher Pitts

Contributing Writers
Amy Balfour, Sandra Bao, Greg Benchwick, Sara Benson, Jennifer Denniston, Bridget Gleeson, Michael Grosberg, Adam Karlin, Beth Kohn, Bradley Mayhew, Carolyn McCarthy, Becky Ohlsen, Zora O'Neill, Kevin Raub, Brendan Sainsbury, Regis St Louis, Ryan Ver Berkmoes, Mara Vorhees, Greg Ward, Karla Zimmerman

Associate Product Director
Angela Tinson

Product Editor
Anne Mason

Book Designer
Jessica Rose

Senior Cartographer
Alison Lyall

Assisting Product Editors
Carolyn Bain, Sarah Billington, Carolyn Boicos, Kate Chapman, Joel Cotterell, Grace Dobell, Bruce Evans, Elizabeth Jones, Kate Kiely, Bella Li, Kate Mathews, Jenna Myers, Catherine Naghten, Katie O'Connell, Alison Ridgway, Kathryn Rowan, Vicky Smith, Luna Soo, Ross Taylor, Saralinda Turner, Tracy Whitmey, Amanda Williamson

Assisting Book Designers
Katherine Marsh, Mazzy Prinsep, Wibowo Rusli

Assisting Cartographers
David Kemp, Valentina Kremenchutskaya

Thanks
Sasha Baskett, Liz Heynes, Campbell McKenzie, Darren O'Connell, Kirsten Rawlings, Dora Whitaker

Cover Researcher
Naomi Parker

Acknowledgments
Climate map data adapted from Peel MC, Finlayson BL & McMahon TA (2007) 'Updated World Map of the Köppen-Geiger Climate Classification', *Hydrology and Earth System Sciences*, 11, 163344
Cover photograph: Bull moose, Glacier National Park, Danita Delimont Stock/AWL

Published by Lonely Planet Publications Pty Ltd
ABN 36 005 607 983
1st edition – Apr 2016
ISBN 978 1 74220 629 5
© Lonely Planet 2016   Photographs © as indicated 2016
10 9 8 7 6 5 4 3 2 1
Printed in China